MANGA	Atsuro Yomino
ORIGINAL STORY	Ichirou Ohkouchi Goro Taniguchi
SCRIPT COOPERATION	Saika Hasumi

ENGLISH PRODUCTION CREDITS

TRANSLATION	Satsuki Yamashita
LETTERING	Keiran O'Leary
EDITOR	Robert Place Napton
PUBLISHER	Ken Iyadomi

CODE GEASS Suzaku of the Counterattack Vol.2
©Atsuro YOMINO 2008
©2006-2008 SUNRISE/PROJECT GEASS, MBS
Character Design ©2006 CLAMP

Originally published in Japan in 2008 by KADOKAWA SHOTEN PUBLISHING CO., LTD., Tokyo.
English translation published by Bandai Entertainment Inc. under the license by Sunrise, Inc.

ISBN-13: 978-1-59409-978-6

Printed in Canada
First Bandai Printing: February 2008

10 9 8 7 6 5 4 3 2 1

JUL 09

CH

Thank you for picking up this book.

It's been two years since they asked me to work on this manga adaptation.

The Suzaku of the Counterattack manga finished before the anime.

It was really hard to draw what Ms. Hasumi wrote for this story, and that caused her and the other staff trouble every month. I would like to take this opportunity to say sorry for that. Once I was done with this manga, I was looking forward to watching the show as a normal viewer, but luckily I was able to be involved one last time. I drew one of the pictures they show at the end of the episode. They told me to choose R2 characters who are out of the ordinary, and I was thinking of drawing Rolo, but I didn't. Instead, I drew that person and that other person. I was really fortunate to be able to do that.

To everyone on the staff, to all my readers, and to those who helped me so much and supported me through the end: MSK, MTK, SKR, ARM, HZM, and SUM...and everybody else....

I appreciate your support from the bottom of my heart.
Thank you very, very much.

200807
ヨミノアツロ☺
Atsuro Yomino

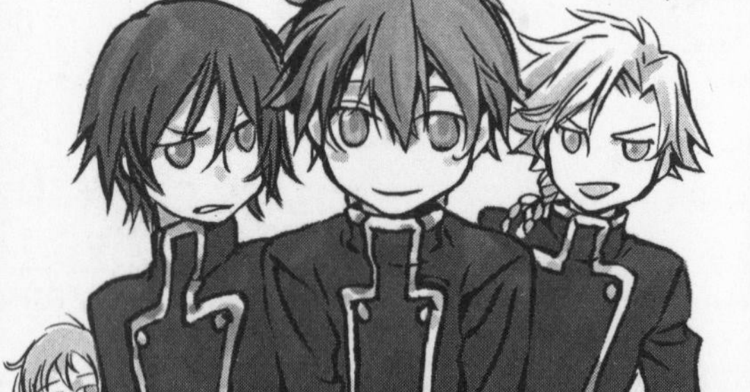

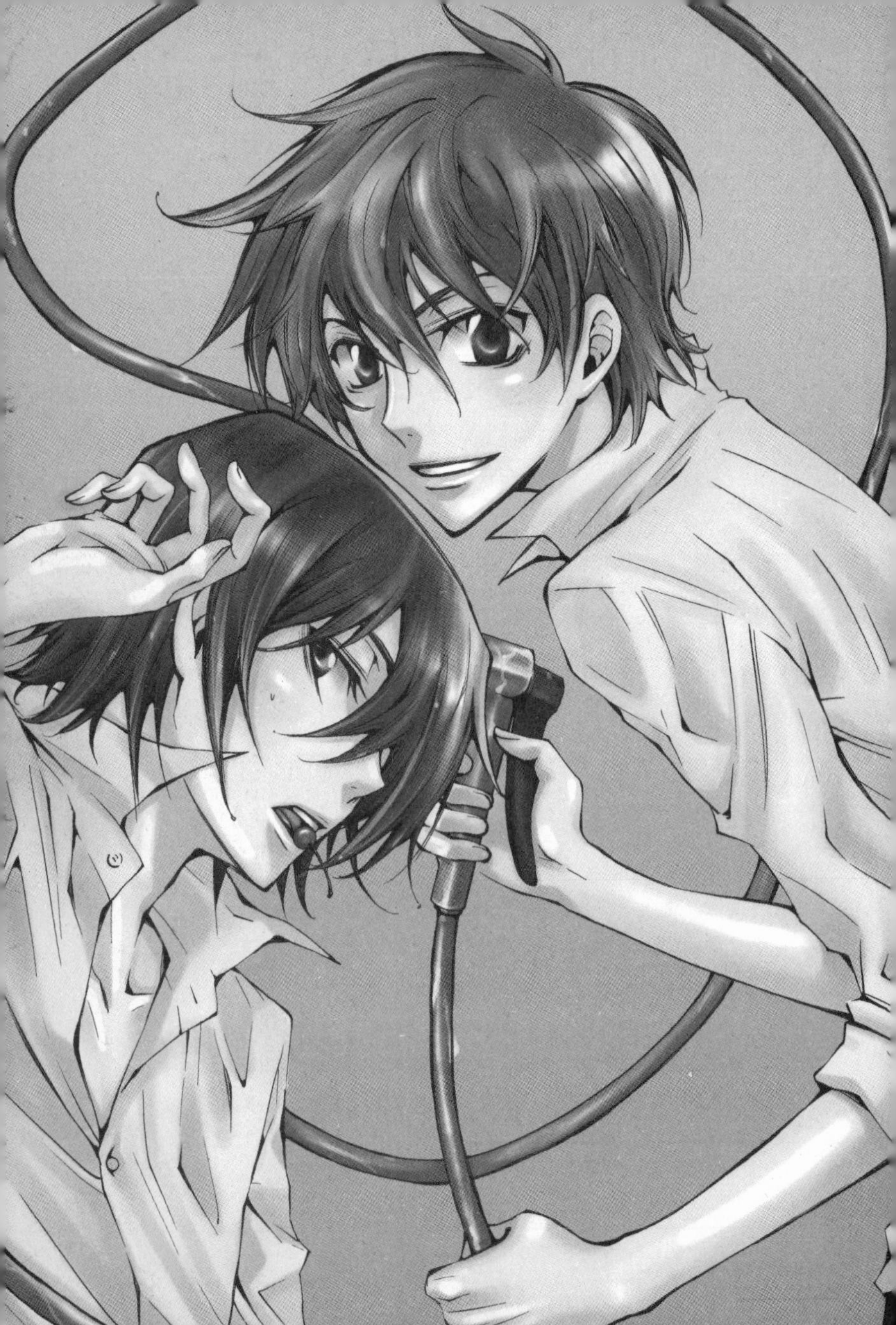

Phase 4

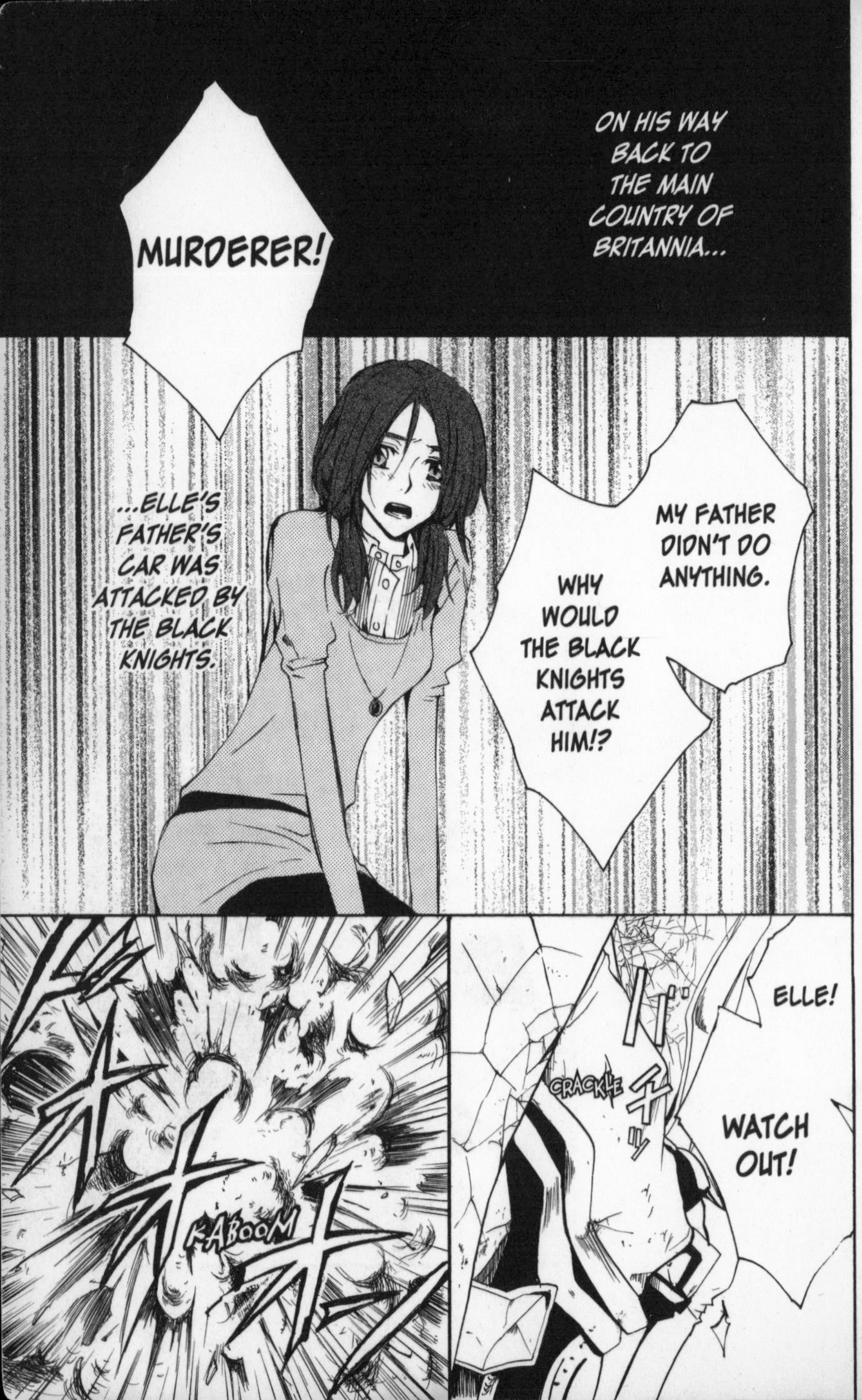
ON HIS WAY BACK TO THE MAIN COUNTRY OF BRITANNIA...
MURDERER!
MY FATHER DIDN'T DO ANYTHING.
WHY WOULD THE BLACK KNIGHTS ATTACK HIM!?
...ELLE'S FATHER'S CAR WAS ATTACKED BY THE BLACK KNIGHTS.
ELLE!
CRACKLE
WATCH OUT!
KABOOM

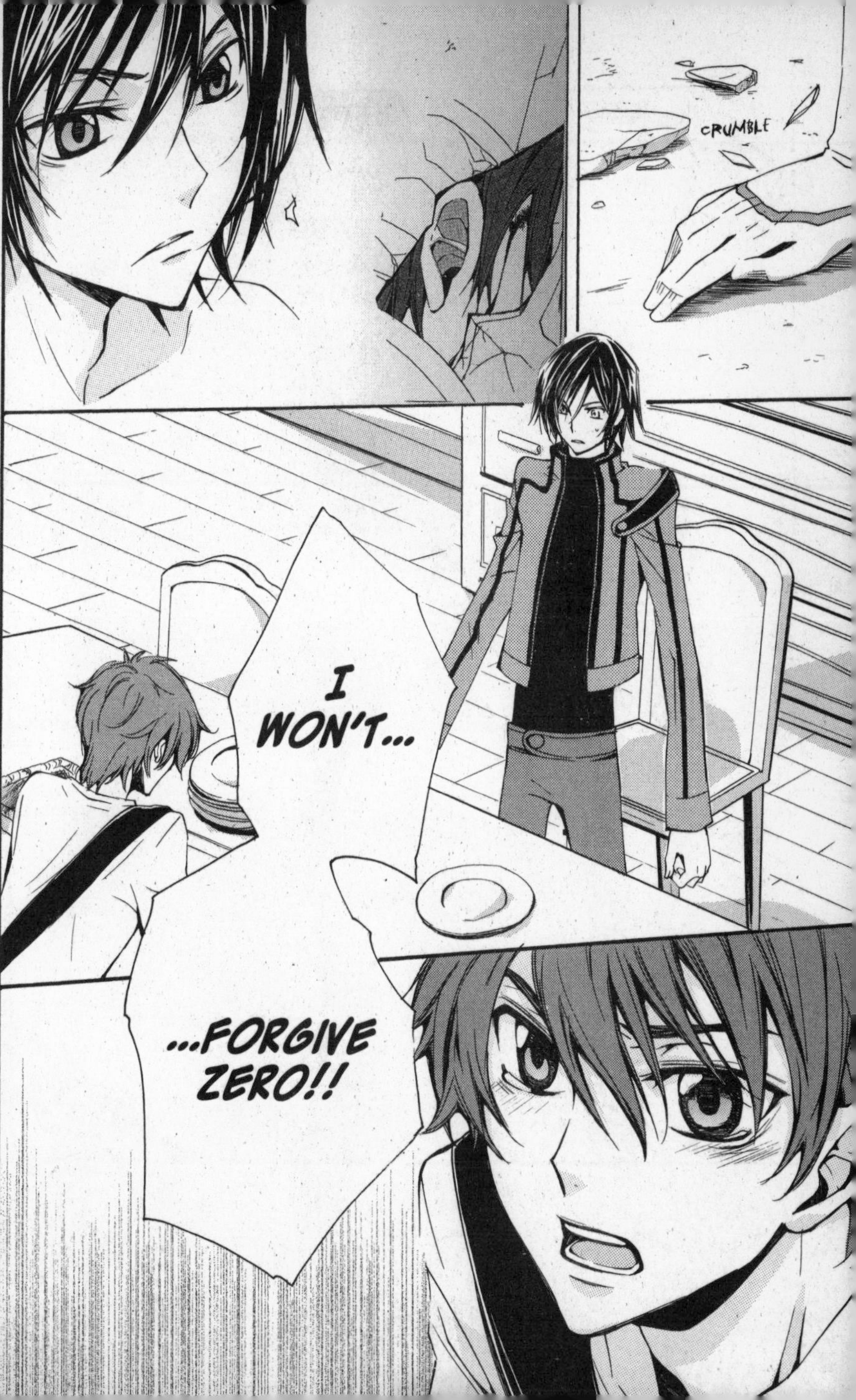
CRUMBLE
I WON'T...
...FORGIVE ZERO!!

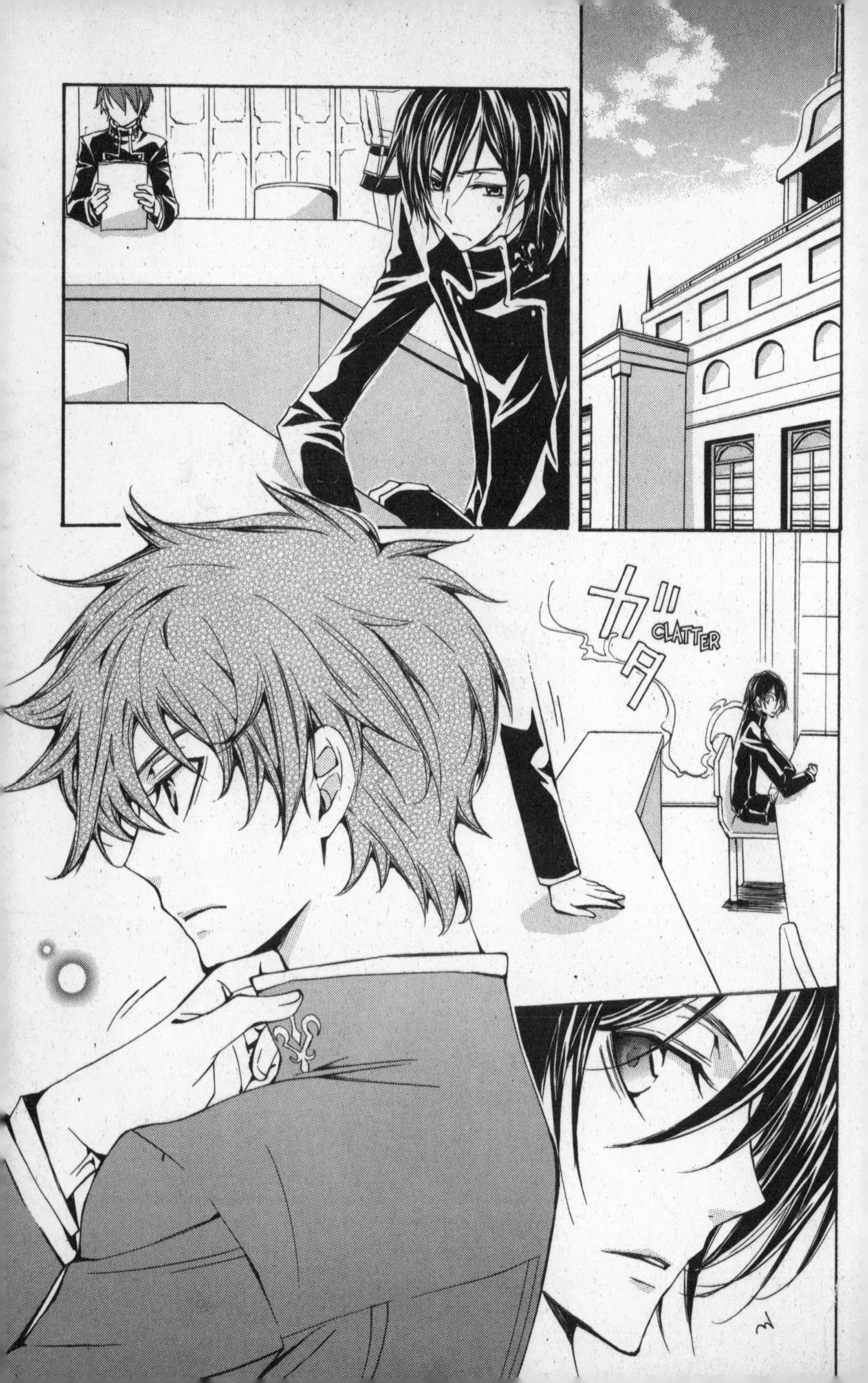
ガタ
CLATTER

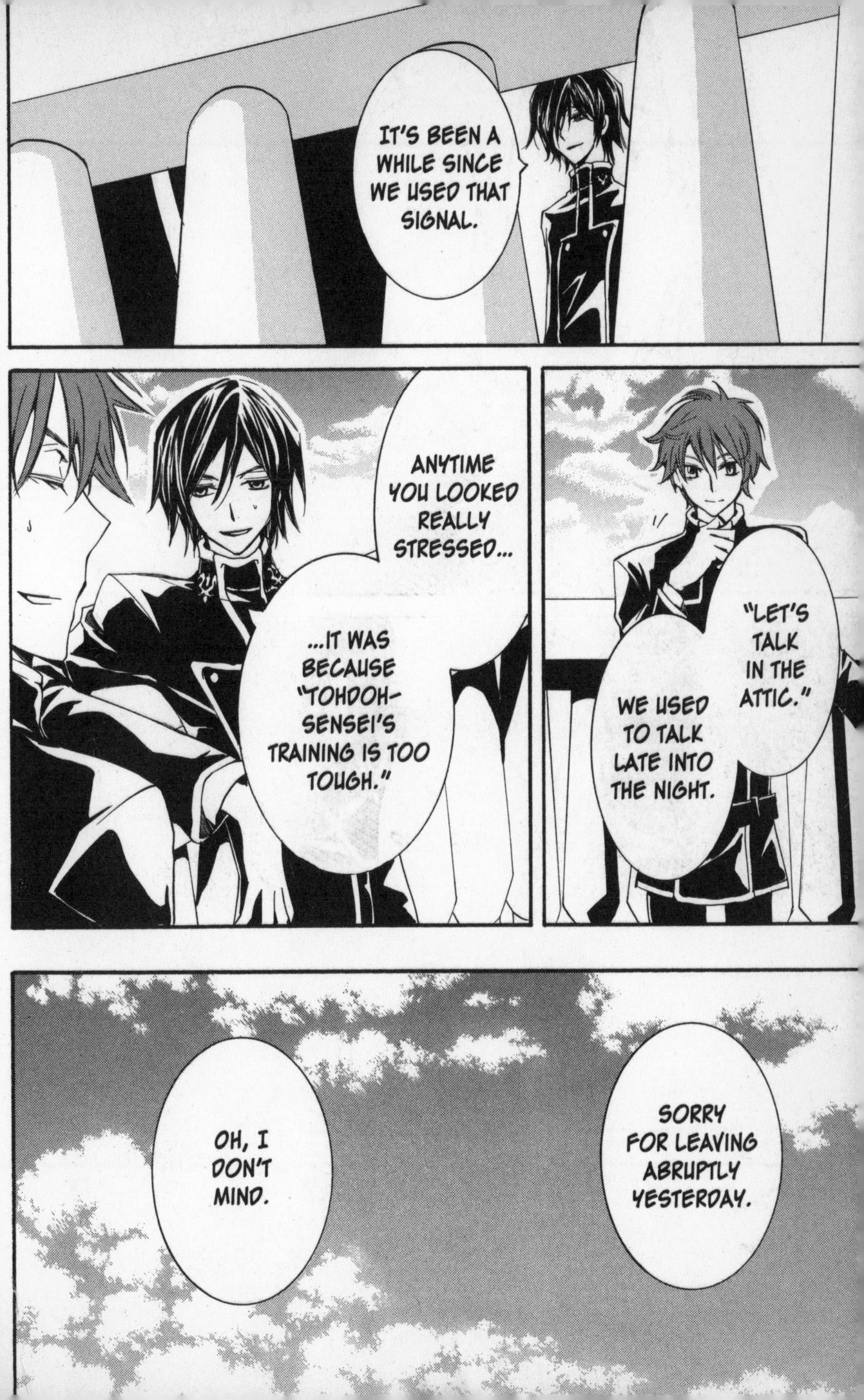
IT'S BEEN A WHILE SINCE WE USED THAT SIGNAL.
"LET'S TALK IN THE ATTIC."
WE USED TO TALK LATE INTO THE NIGHT.
ANYTIME YOU LOOKED REALLY STRESSED...
...IT WAS BECAUSE "TOHDOH-SENSEI'S TRAINING IS TOO TOUGH."
SORRY FOR LEAVING ABRUPTLY YESTERDAY.
OH, I DON'T MIND.

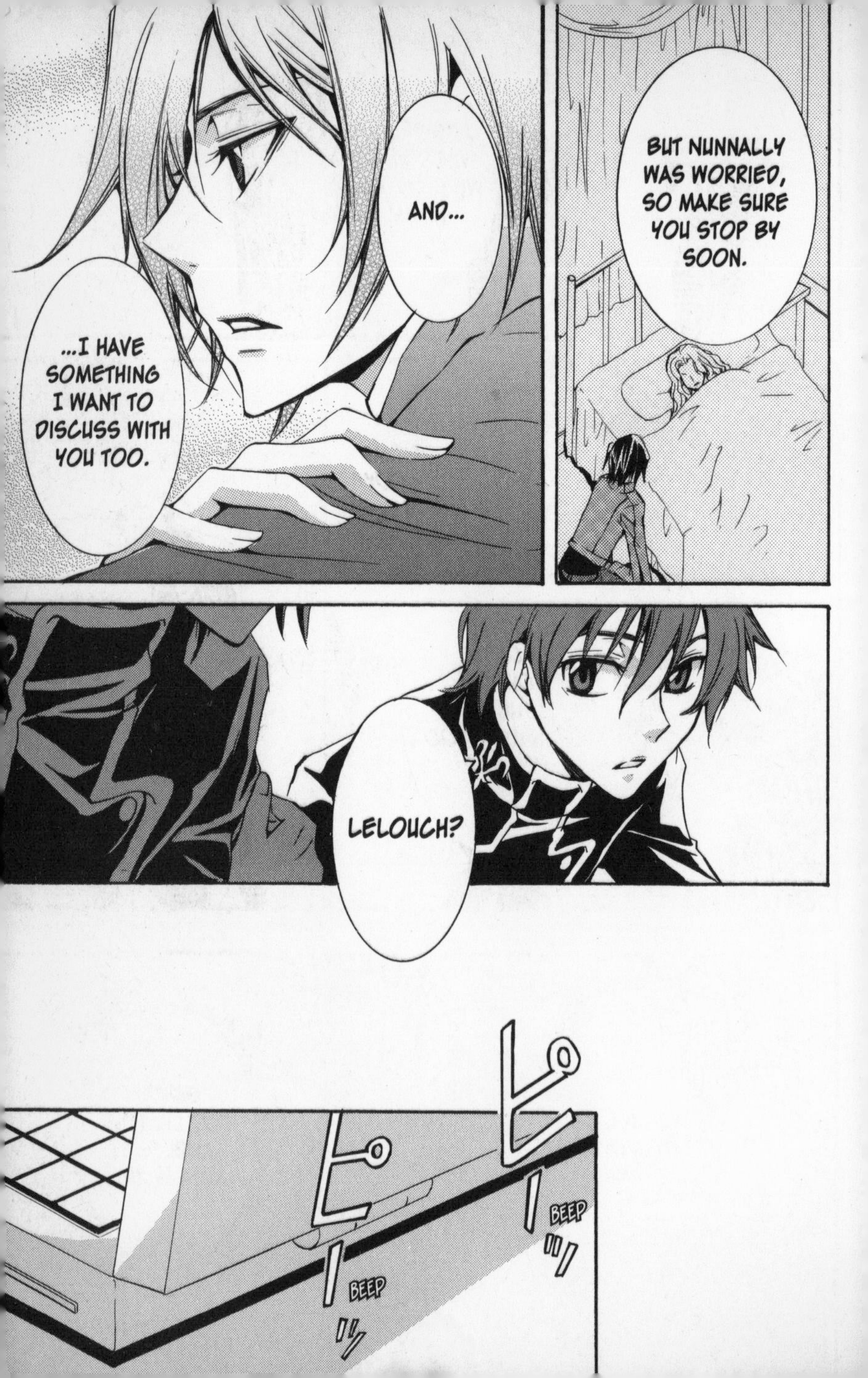
BUT NUNNALLY WAS WORRIED, SO MAKE SURE YOU STOP BY SOON.
AND...
...I HAVE SOMETHING I WANT TO DISCUSS WITH YOU TOO.
LELOUCH?
ピーッ
BEEP
ピーッ
BEEP

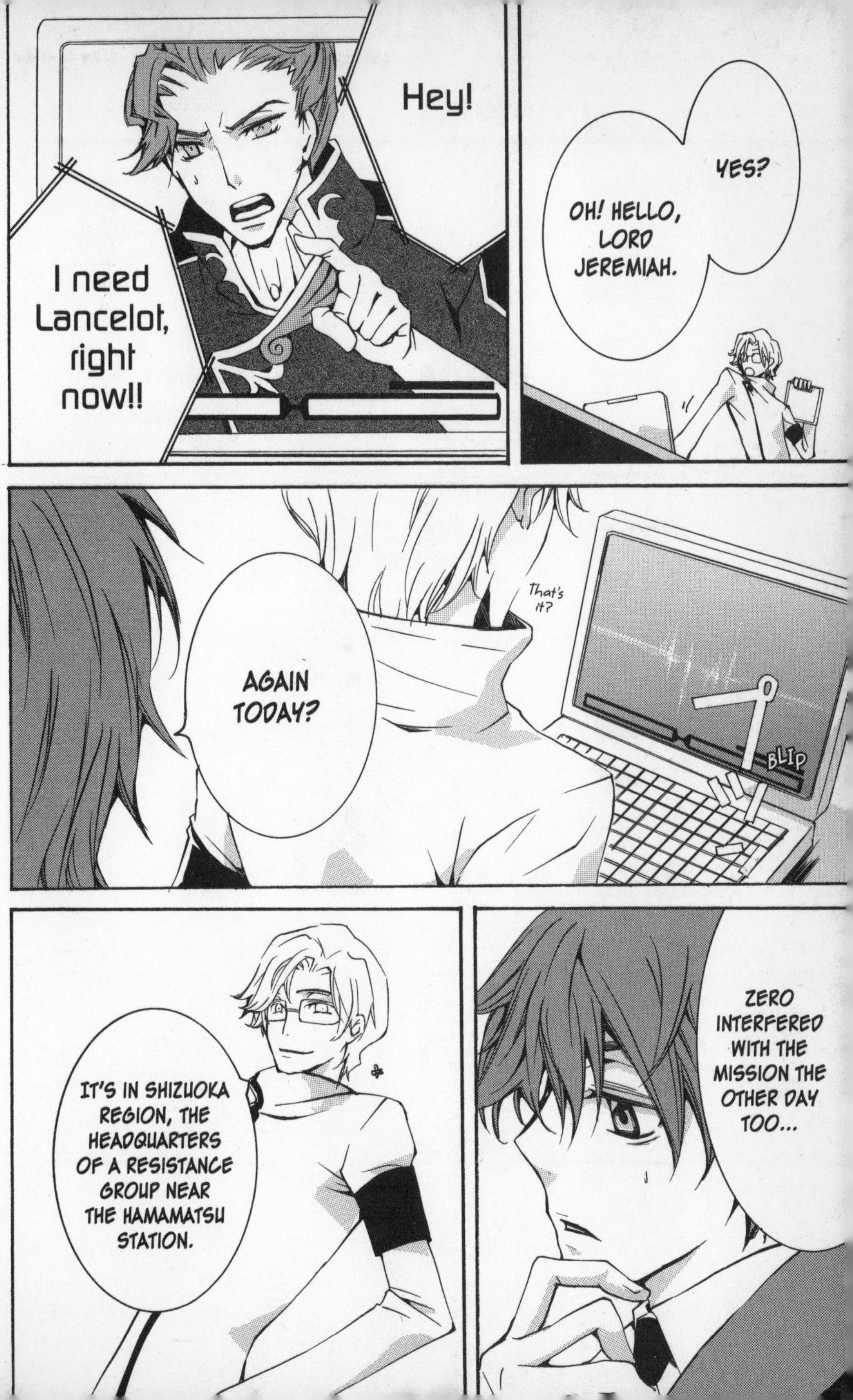
YES?
OH! HELLO, LORD JEREMIAH.
Hey!
I need Lancelot, right now!!
That's it?
AGAIN TODAY?
BLIP
ZERO INTERFERED WITH THE MISSION THE OTHER DAY TOO...
IT'S IN SHIZUOKA REGION, THE HEADQUARTERS OF A RESISTANCE GROUP NEAR THE HAMAMATSU STATION.

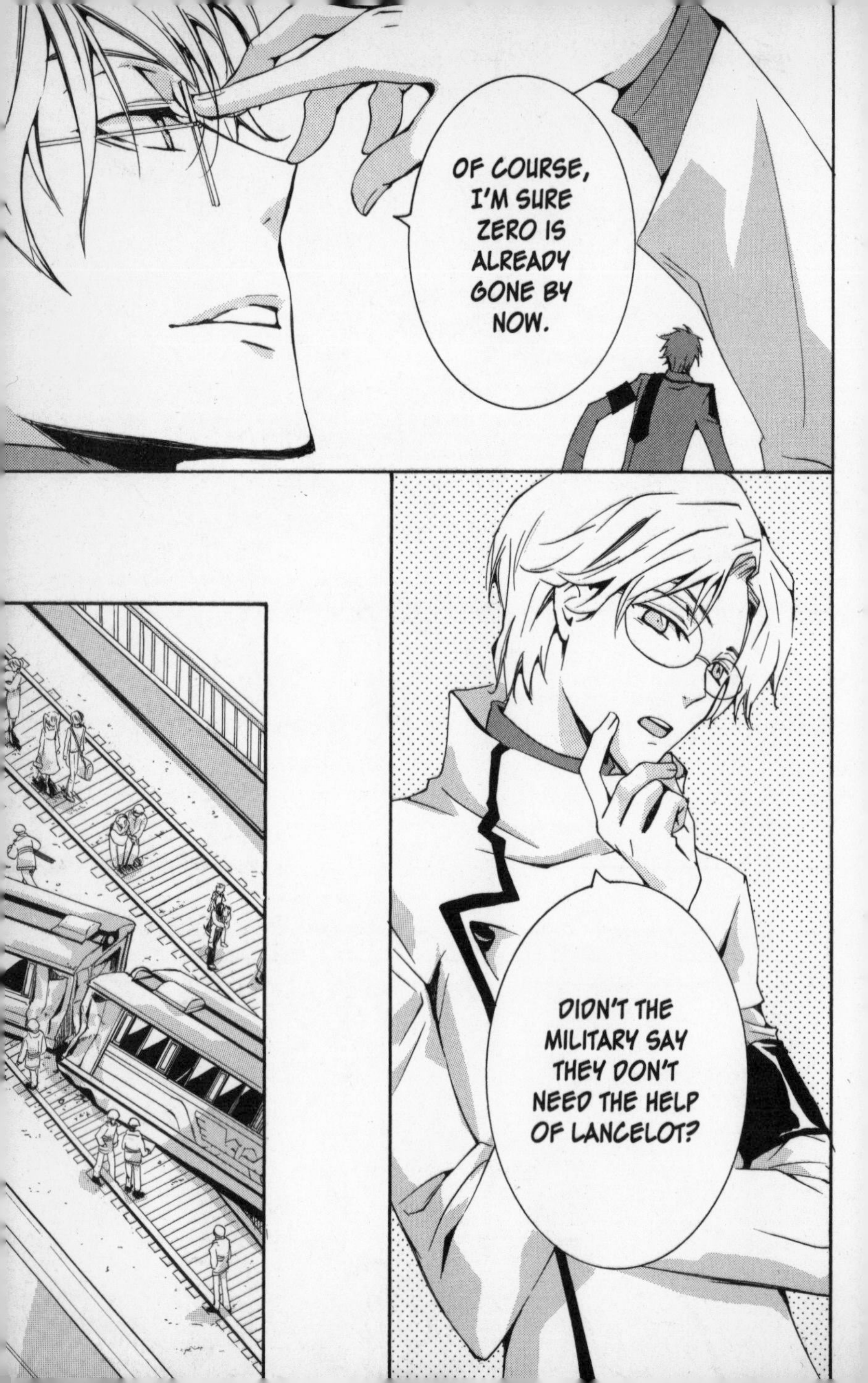
OF COURSE, I'M SURE ZERO IS ALREADY GONE BY NOW.
DIDN'T THE MILITARY SAY THEY DON'T NEED THE HELP OF LANCELOT?

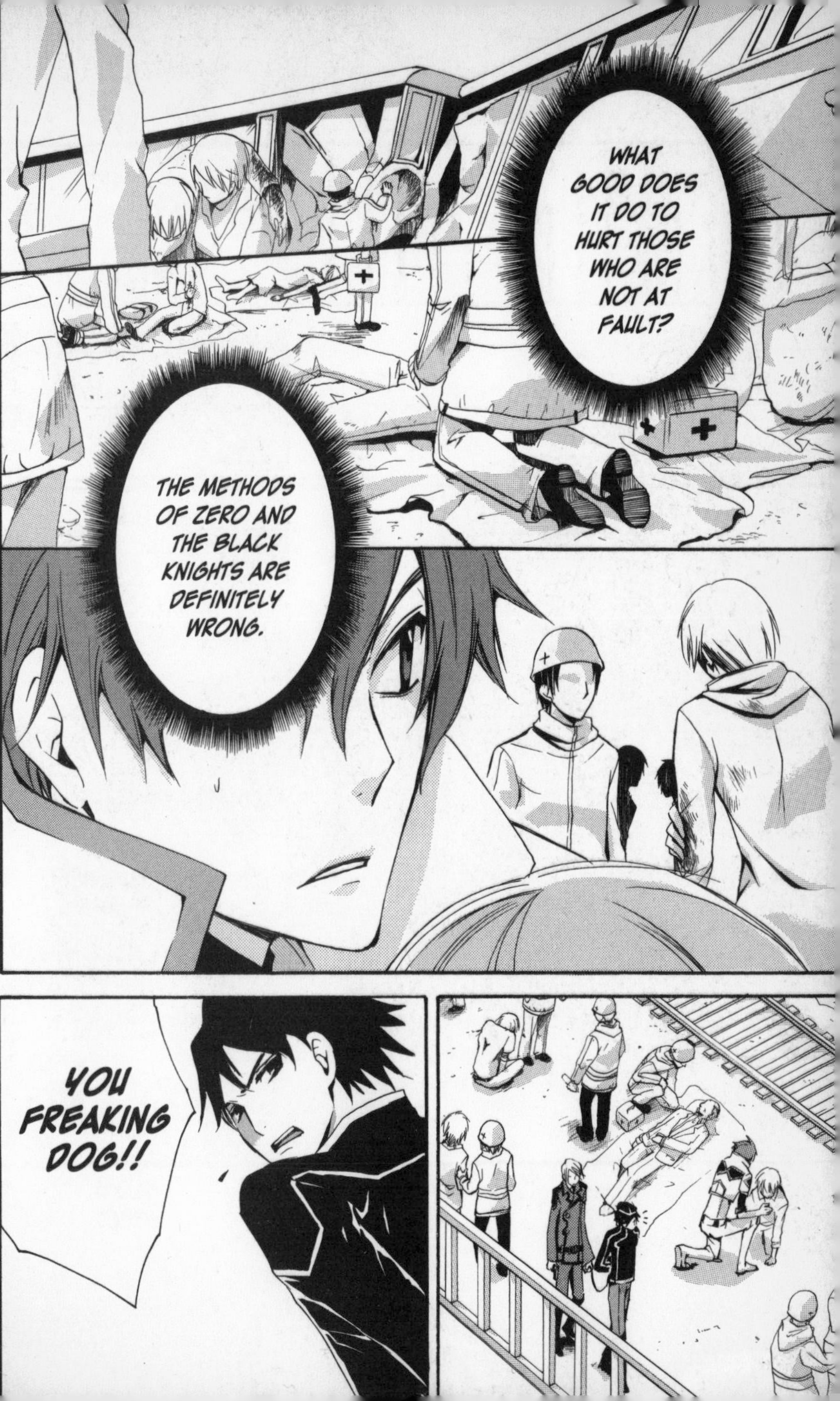
WHAT GOOD DOES IT DO TO HURT THOSE WHO ARE NOT AT FAULT?
THE METHODS OF ZERO AND THE BLACK KNIGHTS ARE DEFINITELY WRONG.
YOU FREAKING DOG!!

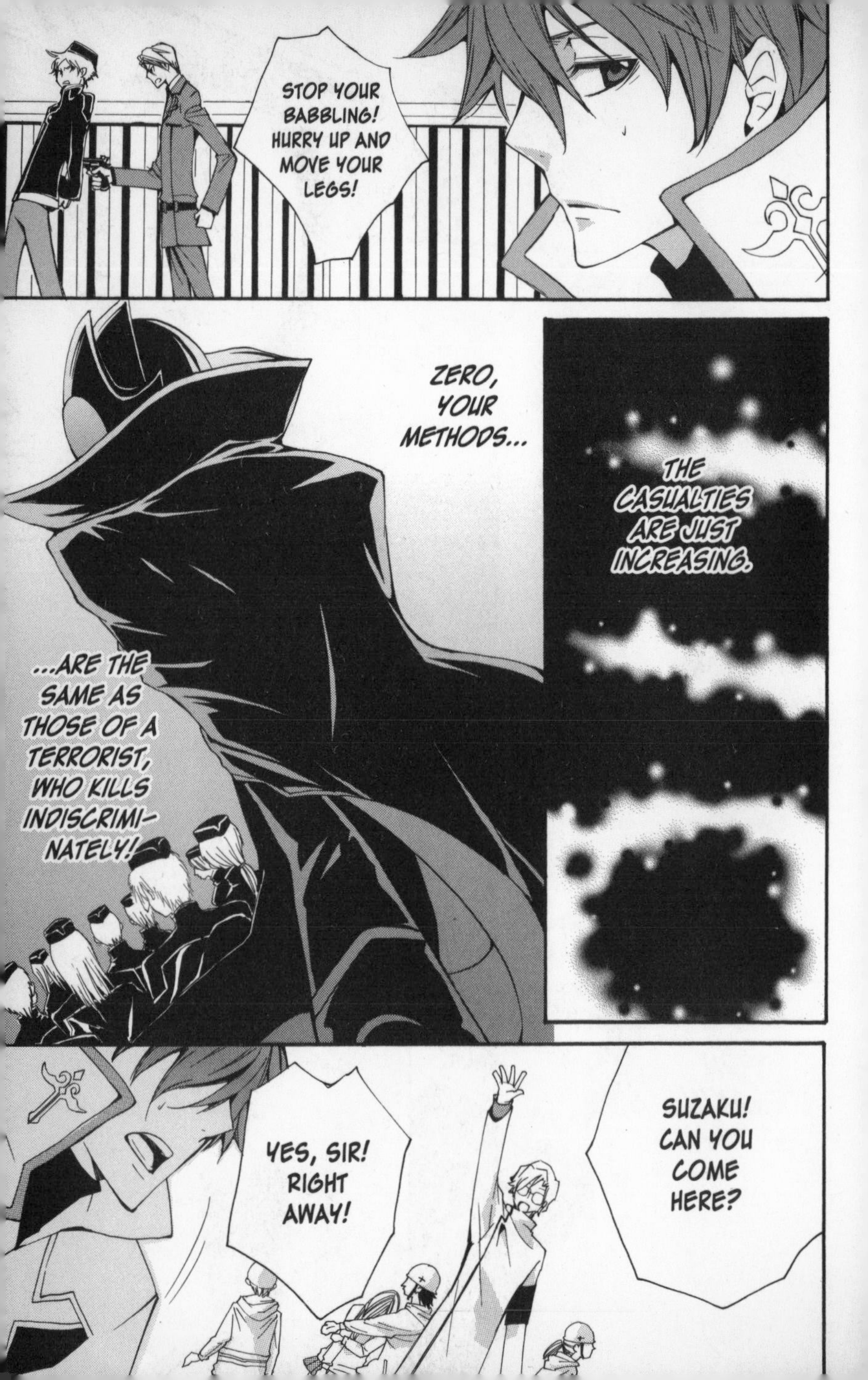
STOP YOUR BABBLING! HURRY UP AND MOVE YOUR LEGS!
THE CASUALTIES ARE JUST INCREASING.
ZERO, YOUR METHODS...
...ARE THE SAME AS THOSE OF A TERRORIST, WHO KILLS INDISCRIMI-NATELY!
SUZAKU! CAN YOU COME HERE?
YES, SIR! RIGHT AWAY!

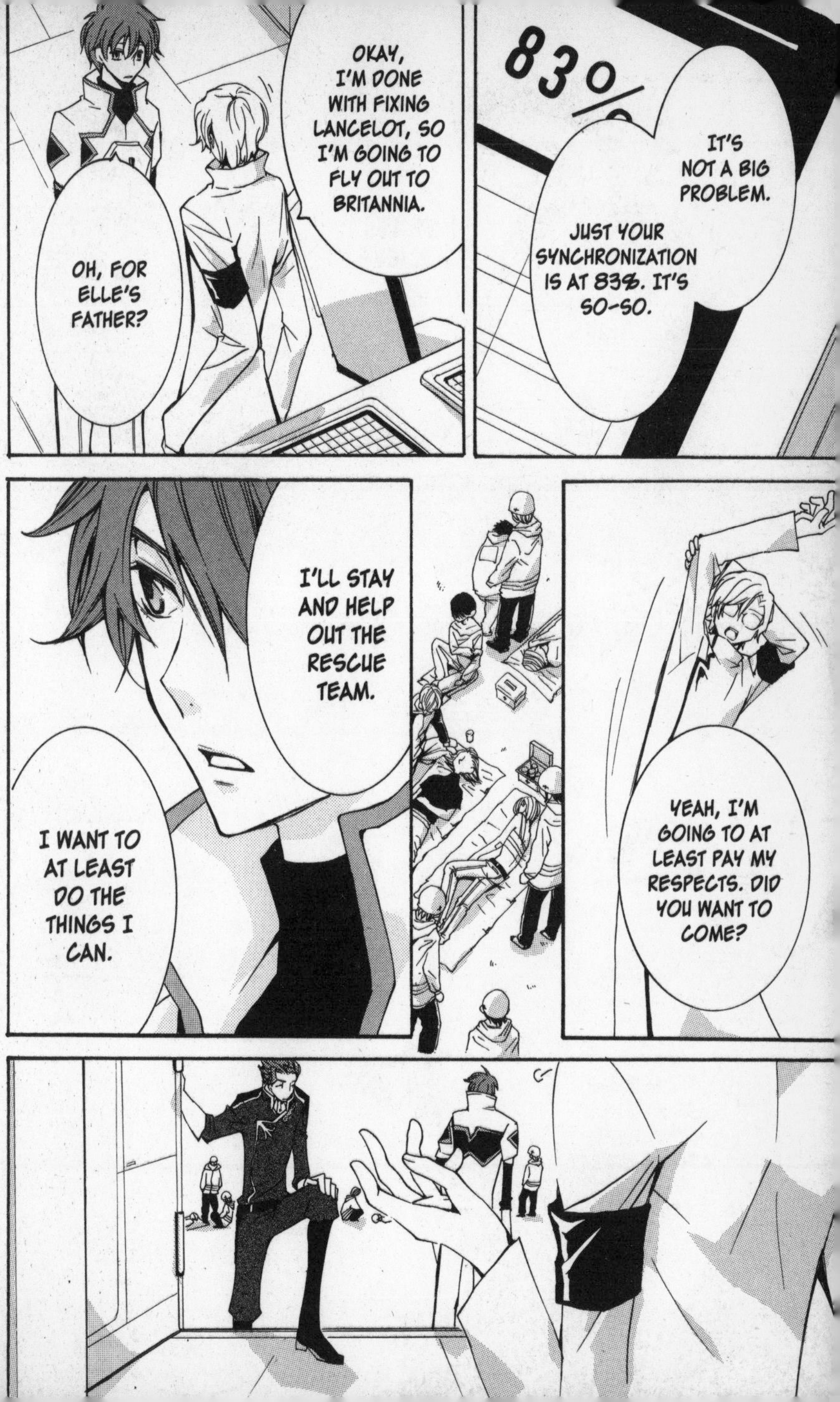
IT'S NOT A BIG PROBLEM.
JUST YOUR SYNCHRONIZATION IS AT 83%. IT'S SO-SO.
OKAY, I'M DONE WITH FIXING LANCELOT, SO I'M GOING TO FLY OUT TO BRITANNIA.
OH, FOR ELLE'S FATHER?
YEAH, I'M GOING TO AT LEAST PAY MY RESPECTS. DID YOU WANT TO COME?
I'LL STAY AND HELP OUT THE RESCUE TEAM.
I WANT TO AT LEAST DO THE THINGS I CAN.

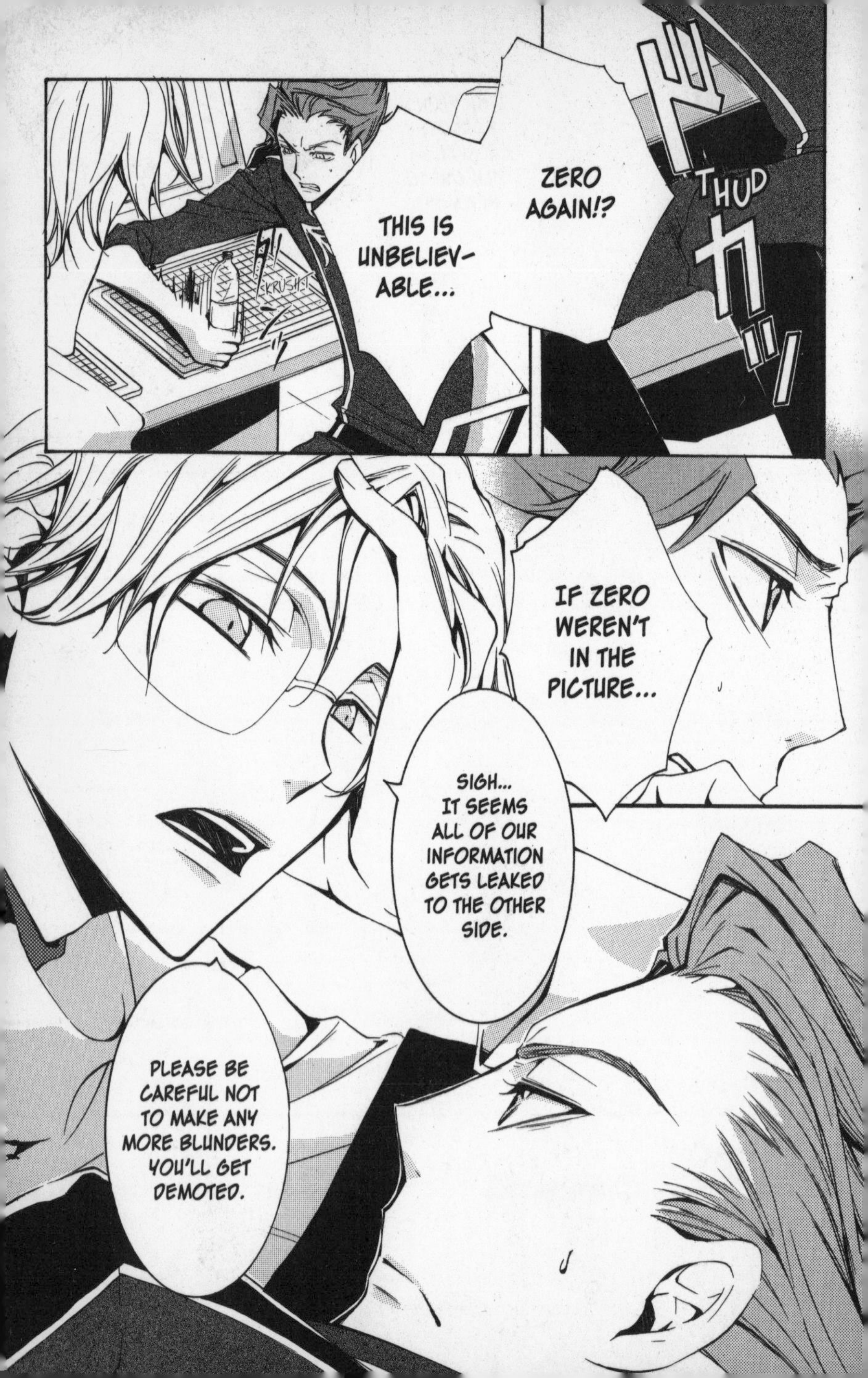
THUD
ZERO AGAIN!?
THIS IS UNBELIEV-ABLE...
KRUSH
IF ZERO WEREN'T IN THE PICTURE...
SIGH... IT SEEMS ALL OF OUR INFORMATION GETS LEAKED TO THE OTHER SIDE.
PLEASE BE CAREFUL NOT TO MAKE ANY MORE BLUNDERS. YOU'LL GET DEMOTED.

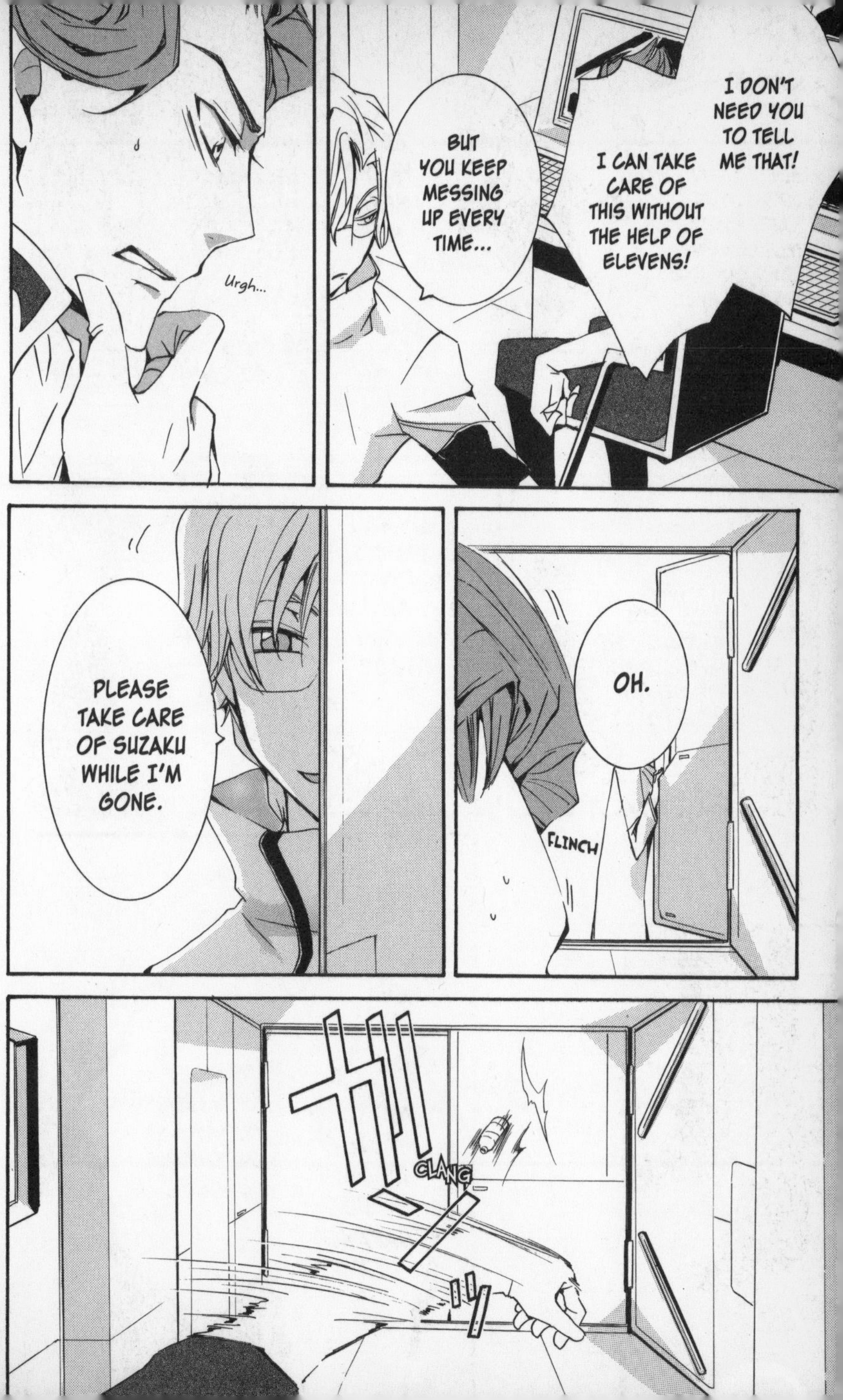
I DON'T NEED YOU TO TELL ME THAT!
I CAN TAKE CARE OF THIS WITHOUT THE HELP OF ELEVENS!
BUT YOU KEEP MESSING UP EVERY TIME...
Urgh...
OH.
FLINCH
PLEASE TAKE CARE OF SUZAKU WHILE I'M GONE.
CLANG

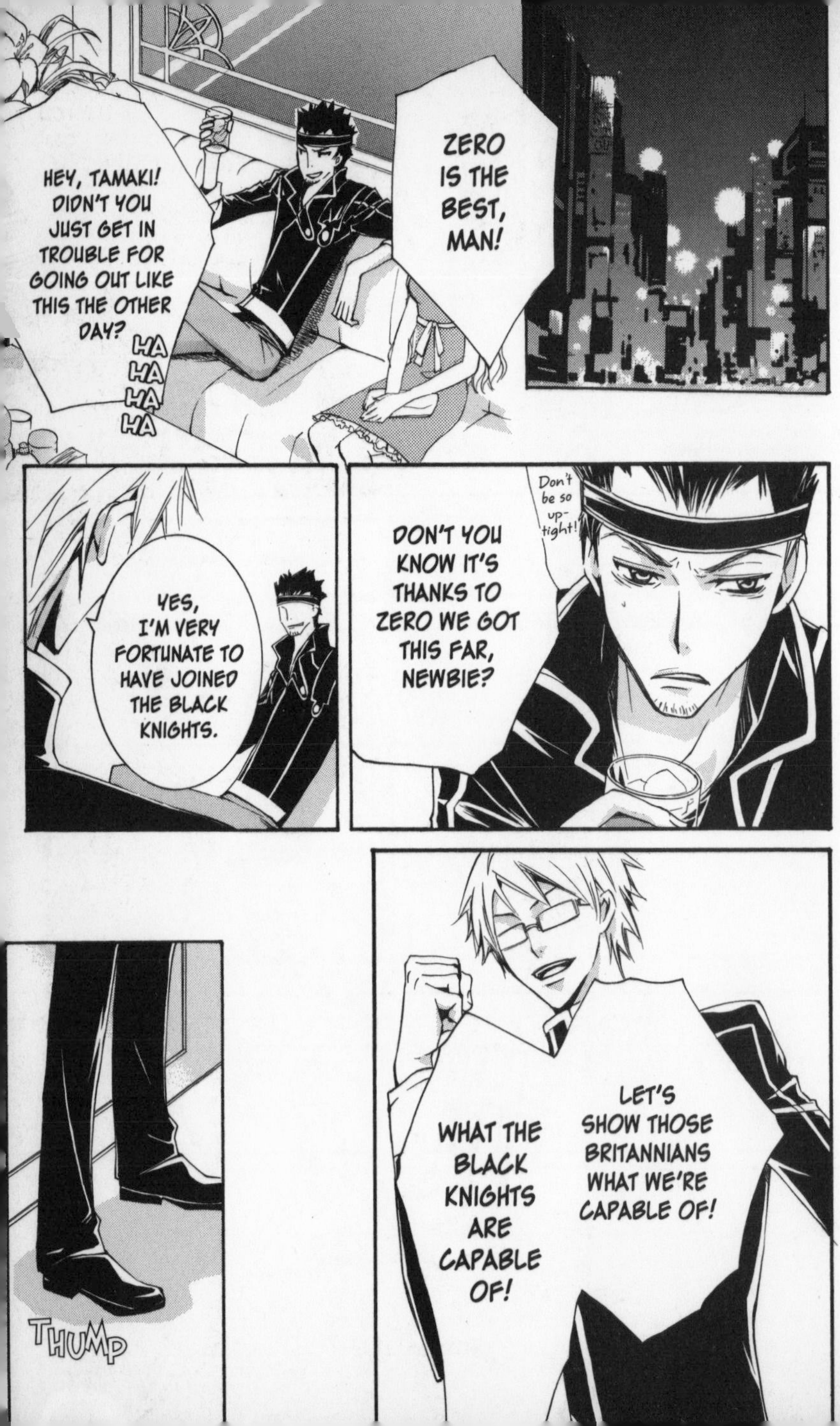
ZERO IS THE BEST, MAN!
HEY, TAMAKI! DIDN'T YOU JUST GET IN TROUBLE FOR GOING OUT LIKE THIS THE OTHER DAY?
HA HA HA HA
Don't be so up-tight!
DON'T YOU KNOW IT'S THANKS TO ZERO WE GOT THIS FAR, NEWBIE?
YES, I'M VERY FORTUNATE TO HAVE JOINED THE BLACK KNIGHTS.
LET'S SHOW THOSE BRITANNIANS WHAT WE'RE CAPABLE OF!
WHAT THE BLACK KNIGHTS ARE CAPABLE OF!
THUMP

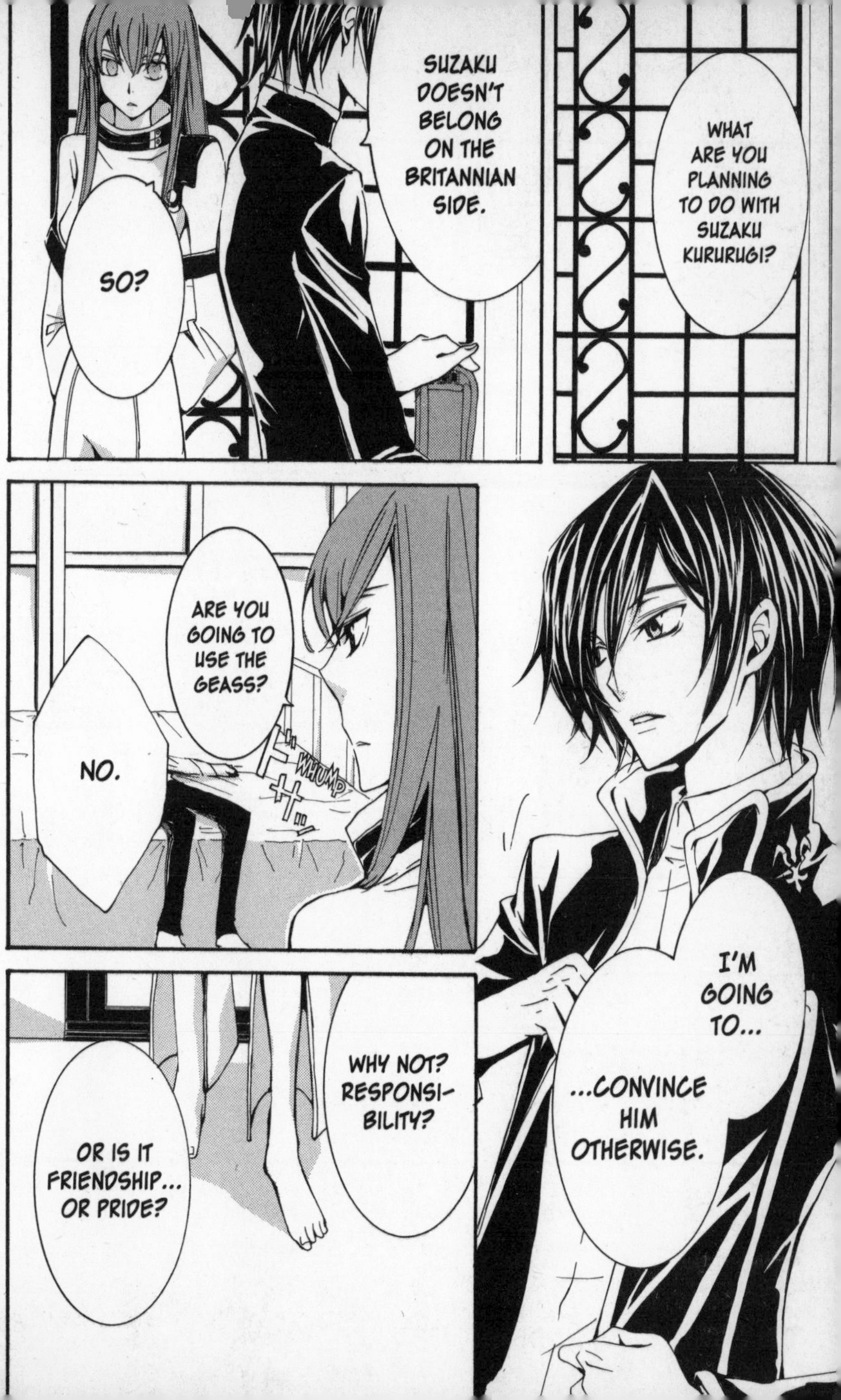
WHAT ARE YOU PLANNING TO DO WITH SUZAKU KURURUGI?
SUZAKU DOESN'T BELONG ON THE BRITANNIAN SIDE.
SO?
I'M GOING TO...
...CONVINCE HIM OTHERWISE.
ARE YOU GOING TO USE THE GEASS?
NO.
WHUMP
WHY NOT? RESPONSI-BILITY?
OR IS IT FRIENDSHIP... OR PRIDE?

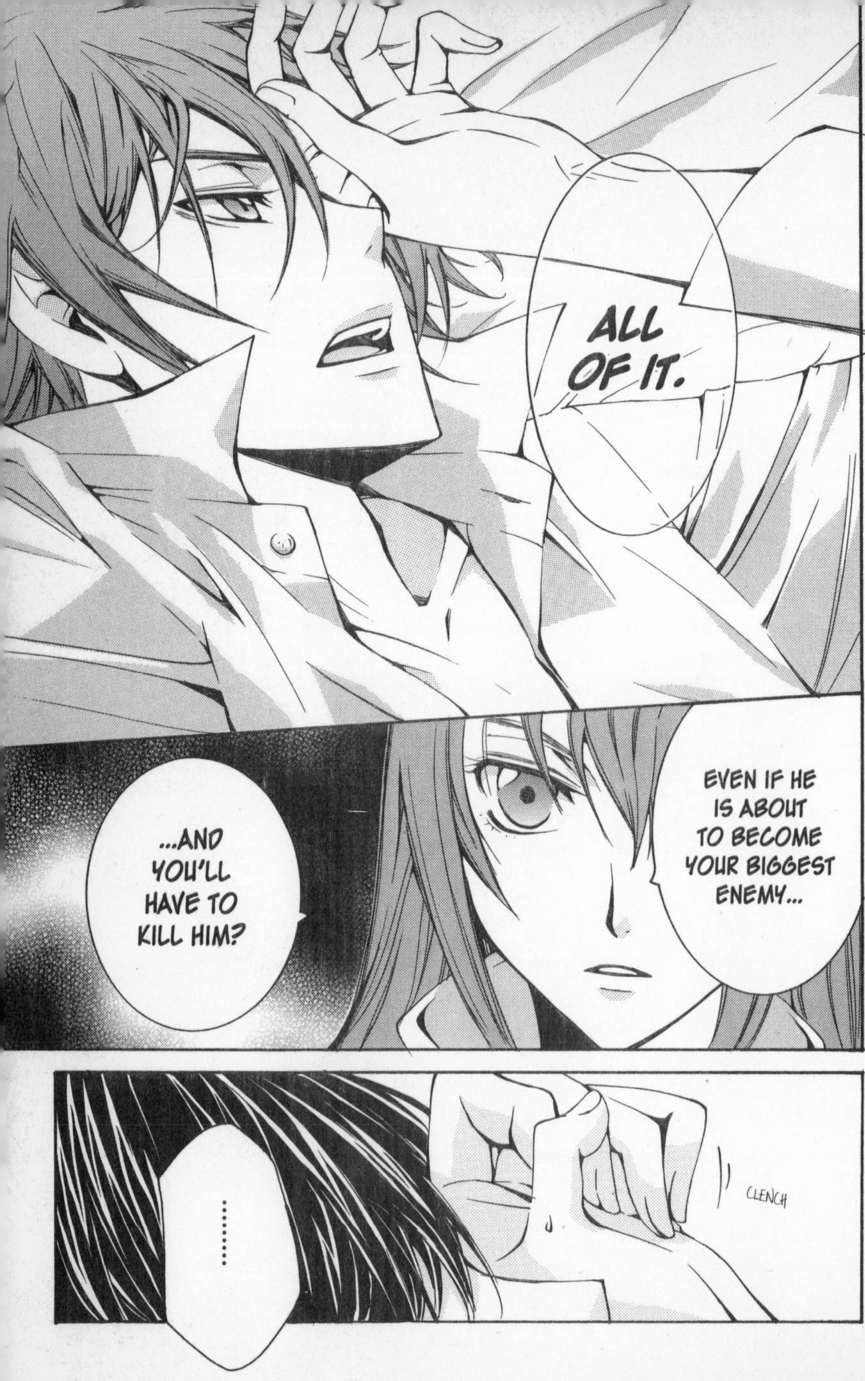
ALL OF IT.
EVEN IF HE IS ABOUT TO BECOME YOUR BIGGEST ENEMY...
...AND YOU'LL HAVE TO KILL HIM?
CLENCH
......

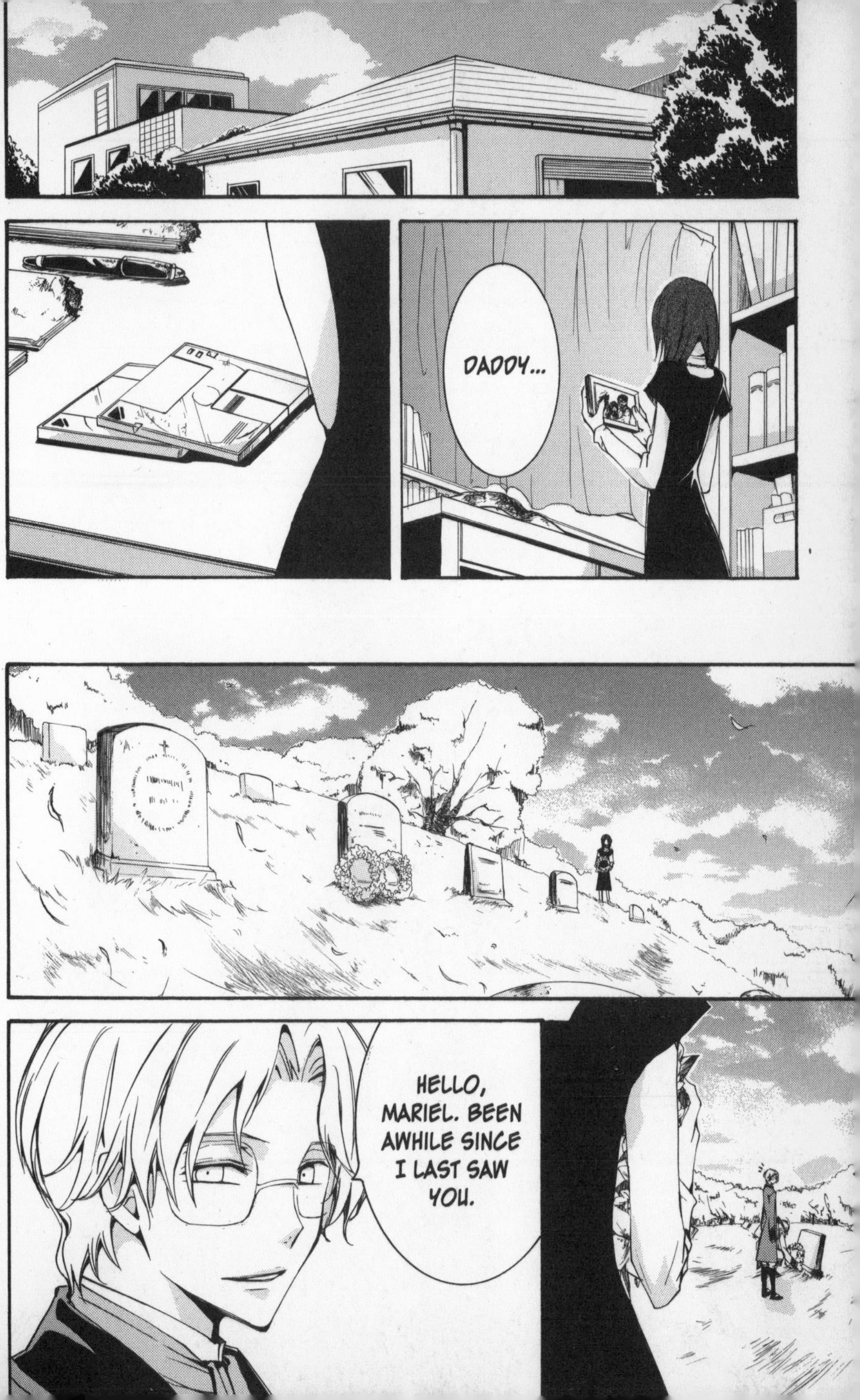
DADDY...
HELLO, MARIEL. BEEN AWHILE SINCE I LAST SAW YOU.

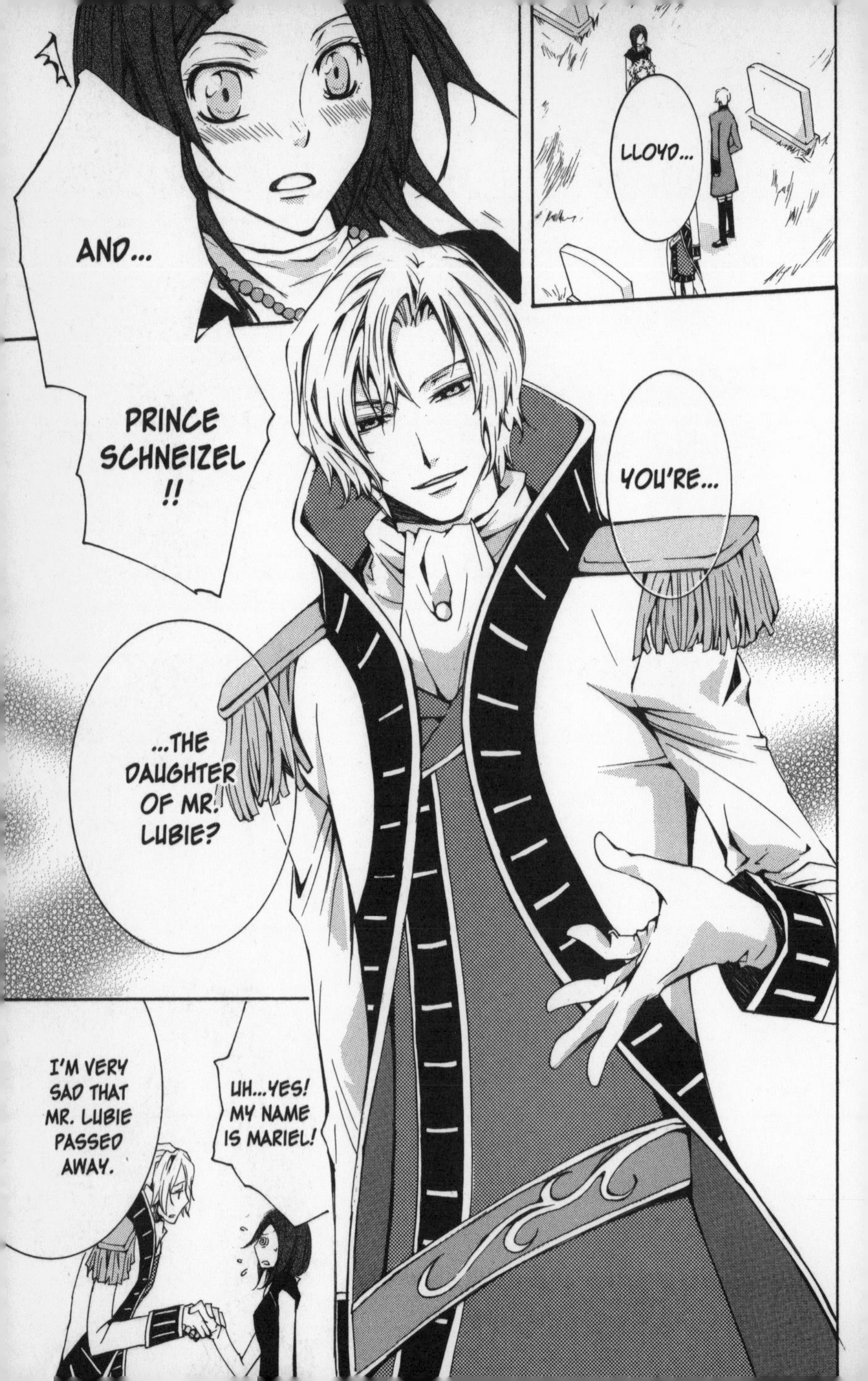
LLOYD...
AND...
PRINCE SCHNEIZEL !!
YOU'RE...
...THE DAUGHTER OF MR. LUBIE?
UH...YES! MY NAME IS MARIEL!
I'M VERY SAD THAT MR. LUBIE PASSED AWAY.

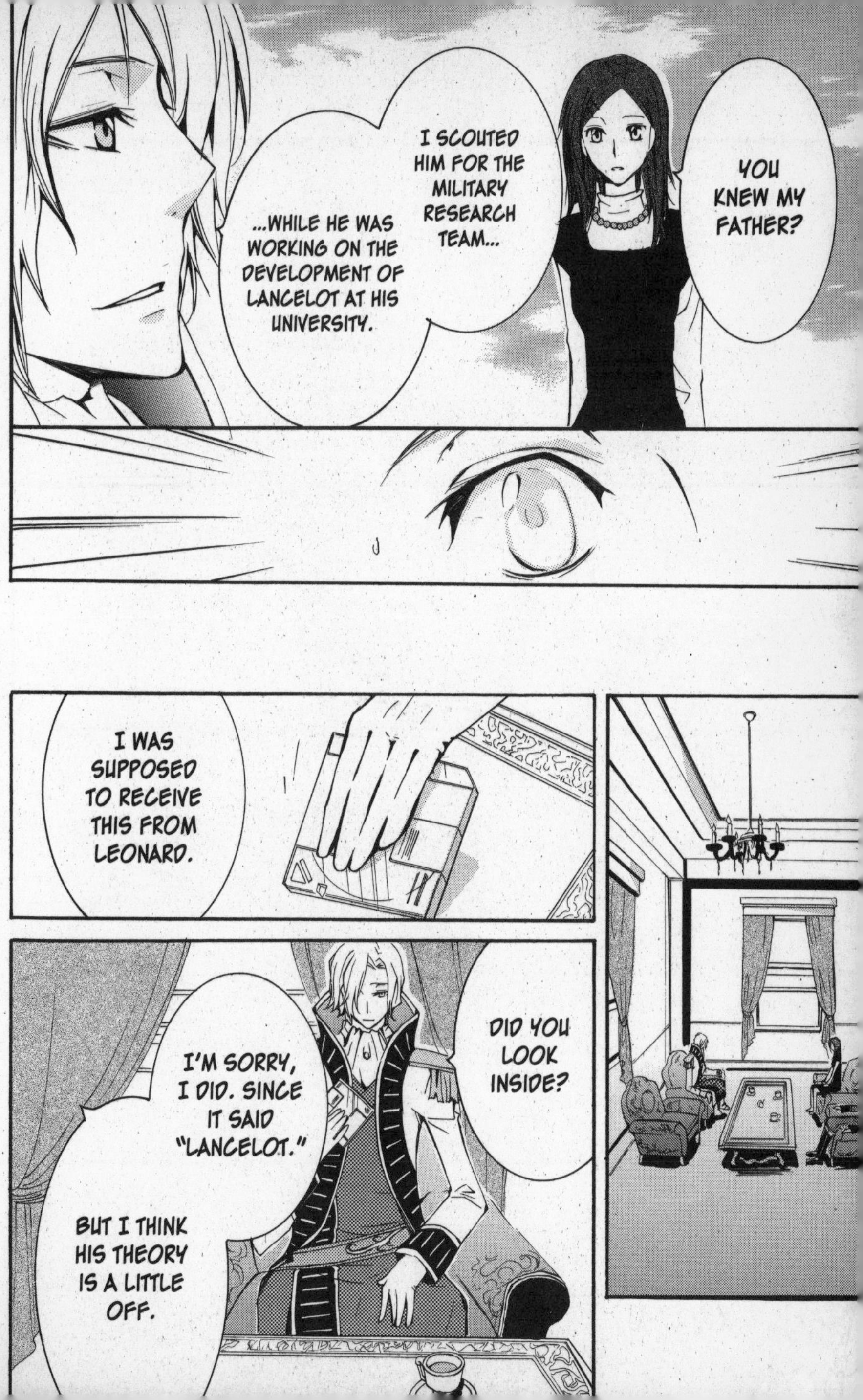
YOU KNEW MY FATHER?
I SCOUTED HIM FOR THE MILITARY RESEARCH TEAM...
...WHILE HE WAS WORKING ON THE DEVELOPMENT OF LANCELOT AT HIS UNIVERSITY.
I WAS SUPPOSED TO RECEIVE THIS FROM LEONARD.
DID YOU LOOK INSIDE?
I'M SORRY, I DID. SINCE IT SAID "LANCELOT."
BUT I THINK HIS THEORY IS A LITTLE OFF.

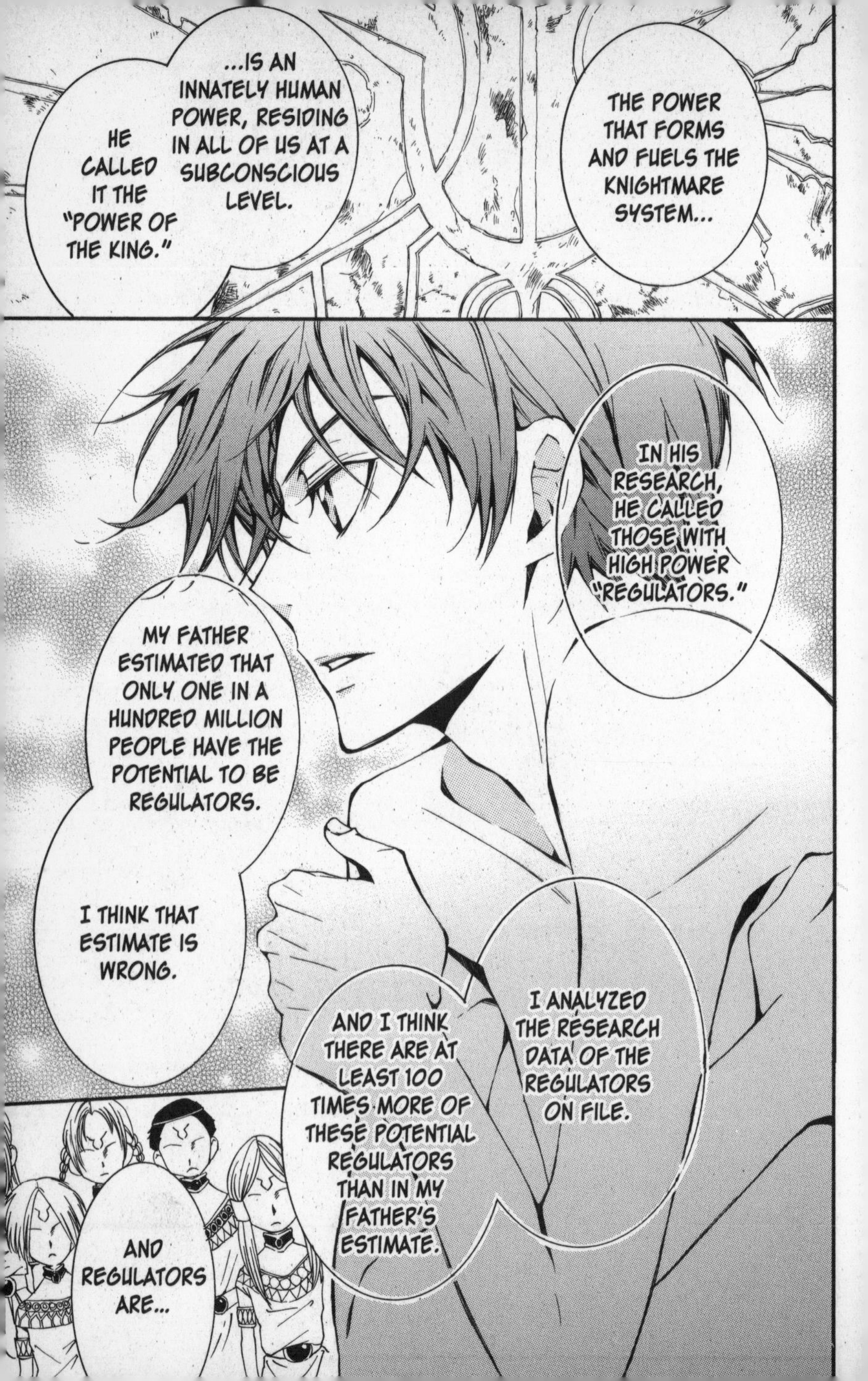
THE POWER THAT FORMS AND FUELS THE KNIGHTMARE SYSTEM...
...IS AN INNATELY HUMAN POWER, RESIDING IN ALL OF US AT A SUBCONSCIOUS LEVEL.
HE CALLED IT THE "POWER OF THE KING."
IN HIS RESEARCH, HE CALLED THOSE WITH HIGH POWER "REGULATORS."
MY FATHER ESTIMATED THAT ONLY ONE IN A HUNDRED MILLION PEOPLE HAVE THE POTENTIAL TO BE REGULATORS.
I THINK THAT ESTIMATE IS WRONG.
I ANALYZED THE RESEARCH DATA OF THE REGULATORS ON FILE.
AND I THINK THERE ARE AT LEAST 100 TIMES MORE OF THESE POTENTIAL REGULATORS THAN IN MY FATHER'S ESTIMATE.
AND REGULATORS ARE...

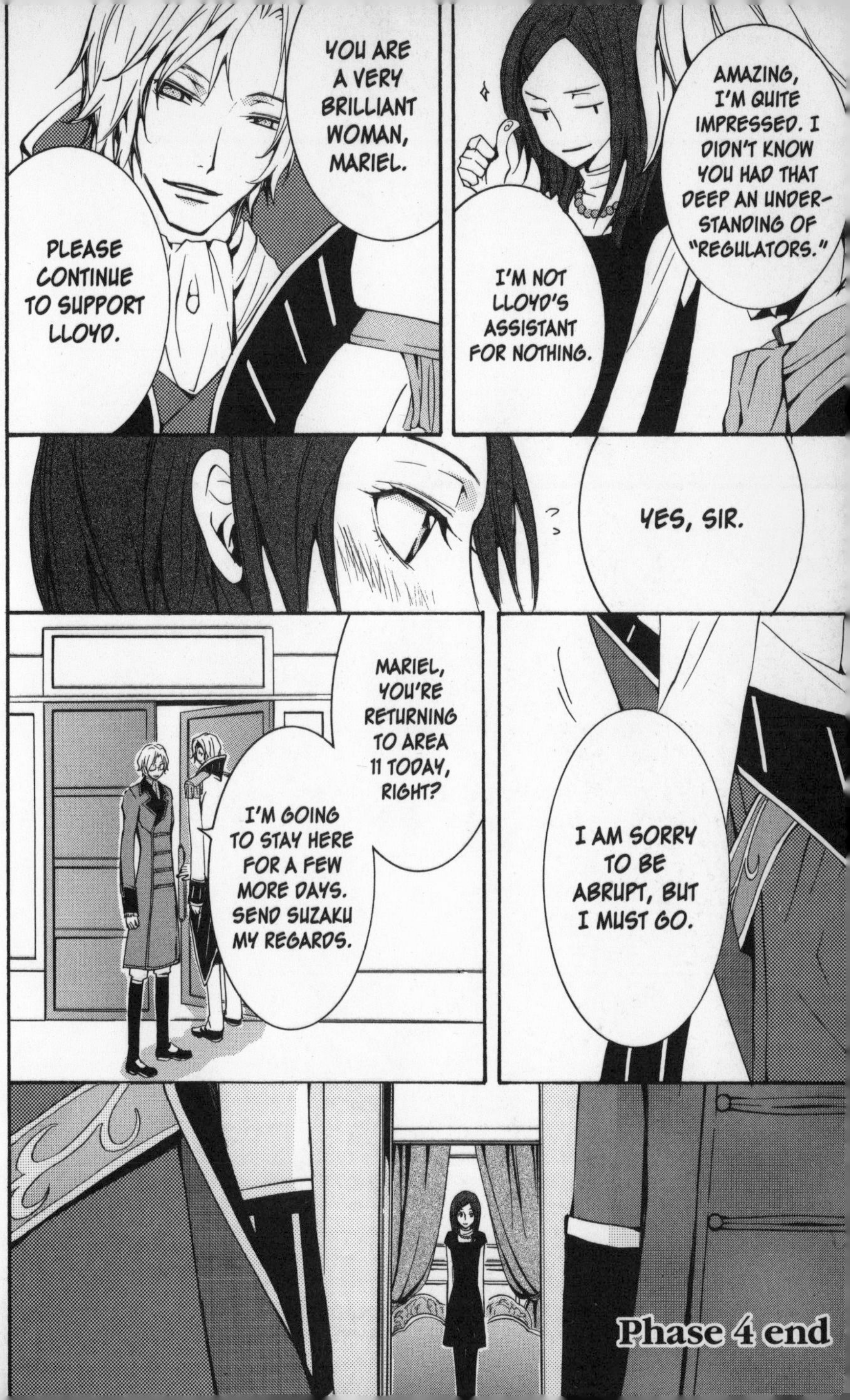
AMAZING, I'M QUITE IMPRESSED. I DIDN'T KNOW YOU HAD THAT DEEP AN UNDER-STANDING OF "REGULATORS."
I'M NOT LLOYD'S ASSISTANT FOR NOTHING.
YOU ARE A VERY BRILLIANT WOMAN, MARIEL.
PLEASE CONTINUE TO SUPPORT LLOYD.
YES, SIR.
I AM SORRY TO BE ABRUPT, BUT I MUST GO.
MARIEL, YOU'RE RETURNING TO AREA 11 TODAY, RIGHT?
I'M GOING TO STAY HERE FOR A FEW MORE DAYS. SEND SUZAKU MY REGARDS.
Phase 4 end

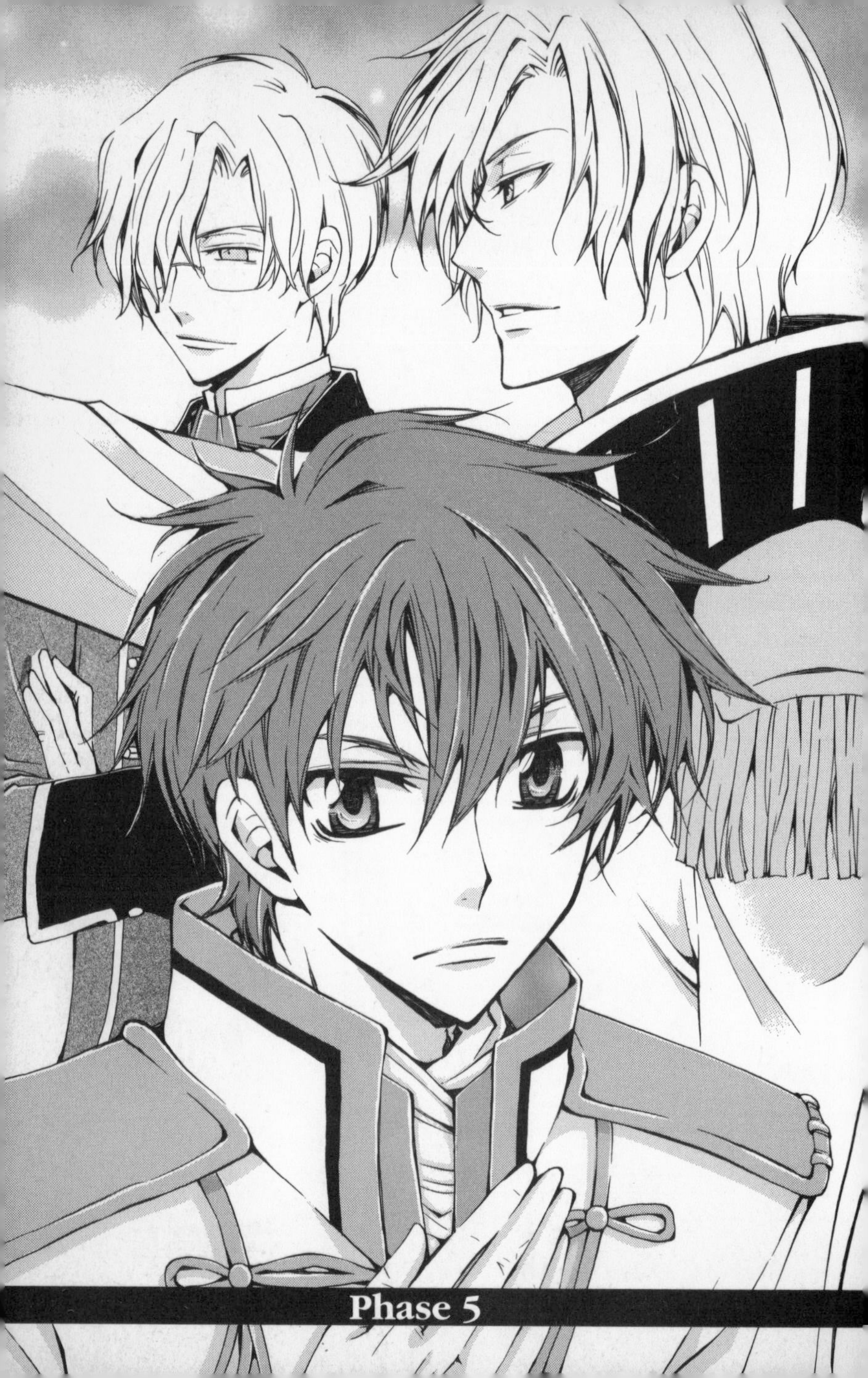

Phase 5

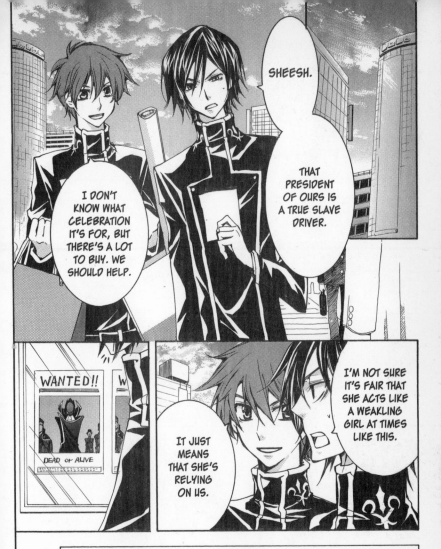

SHEESH.
THAT PRESIDENT OF OURS IS A TRUE SLAVE DRIVER.
I DON'T KNOW WHAT CELEBRATION IT'S FOR, BUT THERE'S A LOT TO BUY. WE SHOULD HELP.
I'M NOT SURE IT'S FAIR THAT SHE ACTS LIKE A WEAKLING GIRL AT TIMES LIKE THIS.
IT JUST MEANS THAT SHE'S RELYING ON US.
WANTED!!
DEAD or ALIVE

About Small Toys

The design on Prince Schneizel's coat, especially the trim, was hard to draw, so I used the little "Chibi Voice Schneizel" toy as reference.

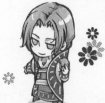

It's pretty handy. But the head is enormous, so it wasn't useful when drawing proportions.

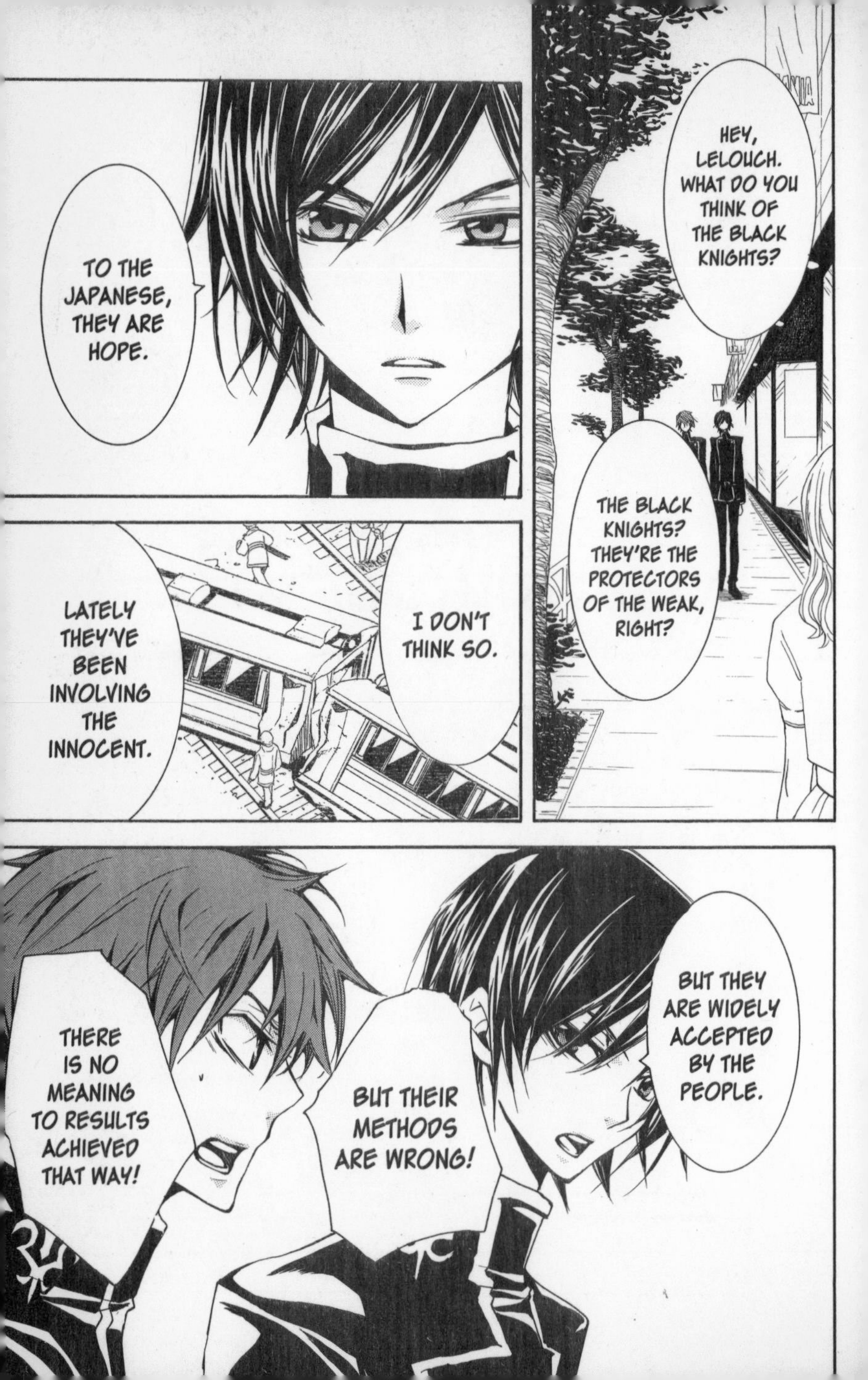
HEY, LELOUCH. WHAT DO YOU THINK OF THE BLACK KNIGHTS?
THE BLACK KNIGHTS? THEY'RE THE PROTECTORS OF THE WEAK, RIGHT?
TO THE JAPANESE, THEY ARE HOPE.
I DON'T THINK SO.
LATELY THEY'VE BEEN INVOLVING THE INNOCENT.
BUT THEY ARE WIDELY ACCEPTED BY THE PEOPLE.
BUT THEIR METHODS ARE WRONG!
THERE IS NO MEANING TO RESULTS ACHIEVED THAT WAY!

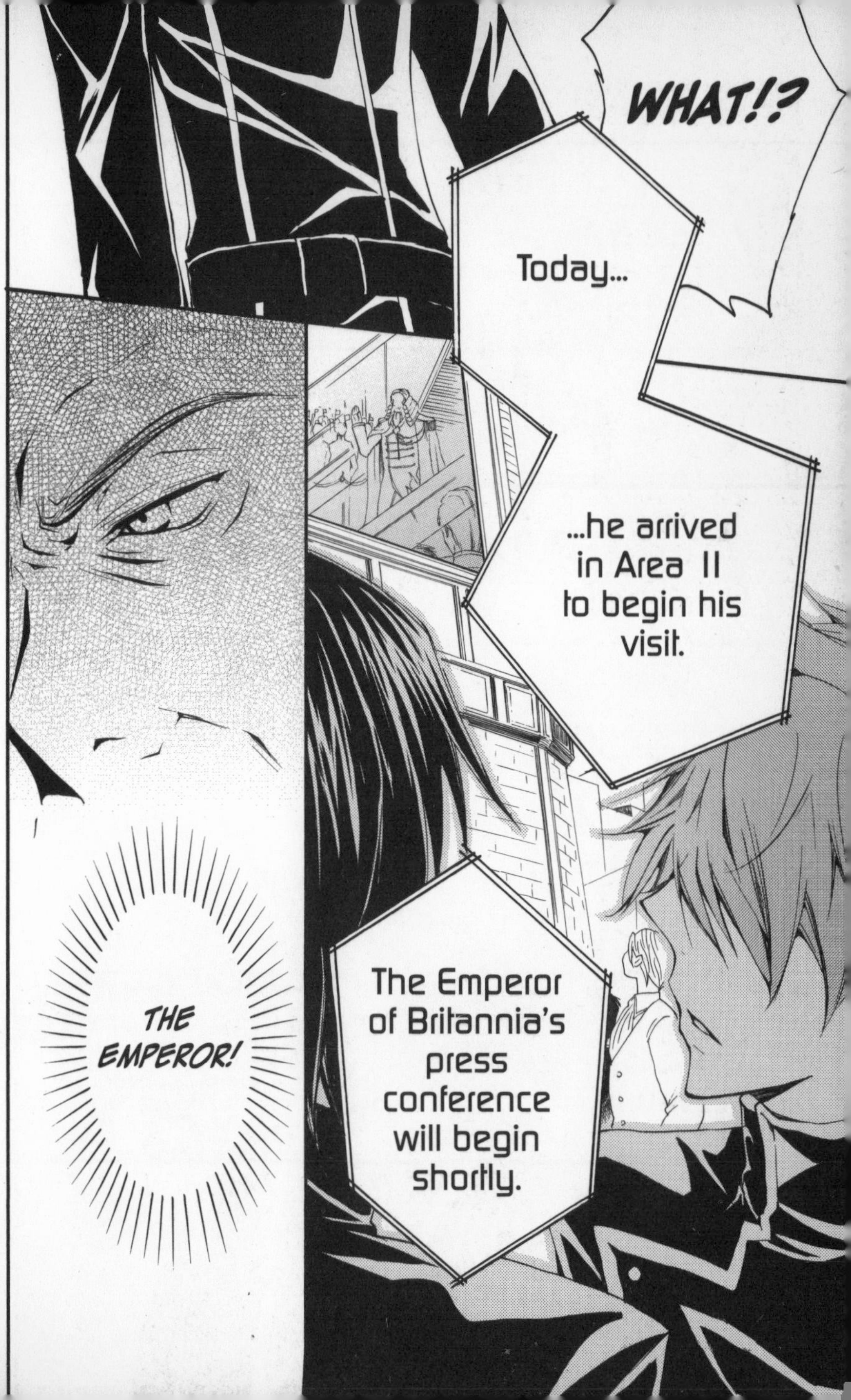
WHAT!?
Today...
...he arrived in Area 11 to begin his visit.
The Emperor of Britannia's press conference will begin shortly.
THE EMPEROR!

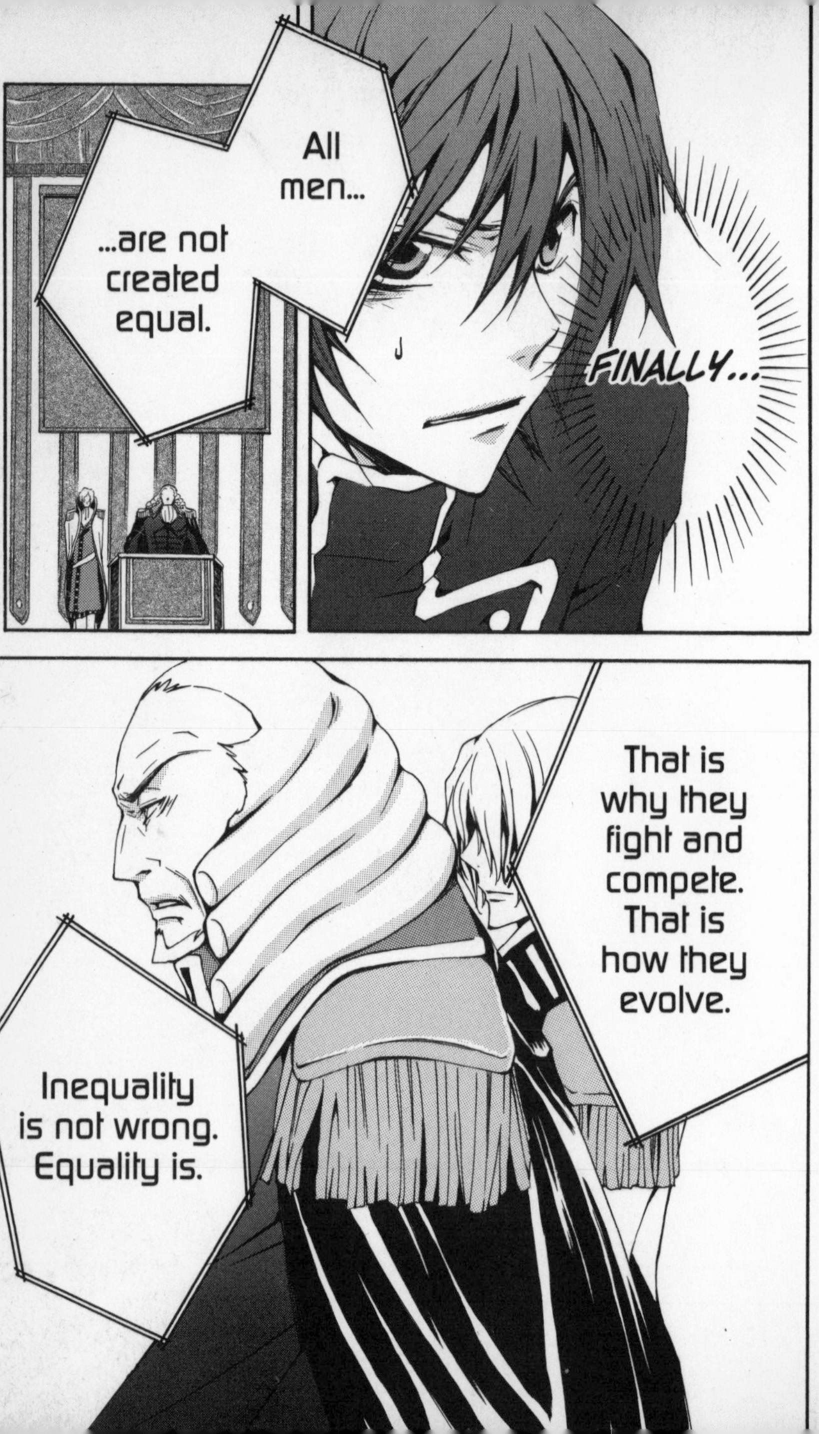
All men...
...are not created equal.
FINALLY...
That is why they fight and compete. That is how they evolve.
Inequality is not wrong. Equality is.

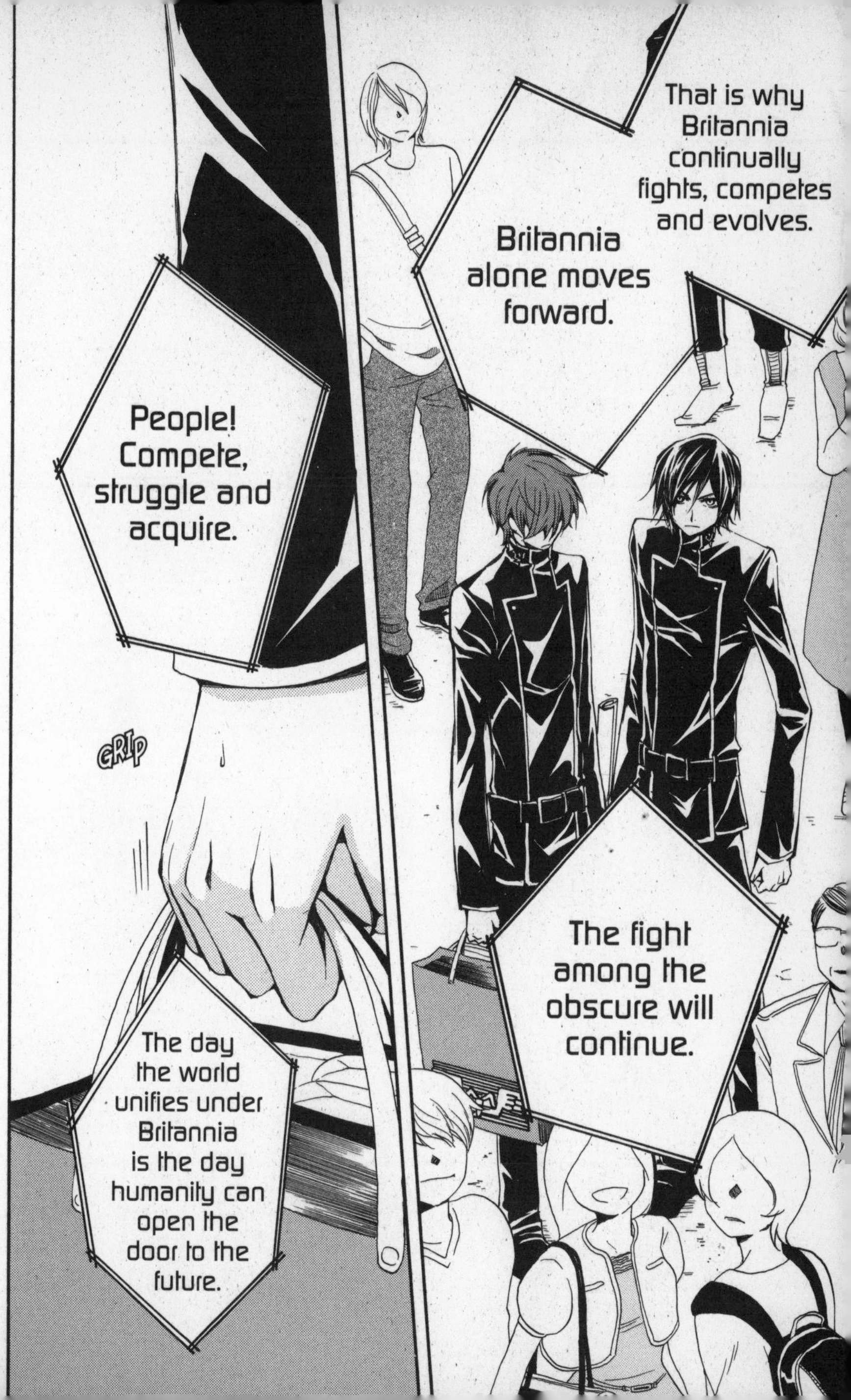
That is why Britannia continually fights, competes and evolves.
Britannia alone moves forward.
The fight among the obscure will continue.
People! Compete, struggle and acquire.
GRIP
The day the world unifies under Britannia is the day humanity can open the door to the future.

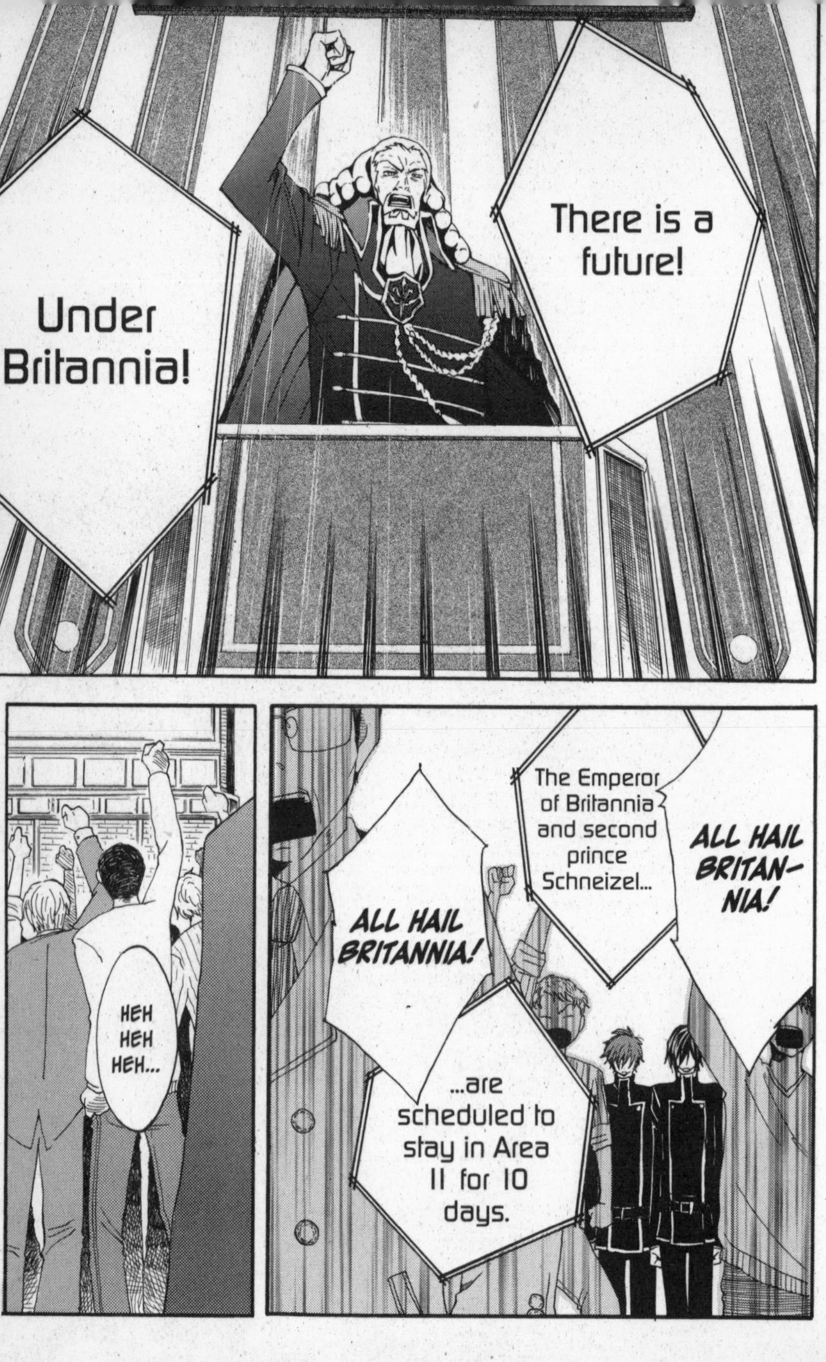
There is a future!
Under Britannia!
ALL HAIL BRITAN-NIA!
The Emperor of Britannia and second prince Schneizel...
ALL HAIL BRITANNIA!
...are scheduled to stay in Area 11 for 10 days.
HEH HEH HEH...

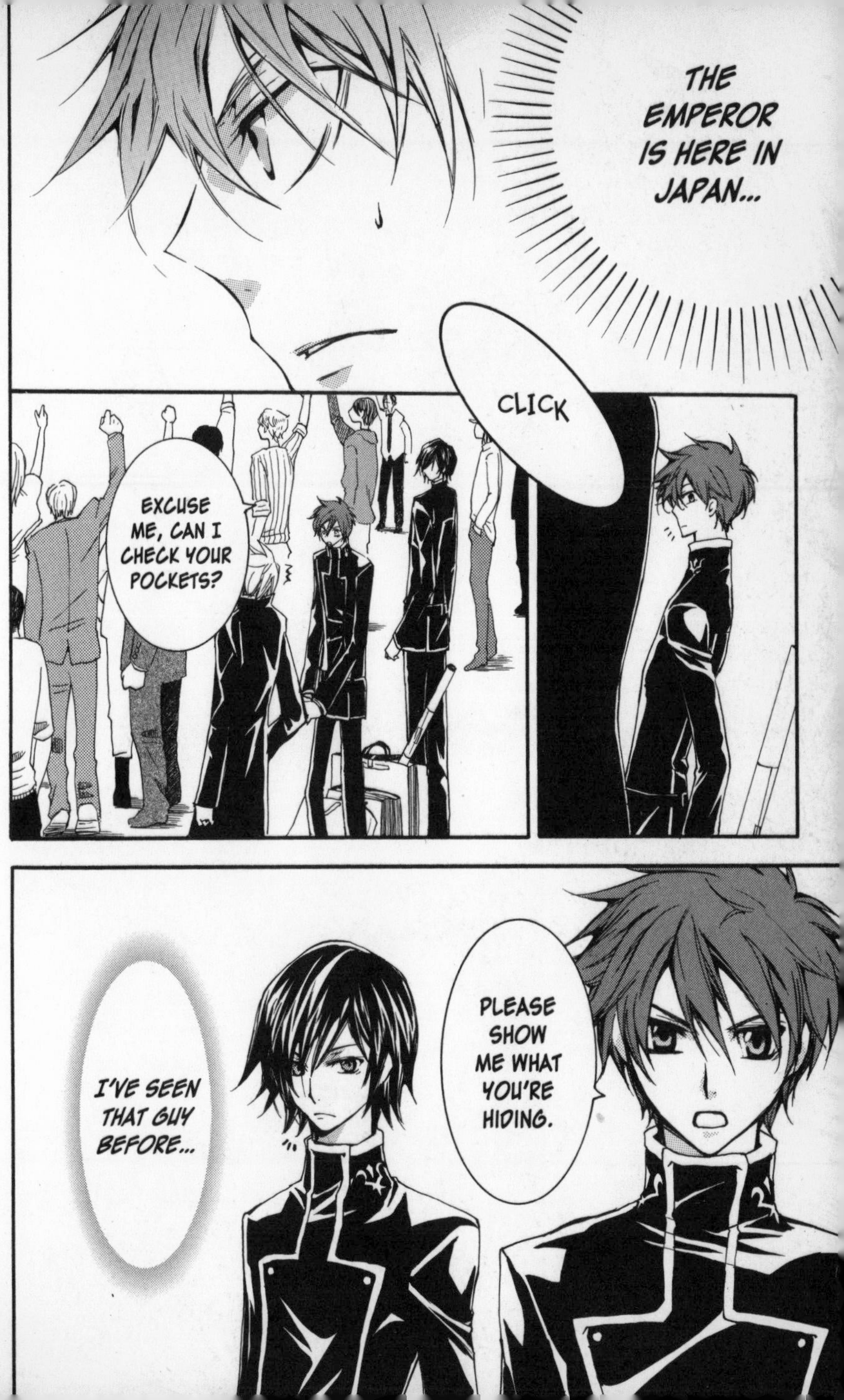
THE EMPEROR IS HERE IN JAPAN...
CLICK
EXCUSE ME, CAN I CHECK YOUR POCKETS?
PLEASE SHOW ME WHAT YOU'RE HIDING.
I'VE SEEN THAT GUY BEFORE...

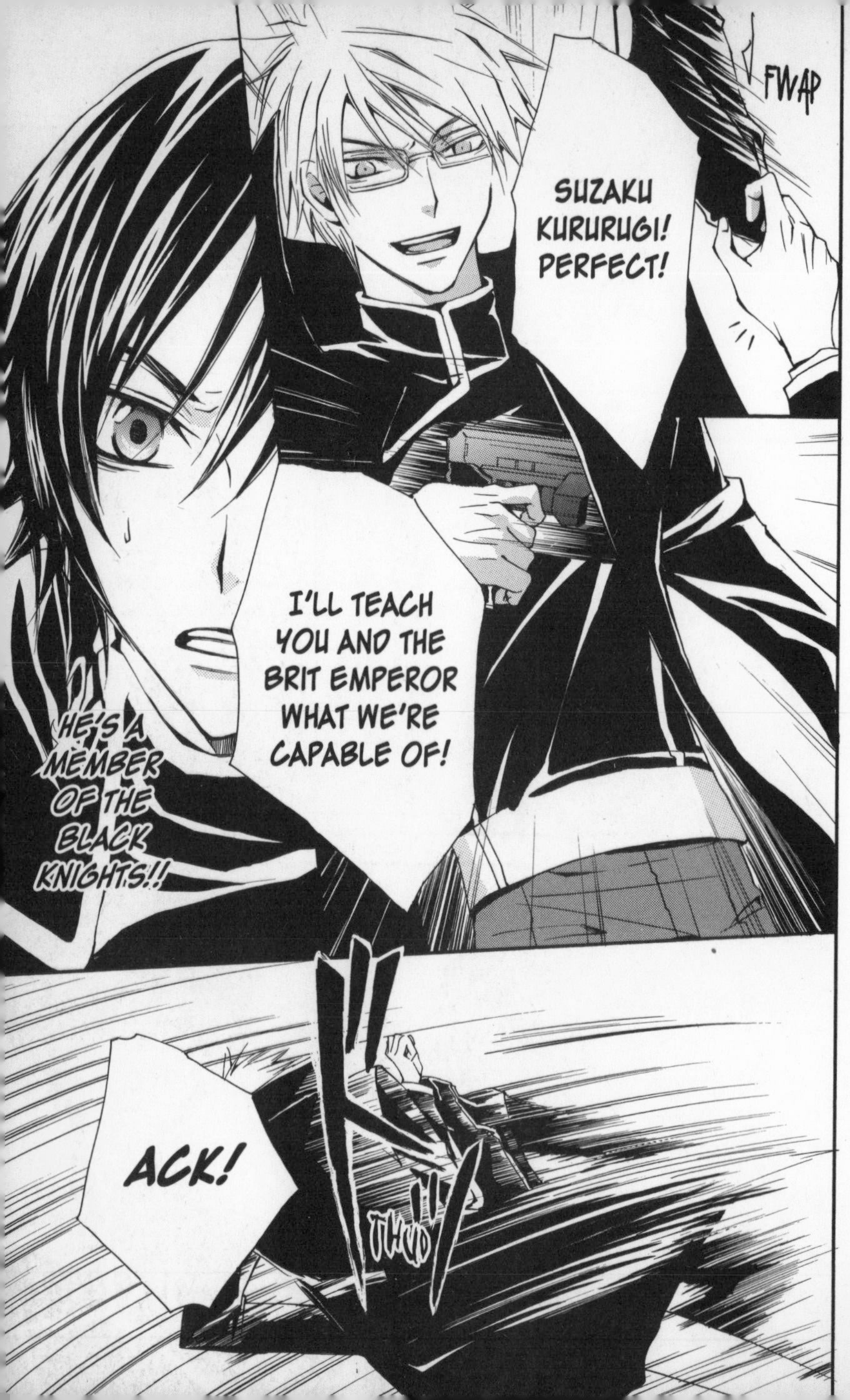
FWAP
SUZAKU KURURUGI! PERFECT!
I'LL TEACH YOU AND THE BRIT EMPEROR WHAT WE'RE CAPABLE OF!
HE'S A MEMBER OF THE BLACK KNIGHTS!!
ACK!
THUD!!

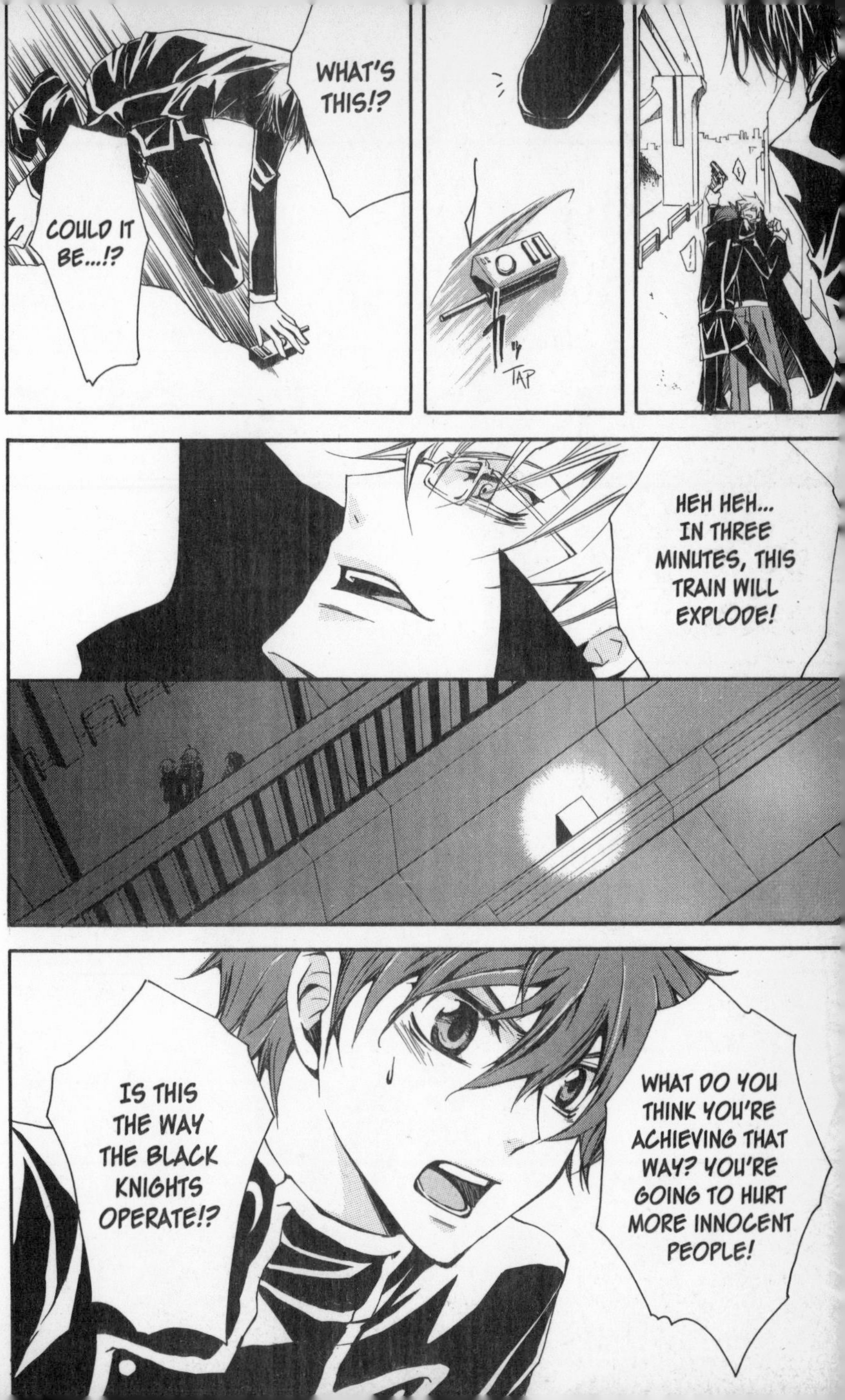
TAP
WHAT'S THIS!?
COULD IT BE...!?
HEH HEH... IN THREE MINUTES, THIS TRAIN WILL EXPLODE!
WHAT DO YOU THINK YOU'RE ACHIEVING THAT WAY? YOU'RE GOING TO HURT MORE INNOCENT PEOPLE!
IS THIS THE WAY THE BLACK KNIGHTS OPERATE!?

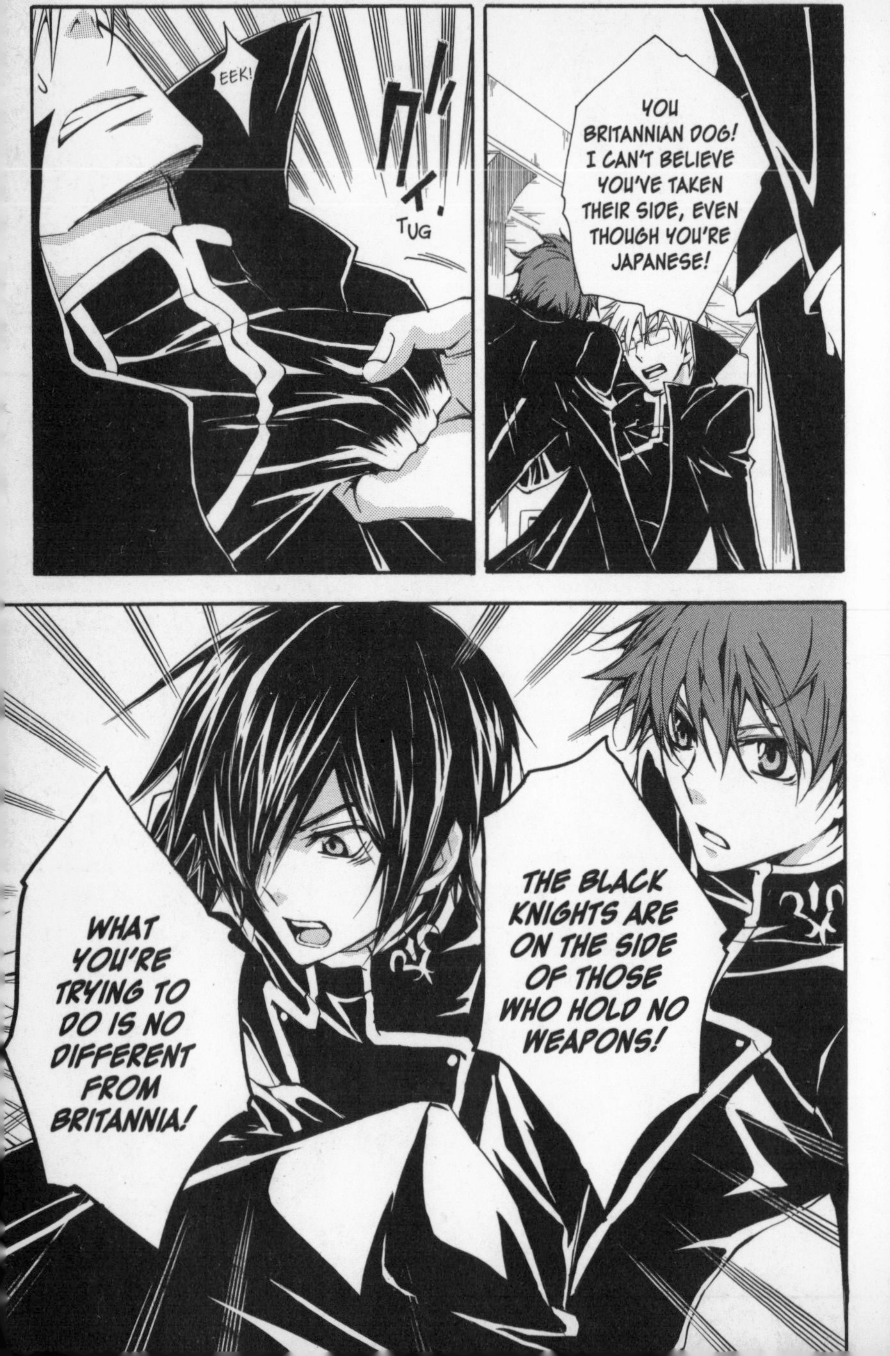
YOU BRITANNIAN DOG! I CAN'T BELIEVE YOU'VE TAKEN THEIR SIDE, EVEN THOUGH YOU'RE JAPANESE!
EEK!
グイ!
TUG
THE BLACK KNIGHTS ARE ON THE SIDE OF THOSE WHO HOLD NO WEAPONS!
WHAT YOU'RE TRYING TO DO IS NO DIFFERENT FROM BRITANNIA!

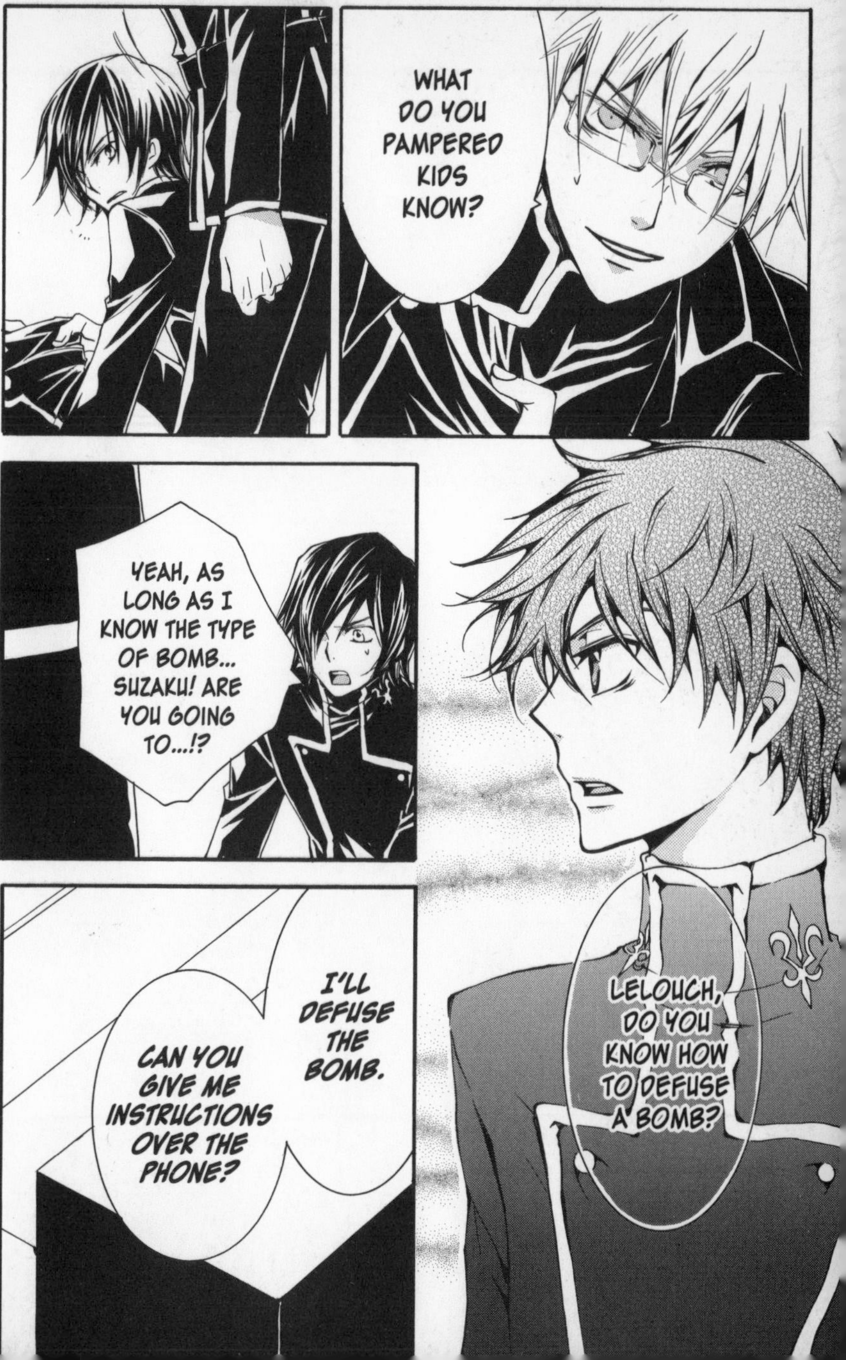
WHAT DO YOU PAMPERED KIDS KNOW?
LELOUCH, DO YOU KNOW HOW TO DEFUSE A BOMB?
YEAH, AS LONG AS I KNOW THE TYPE OF BOMB... SUZAKU! ARE YOU GOING TO...!?
I'LL DEFUSE THE BOMB.
CAN YOU GIVE ME INSTRUCTIONS OVER THE PHONE?

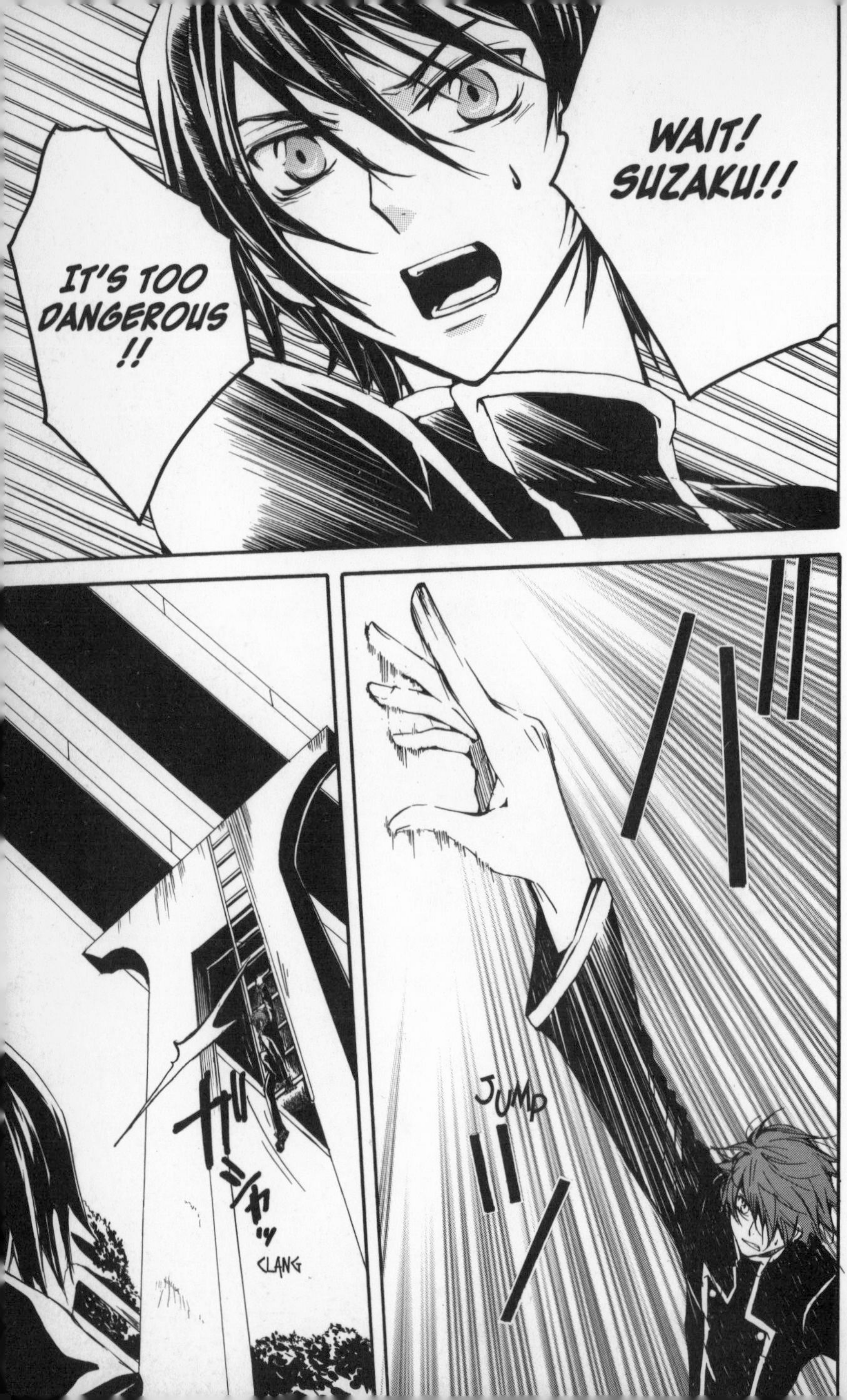
WAIT! SUZAKU!!
IT'S TOO DANGEROUS !!
JUMP
CLANG

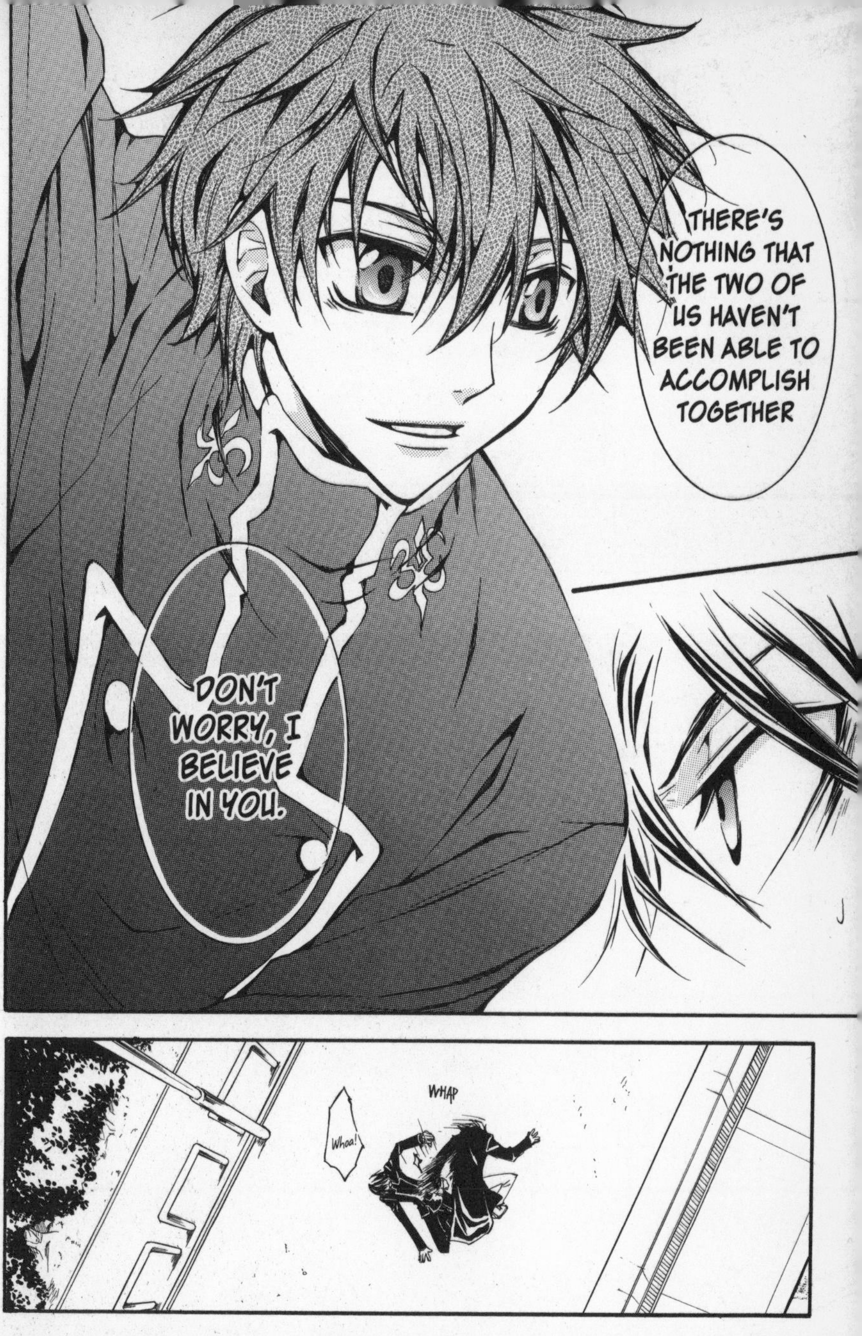
THERE'S NOTHING THAT THE TWO OF US HAVEN'T BEEN ABLE TO ACCOMPLISH TOGETHER
DON'T WORRY, I BELIEVE IN YOU.
WHAP
Whoa!

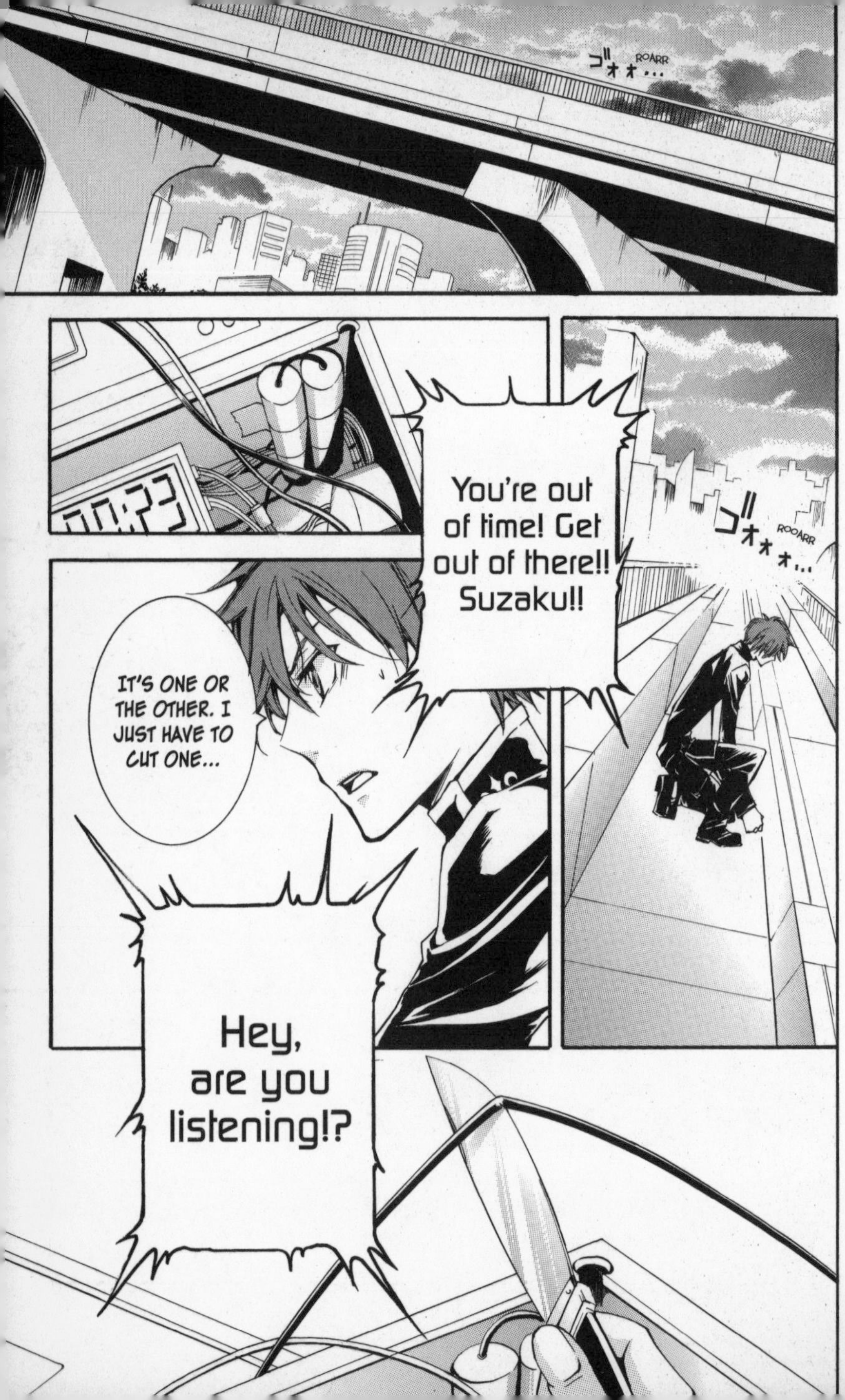
ゴォォ...
ROARR
ゴォォォ...
ROOARR
You're out of time! Get out of there!! Suzaku!!
IT'S ONE OR THE OTHER. I JUST HAVE TO CUT ONE...
Hey, are you listening!?

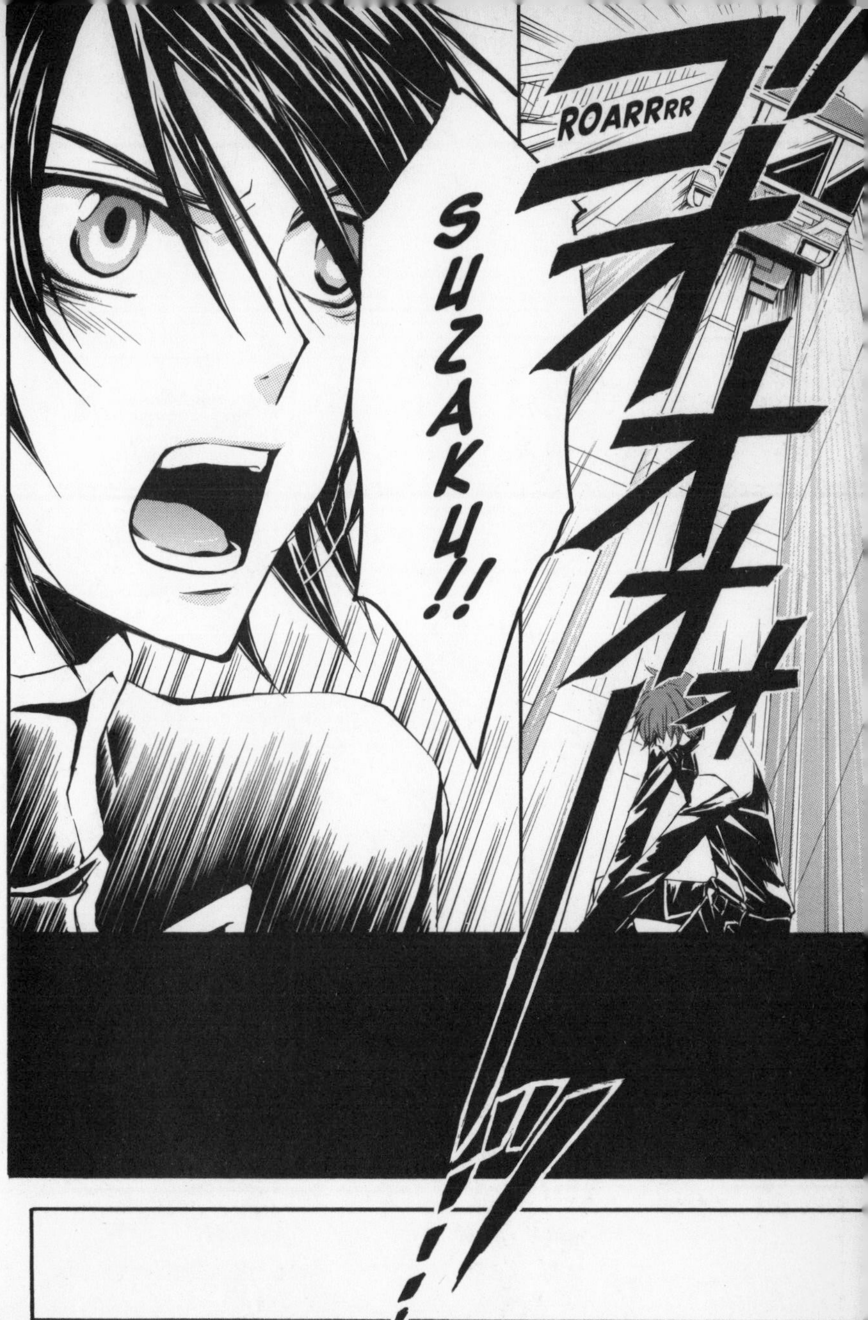
ROARRrr
SUZAKU!!

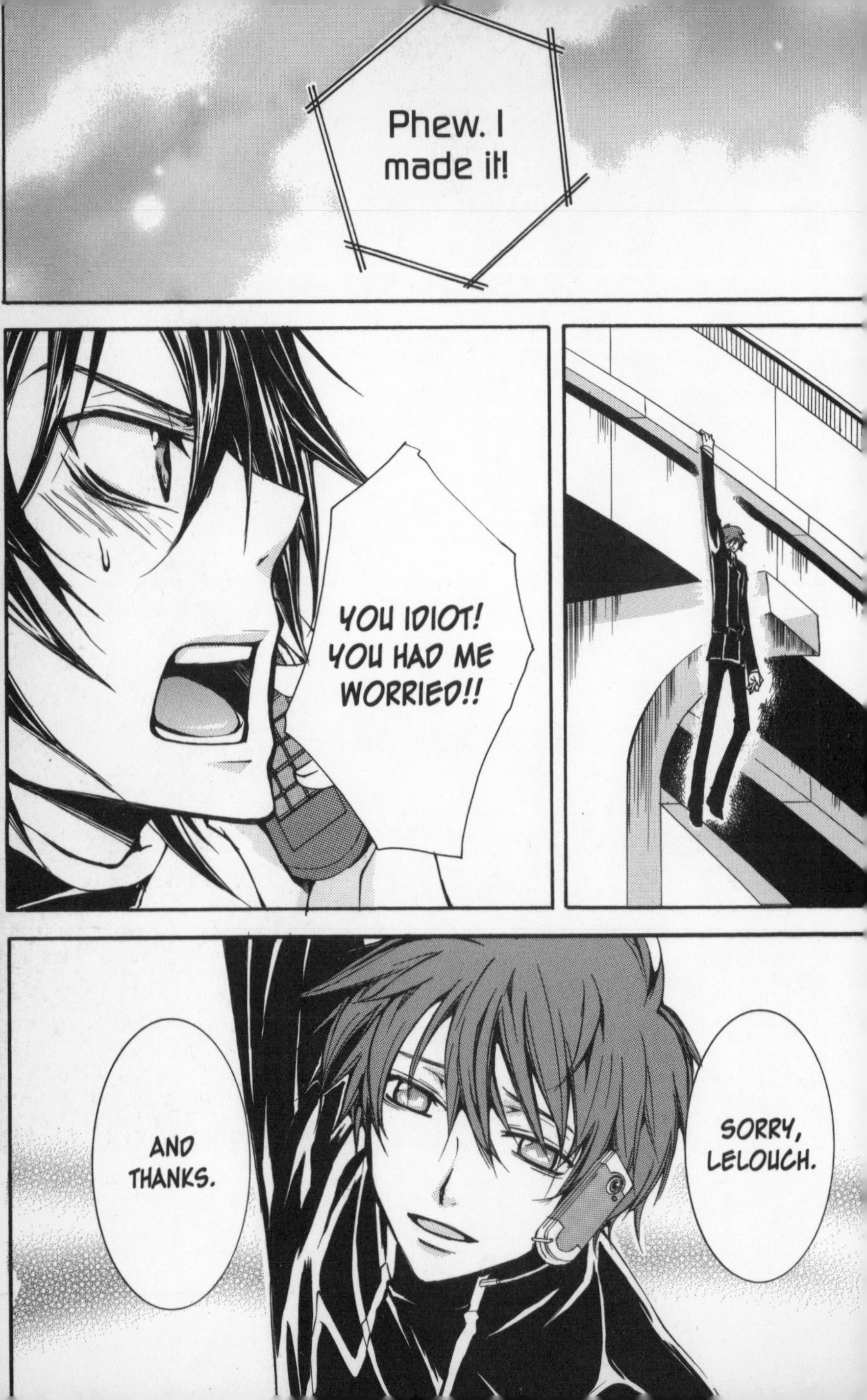
Phew. I made it!
YOU IDIOT! YOU HAD ME WORRIED!!
SORRY, LELOUCH.
AND THANKS.

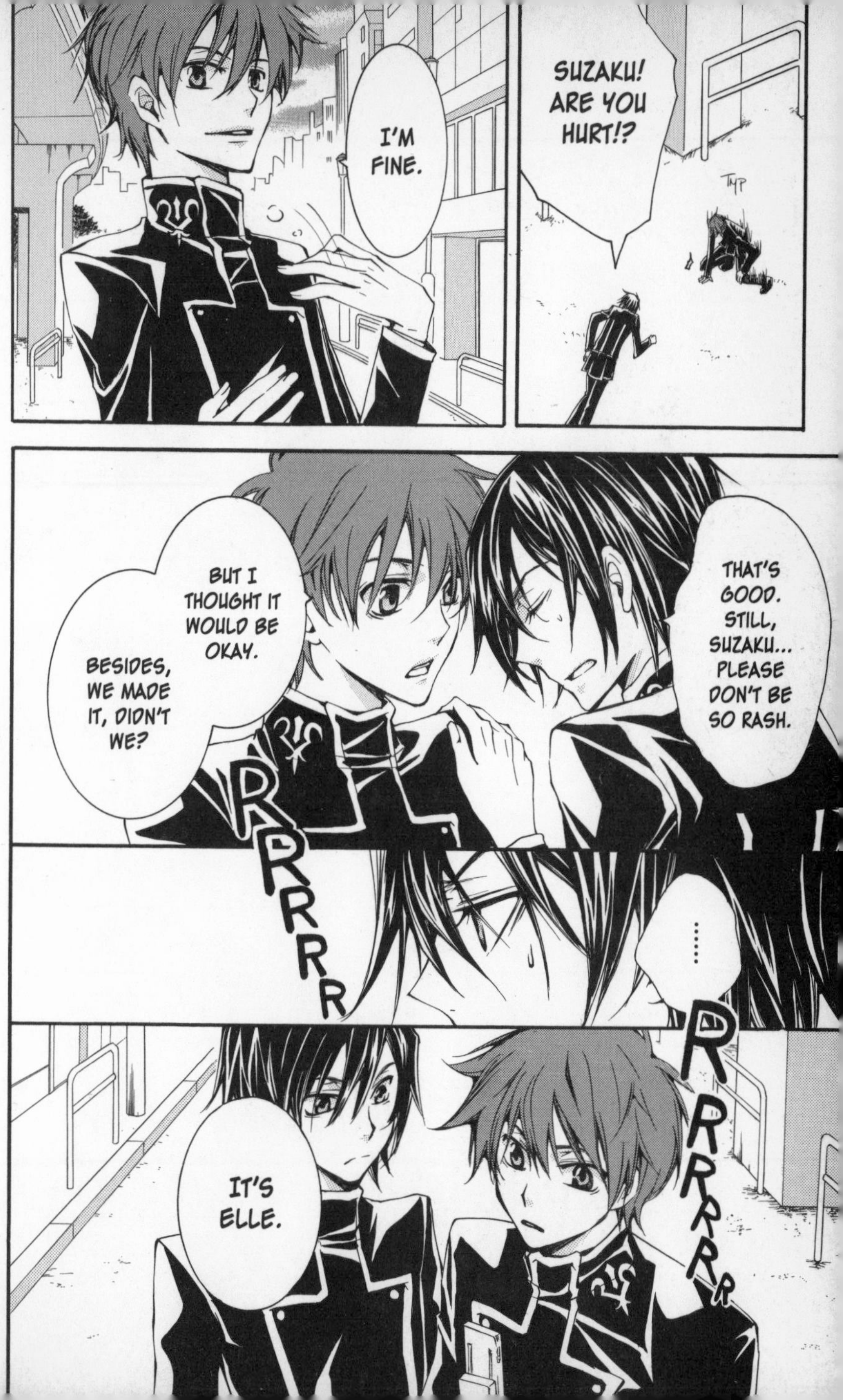
SUZAKU! ARE YOU HURT!?
TMP
I'M FINE.
THAT'S GOOD. STILL, SUZAKU... PLEASE DON'T BE SO RASH.
BUT I THOUGHT IT WOULD BE OKAY.
BESIDES, WE MADE IT, DIDN'T WE?
RRRRRR
......
RRRRRR
IT'S ELLE.

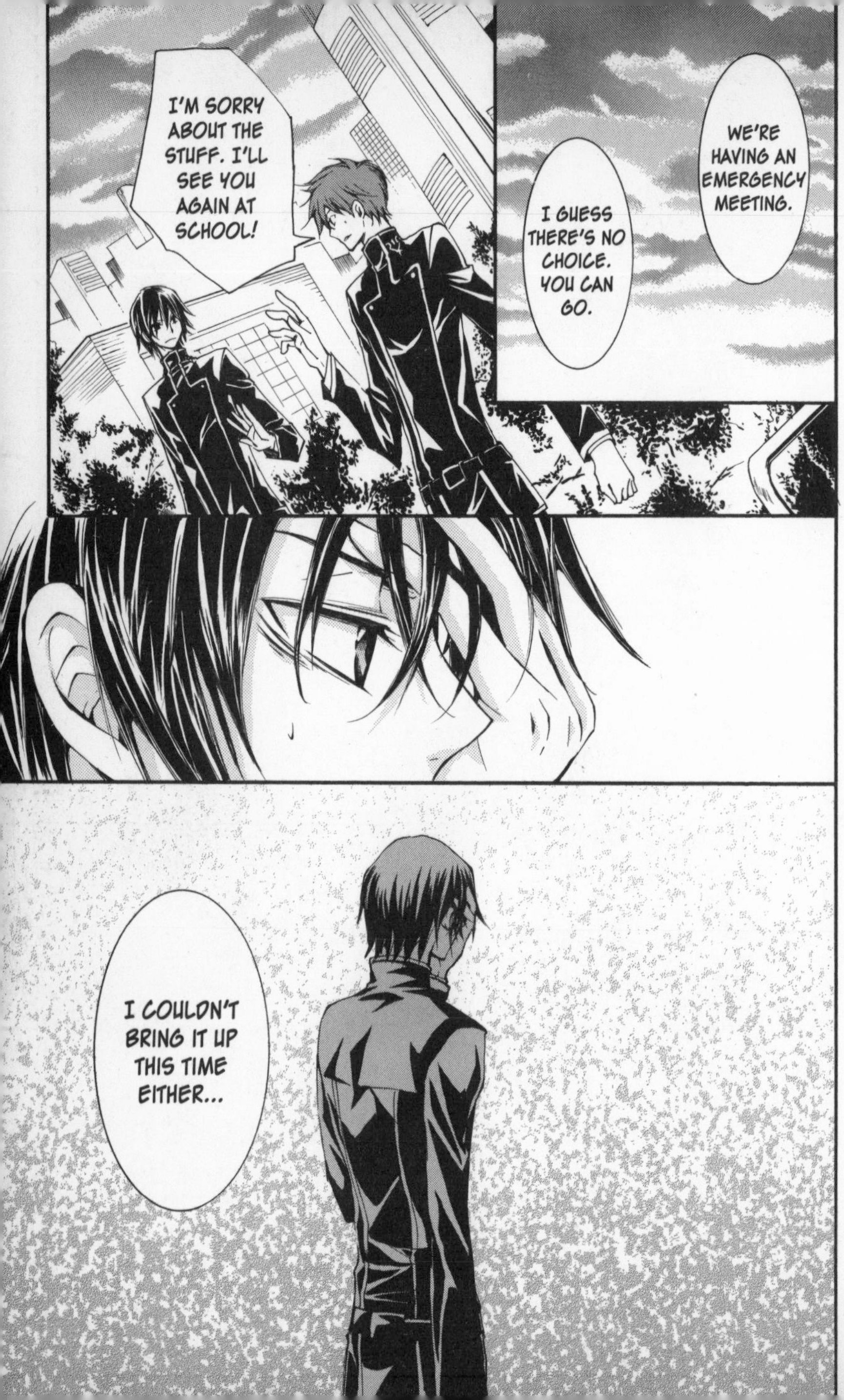
WE'RE HAVING AN EMERGENCY MEETING.
I GUESS THERE'S NO CHOICE. YOU CAN GO.
I'M SORRY ABOUT THE STUFF. I'LL SEE YOU AGAIN AT SCHOOL!
I COULDN'T BRING IT UP THIS TIME EITHER...

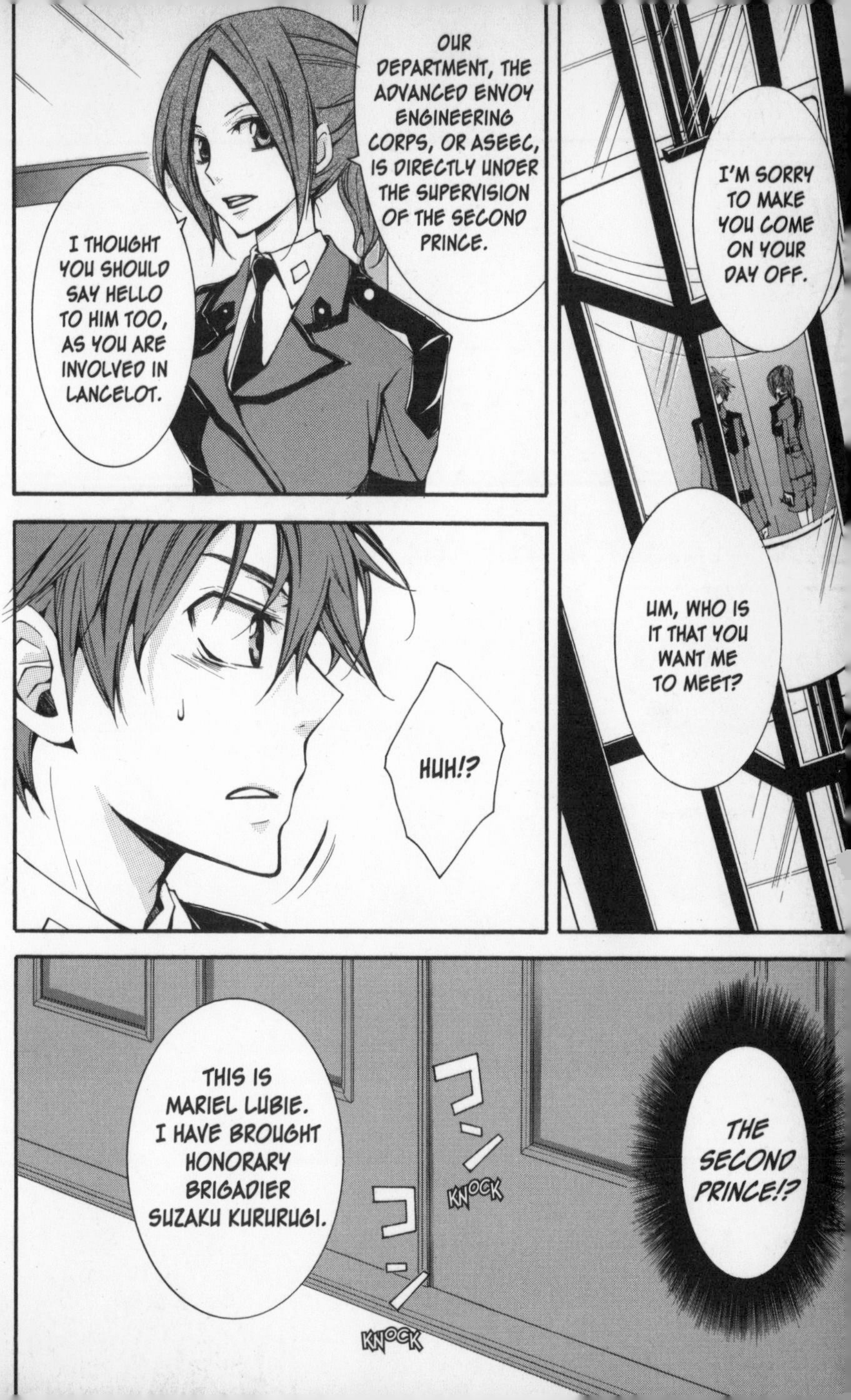
I'M SORRY TO MAKE YOU COME ON YOUR DAY OFF.
UM, WHO IS IT THAT YOU WANT ME TO MEET?
OUR DEPARTMENT, THE ADVANCED ENVOY ENGINEERING CORPS, OR ASEEC, IS DIRECTLY UNDER THE SUPERVISION OF THE SECOND PRINCE.
I THOUGHT YOU SHOULD SAY HELLO TO HIM TOO, AS YOU ARE INVOLVED IN LANCELOT.
HUH!?
THE SECOND PRINCE!?
KNOCK
THIS IS MARIEL LUBIE. I HAVE BROUGHT HONORARY BRIGADIER SUZAKU KURURUGI.
KNOCK

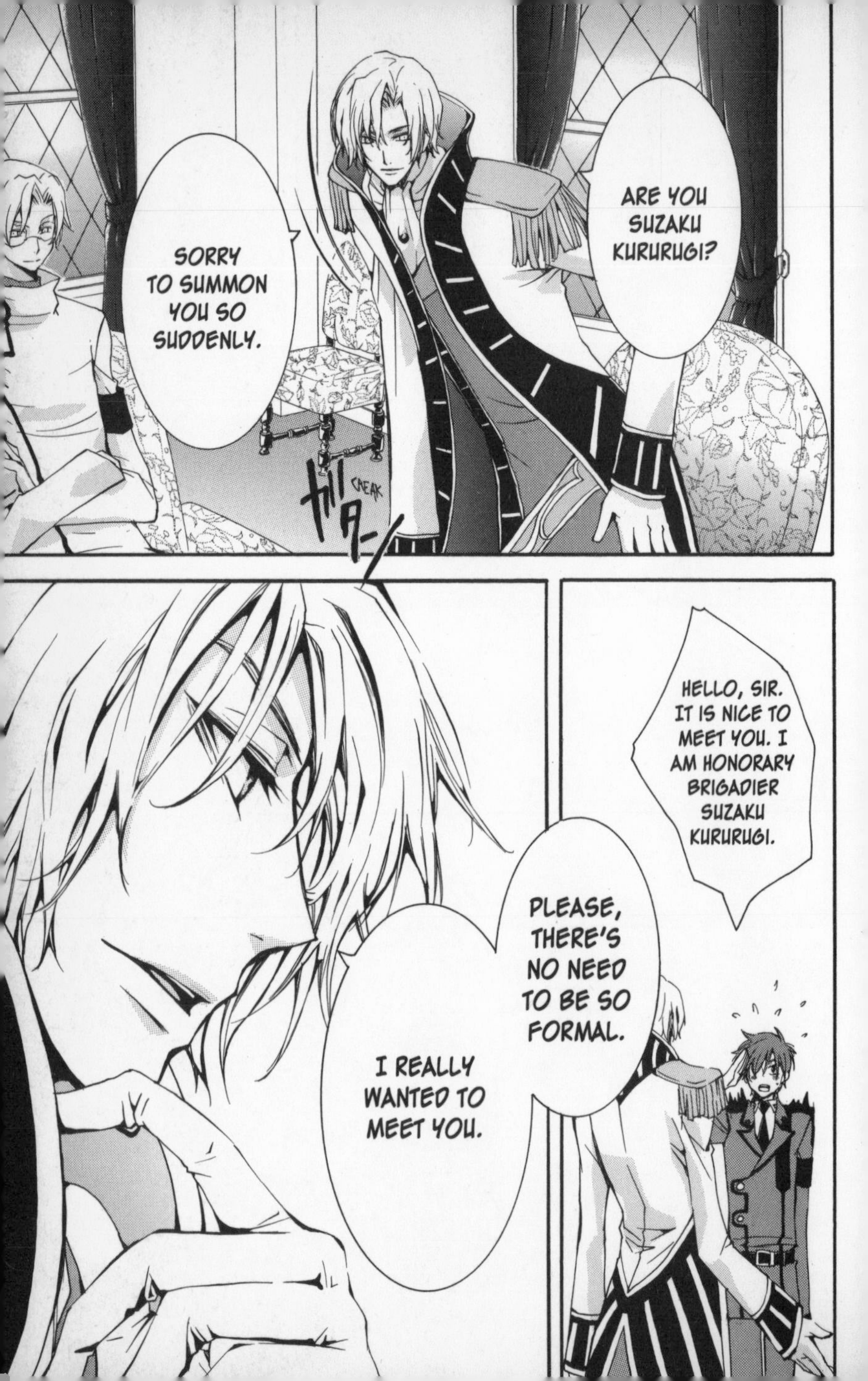
ARE YOU SUZAKU KURURUGI?
SORRY TO SUMMON YOU SO SUDDENLY.
CREAK
HELLO, SIR. IT IS NICE TO MEET YOU. I AM HONORARY BRIGADIER SUZAKU KURURUGI.
PLEASE, THERE'S NO NEED TO BE SO FORMAL.
I REALLY WANTED TO MEET YOU.

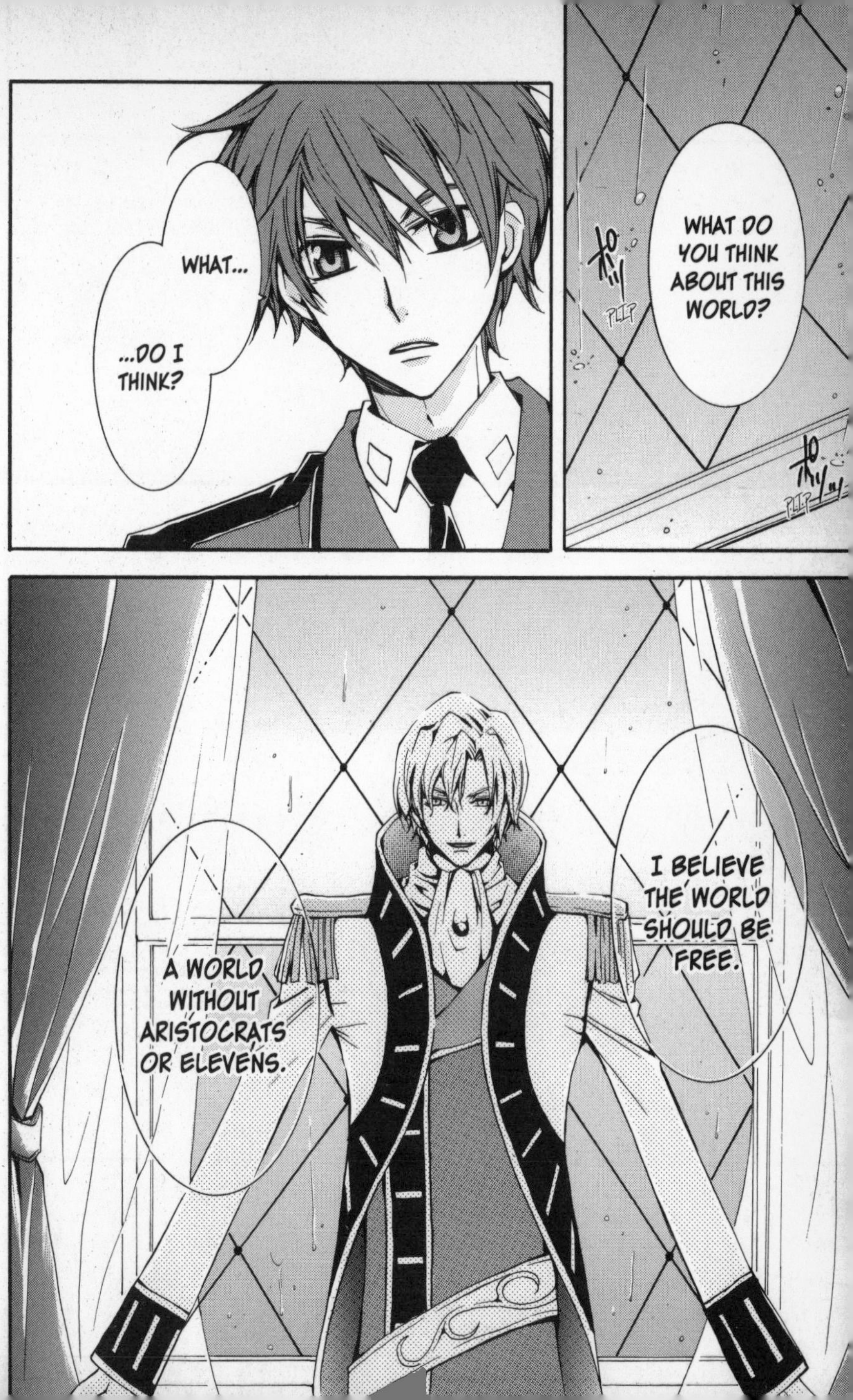
WHAT DO YOU THINK ABOUT THIS WORLD?
PLIP
PLIP
WHAT...
...DO I THINK?
I BELIEVE THE WORLD SHOULD BE FREE.
A WORLD WITHOUT ARISTOCRATS OR ELEVENS.

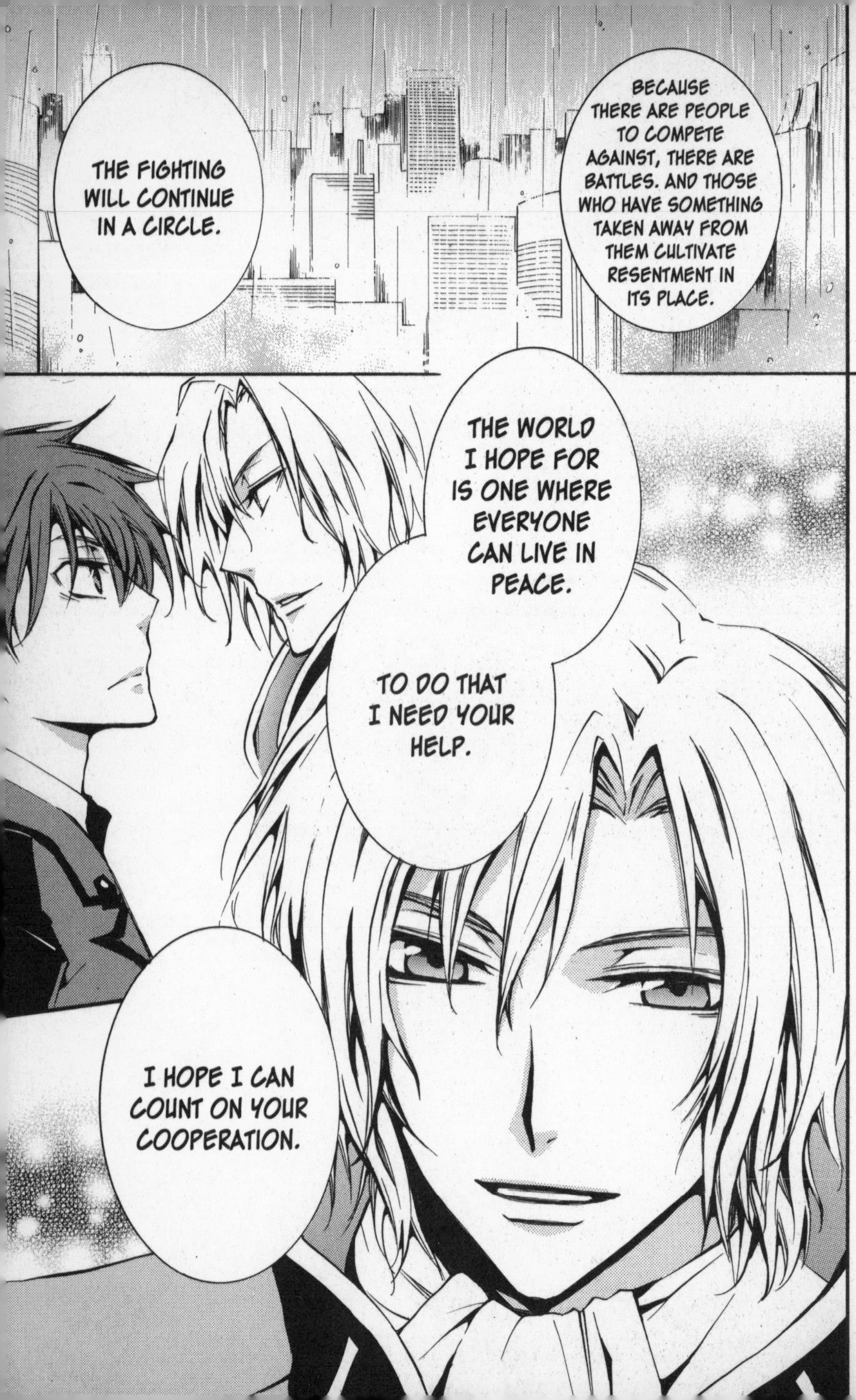
BECAUSE THERE ARE PEOPLE TO COMPETE AGAINST, THERE ARE BATTLES. AND THOSE WHO HAVE SOMETHING TAKEN AWAY FROM THEM CULTIVATE RESENTMENT IN ITS PLACE.
THE FIGHTING WILL CONTINUE IN A CIRCLE.
THE WORLD I HOPE FOR IS ONE WHERE EVERYONE CAN LIVE IN PEACE.
TO DO THAT I NEED YOUR HELP.
I HOPE I CAN COUNT ON YOUR COOPERATION.

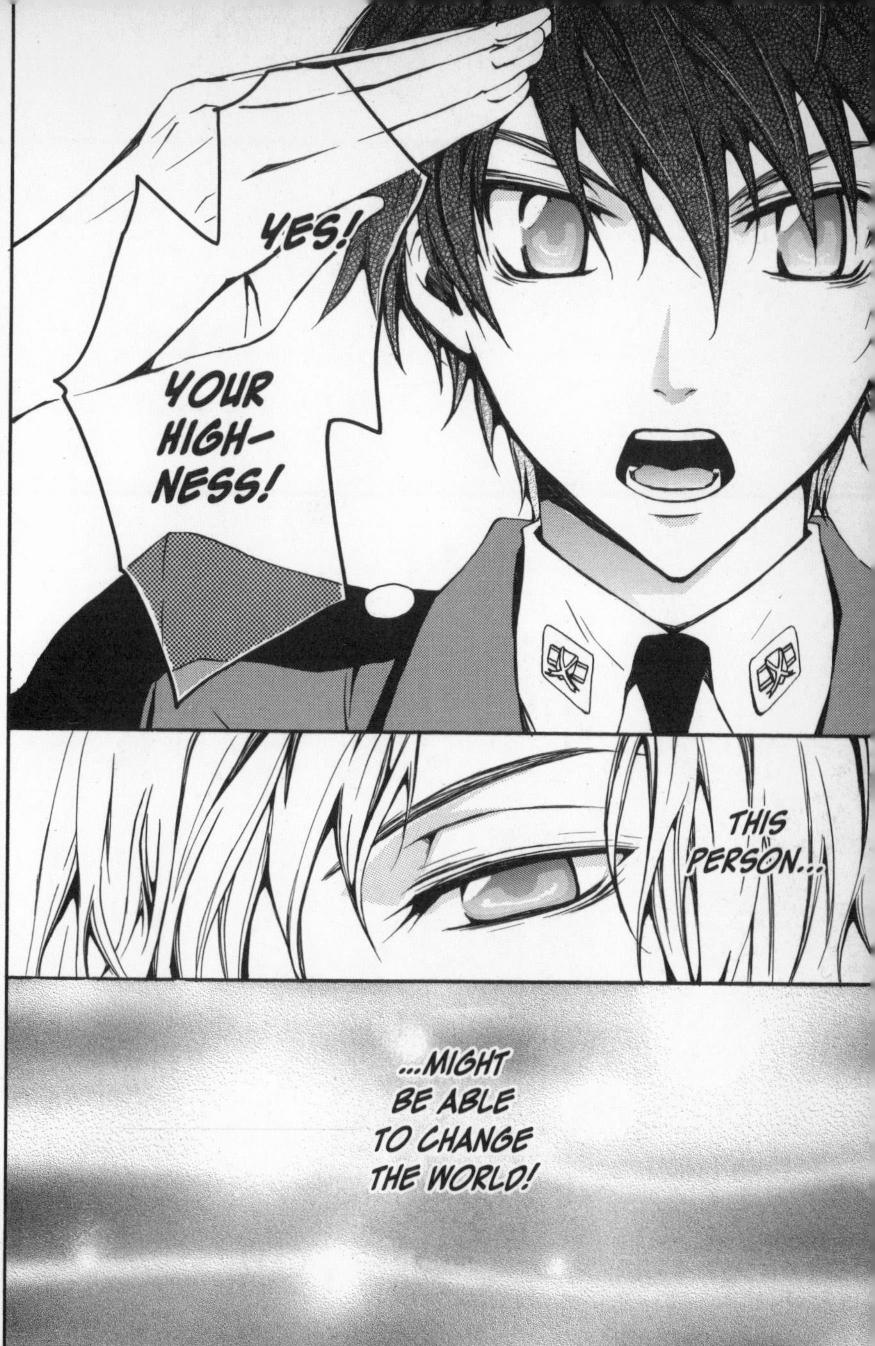
YES!
YOUR HIGH-NESS!
THIS PERSON...
...MIGHT BE ABLE TO CHANGE THE WORLD!

Phase 5 end

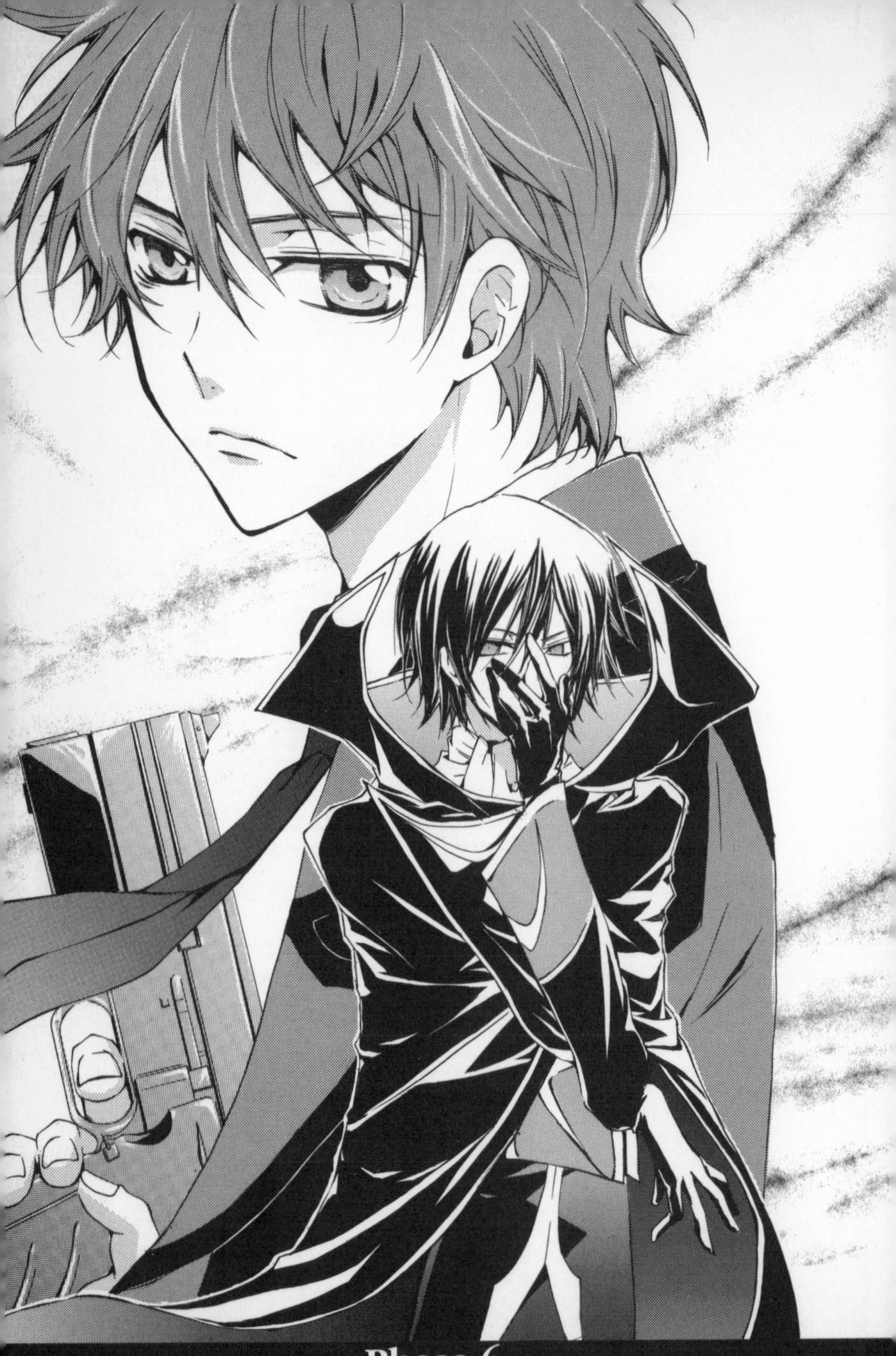

Phase 6

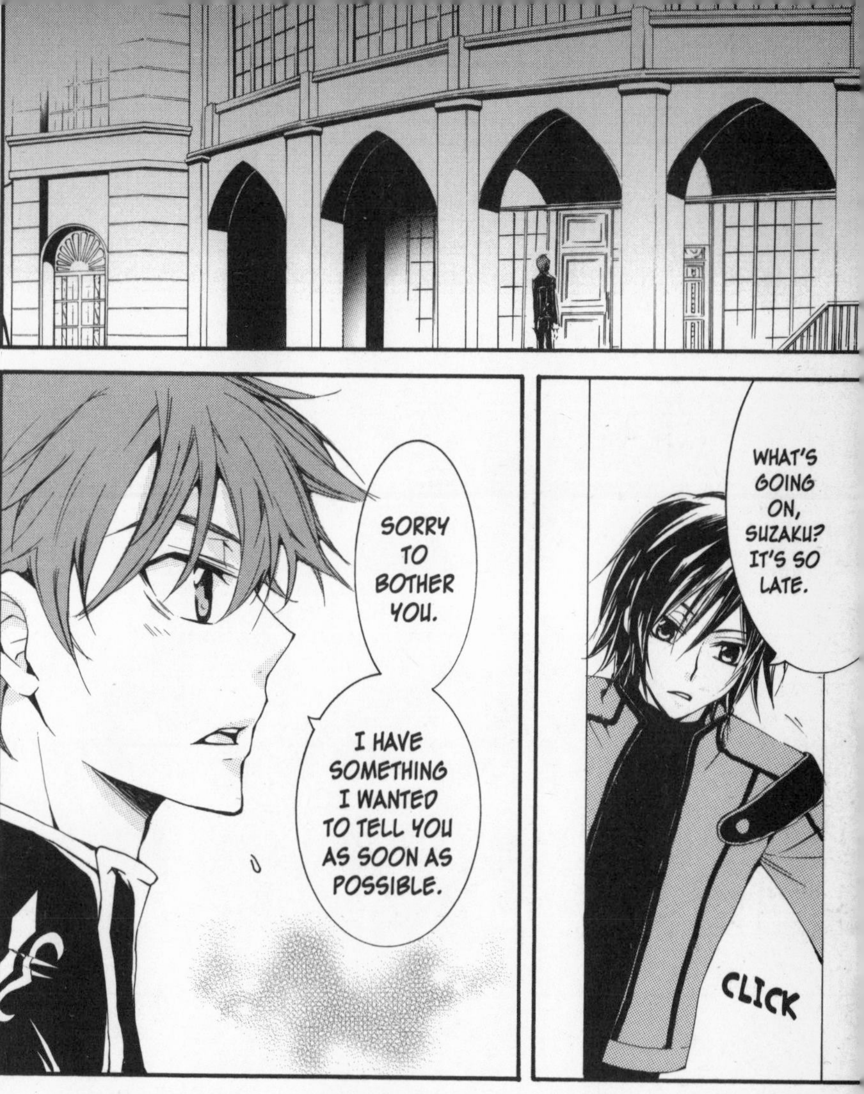
WHAT'S GOING ON, SUZAKU? IT'S SO LATE.
CLICK
SORRY TO BOTHER YOU.
I HAVE SOMETHING I WANTED TO TELL YOU AS SOON AS POSSIBLE.

I went to Bandai Hobby Center, the sacred land of plastic models, to visit.

The Guren that was displayed at the entrance was pretty awesome-looking.

The day I went was very sunny, and I got sunburned. I still have tan lines from my shoes.

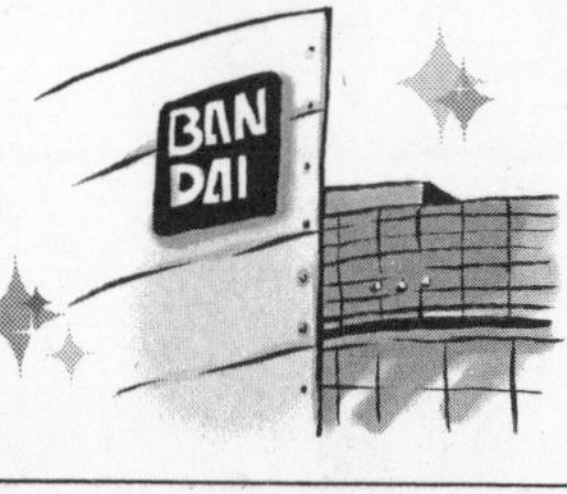
BAN DAI

Lately I don't even have time to build plastic models, and all I am left with is a mountain of incomplete models.

When can I play with my Vincent?

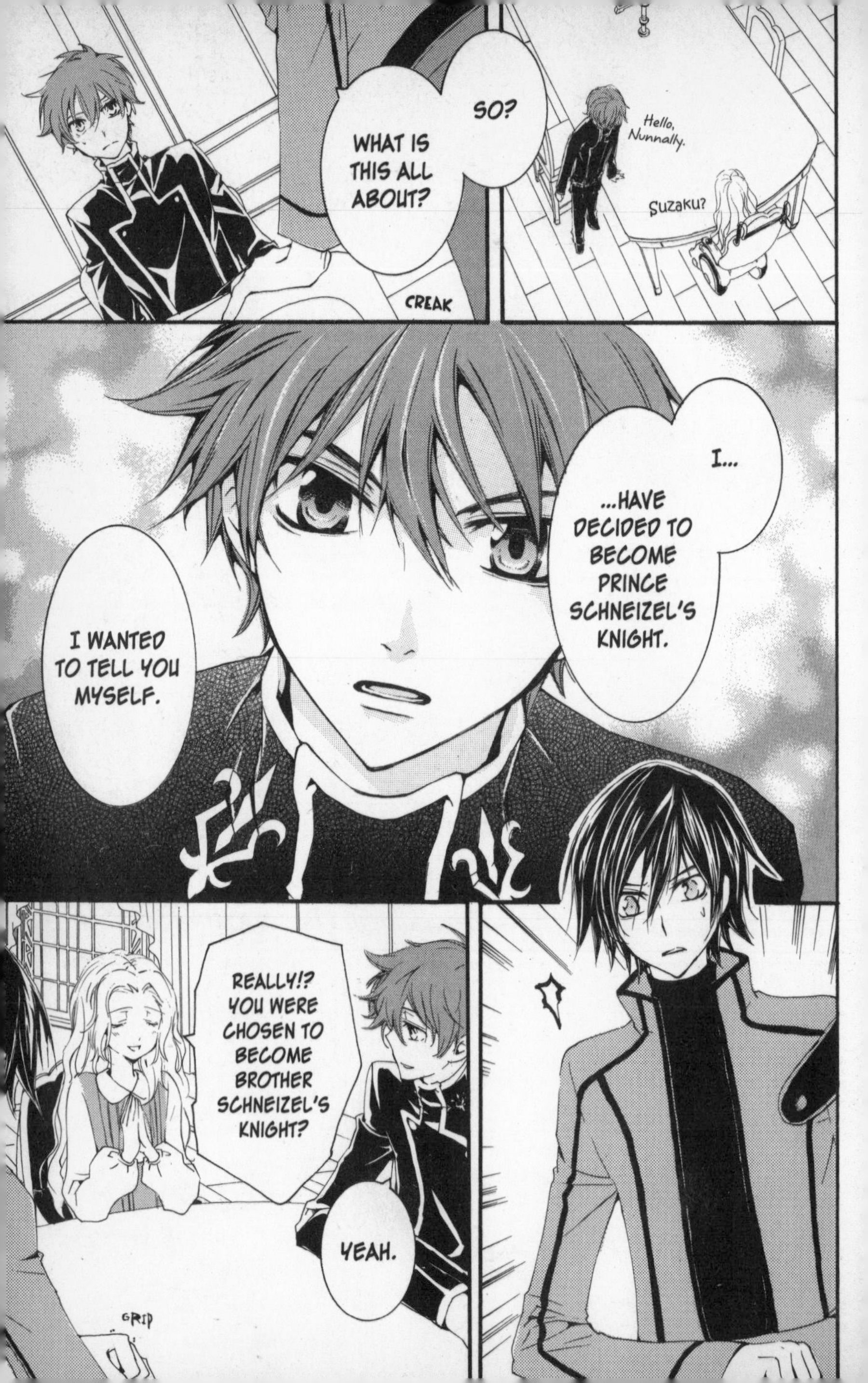
Hello, Nunnally.
Suzaku?
SO?
WHAT IS THIS ALL ABOUT?
CREAK
I...
...HAVE DECIDED TO BECOME PRINCE SCHNEIZEL'S KNIGHT.
I WANTED TO TELL YOU MYSELF.
REALLY!? YOU WERE CHOSEN TO BECOME BROTHER SCHNEIZEL'S KNIGHT?
YEAH.
GRIP

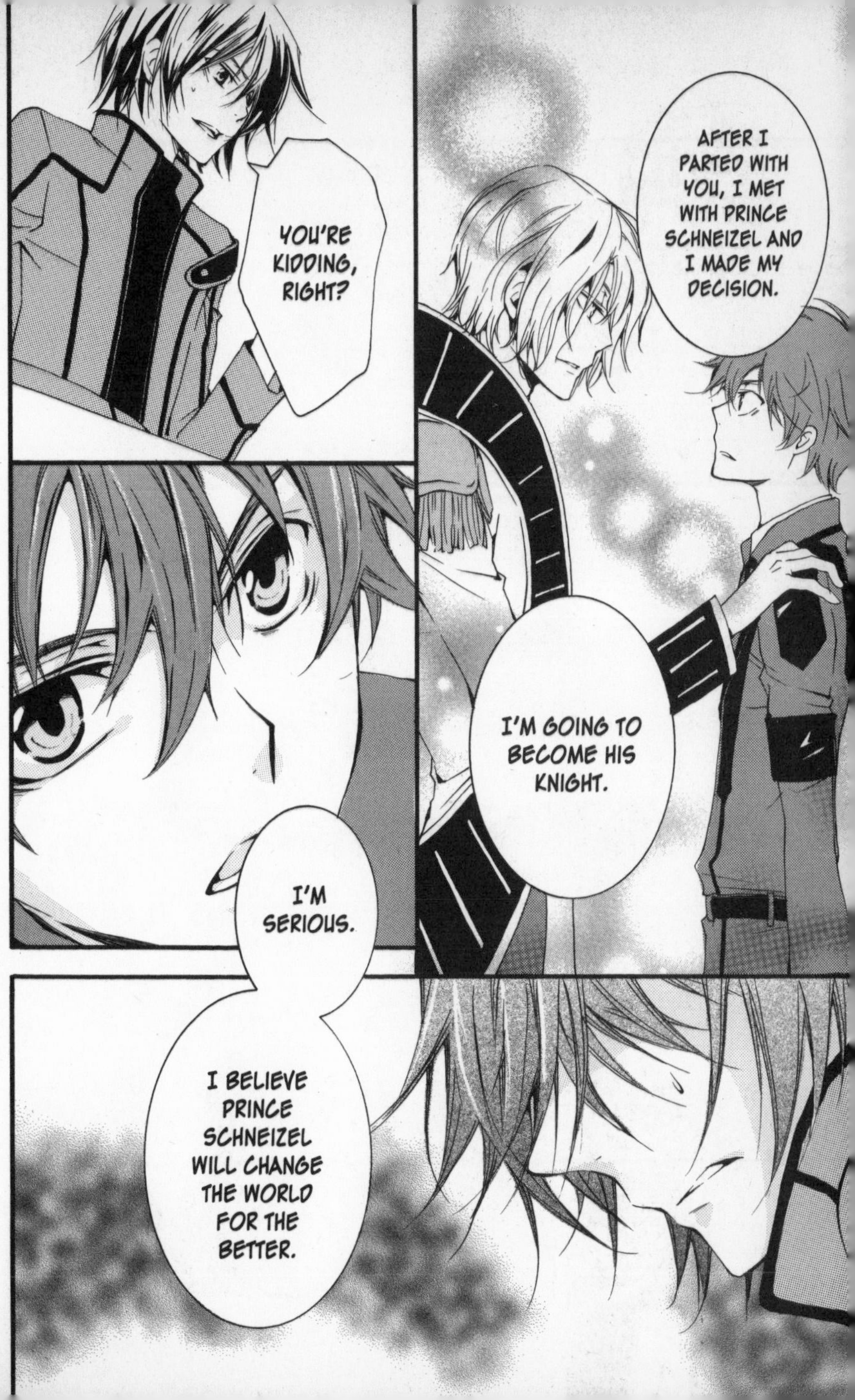
AFTER I PARTED WITH YOU, I MET WITH PRINCE SCHNEIZEL AND I MADE MY DECISION.
I'M GOING TO BECOME HIS KNIGHT.
YOU'RE KIDDING, RIGHT?
I'M SERIOUS.
I BELIEVE PRINCE SCHNEIZEL WILL CHANGE THE WORLD FOR THE BETTER.

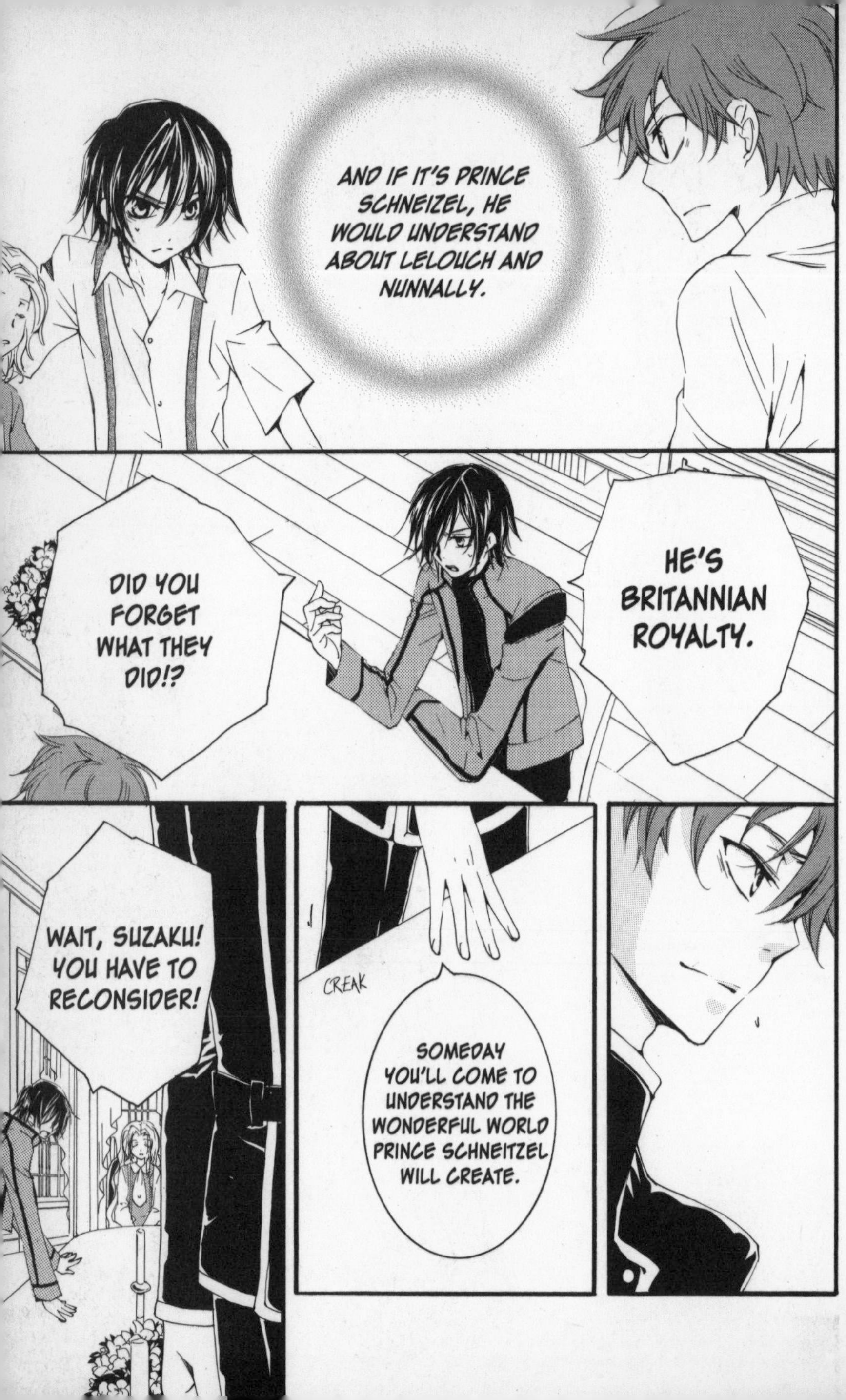
AND IF IT'S PRINCE SCHNEIZEL, HE WOULD UNDERSTAND ABOUT LELOUCH AND NUNNALLY.
HE'S BRITANNIAN ROYALTY.
DID YOU FORGET WHAT THEY DID!?
CREAK
SOMEDAY YOU'LL COME TO UNDERSTAND THE WONDERFUL WORLD PRINCE SCHNEITZEL WILL CREATE.
WAIT, SUZAKU! YOU HAVE TO RECONSIDER!

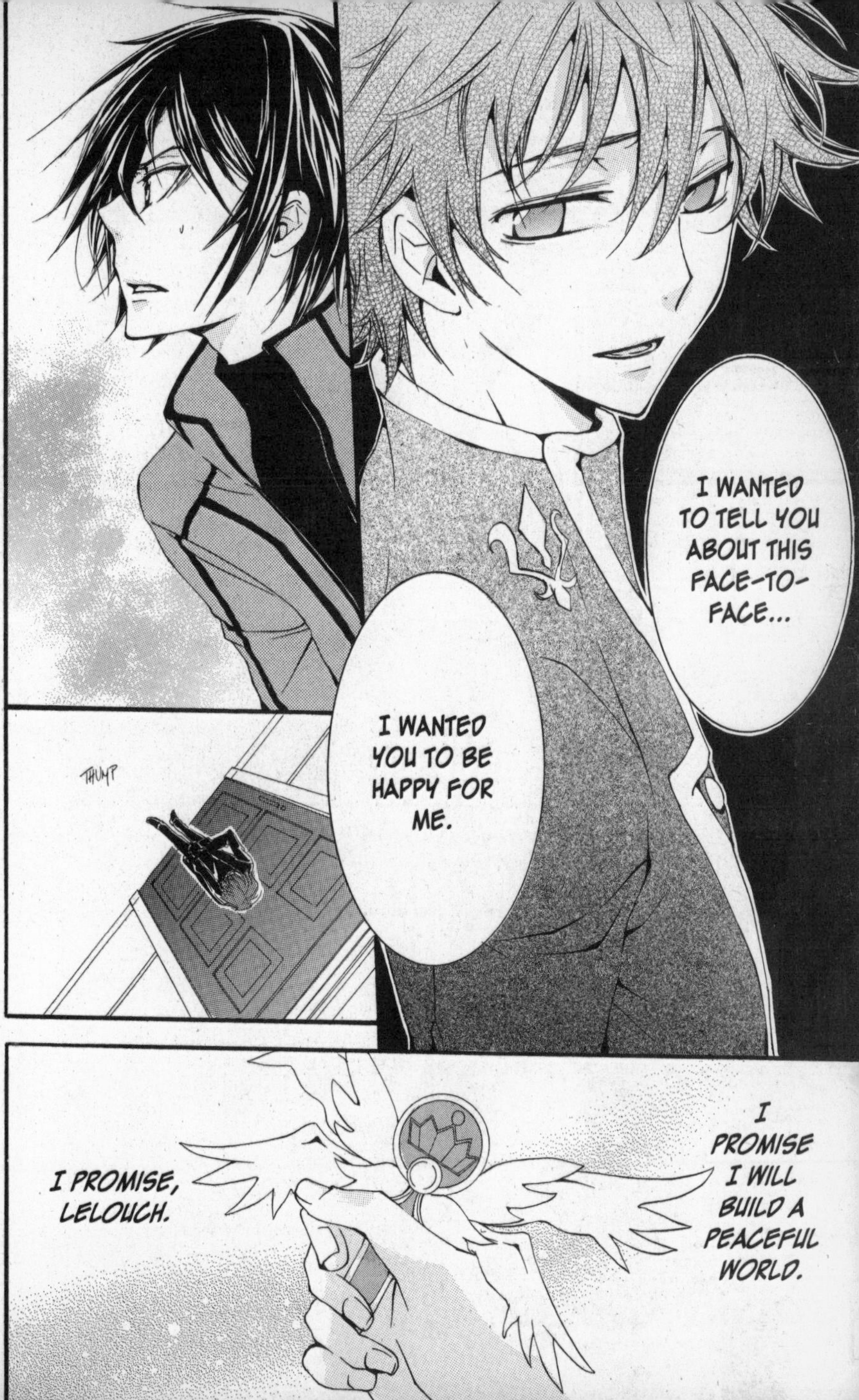
I WANTED TO TELL YOU ABOUT THIS FACE-TO-FACE...
I WANTED YOU TO BE HAPPY FOR ME.
THUMP
I PROMISE I WILL BUILD A PEACEFUL WORLD.
I PROMISE, LELOUCH.

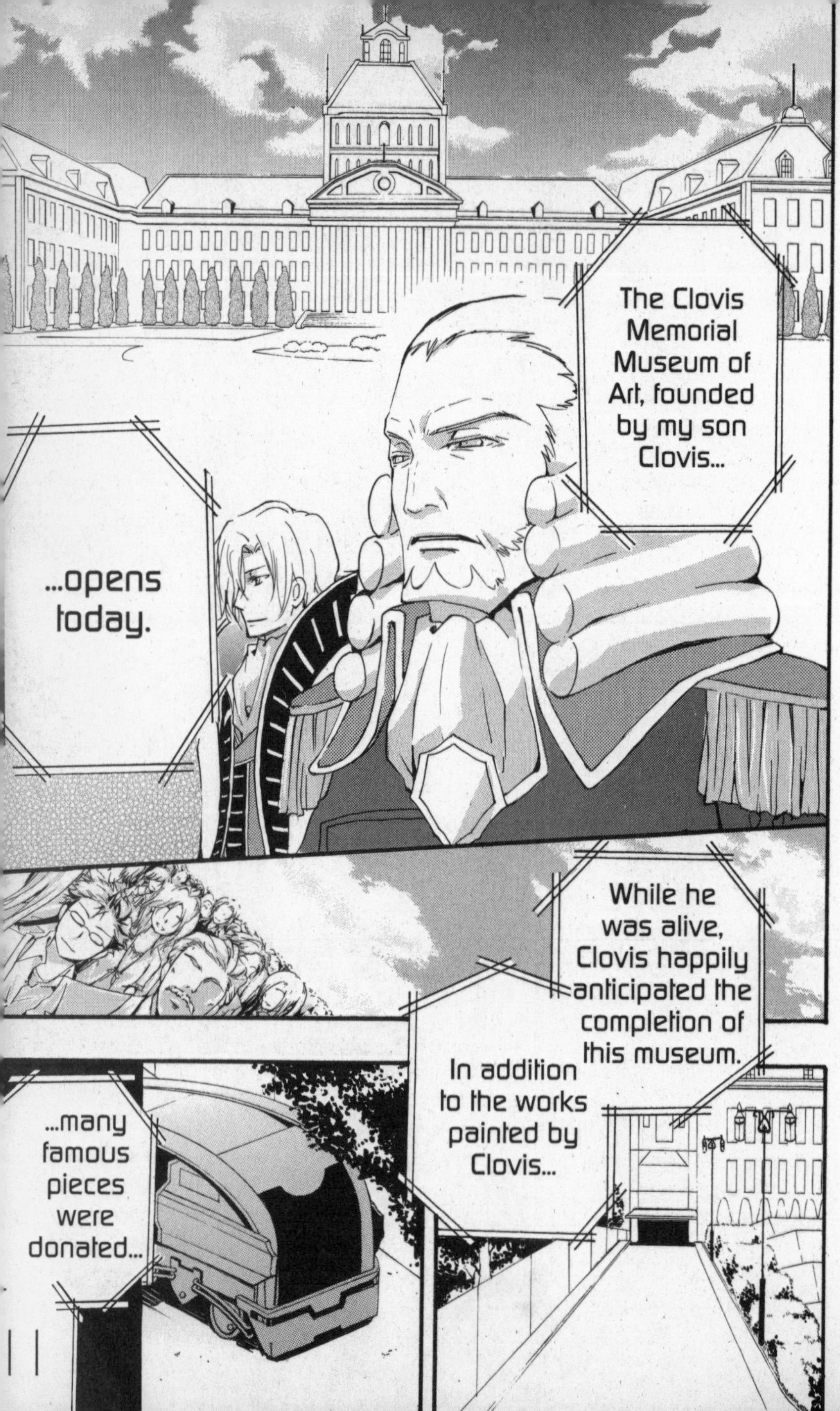
The Clovis Memorial Museum of Art, founded by my son Clovis...
...opens today.
While he was alive, Clovis happily anticipated the completion of this museum.
In addition to the works painted by Clovis...
...many famous pieces were donated...

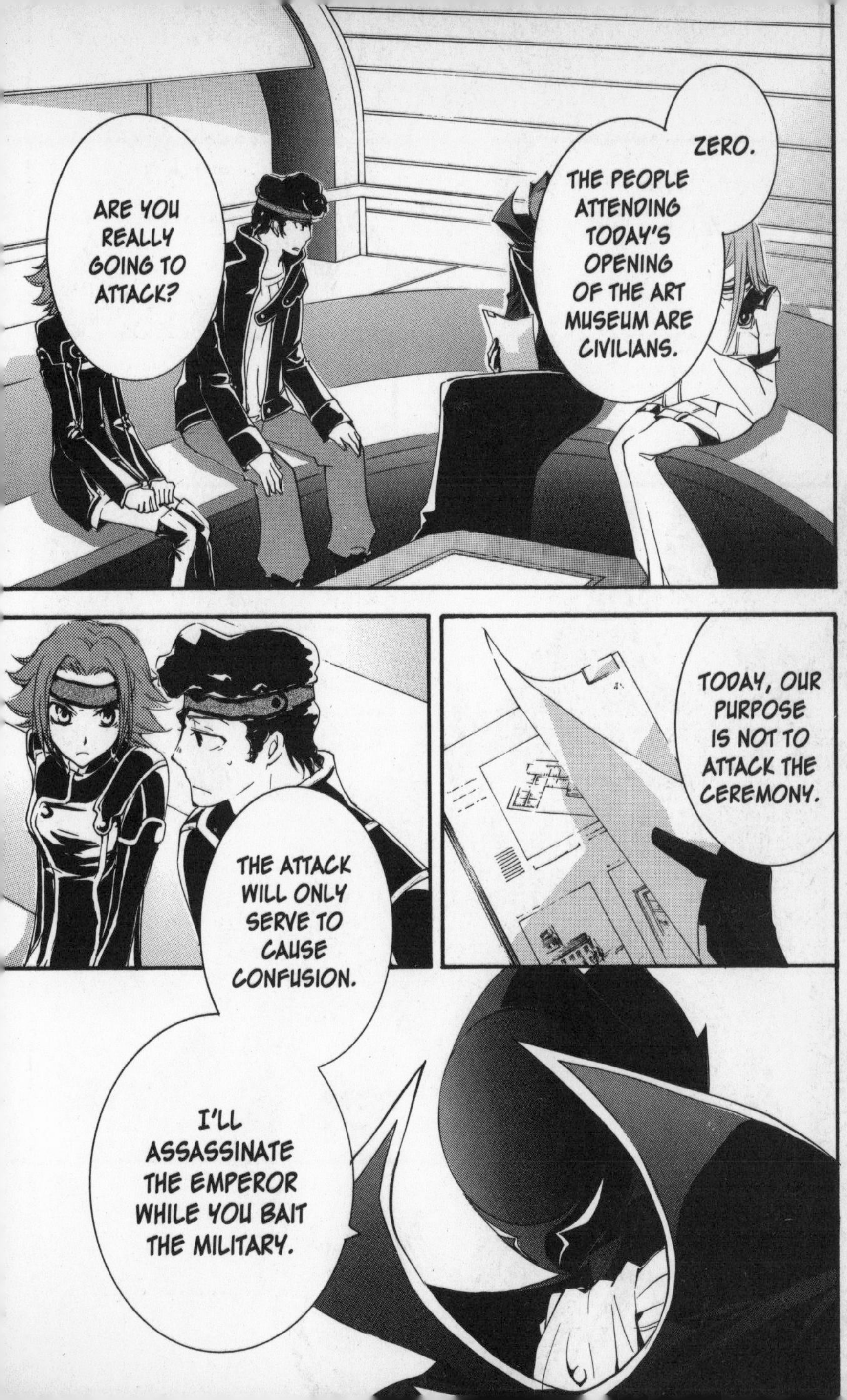
ZERO.
THE PEOPLE ATTENDING TODAY'S OPENING OF THE ART MUSEUM ARE CIVILIANS.
ARE YOU REALLY GOING TO ATTACK?
TODAY, OUR PURPOSE IS NOT TO ATTACK THE CEREMONY.
THE ATTACK WILL ONLY SERVE TO CAUSE CONFUSION.
I'LL ASSASSINATE THE EMPEROR WHILE YOU BAIT THE MILITARY.

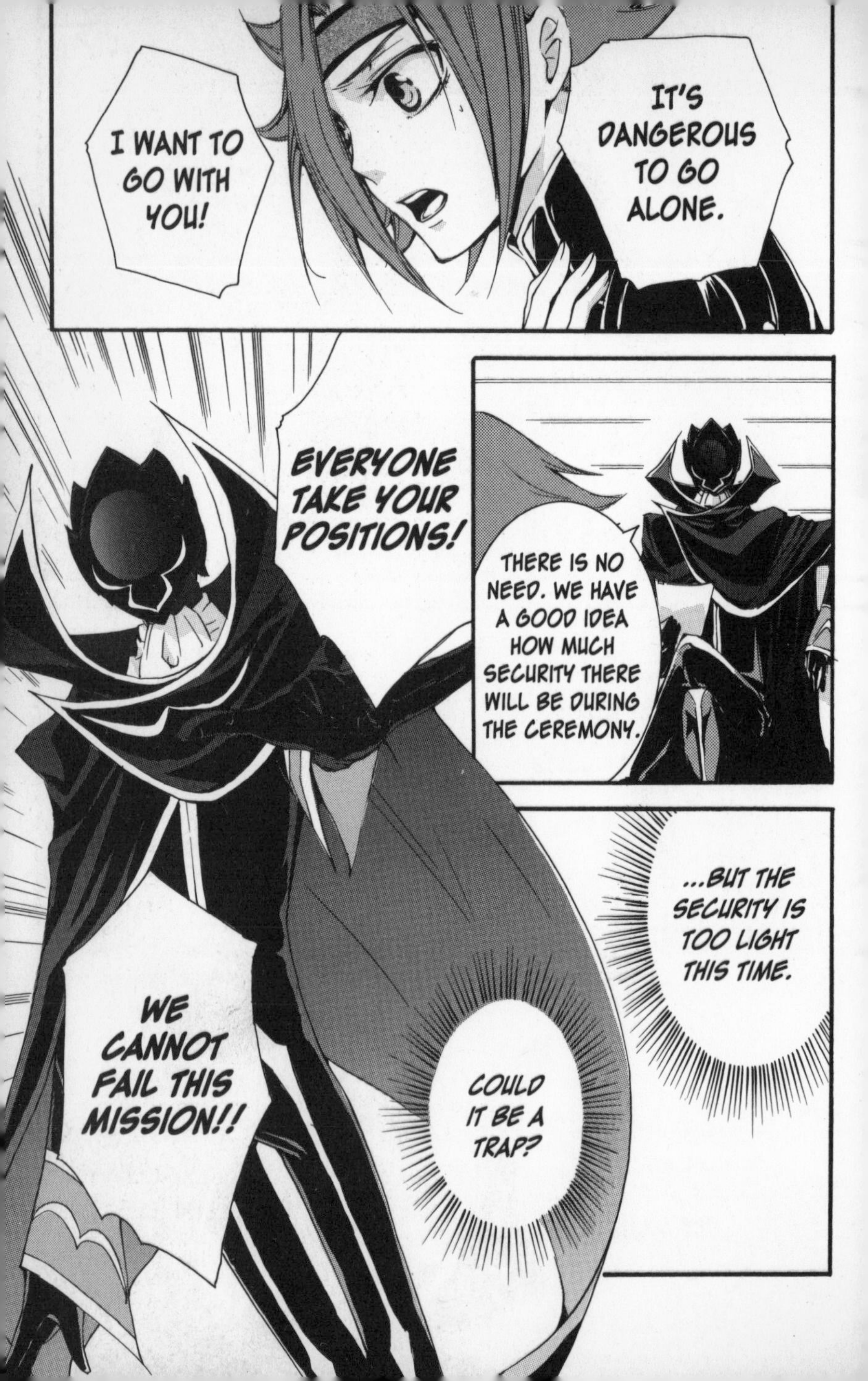
IT'S DANGEROUS TO GO ALONE.
I WANT TO GO WITH YOU!
THERE IS NO NEED. WE HAVE A GOOD IDEA HOW MUCH SECURITY THERE WILL BE DURING THE CEREMONY.
...BUT THE SECURITY IS TOO LIGHT THIS TIME.
COULD IT BE A TRAP?
EVERYONE TAKE YOUR POSITIONS!
WE CANNOT FAIL THIS MISSION!!

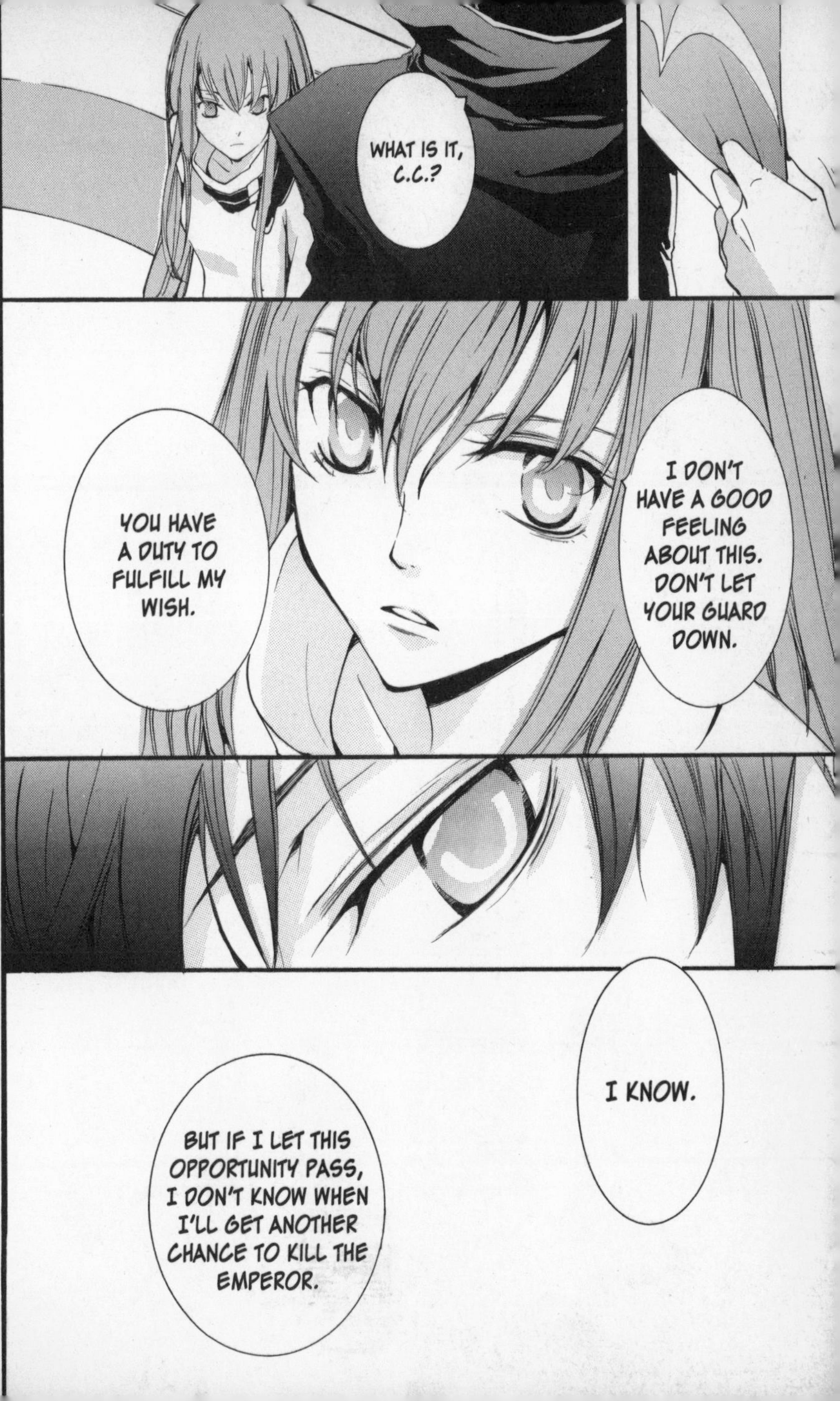
WHAT IS IT, C.C.?
I DON'T HAVE A GOOD FEELING ABOUT THIS. DON'T LET YOUR GUARD DOWN.
YOU HAVE A DUTY TO FULFILL MY WISH.
I KNOW.
BUT IF I LET THIS OPPORTUNITY PASS, I DON'T KNOW WHEN I'LL GET ANOTHER CHANCE TO KILL THE EMPEROR.

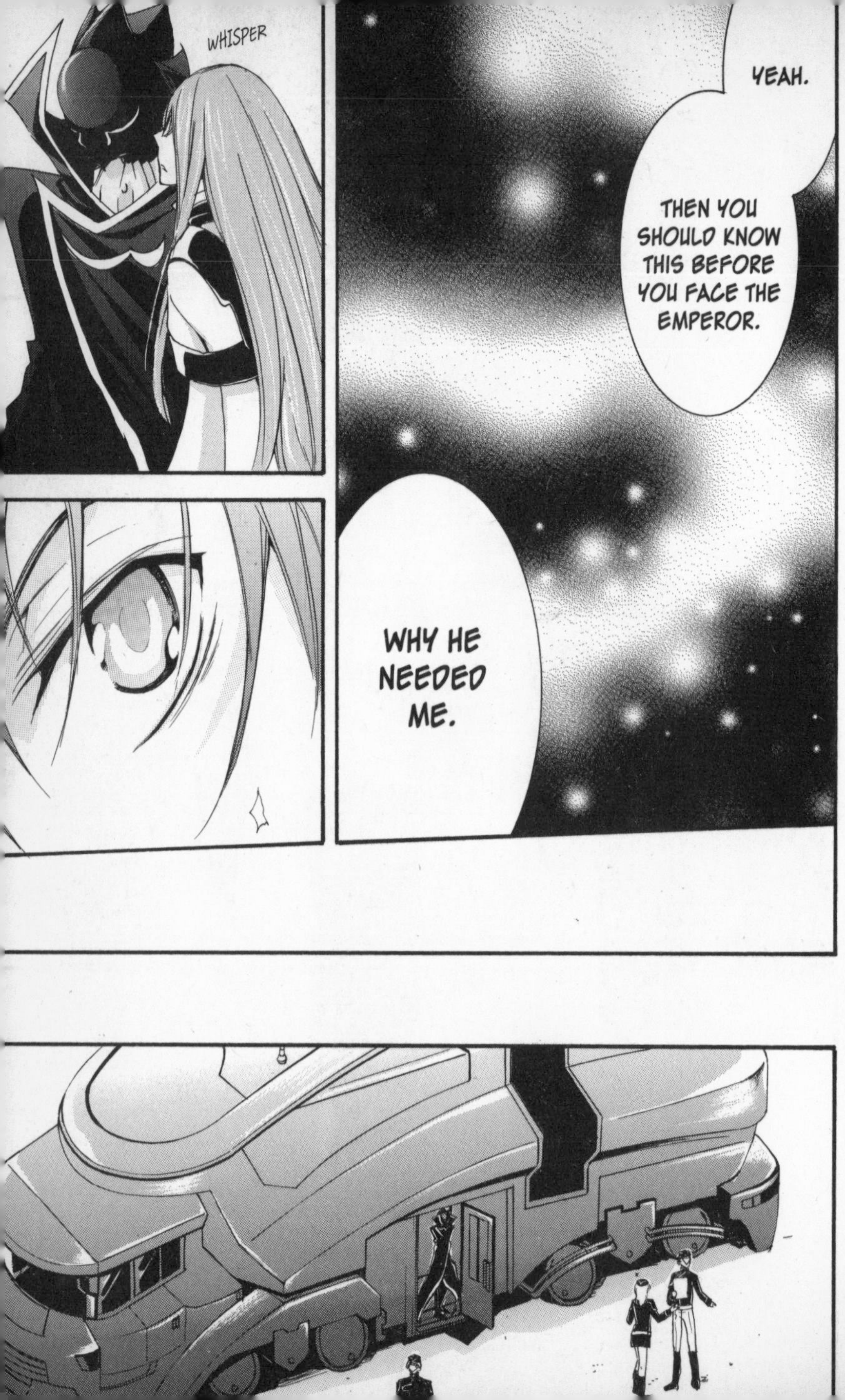
YEAH.
THEN YOU SHOULD KNOW THIS BEFORE YOU FACE THE EMPEROR.
WHY HE NEEDED ME.
WHISPER

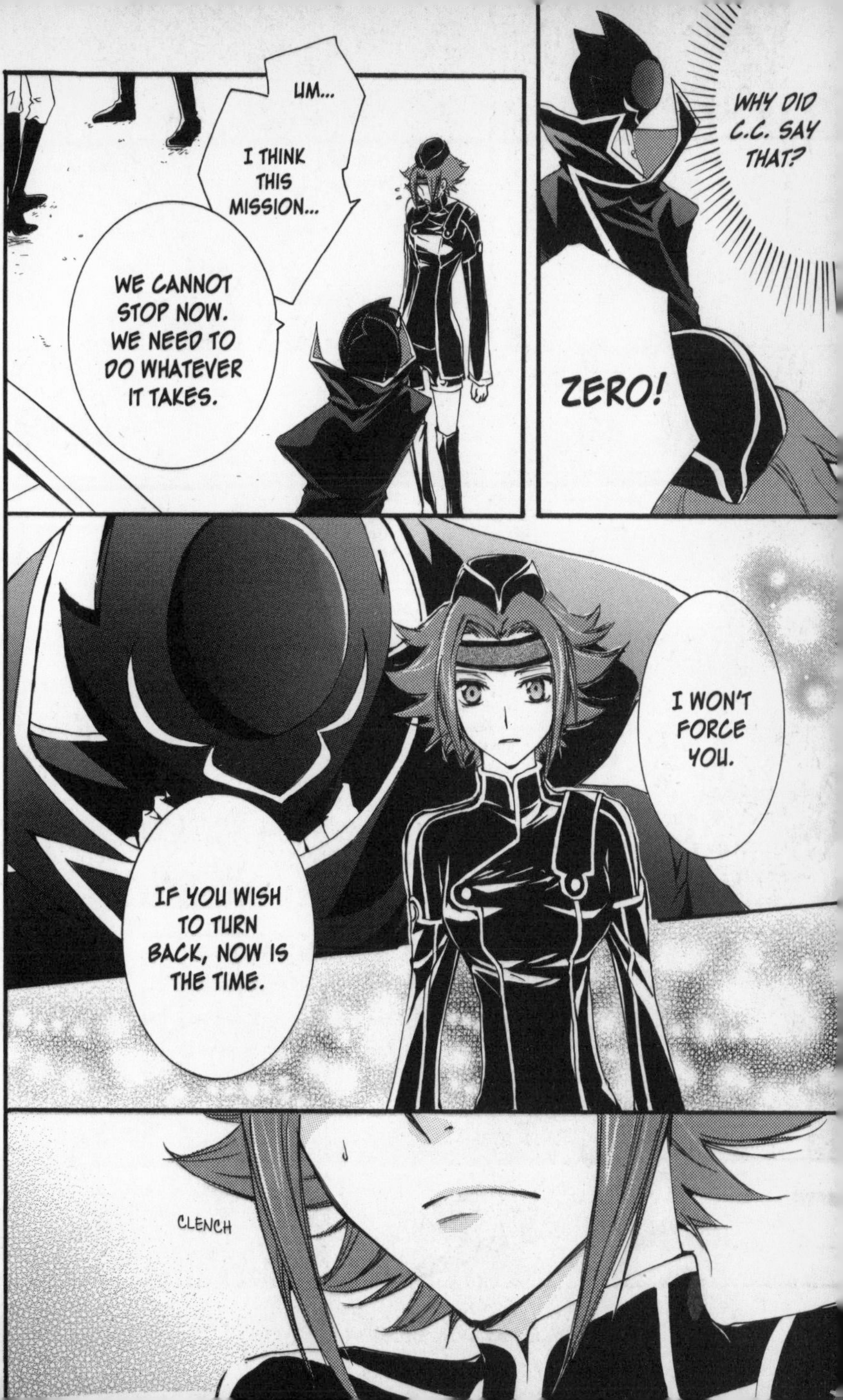
WHY DID C.C. SAY THAT?
ZERO!
UM...
I THINK THIS MISSION...
WE CANNOT STOP NOW. WE NEED TO DO WHATEVER IT TAKES.
I WON'T FORCE YOU.
IF YOU WISH TO TURN BACK, NOW IS THE TIME.
CLENCH

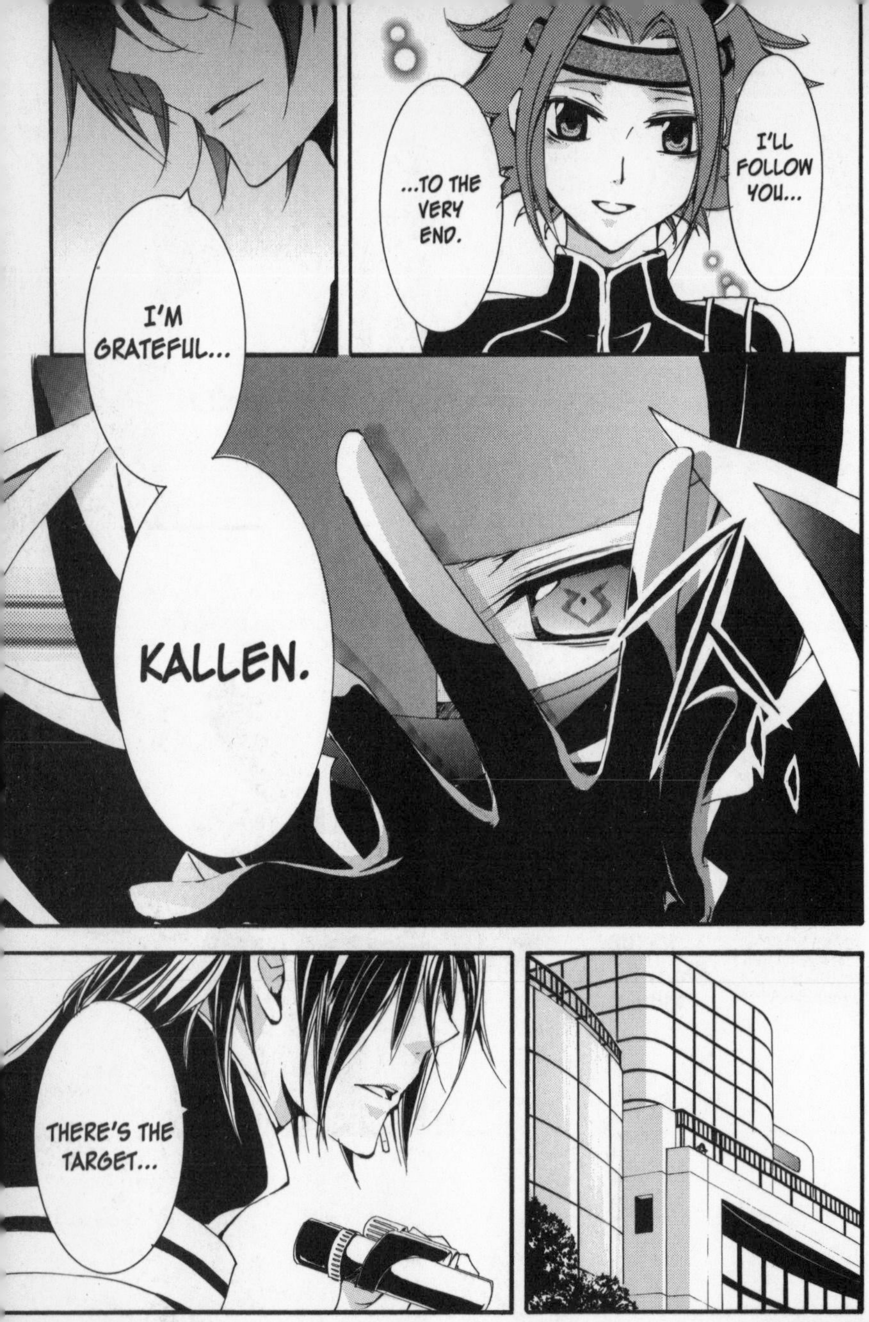
I'LL FOLLOW YOU...
...TO THE VERY END.
I'M GRATEFUL...
KALLEN.
THERE'S THE TARGET...

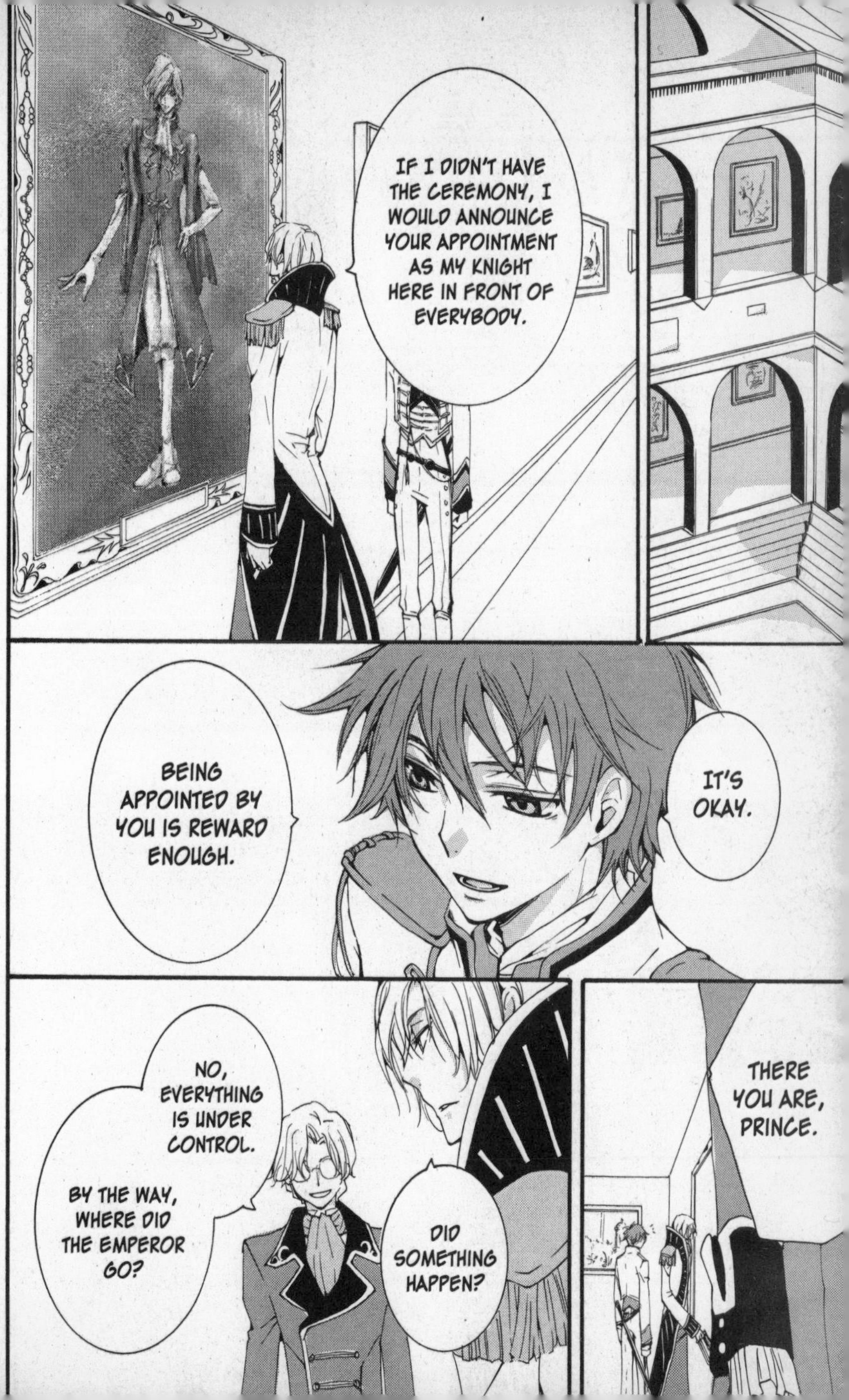
IF I DIDN'T HAVE THE CEREMONY, I WOULD ANNOUNCE YOUR APPOINTMENT AS MY KNIGHT HERE IN FRONT OF EVERYBODY.
IT'S OKAY.
BEING APPOINTED BY YOU IS REWARD ENOUGH.
THERE YOU ARE, PRINCE.
DID SOMETHING HAPPEN?
NO, EVERYTHING IS UNDER CONTROL.
BY THE WAY, WHERE DID THE EMPEROR GO?

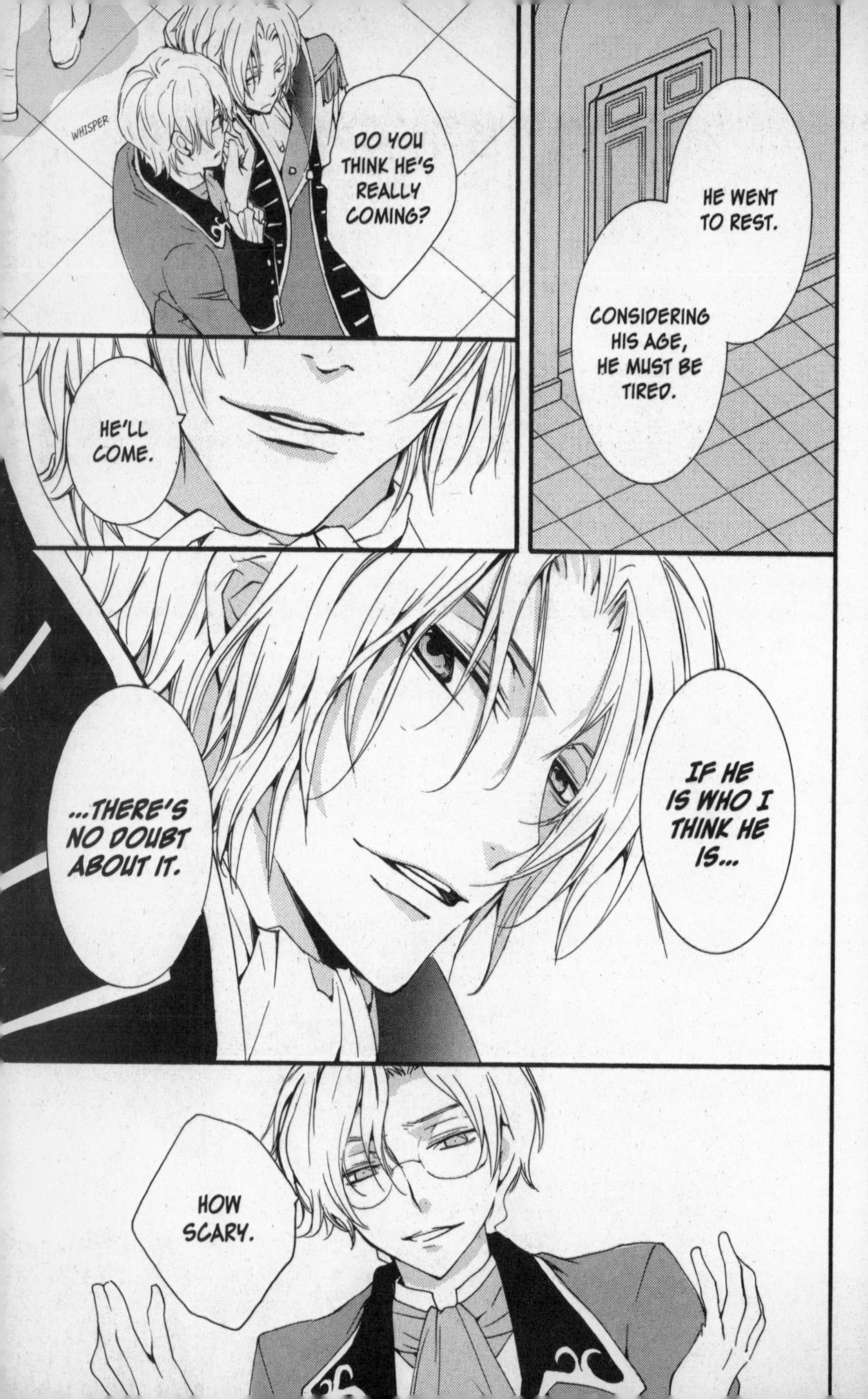
HE WENT TO REST.
CONSIDERING HIS AGE, HE MUST BE TIRED.
DO YOU THINK HE'S REALLY COMING?
WHISPER
HE'LL COME.
IF HE IS WHO I THINK HE IS...
...THERE'S NO DOUBT ABOUT IT.
HOW SCARY.

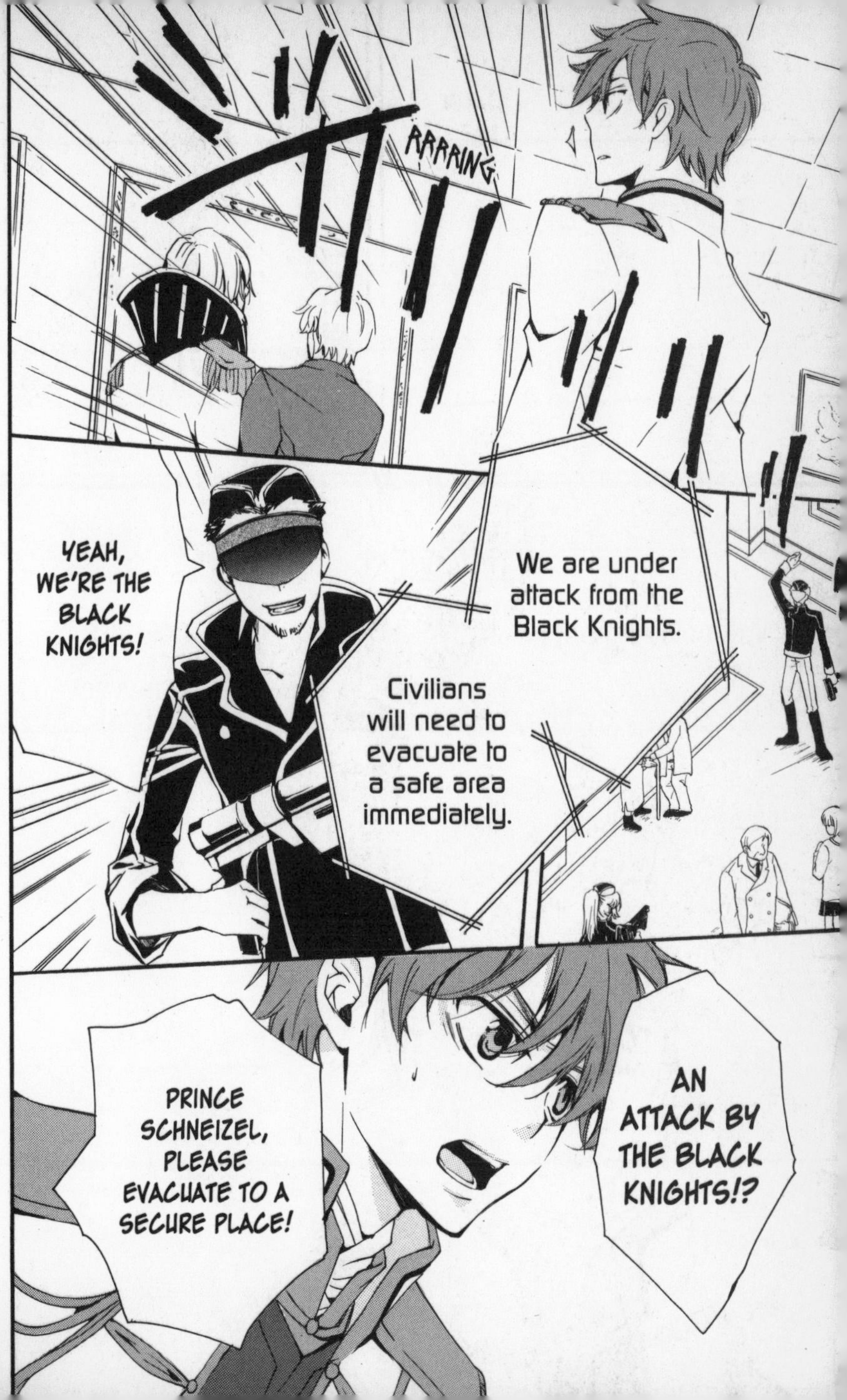
RRRRING
We are under attack from the Black Knights.
Civilians will need to evacuate to a safe area immediately.
YEAH, WE'RE THE BLACK KNIGHTS!
AN ATTACK BY THE BLACK KNIGHTS!?
PRINCE SCHNEIZEL, PLEASE EVACUATE TO A SECURE PLACE!

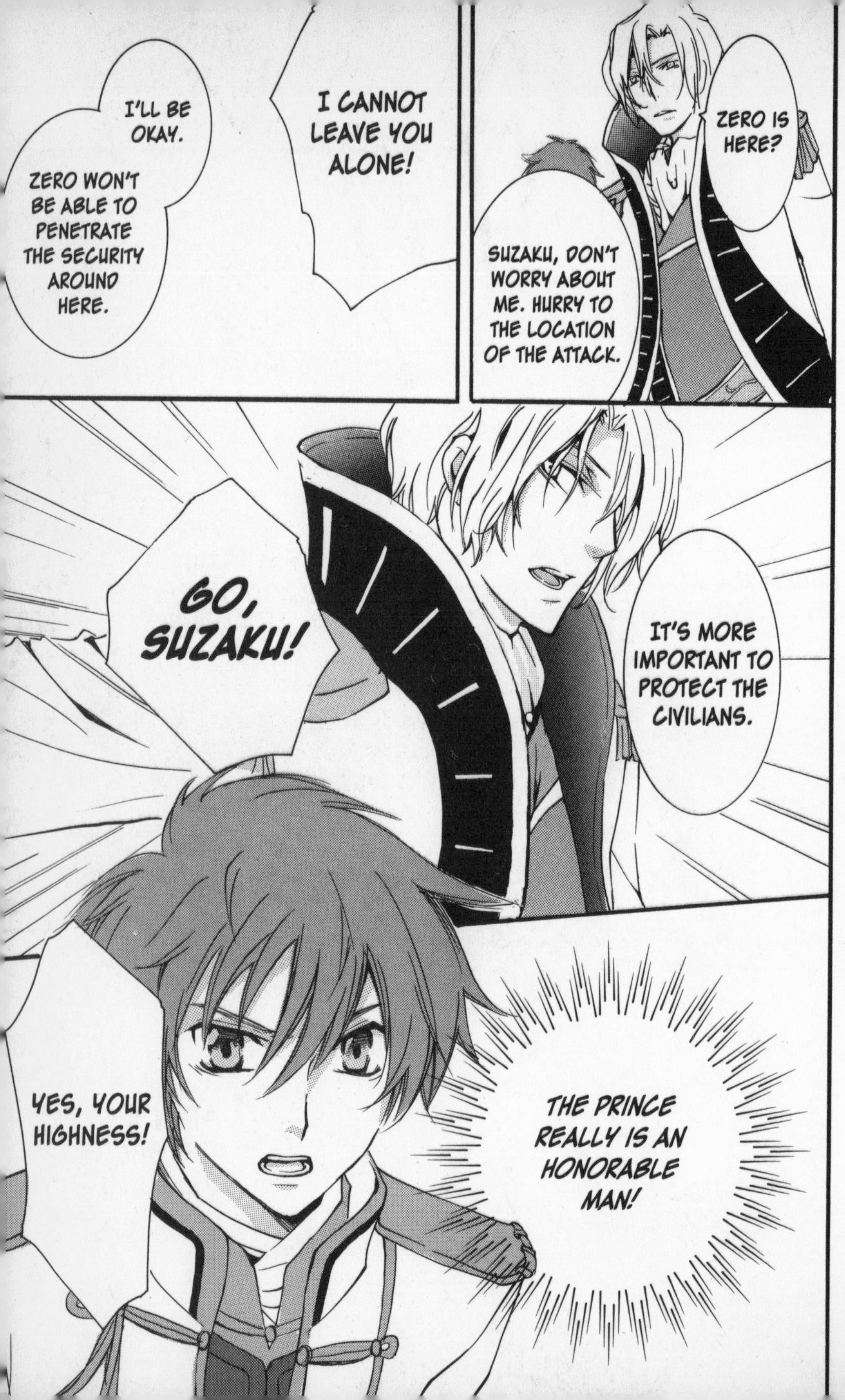
ZERO IS HERE?
SUZAKU, DON'T WORRY ABOUT ME. HURRY TO THE LOCATION OF THE ATTACK.
I CANNOT LEAVE YOU ALONE!
I'LL BE OKAY.
ZERO WON'T BE ABLE TO PENETRATE THE SECURITY AROUND HERE.
IT'S MORE IMPORTANT TO PROTECT THE CIVILIANS.
GO, SUZAKU!
THE PRINCE REALLY IS AN HONORABLE MAN!
YES, YOUR HIGHNESS!

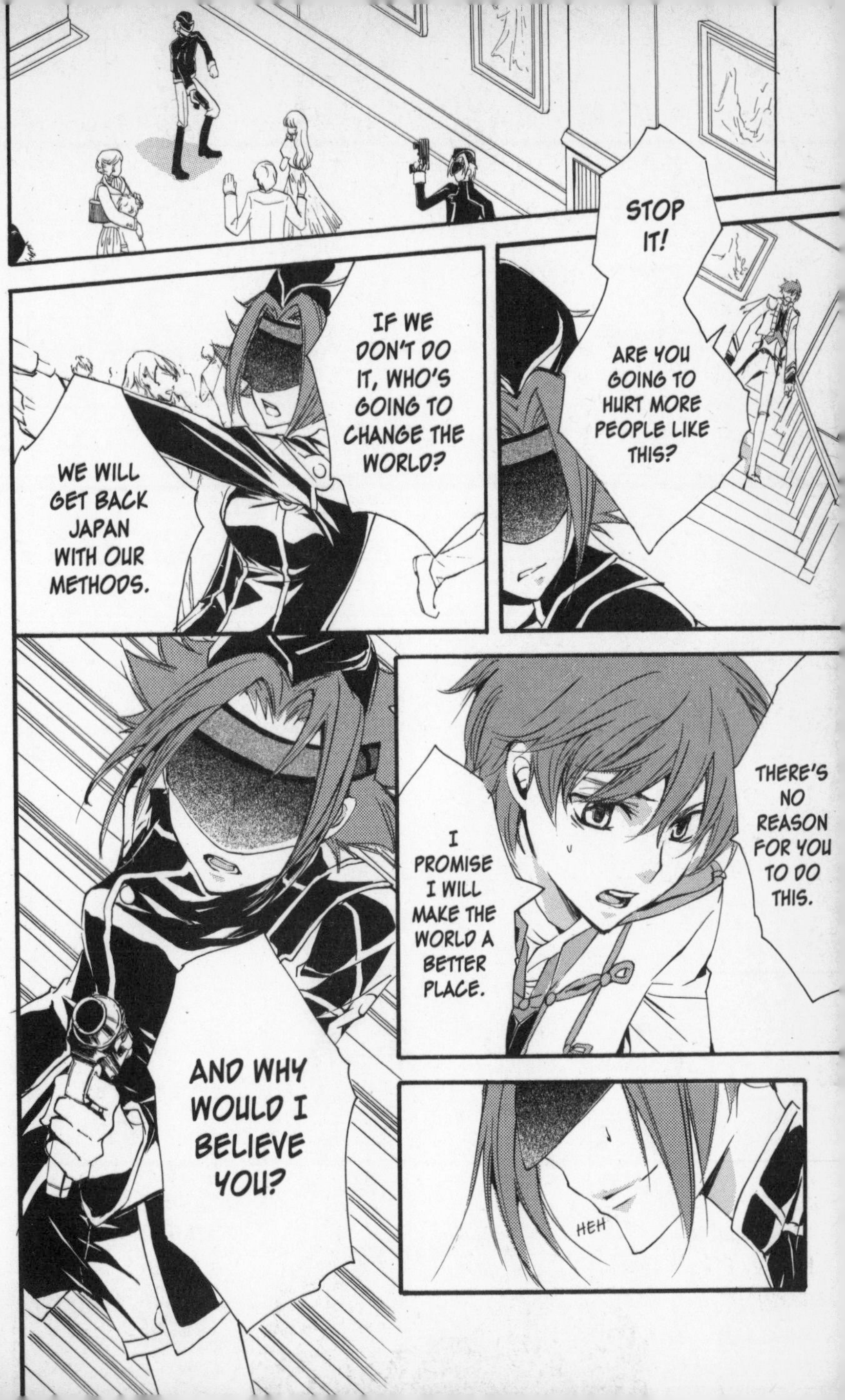
STOP IT!
ARE YOU GOING TO HURT MORE PEOPLE LIKE THIS?
IF WE DON'T DO IT, WHO'S GOING TO CHANGE THE WORLD?
WE WILL GET BACK JAPAN WITH OUR METHODS.
THERE'S NO REASON FOR YOU TO DO THIS.
I PROMISE I WILL MAKE THE WORLD A BETTER PLACE.
HEH
AND WHY WOULD I BELIEVE YOU?

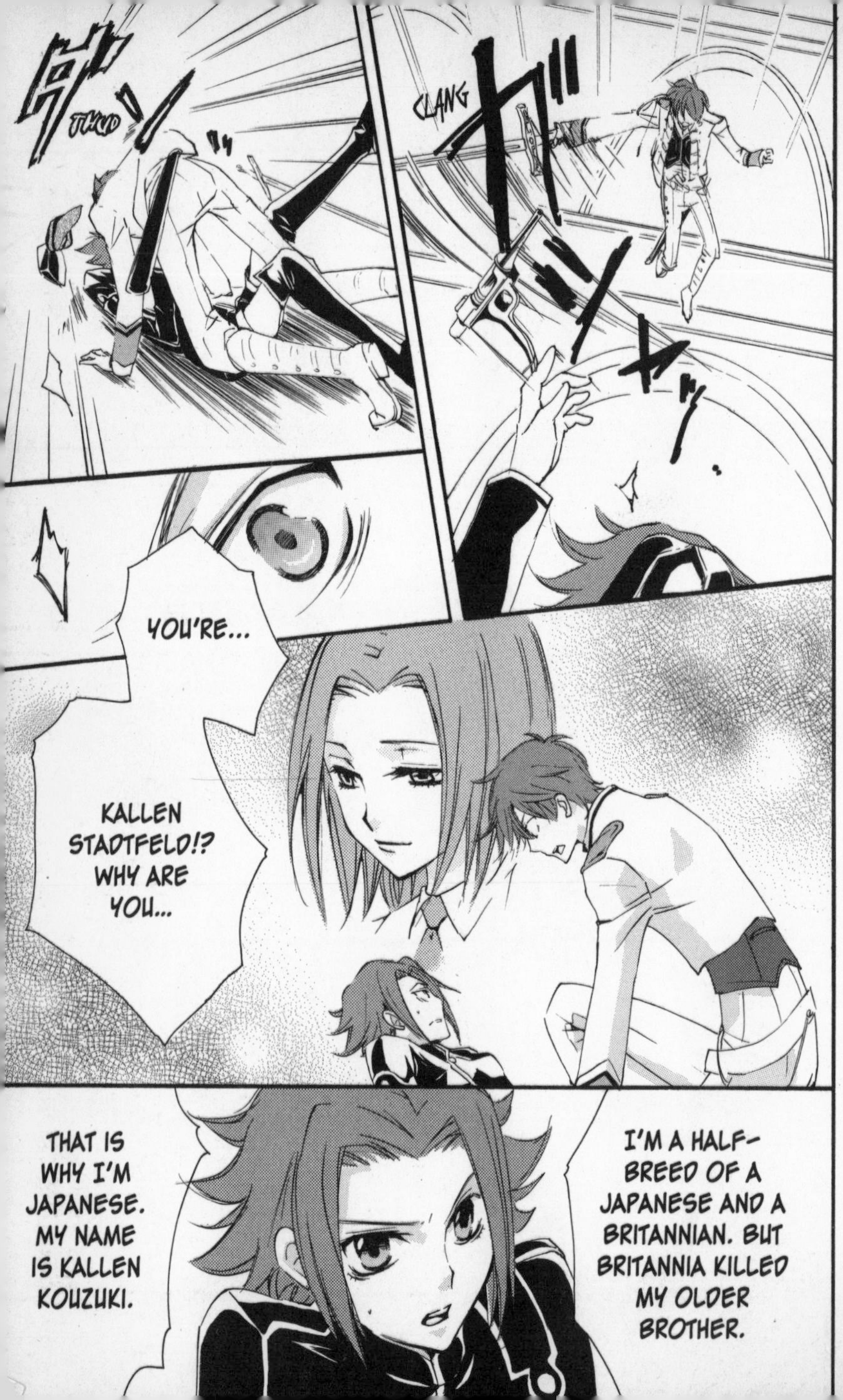
CLANG
THUD
YOU'RE...
KALLEN STADTFELD!? WHY ARE YOU...
I'M A HALF-BREED OF A JAPANESE AND A BRITANNIAN. BUT BRITANNIA KILLED MY OLDER BROTHER.
THAT IS WHY I'M JAPANESE. MY NAME IS KALLEN KOUZUKI.

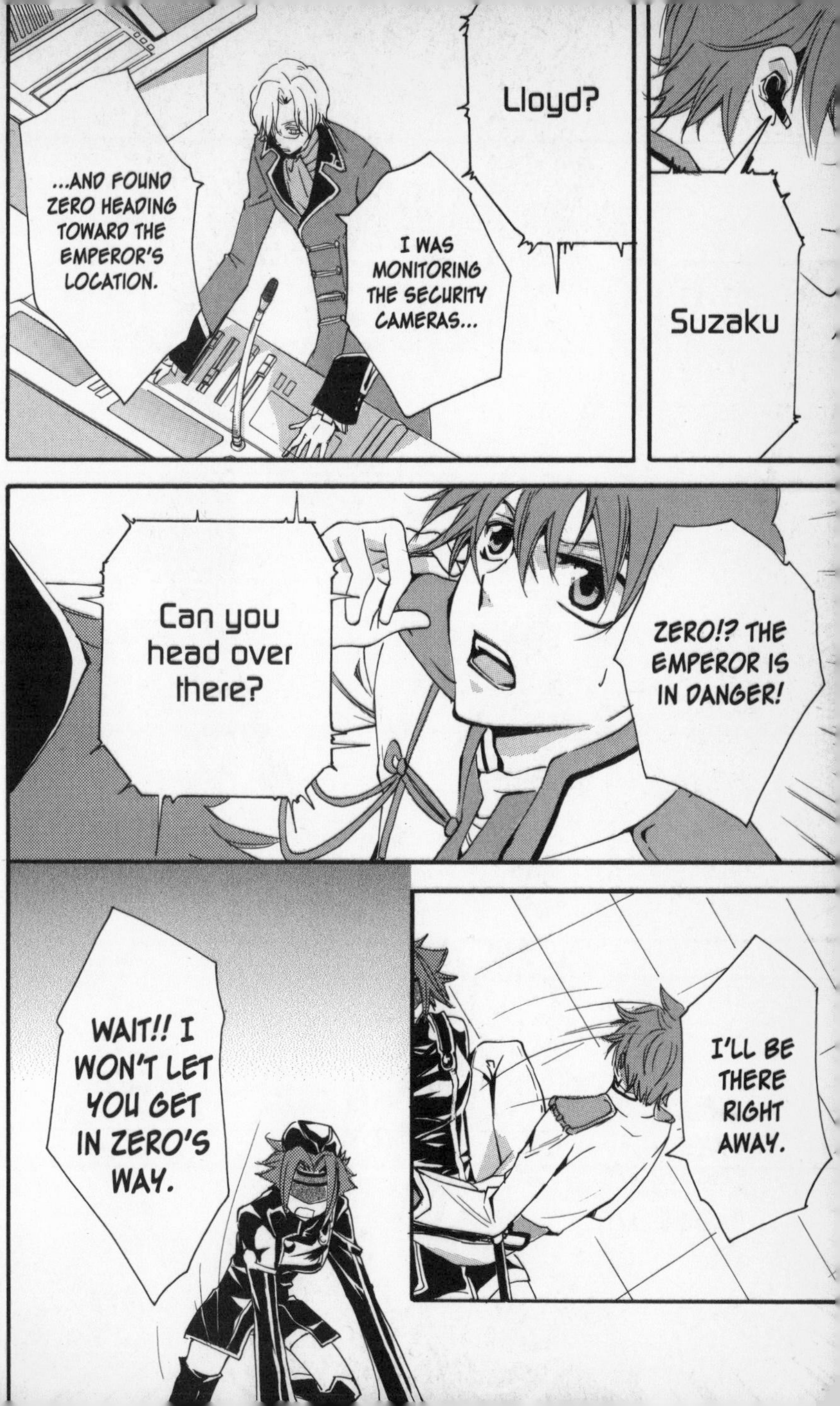
Suzaku
Lloyd?
I WAS MONITORING THE SECURITY CAMERAS...
...AND FOUND ZERO HEADING TOWARD THE EMPEROR'S LOCATION.
ZERO!? THE EMPEROR IS IN DANGER!
Can you head over there?
I'LL BE THERE RIGHT AWAY.
WAIT!! I WON'T LET YOU GET IN ZERO'S WAY.

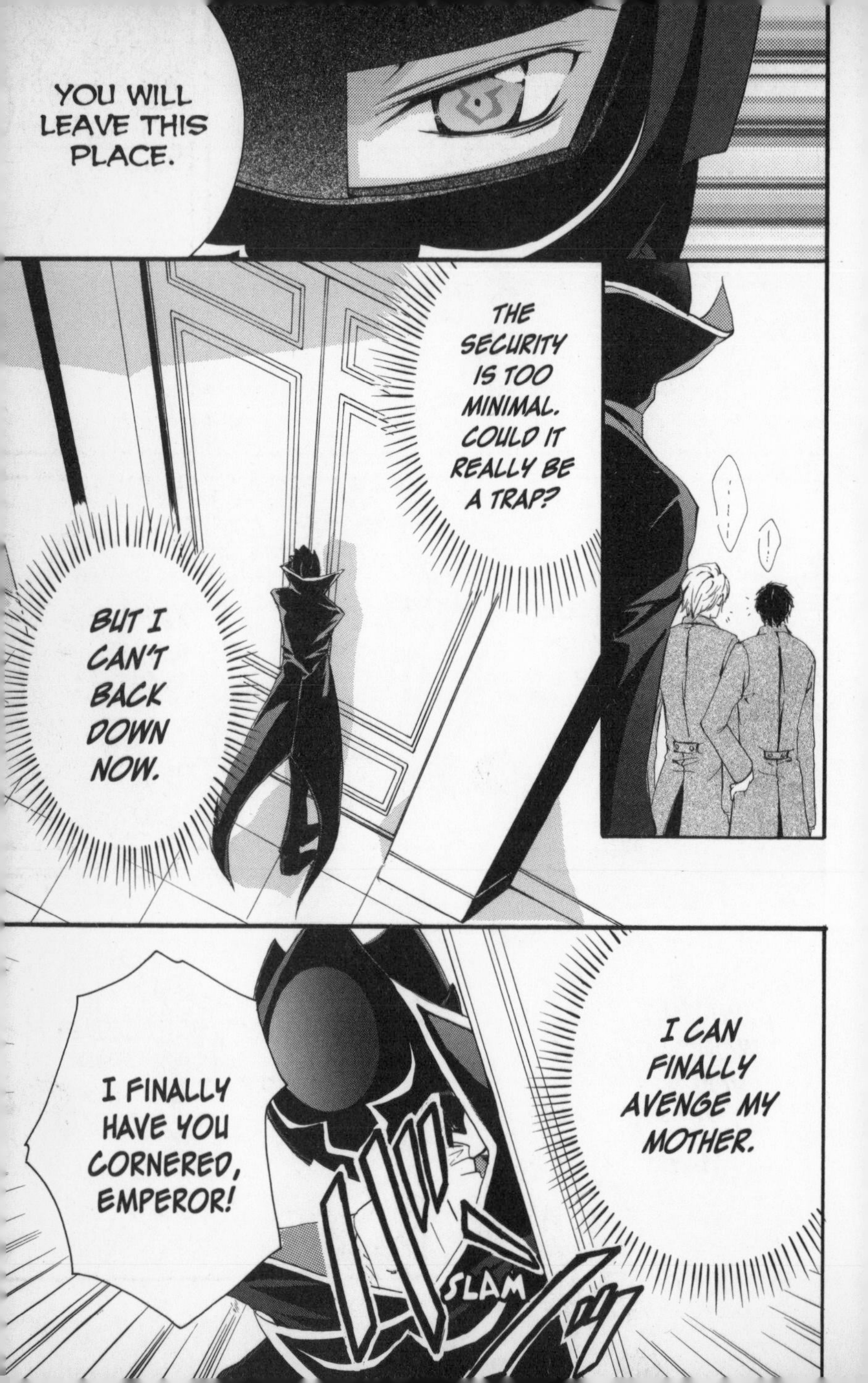
YOU WILL LEAVE THIS PLACE.
THE SECURITY IS TOO MINIMAL. COULD IT REALLY BE A TRAP?
BUT I CAN'T BACK DOWN NOW.
I CAN FINALLY AVENGE MY MOTHER.
I FINALLY HAVE YOU CORNERED, EMPEROR!
SLAM

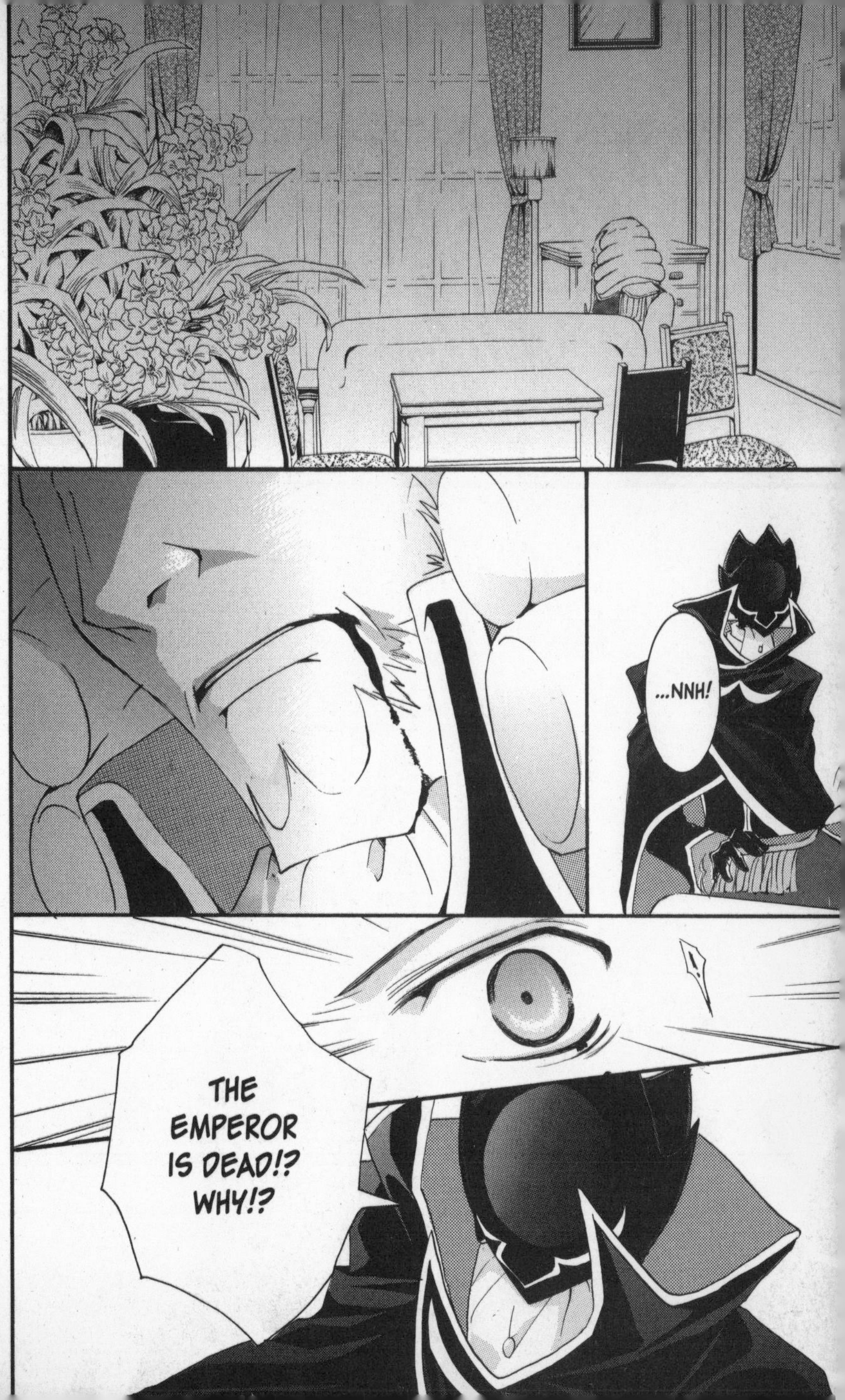
...NNH!
!
THE EMPEROR IS DEAD!? WHY!?

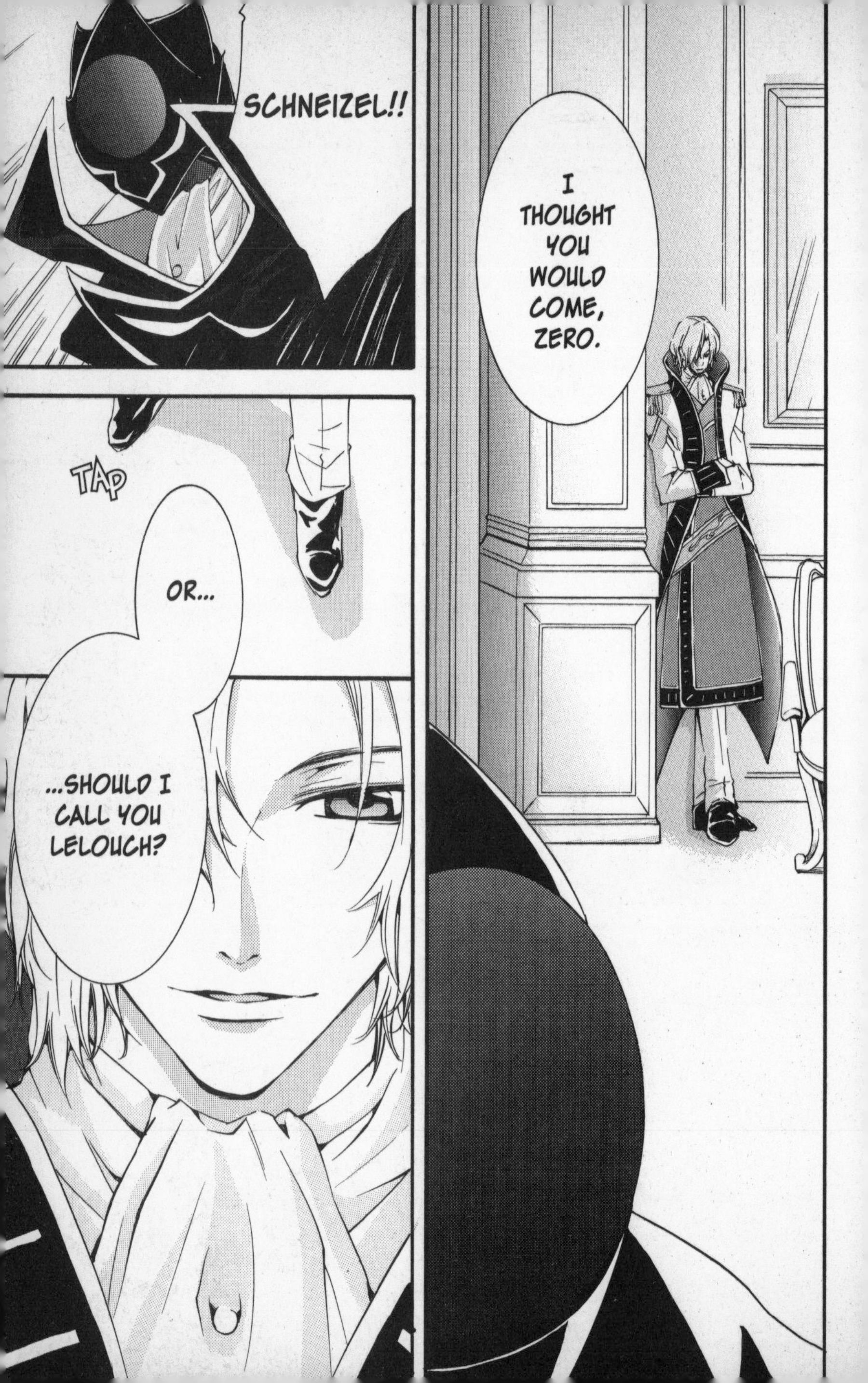
I THOUGHT YOU WOULD COME, ZERO.
SCHNEIZEL!!
TAP
OR...
...SHOULD I CALL YOU LELOUCH?

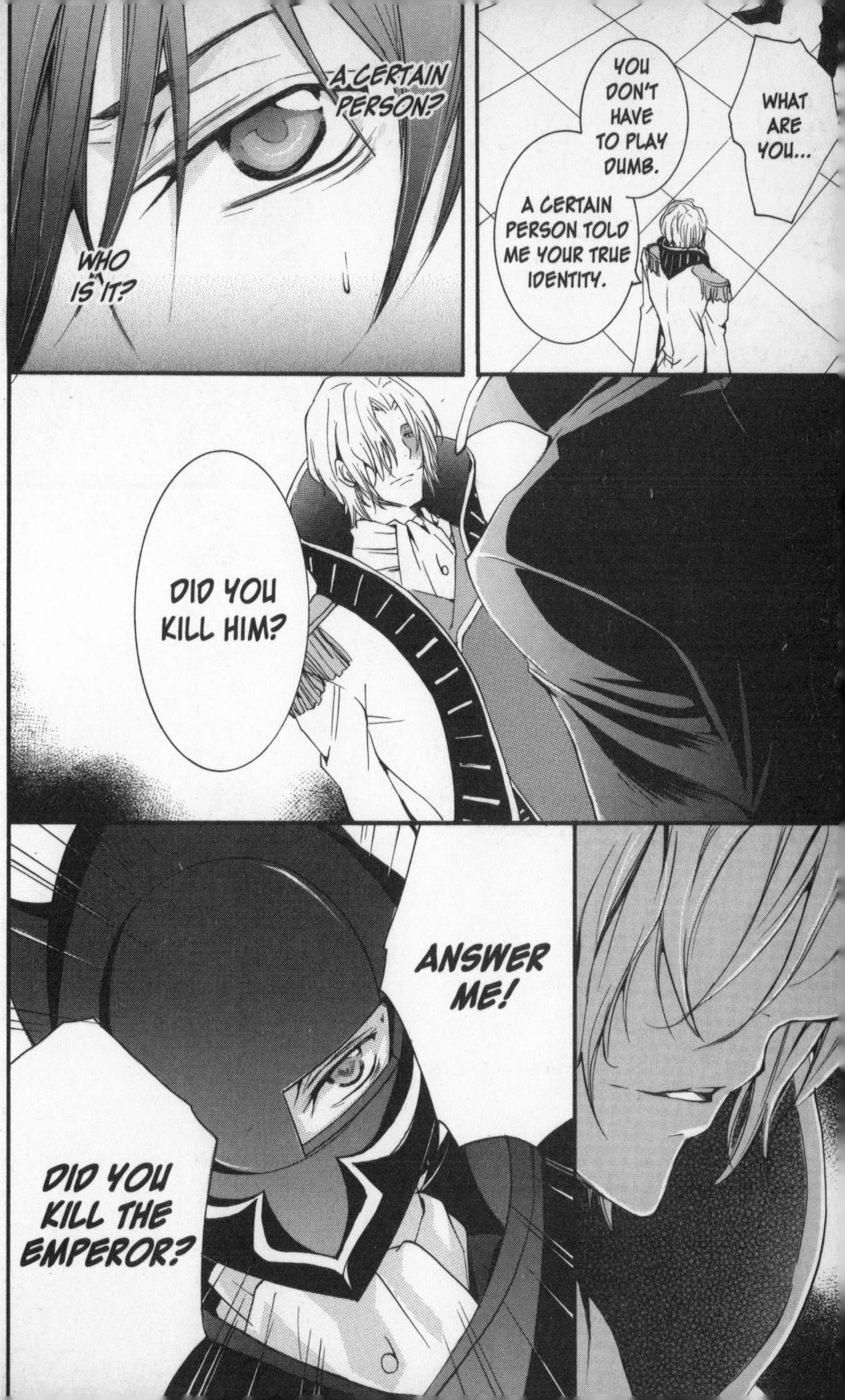
WHAT ARE YOU...
YOU DON'T HAVE TO PLAY DUMB.
A CERTAIN PERSON TOLD ME YOUR TRUE IDENTITY.
A CERTAIN PERSON?
WHO IS IT?
DID YOU KILL HIM?
ANSWER ME!
DID YOU KILL THE EMPEROR?

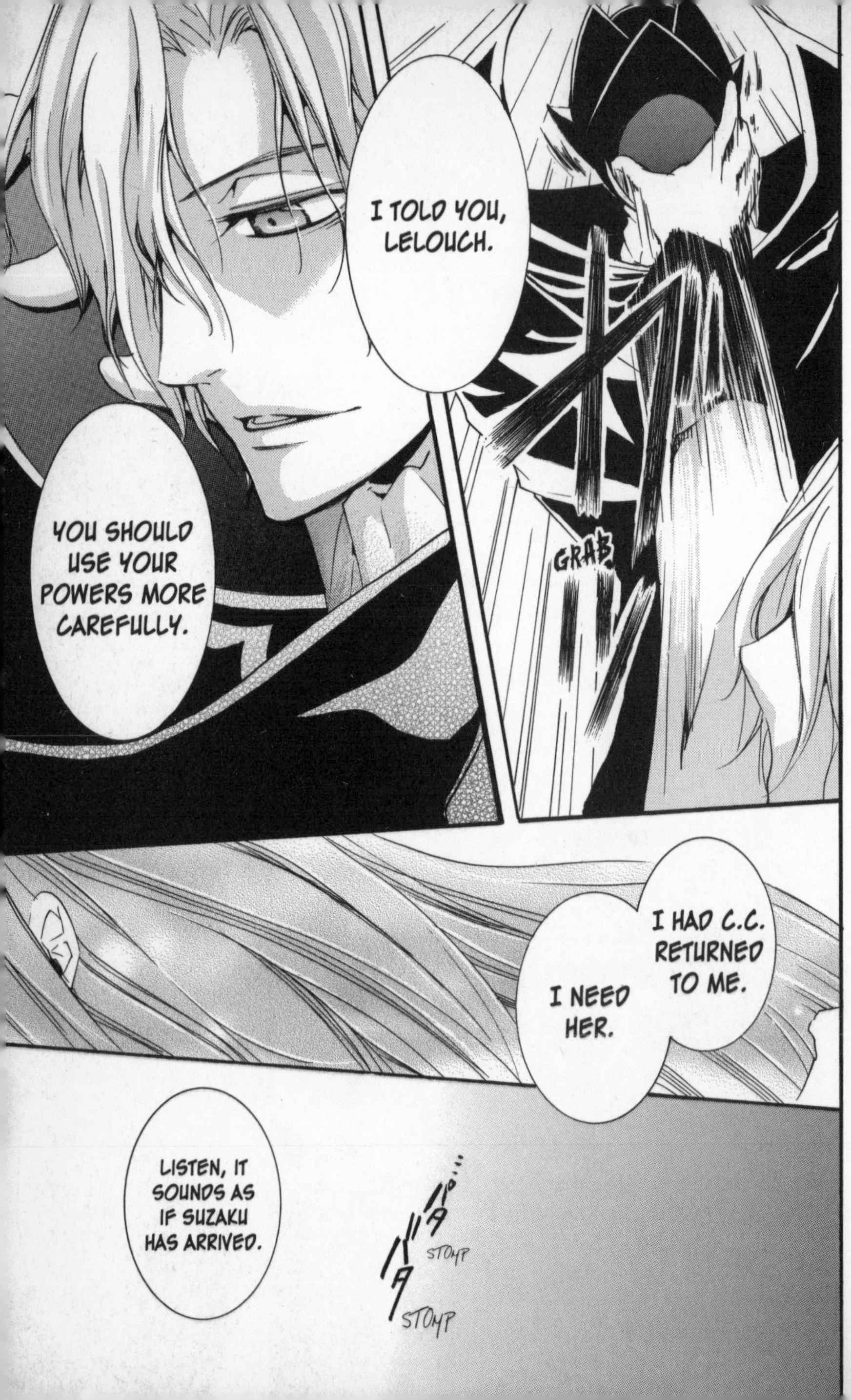
GRAB
I TOLD YOU, LELOUCH.
YOU SHOULD USE YOUR POWERS MORE CAREFULLY.
I HAD C.C. RETURNED TO ME.
I NEED HER.
STOMP
STOMP
LISTEN, IT SOUNDS AS IF SUZAKU HAS ARRIVED.

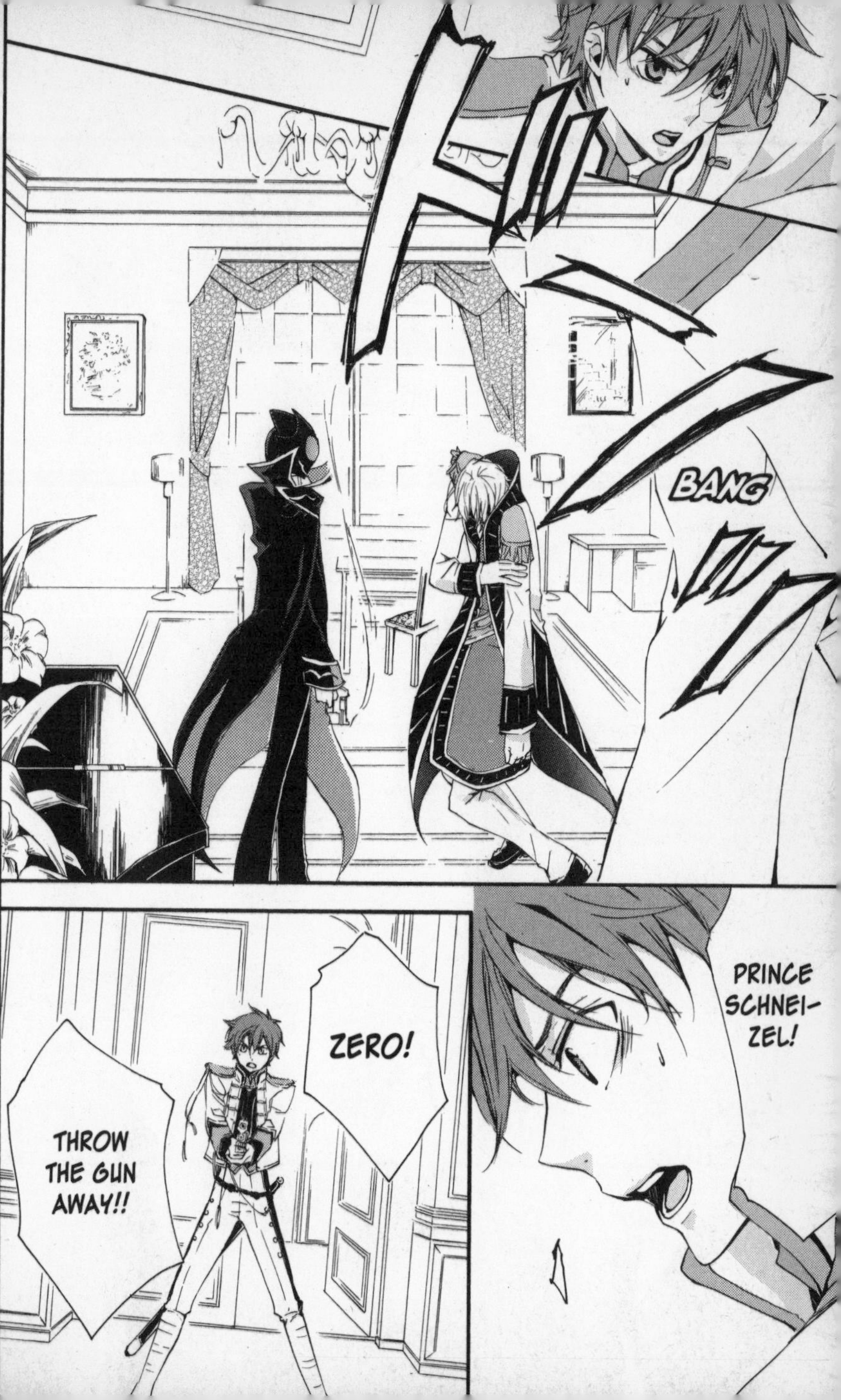
BANG
PRINCE SCHNEIZEL!
ZERO!
THROW THE GUN AWAY!!

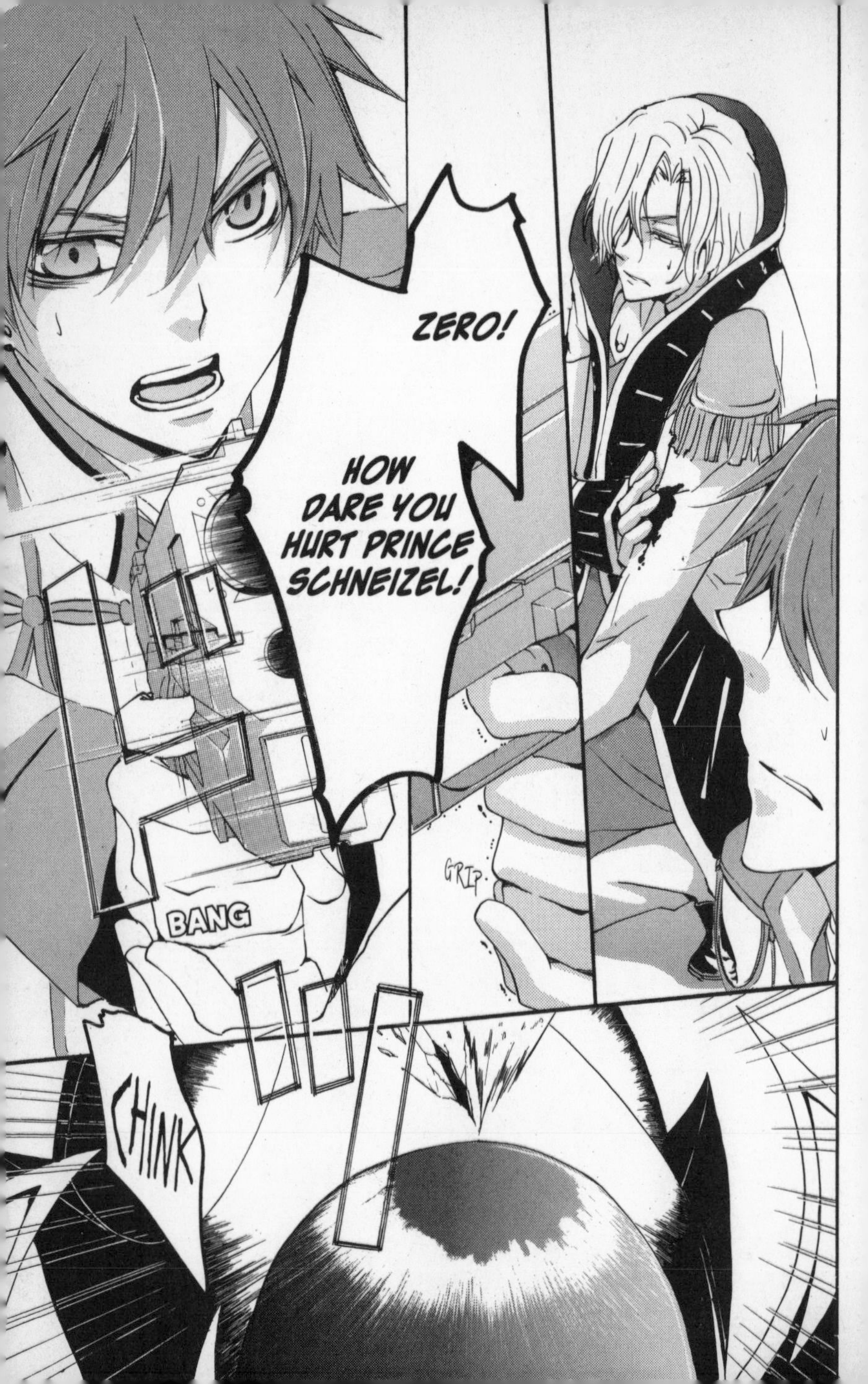
GRIP
ZERO!
HOW DARE YOU HURT PRINCE SCHNEIZEL!
BANG
CHINK

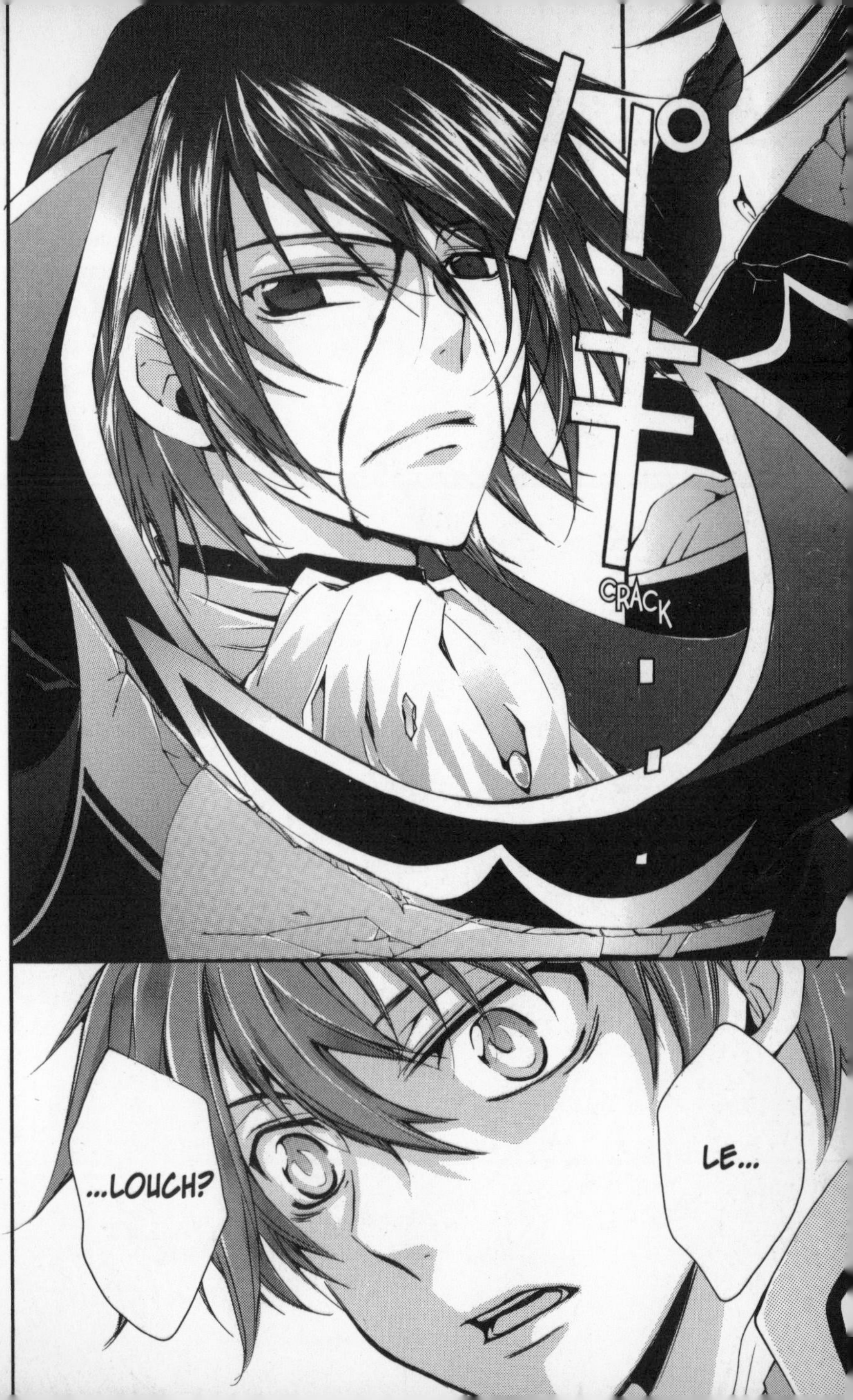
パキ
CRACK
LE...
...LOUCH?

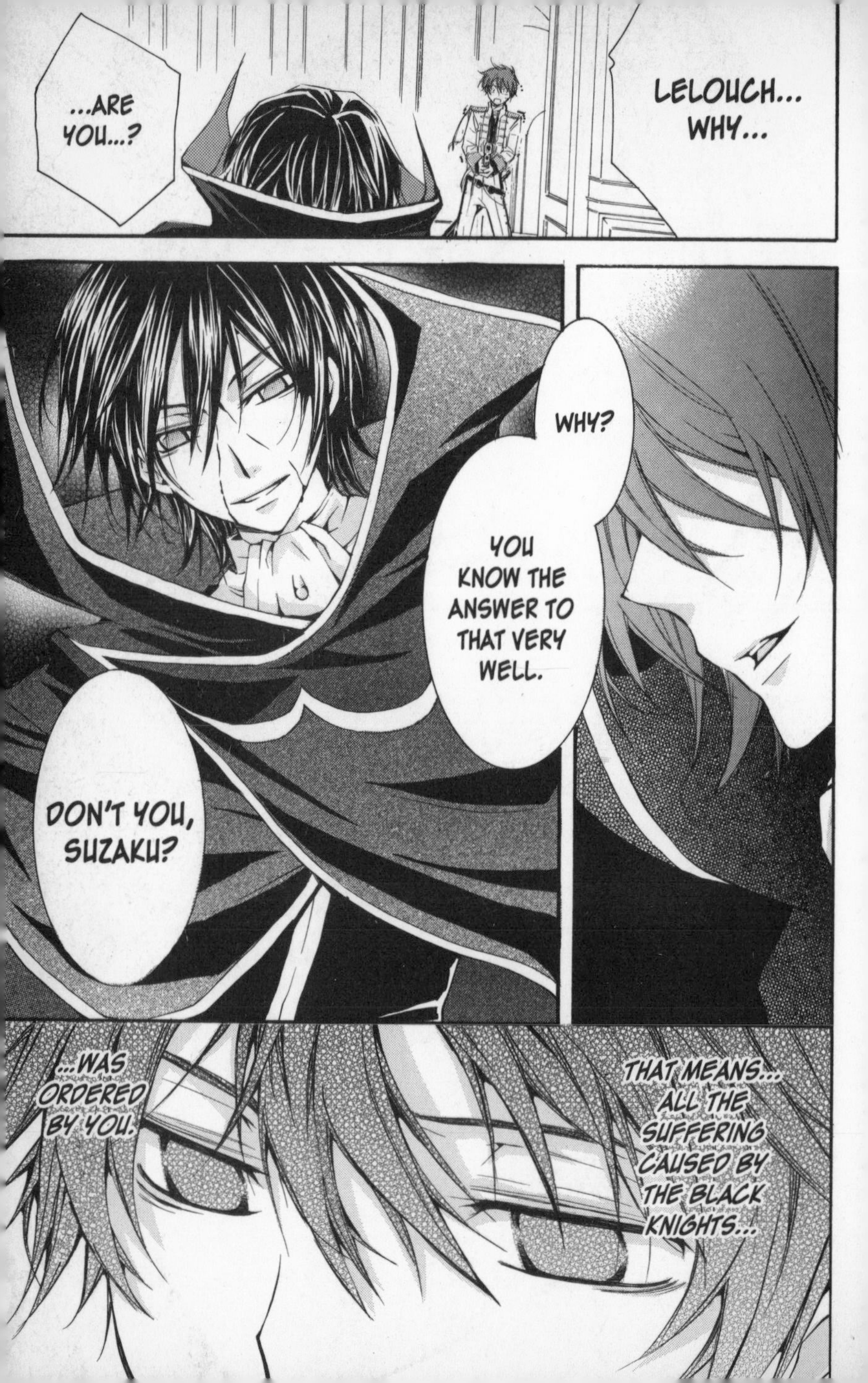
LELOUCH... WHY...
...ARE YOU...?
WHY?
YOU KNOW THE ANSWER TO THAT VERY WELL.
DON'T YOU, SUZAKU?
THAT MEANS... ALL THE SUFFERING CAUSED BY THE BLACK KNIGHTS...
...WAS ORDERED BY YOU.

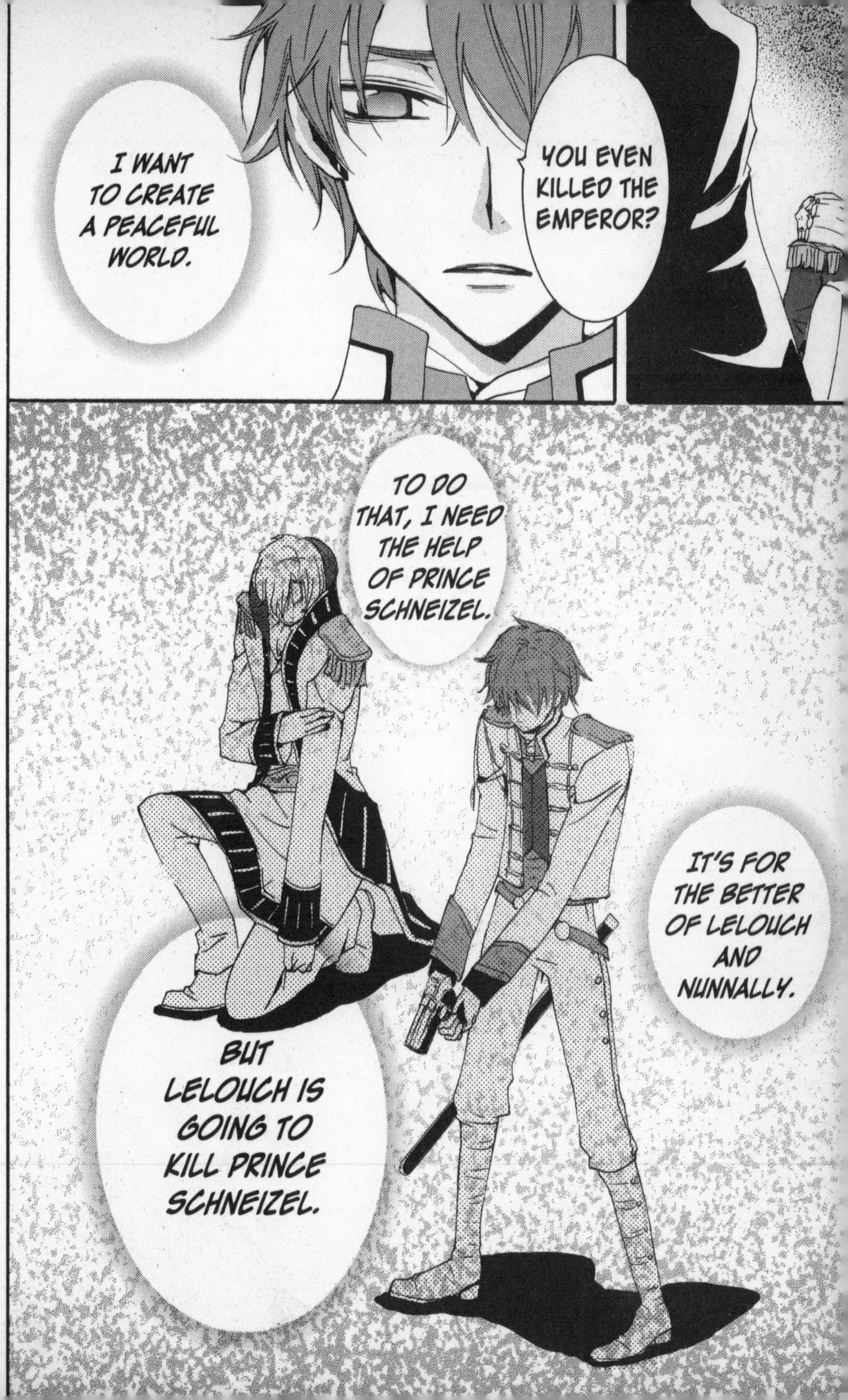
YOU EVEN KILLED THE EMPEROR?
I WANT TO CREATE A PEACEFUL WORLD.
TO DO THAT, I NEED THE HELP OF PRINCE SCHNEIZEL.
IT'S FOR THE BETTER OF LELOUCH AND NUNNALLY.
BUT LELOUCH IS GOING TO KILL PRINCE SCHNEIZEL.

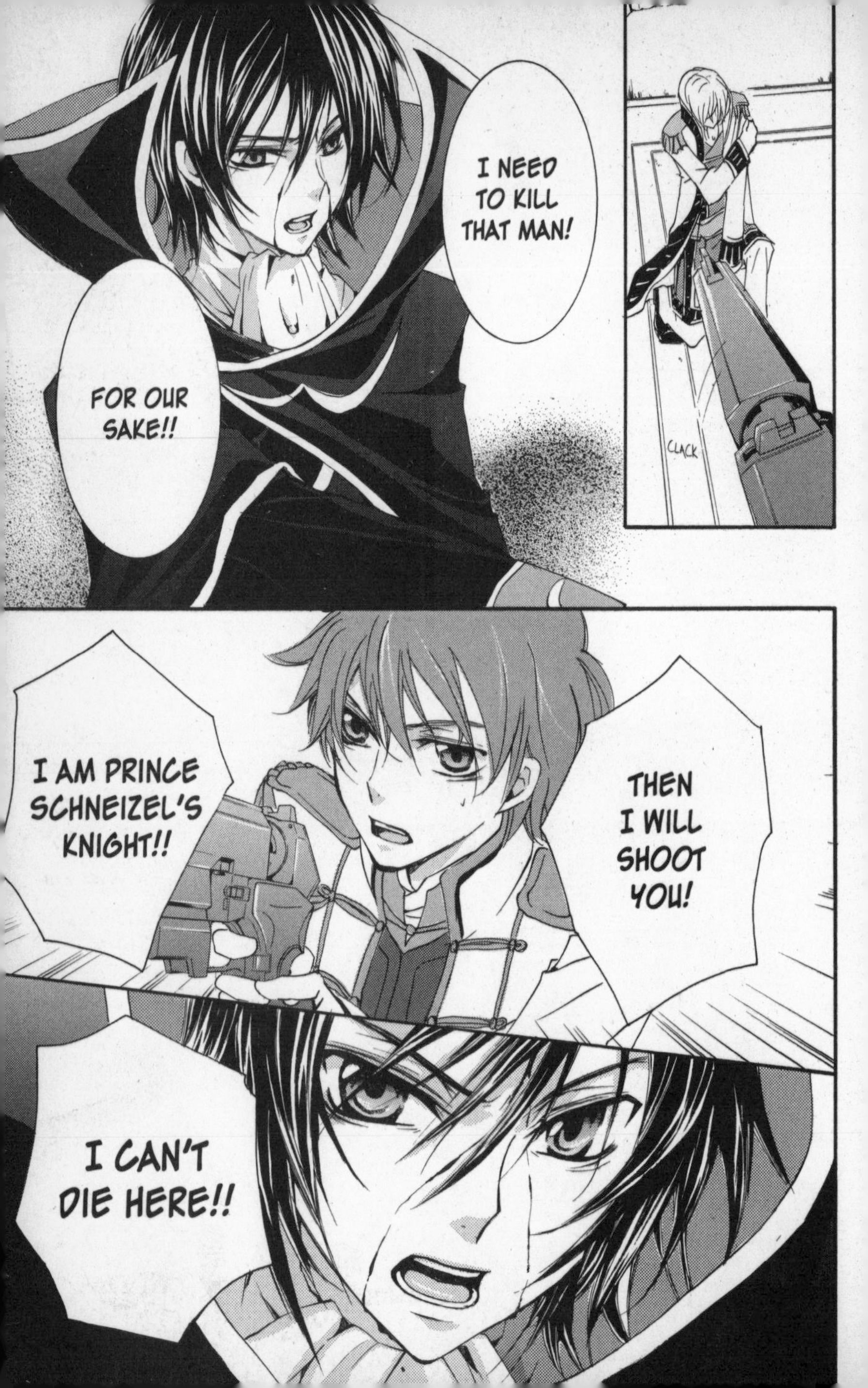
CLACK
I NEED TO KILL THAT MAN!
FOR OUR SAKE!!
THEN I WILL SHOOT YOU!
I AM PRINCE SCHNEIZEL'S KNIGHT!!
I CAN'T DIE HERE!!

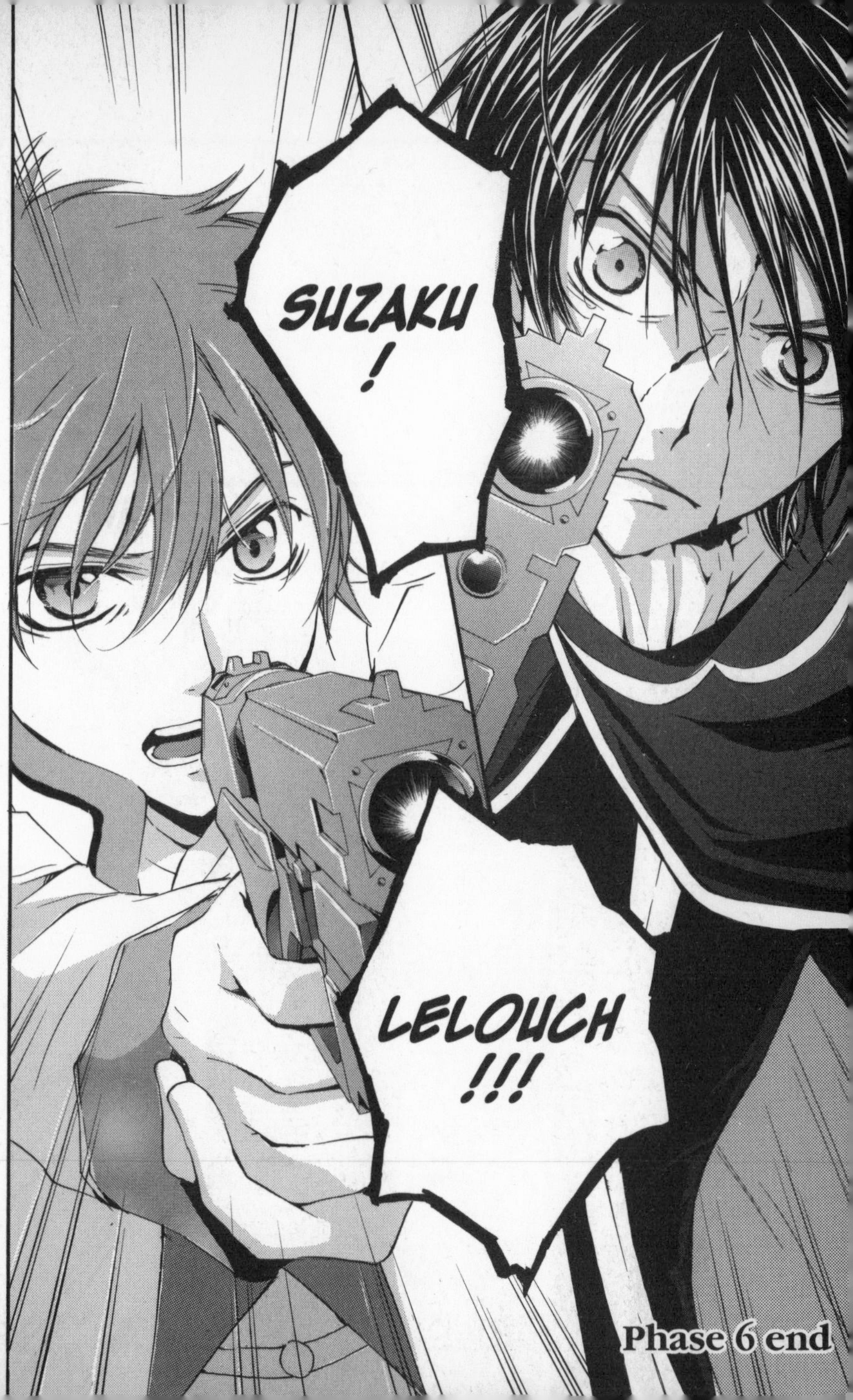
SUZAKU !
LELOUCH !!!

Phase 6 end

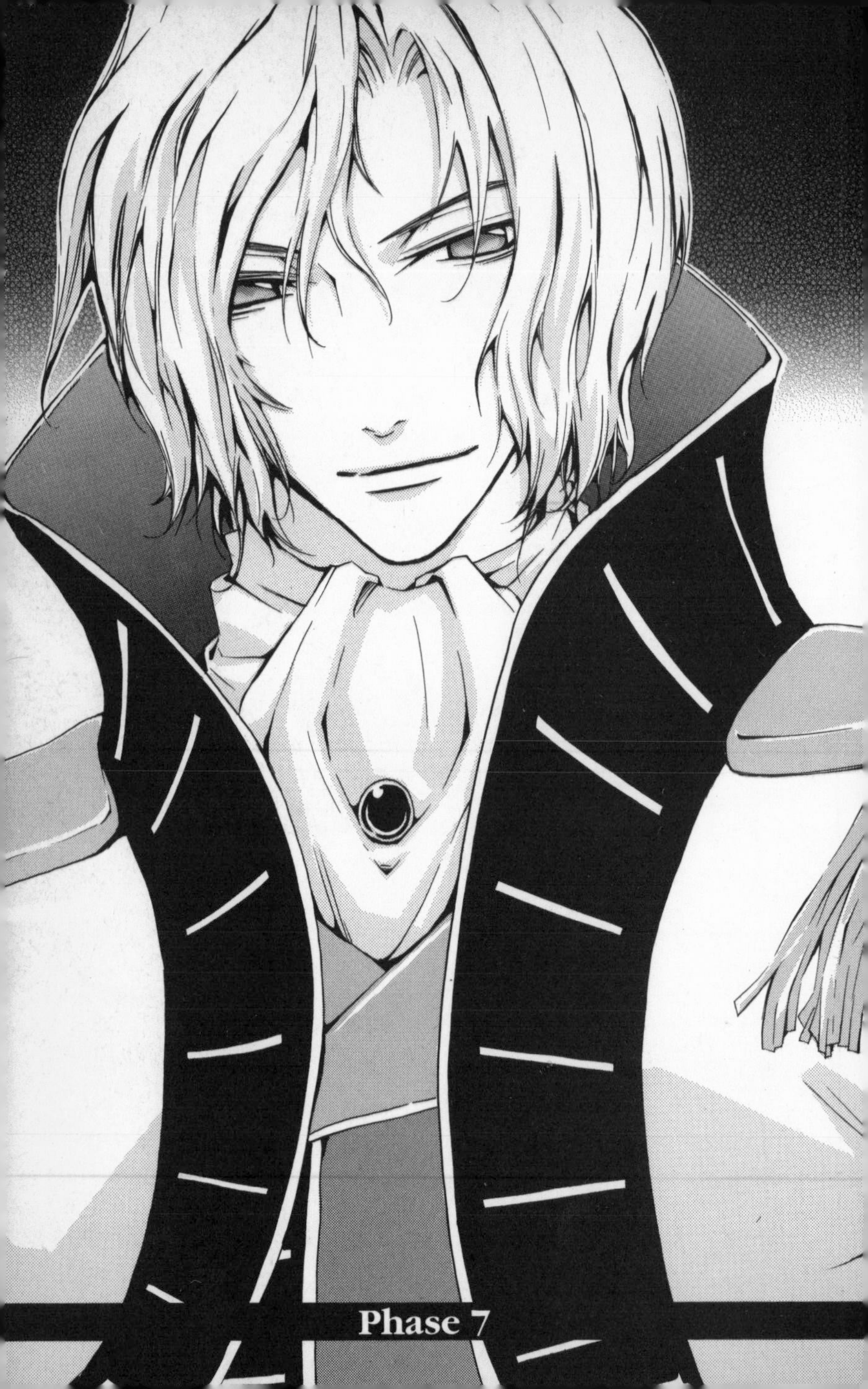

Phase 7

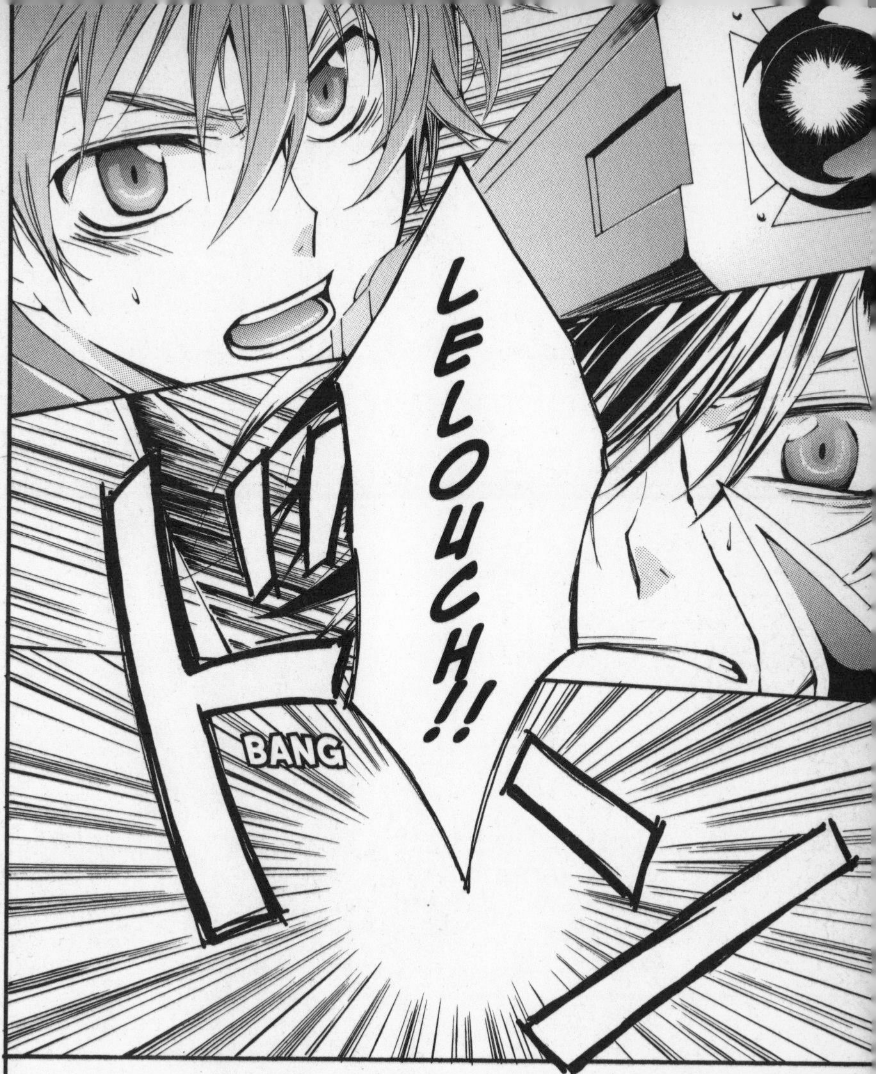
LELOUCH!!
BANG

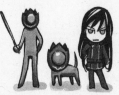

About Small Toys
Part 2

Figures these days often have interchangeable parts, so my bookshelf might have a Xingke dressed up as a student, or a dog dressed up as Zero, and it is major chaos.

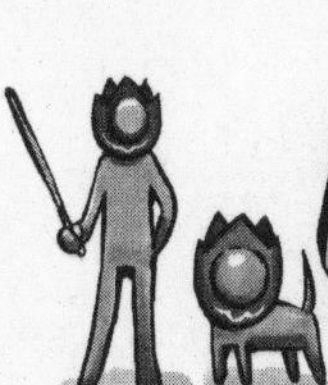

The parts that are especially useful are Zero's head, the various school uniforms, the clothing of the Rounds, and Euphy's legs. I wish I had one more of Rolo's body.

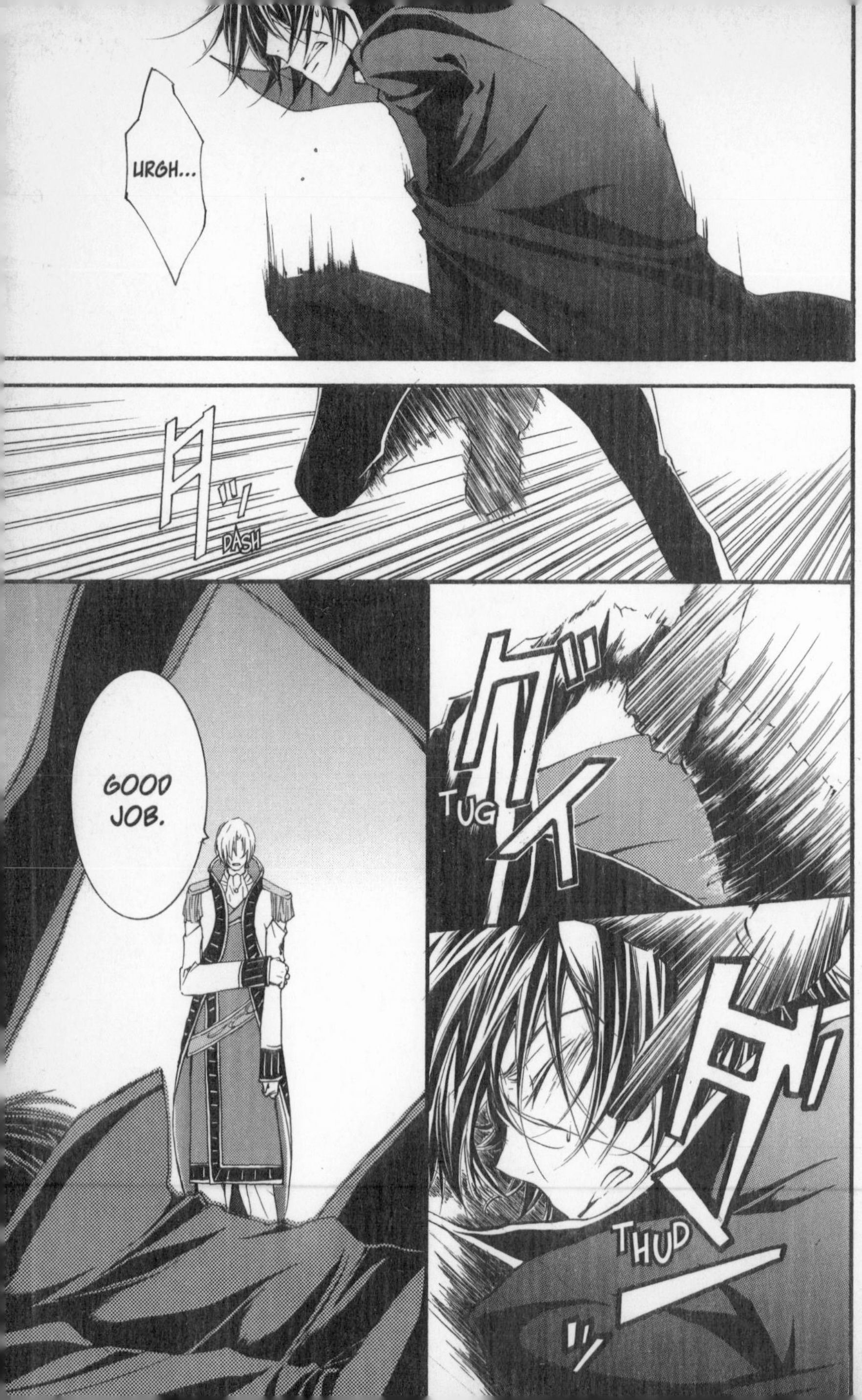
URGH...
DASH
TUG
THUD
GOOD JOB.

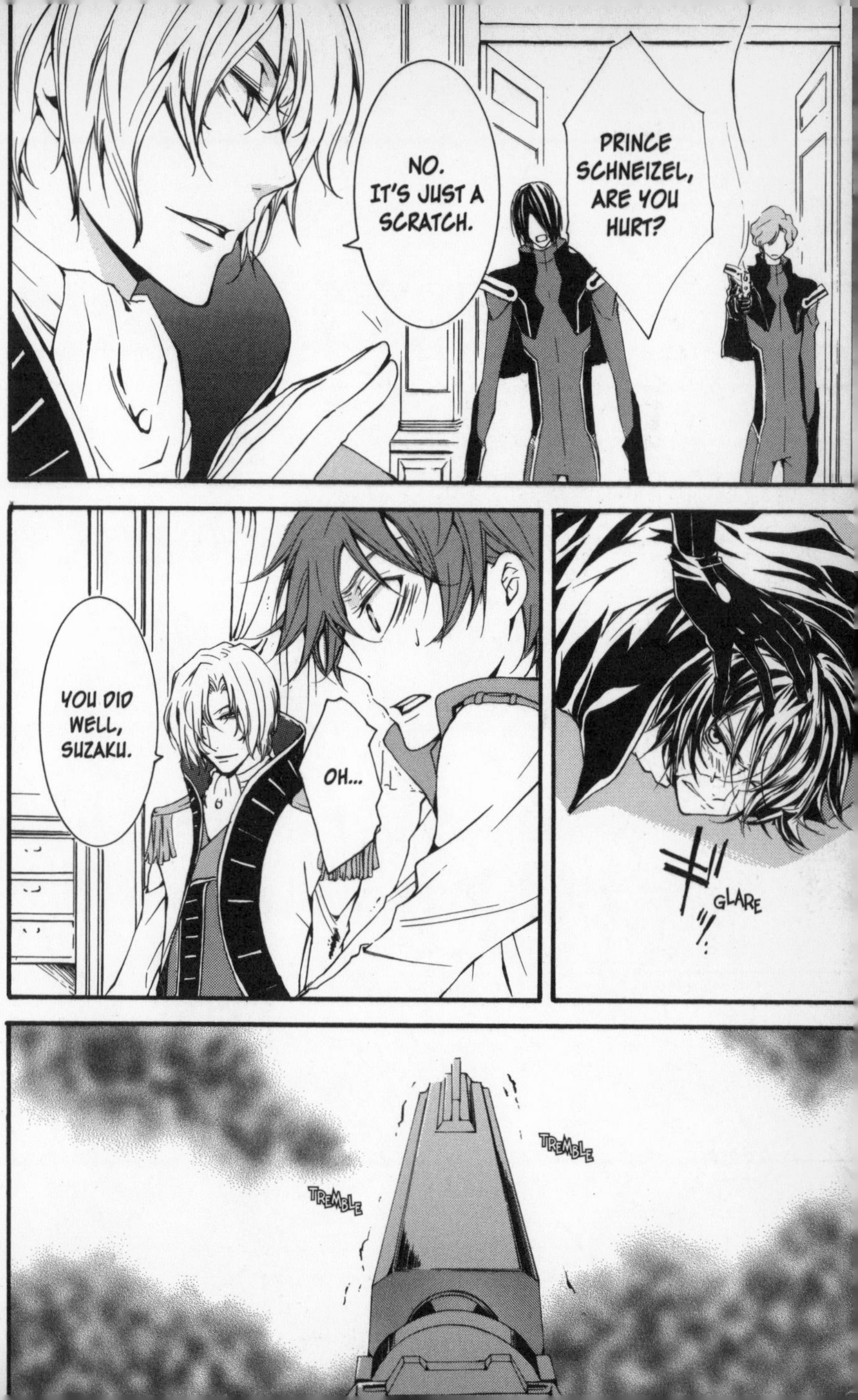
PRINCE SCHNEIZEL, ARE YOU HURT?
NO. IT'S JUST A SCRATCH.
GLARE
YOU DID WELL, SUZAKU.
OH...
TREMBLE
TREMBLE

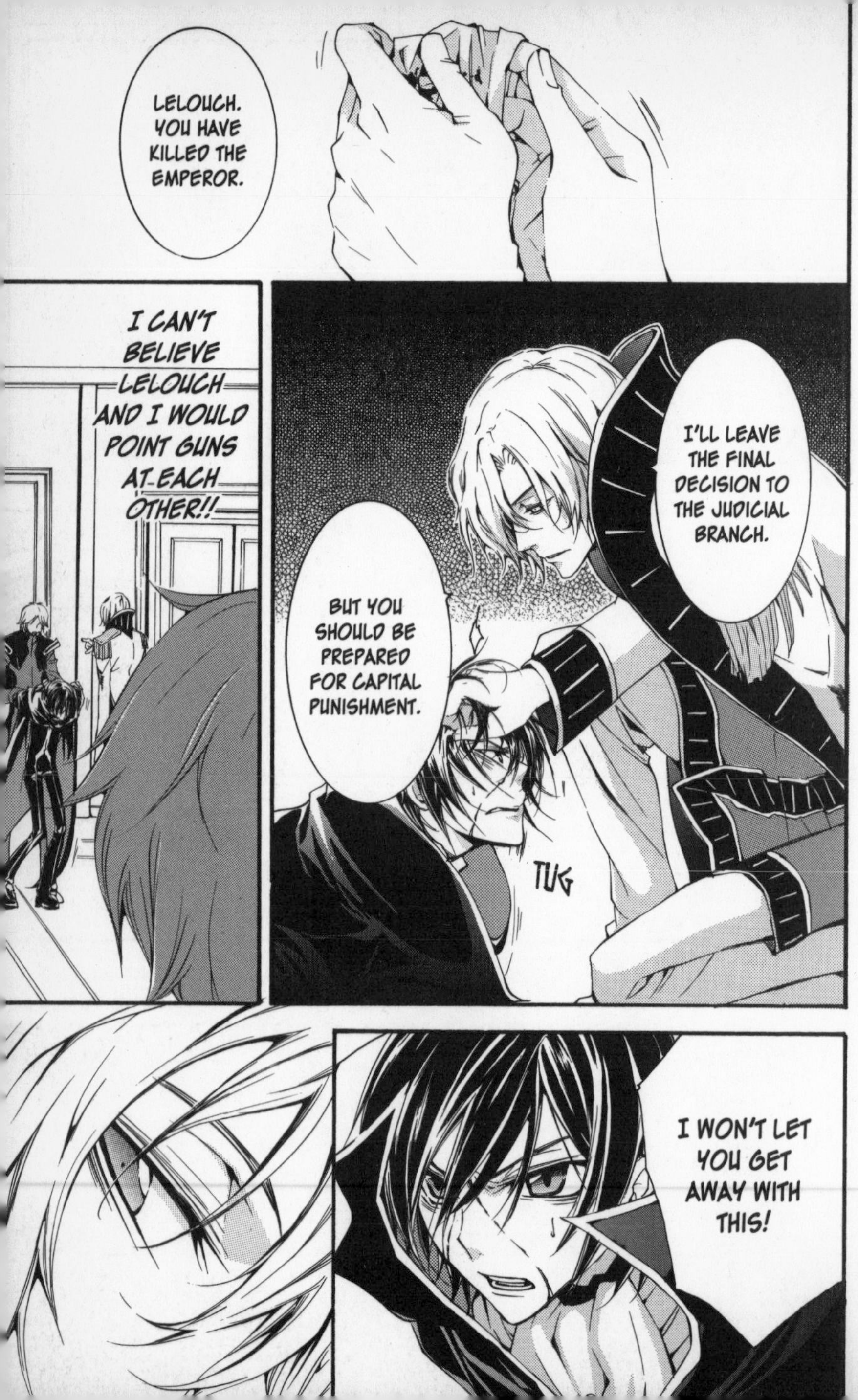
LELOUCH. YOU HAVE KILLED THE EMPEROR.
I'LL LEAVE THE FINAL DECISION TO THE JUDICIAL BRANCH.
BUT YOU SHOULD BE PREPARED FOR CAPITAL PUNISHMENT.
TUG
I CAN'T BELIEVE LELOUCH AND I WOULD POINT GUNS AT EACH OTHER!!
I WON'T LET YOU GET AWAY WITH THIS!

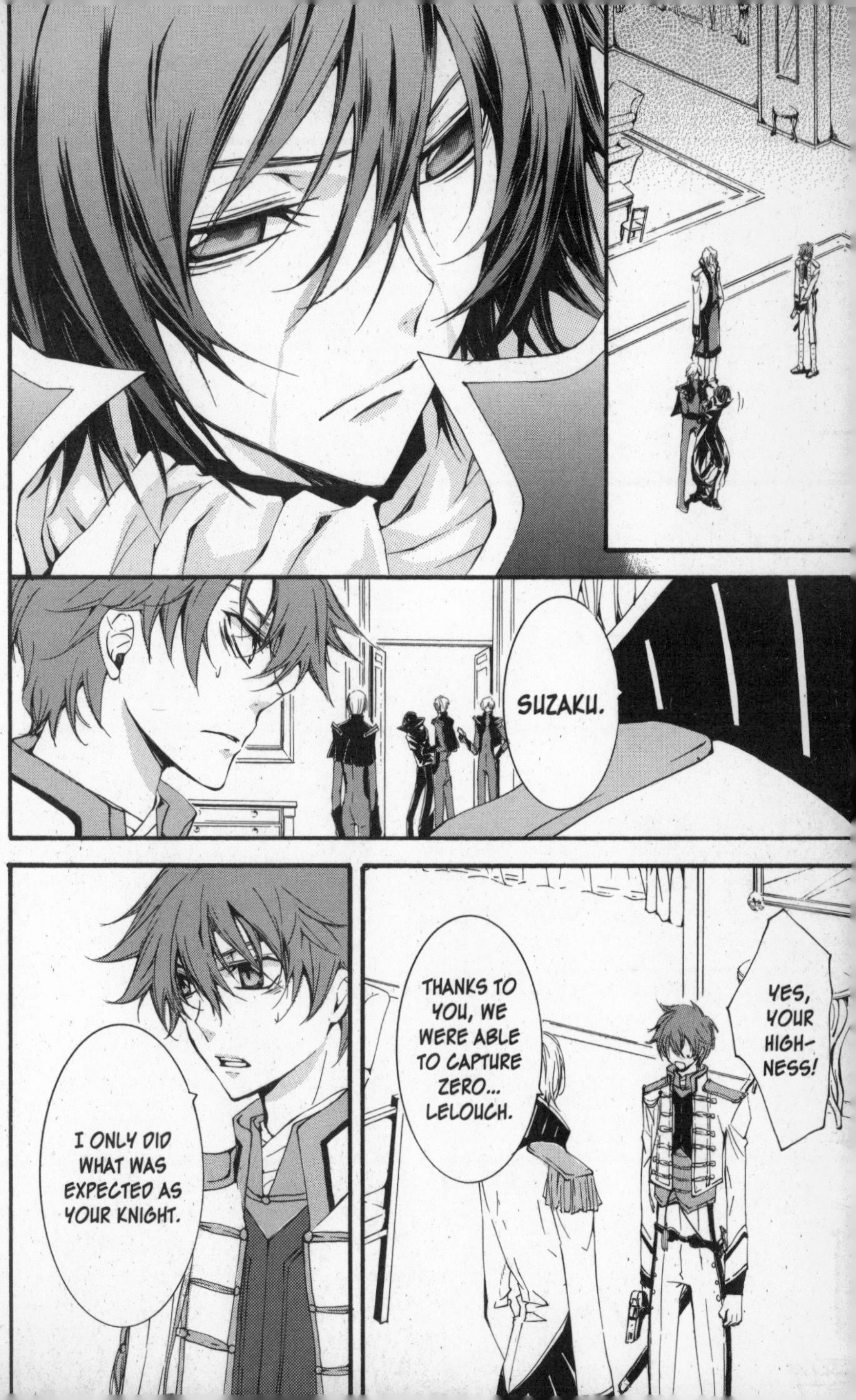
SUZAKU.
YES, YOUR HIGH-NESS!
THANKS TO YOU, WE WERE ABLE TO CAPTURE ZERO... LELOUCH.
I ONLY DID WHAT WAS EXPECTED AS YOUR KNIGHT.

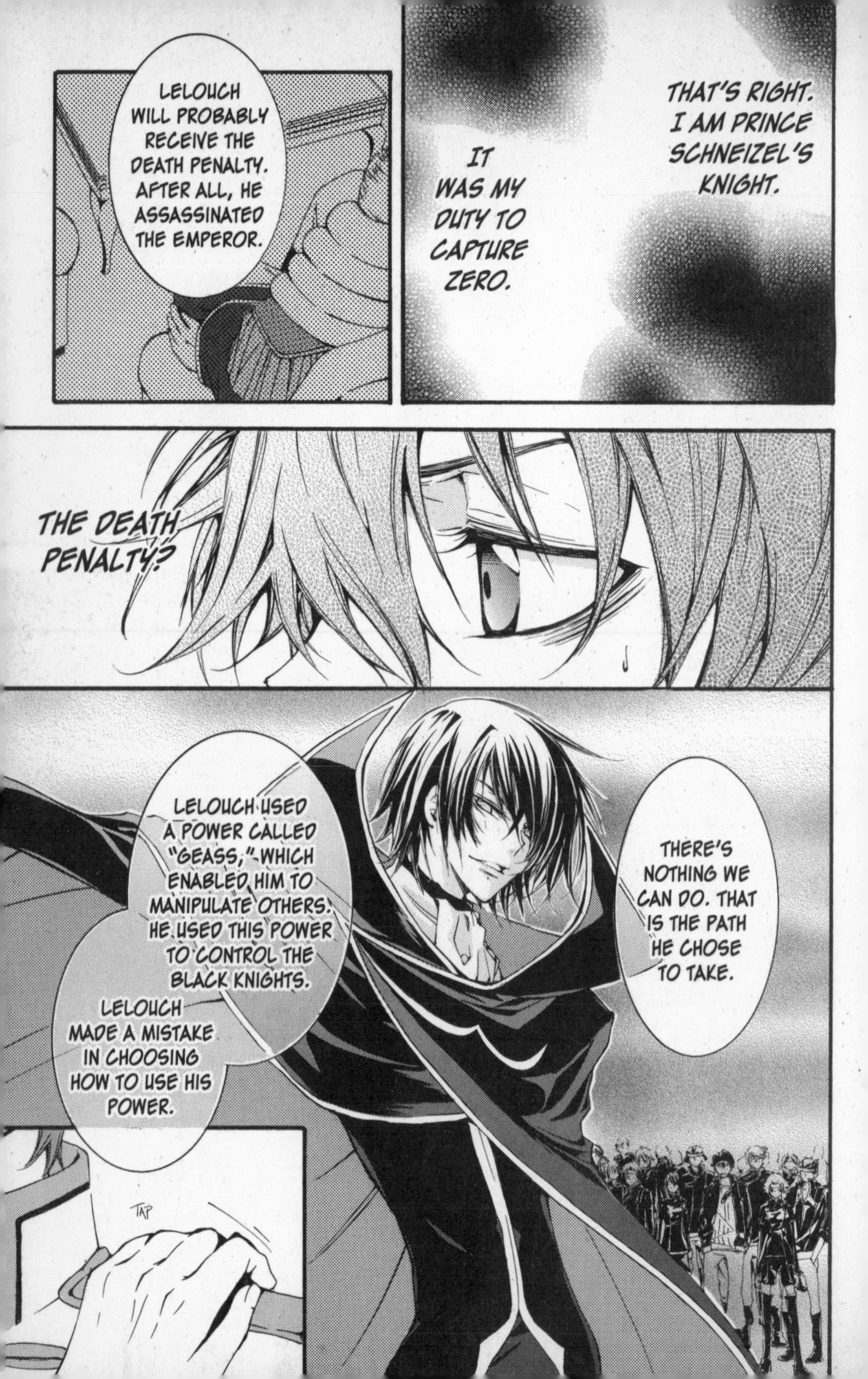
THAT'S RIGHT. I AM PRINCE SCHNEIZEL'S KNIGHT.
IT WAS MY DUTY TO CAPTURE ZERO.
LELOUCH WILL PROBABLY RECEIVE THE DEATH PENALTY. AFTER ALL, HE ASSASSINATED THE EMPEROR.
THE DEATH PENALTY?
THERE'S NOTHING WE CAN DO. THAT IS THE PATH HE CHOSE TO TAKE.
LELOUCH USED A POWER CALLED "GEASS," WHICH ENABLED HIM TO MANIPULATE OTHERS. HE USED THIS POWER TO CONTROL THE BLACK KNIGHTS.
LELOUCH MADE A MISTAKE IN CHOOSING HOW TO USE HIS POWER.
TAP

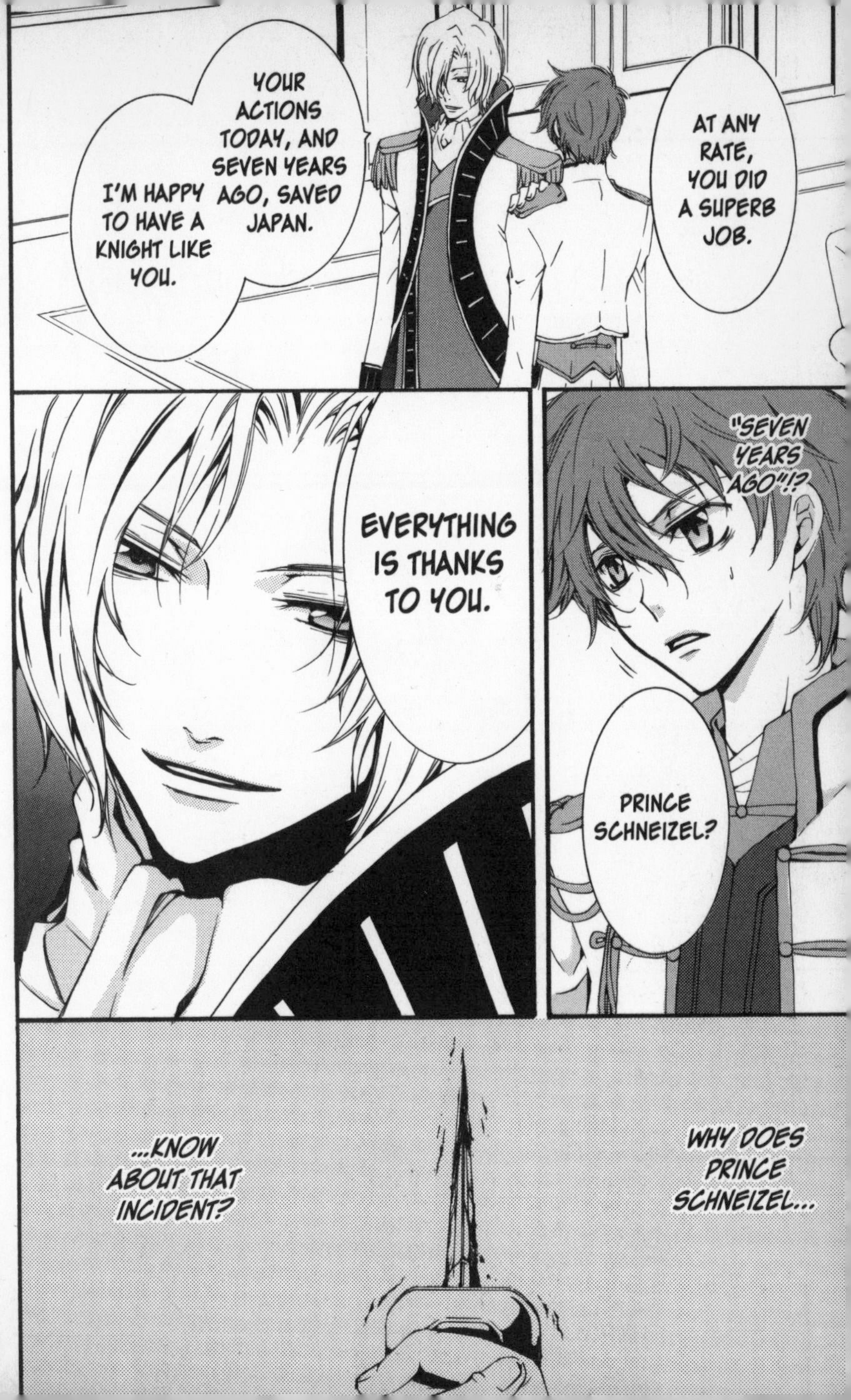
AT ANY RATE, YOU DID A SUPERB JOB.
YOUR ACTIONS TODAY, AND SEVEN YEARS AGO, SAVED JAPAN.
I'M HAPPY TO HAVE A KNIGHT LIKE YOU.
"SEVEN YEARS AGO"!?
PRINCE SCHNEIZEL?
EVERYTHING IS THANKS TO YOU.
WHY DOES PRINCE SCHNEIZEL...
...KNOW ABOUT THAT INCIDENT?

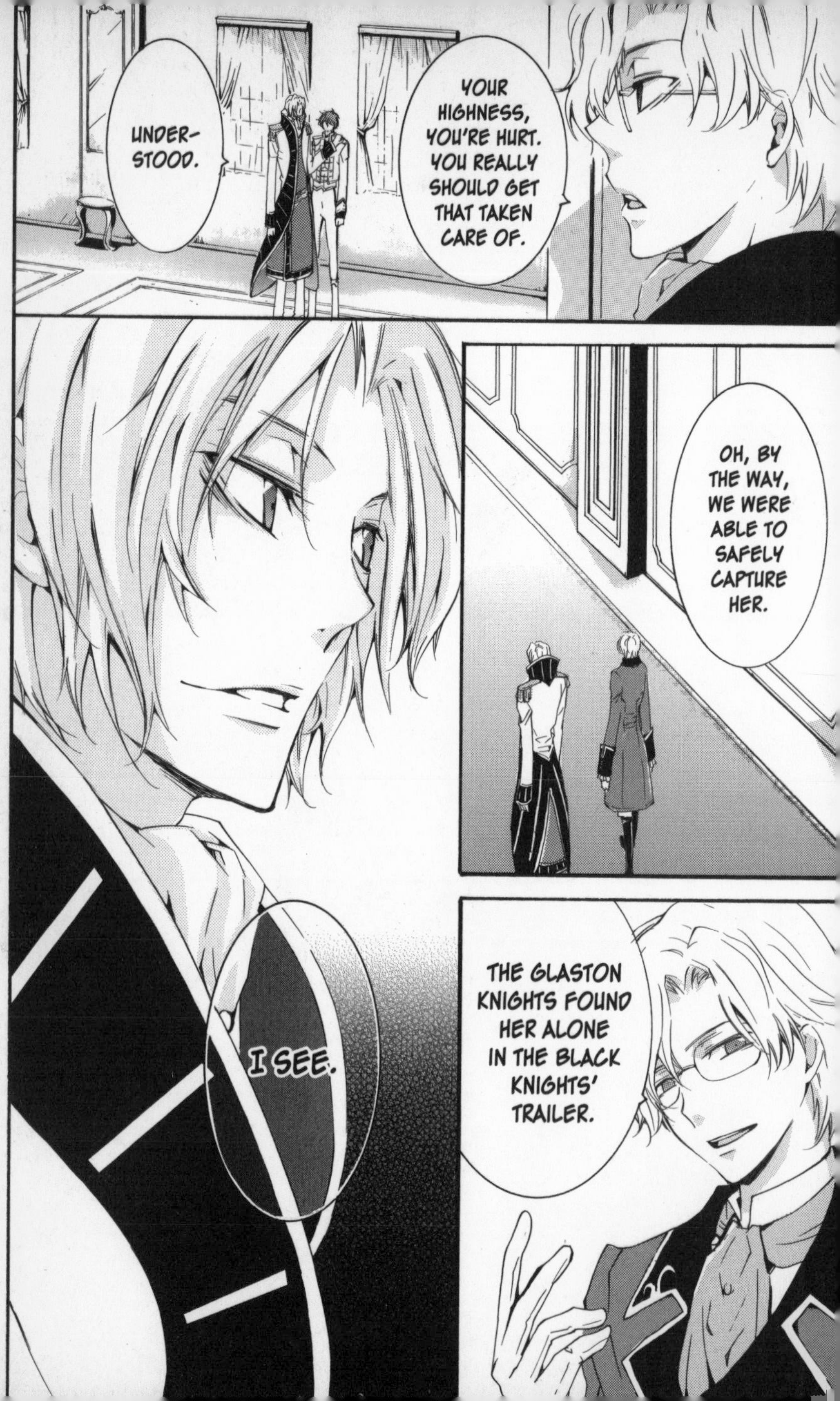
YOUR HIGHNESS, YOU'RE HURT. YOU REALLY SHOULD GET THAT TAKEN CARE OF.
UNDER-STOOD.
OH, BY THE WAY, WE WERE ABLE TO SAFELY CAPTURE HER.
THE GLASTON KNIGHTS FOUND HER ALONE IN THE BLACK KNIGHTS' TRAILER.
I SEE.

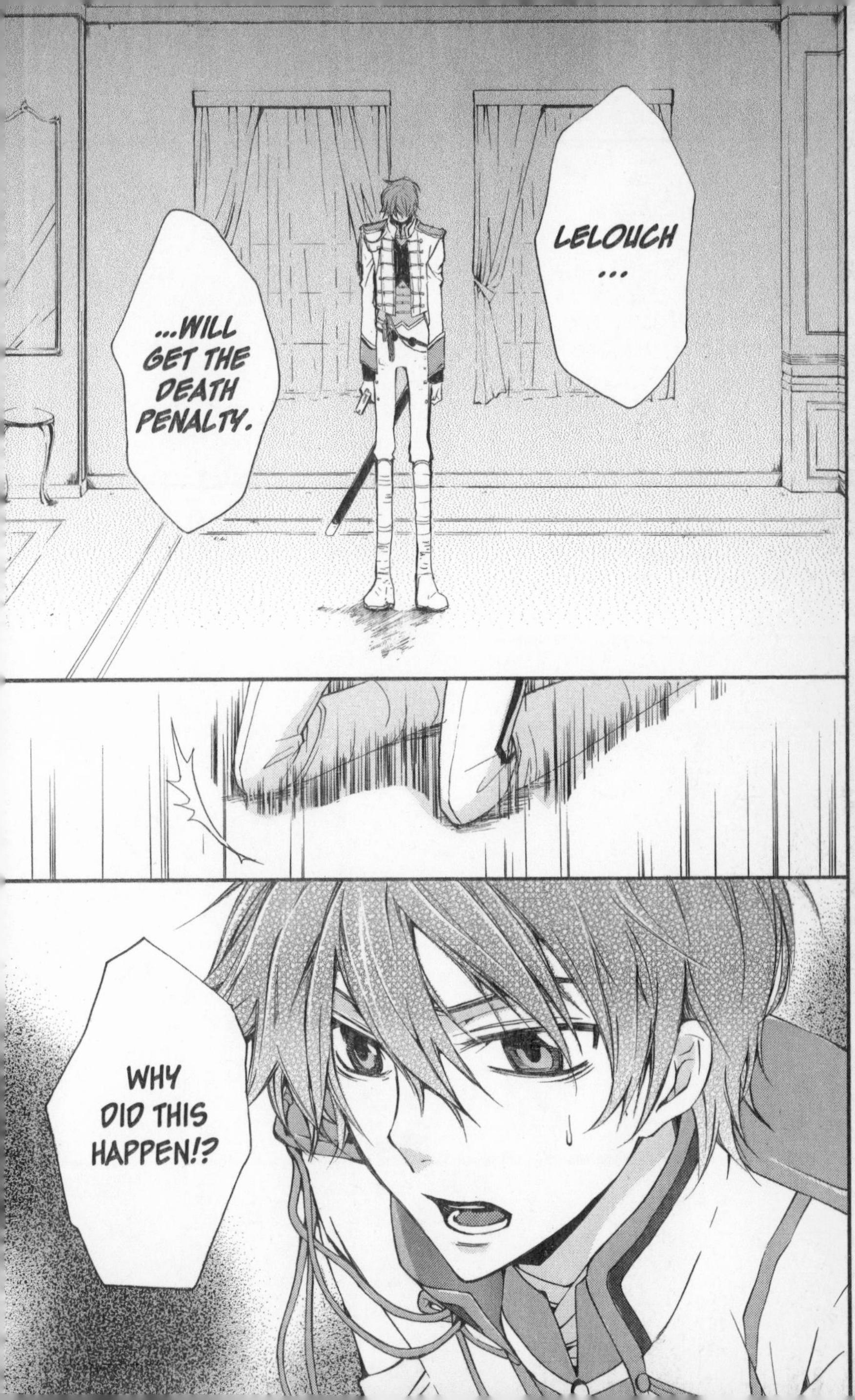
LELOUCH ...
...WILL GET THE DEATH PENALTY.
WHY DID THIS HAPPEN!?

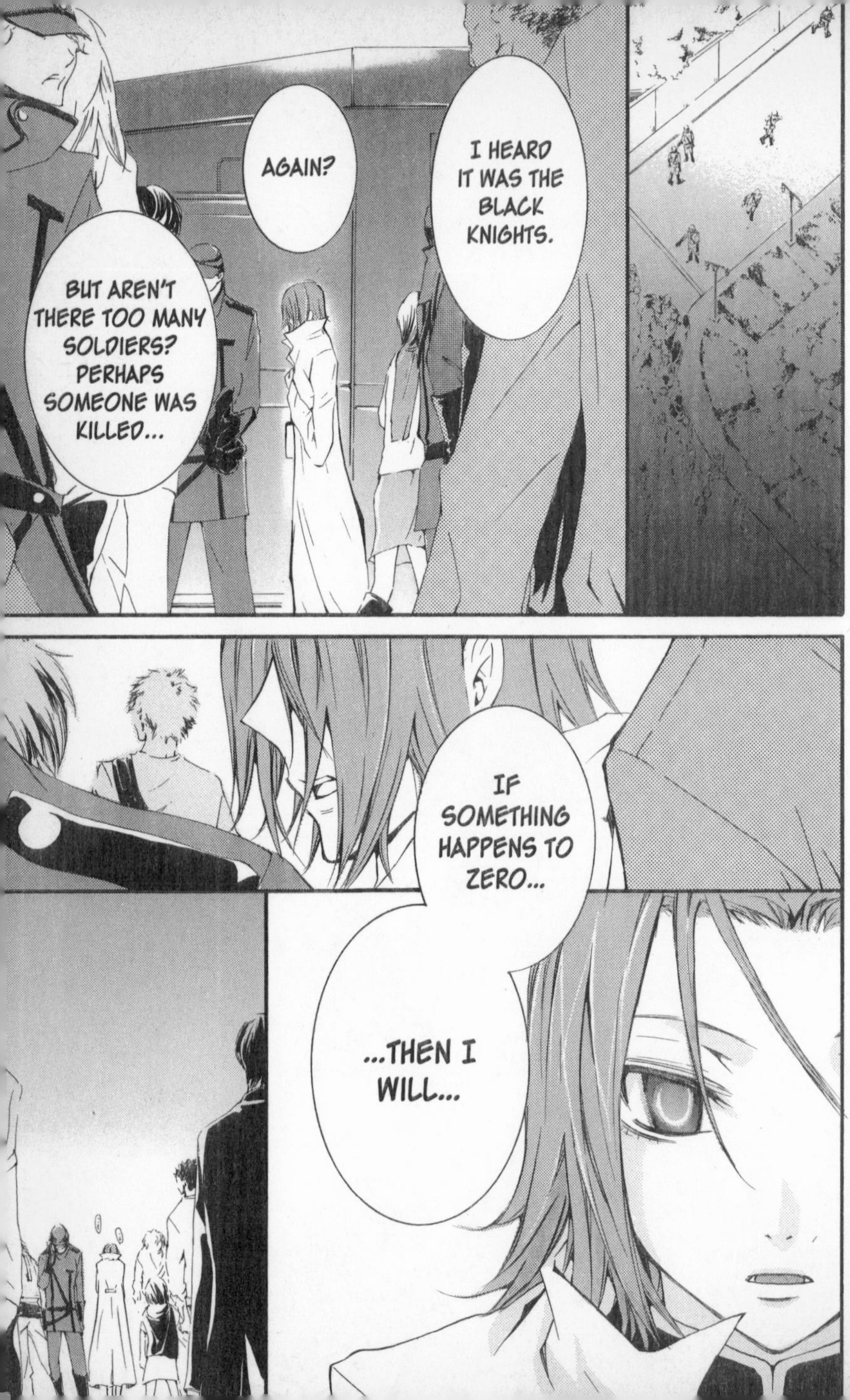
I HEARD IT WAS THE BLACK KNIGHTS.
AGAIN?
BUT AREN'T THERE TOO MANY SOLDIERS? PERHAPS SOMEONE WAS KILLED...
IF SOMETHING HAPPENS TO ZERO...
...THEN I WILL...

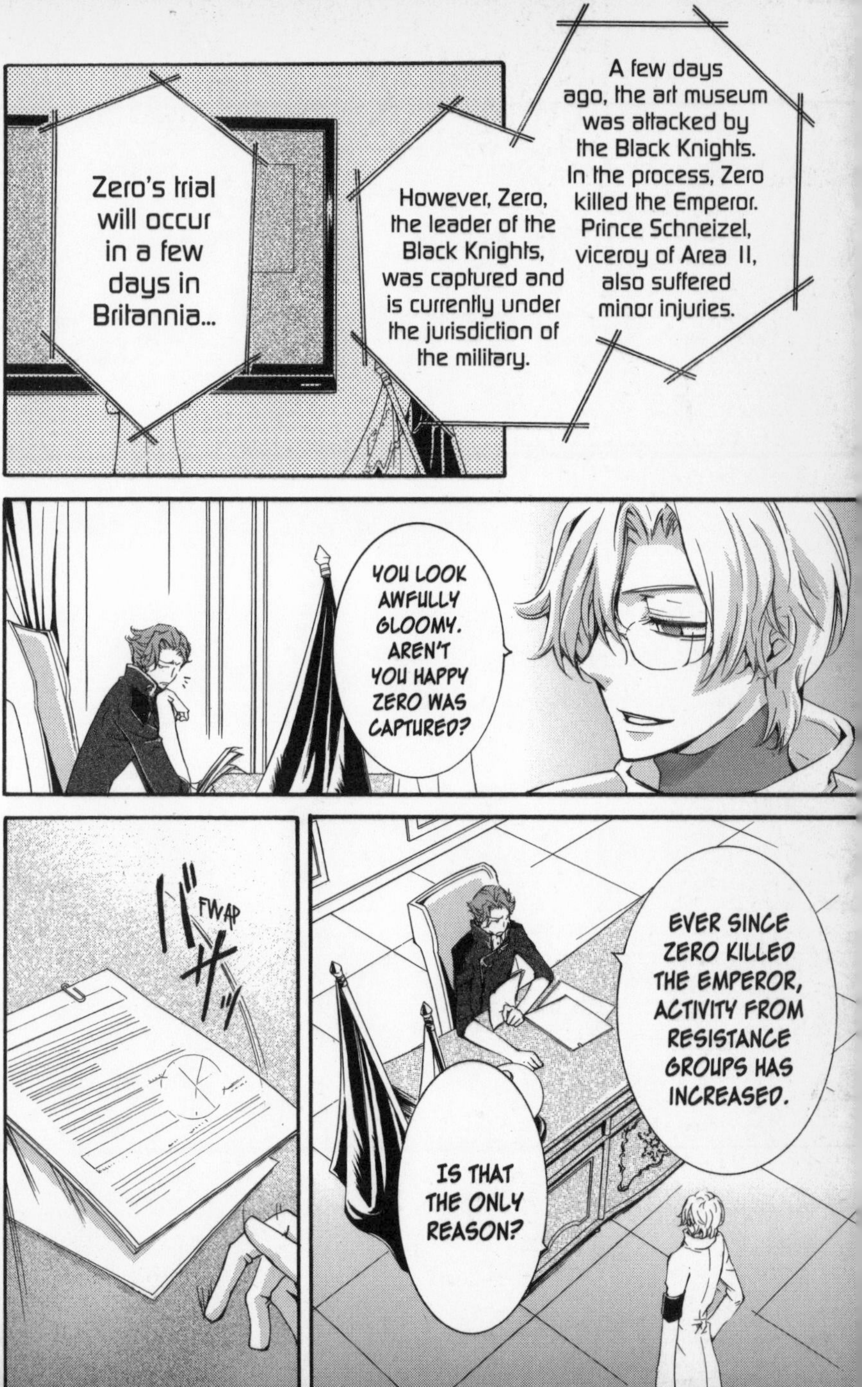
A few days ago, the art museum was attacked by the Black Knights. In the process, Zero killed the Emperor. Prince Schneizel, viceroy of Area 11, also suffered minor injuries.
However, Zero, the leader of the Black Knights, was captured and is currently under the jurisdiction of the military.
Zero's trial will occur in a few days in Britannia...
YOU LOOK AWFULLY GLOOMY. AREN'T YOU HAPPY ZERO WAS CAPTURED?
EVER SINCE ZERO KILLED THE EMPEROR, ACTIVITY FROM RESISTANCE GROUPS HAS INCREASED.
IS THAT THE ONLY REASON?
バサッ
FWAP

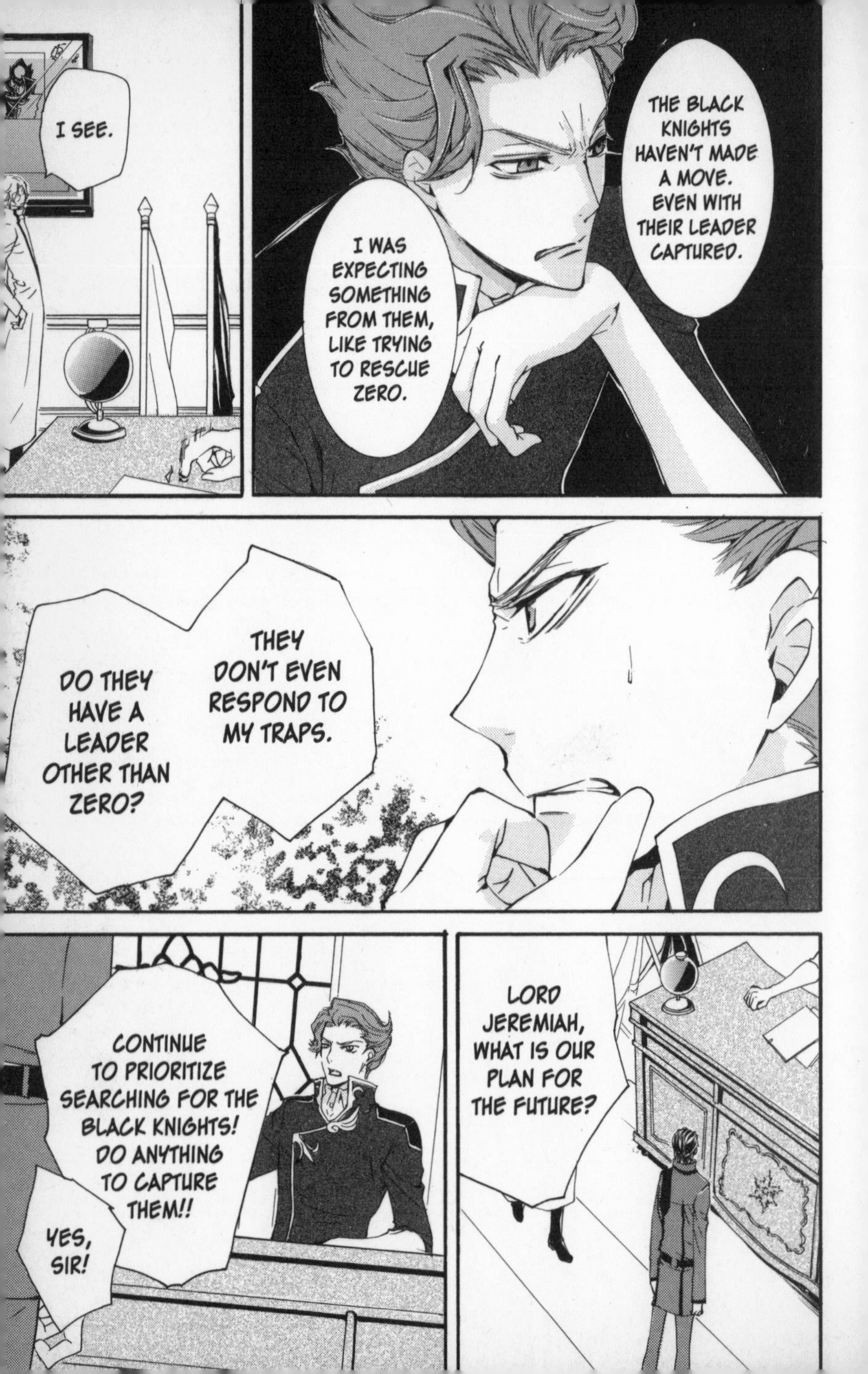
THE BLACK KNIGHTS HAVEN'T MADE A MOVE. EVEN WITH THEIR LEADER CAPTURED.
I WAS EXPECTING SOMETHING FROM THEM, LIKE TRYING TO RESCUE ZERO.
I SEE.
THEY DON'T EVEN RESPOND TO MY TRAPS.
DO THEY HAVE A LEADER OTHER THAN ZERO?
LORD JEREMIAH, WHAT IS OUR PLAN FOR THE FUTURE?
CONTINUE TO PRIORITIZE SEARCHING FOR THE BLACK KNIGHTS! DO ANYTHING TO CAPTURE THEM!!
YES, SIR!

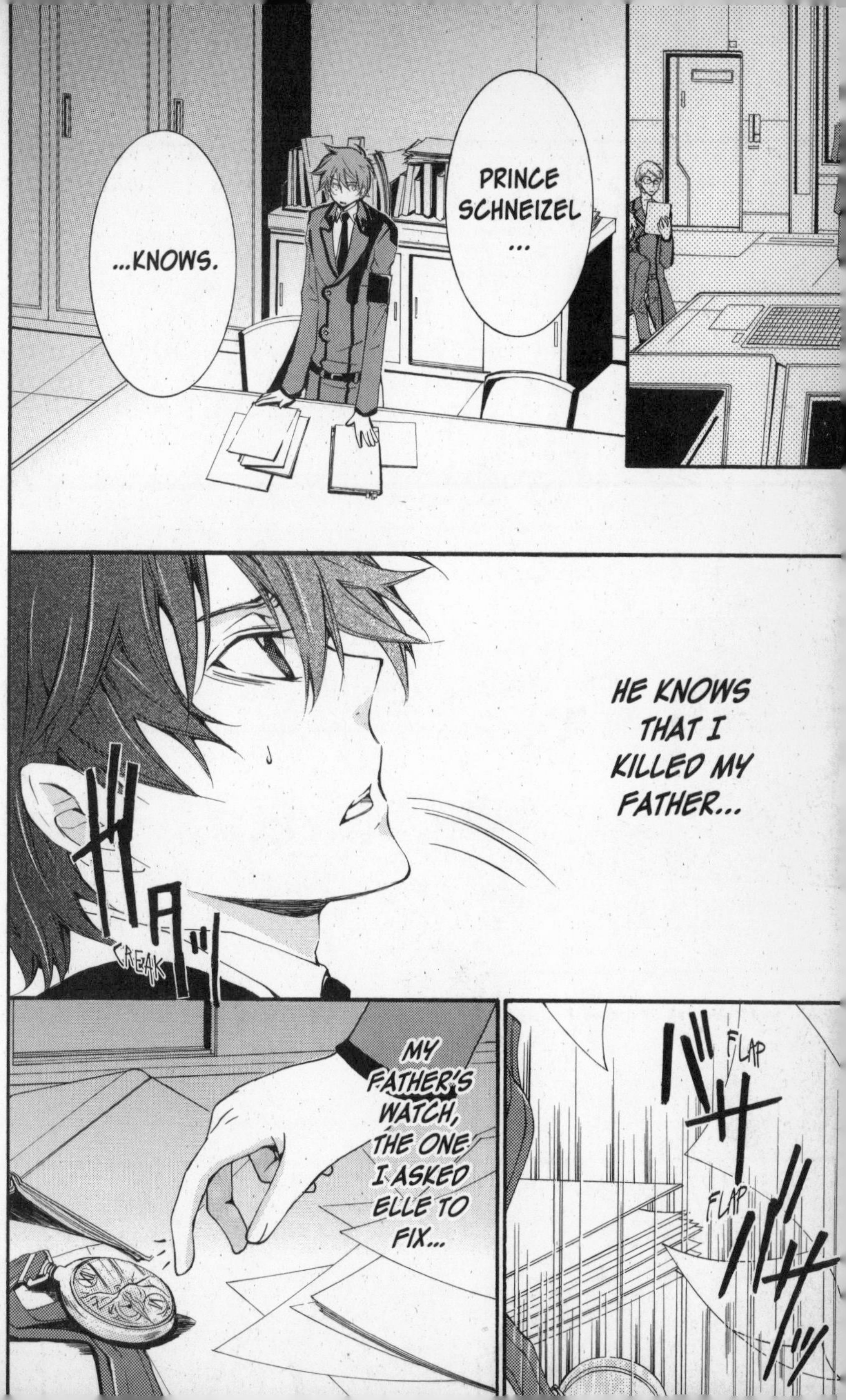
PRINCE SCHNEIZEL ...
...KNOWS.
HE KNOWS THAT I KILLED MY FATHER...
CREAK
FLAP
FLAP
MY FATHER'S WATCH, THE ONE I ASKED ELLE TO FIX...

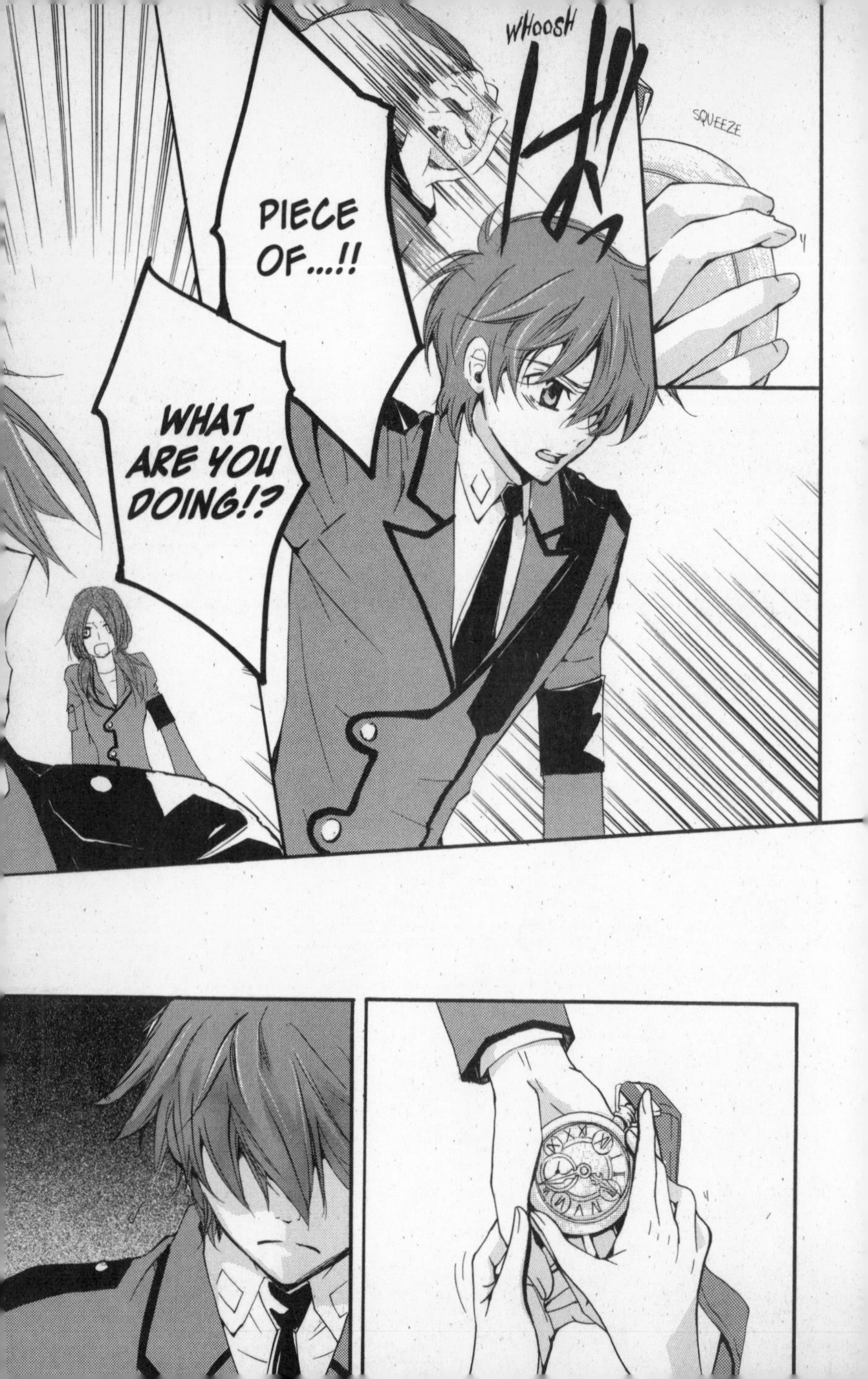
WHOOSH
SQUEEZE
PIECE OF...!!
WHAT ARE YOU DOING!?

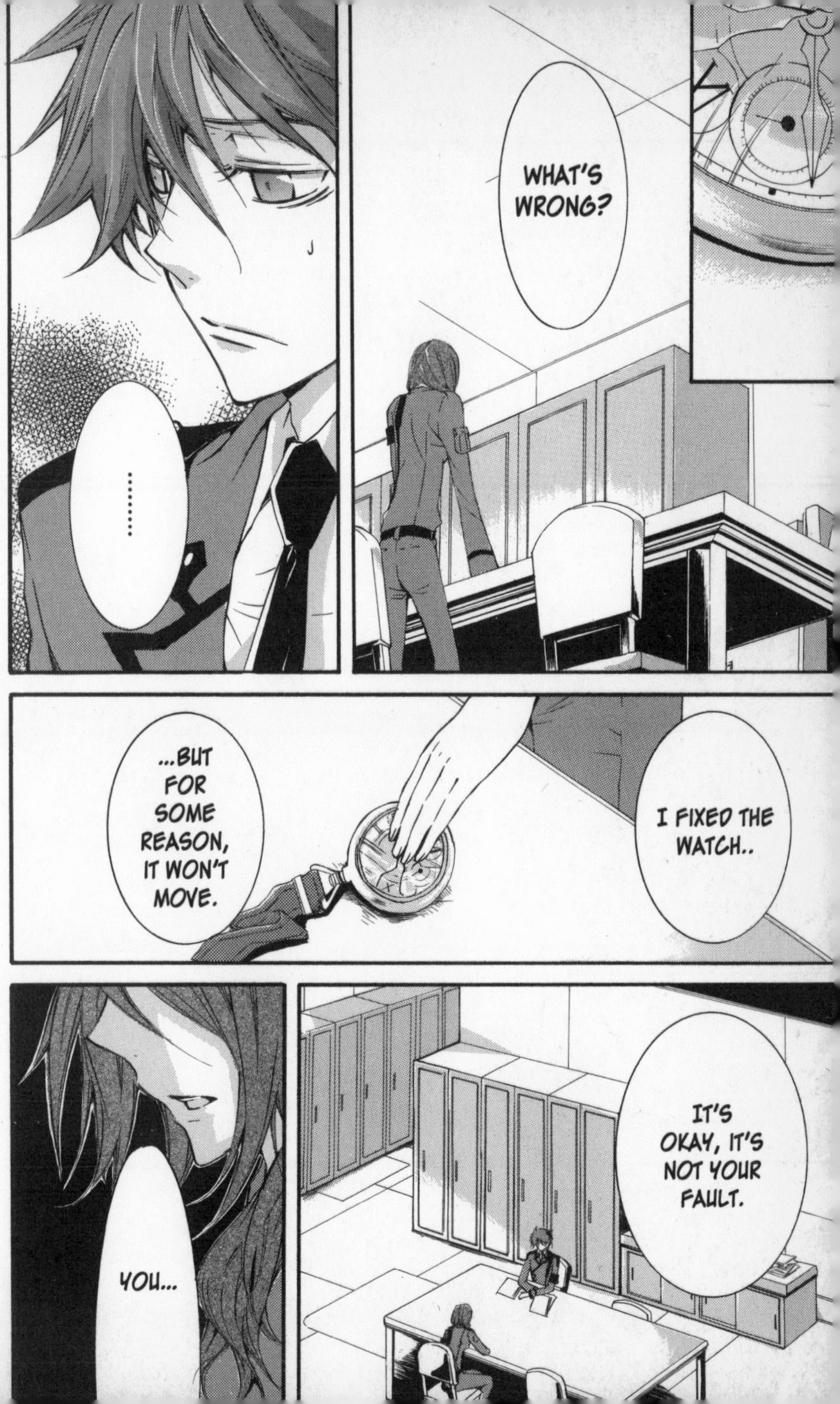
WHAT'S WRONG?
......
I FIXED THE WATCH..
...BUT FOR SOME REASON, IT WON'T MOVE.
IT'S OKAY, IT'S NOT YOUR FAULT.
YOU...

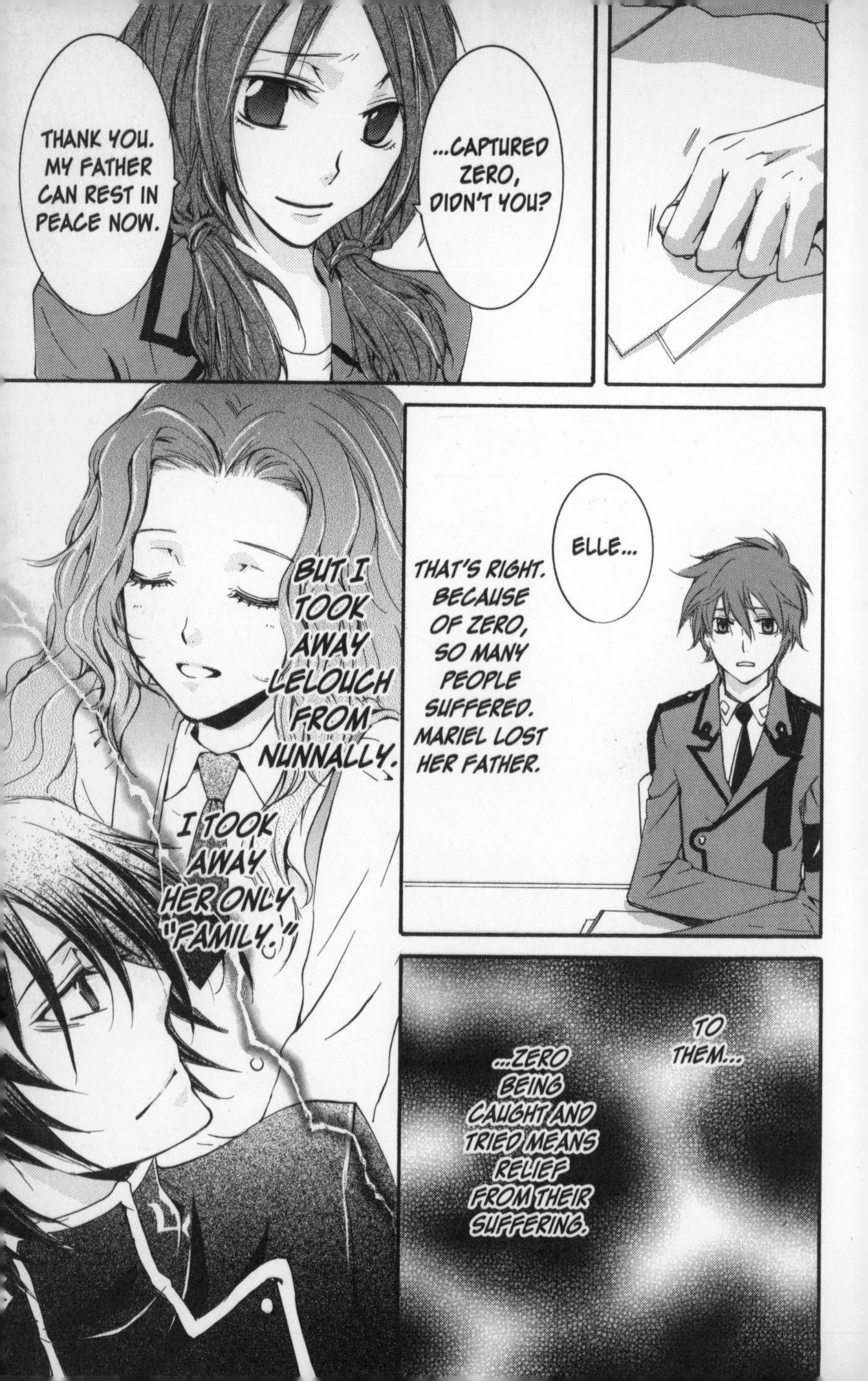
...CAPTURED ZERO, DIDN'T YOU?
THANK YOU. MY FATHER CAN REST IN PEACE NOW.
ELLE...
THAT'S RIGHT. BECAUSE OF ZERO, SO MANY PEOPLE SUFFERED. MARIEL LOST HER FATHER.
TO THEM...
...ZERO BEING CAUGHT AND TRIED MEANS RELIEF FROM THEIR SUFFERING.
BUT I TOOK AWAY LELOUCH FROM NUNNALLY.
I TOOK AWAY HER ONLY "FAMILY."

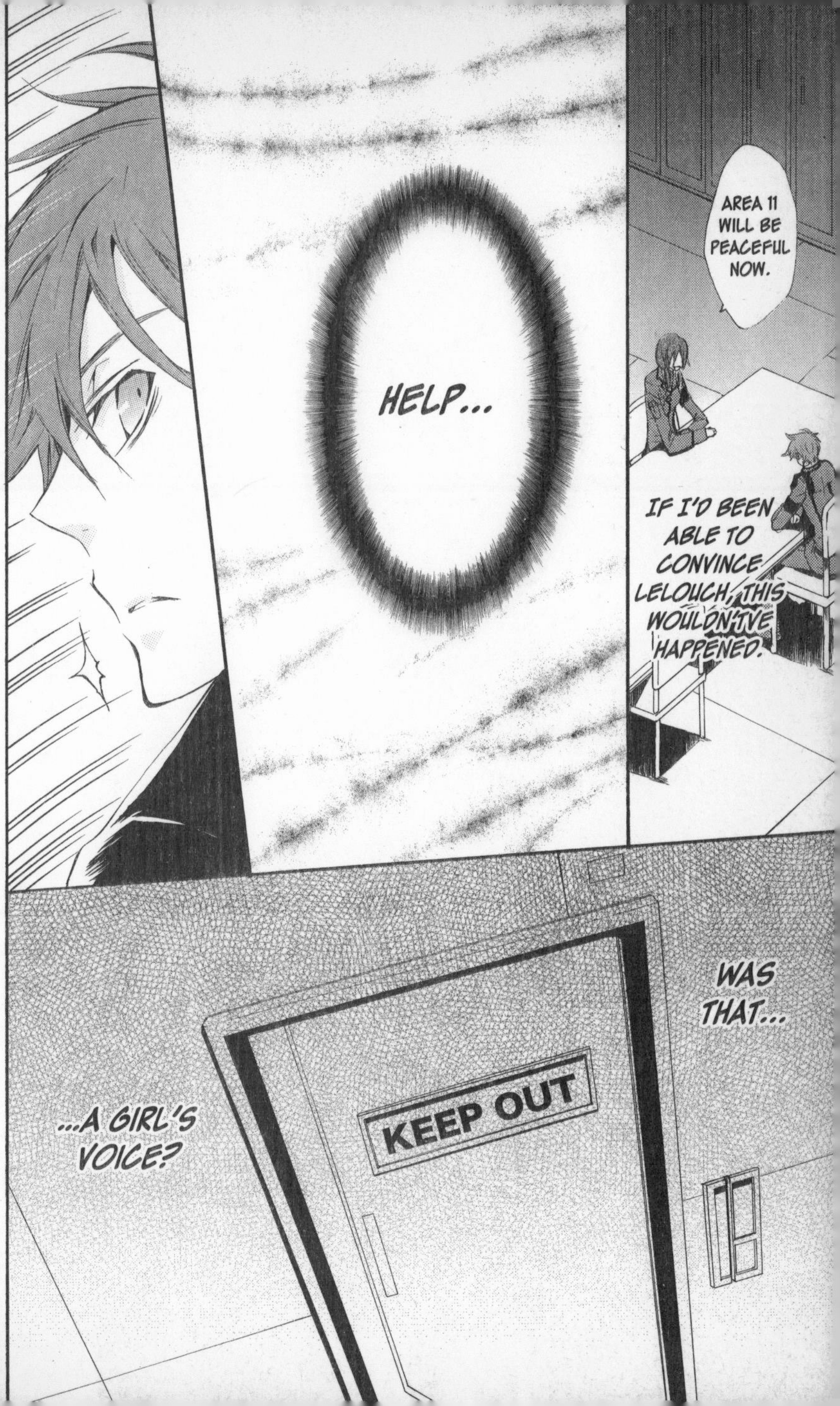
AREA 11 WILL BE PEACEFUL NOW.
IF I'D BEEN ABLE TO CONVINCE LELOUCH, THIS WOULDN'T'VE HAPPENED.
HELP...
WAS THAT...
KEEP OUT
...A GIRL'S VOICE?

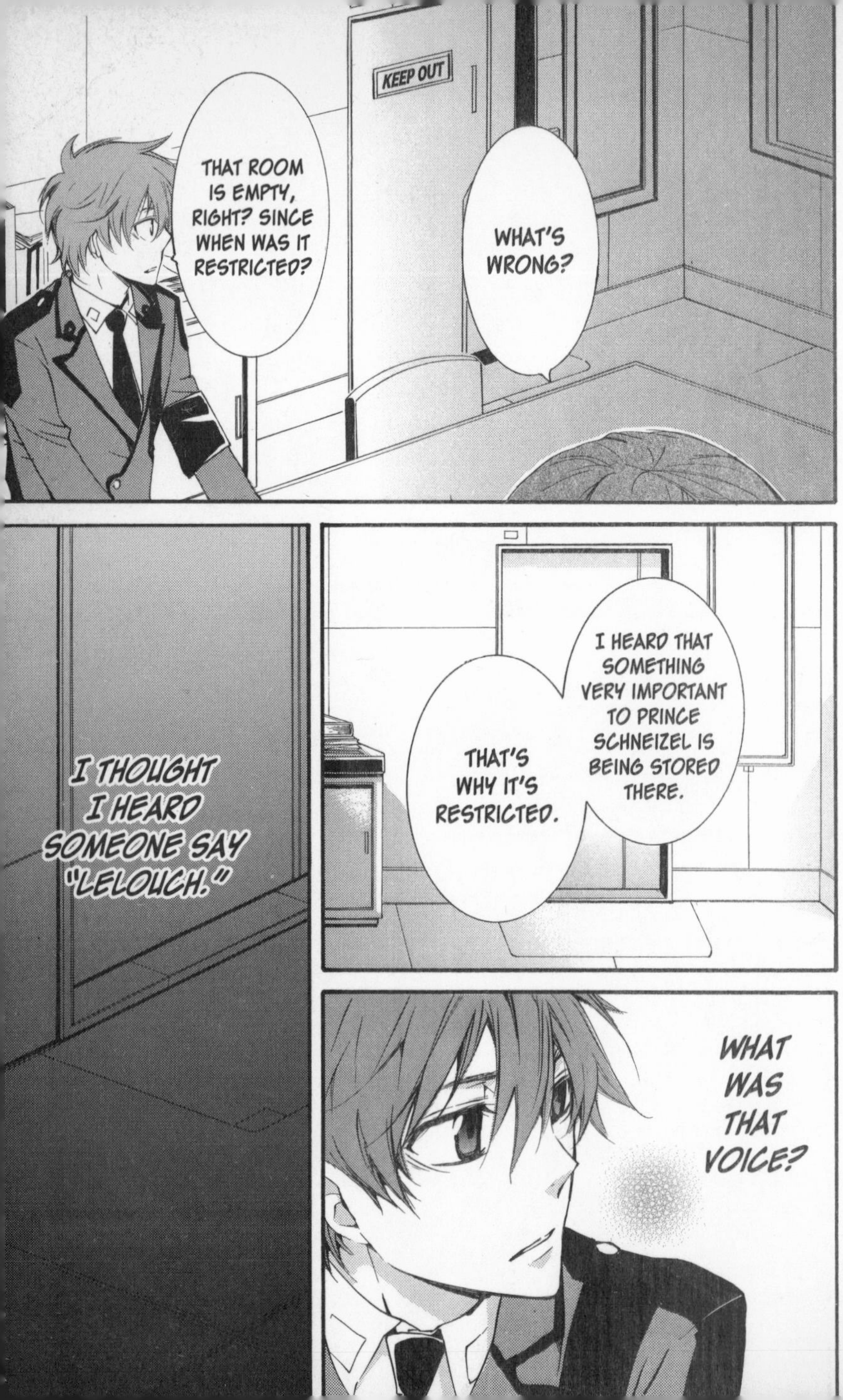
KEEP OUT
WHAT'S WRONG?
THAT ROOM IS EMPTY, RIGHT? SINCE WHEN WAS IT RESTRICTED?
I HEARD THAT SOMETHING VERY IMPORTANT TO PRINCE SCHNEIZEL IS BEING STORED THERE.
THAT'S WHY IT'S RESTRICTED.
WHAT WAS THAT VOICE?
I THOUGHT I HEARD SOMEONE SAY "LELOUCH."

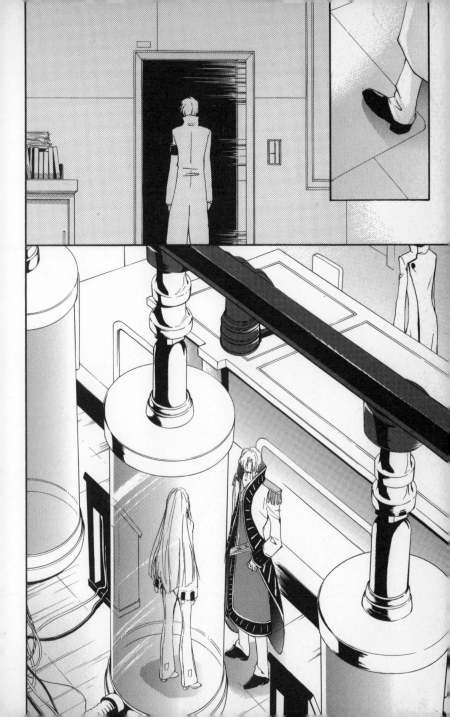

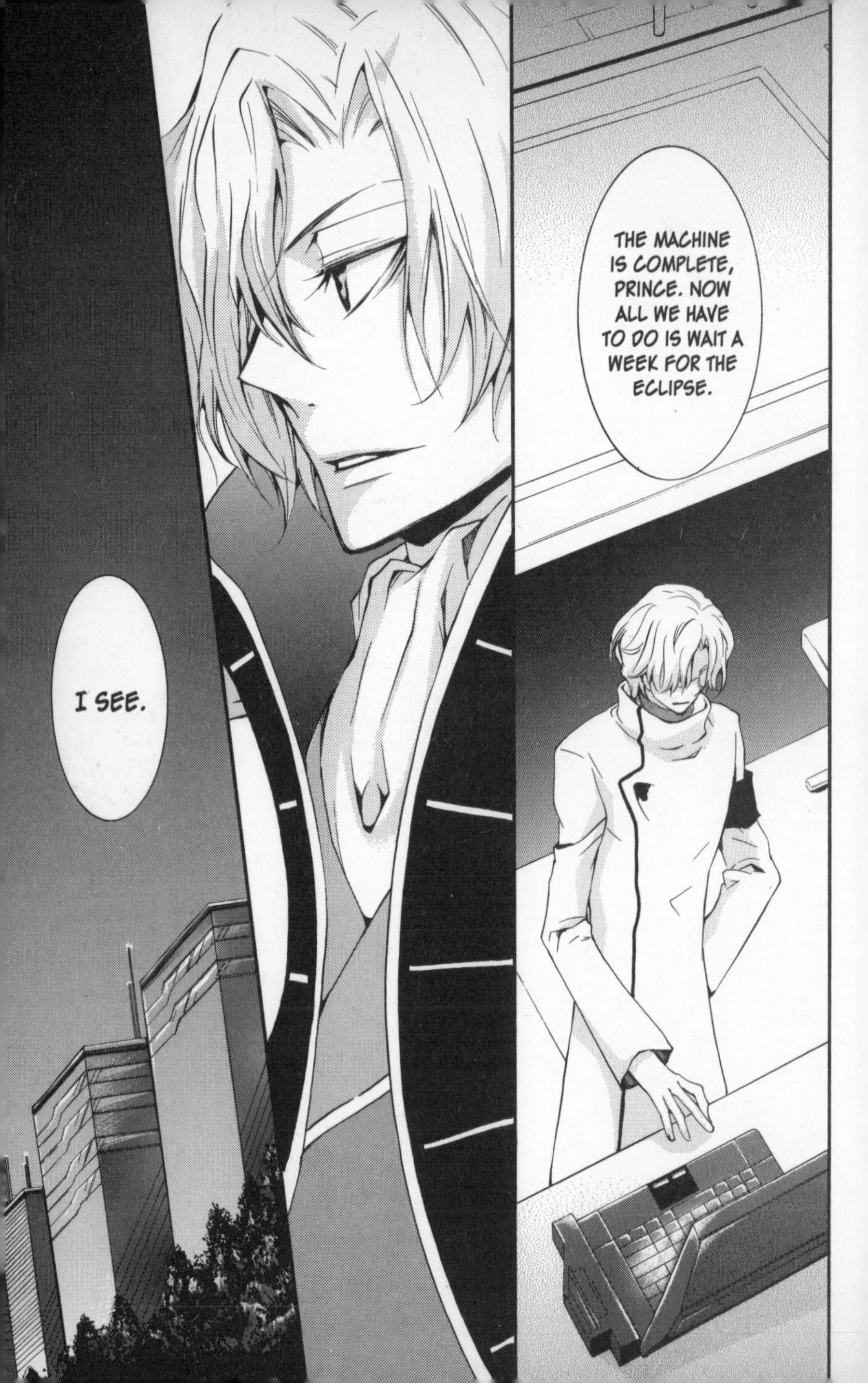
THE MACHINE IS COMPLETE, PRINCE. NOW ALL WE HAVE TO DO IS WAIT A WEEK FOR THE ECLIPSE.
I SEE.

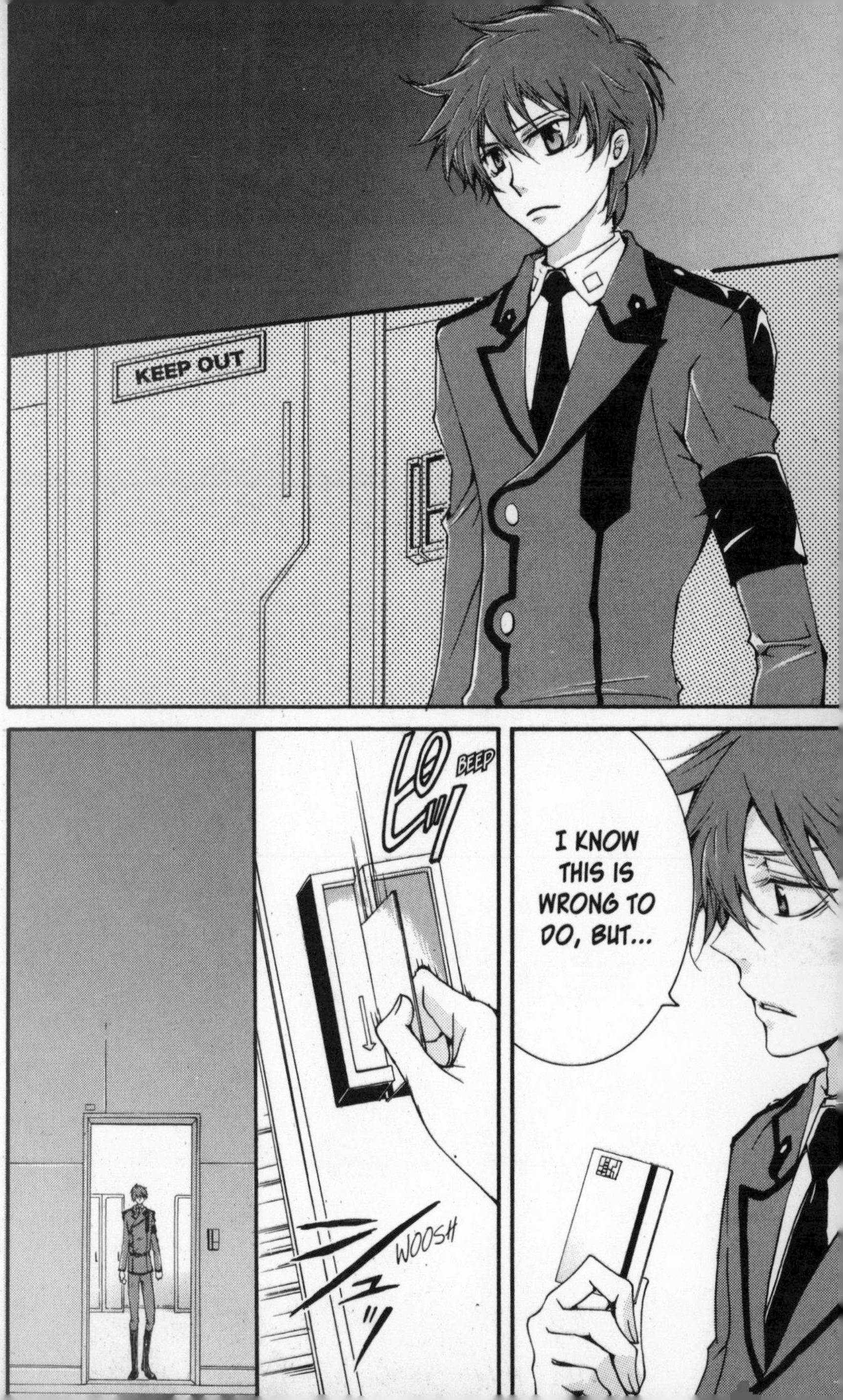
KEEP OUT
I KNOW THIS IS WRONG TO DO, BUT...
BEEP
WOOSH

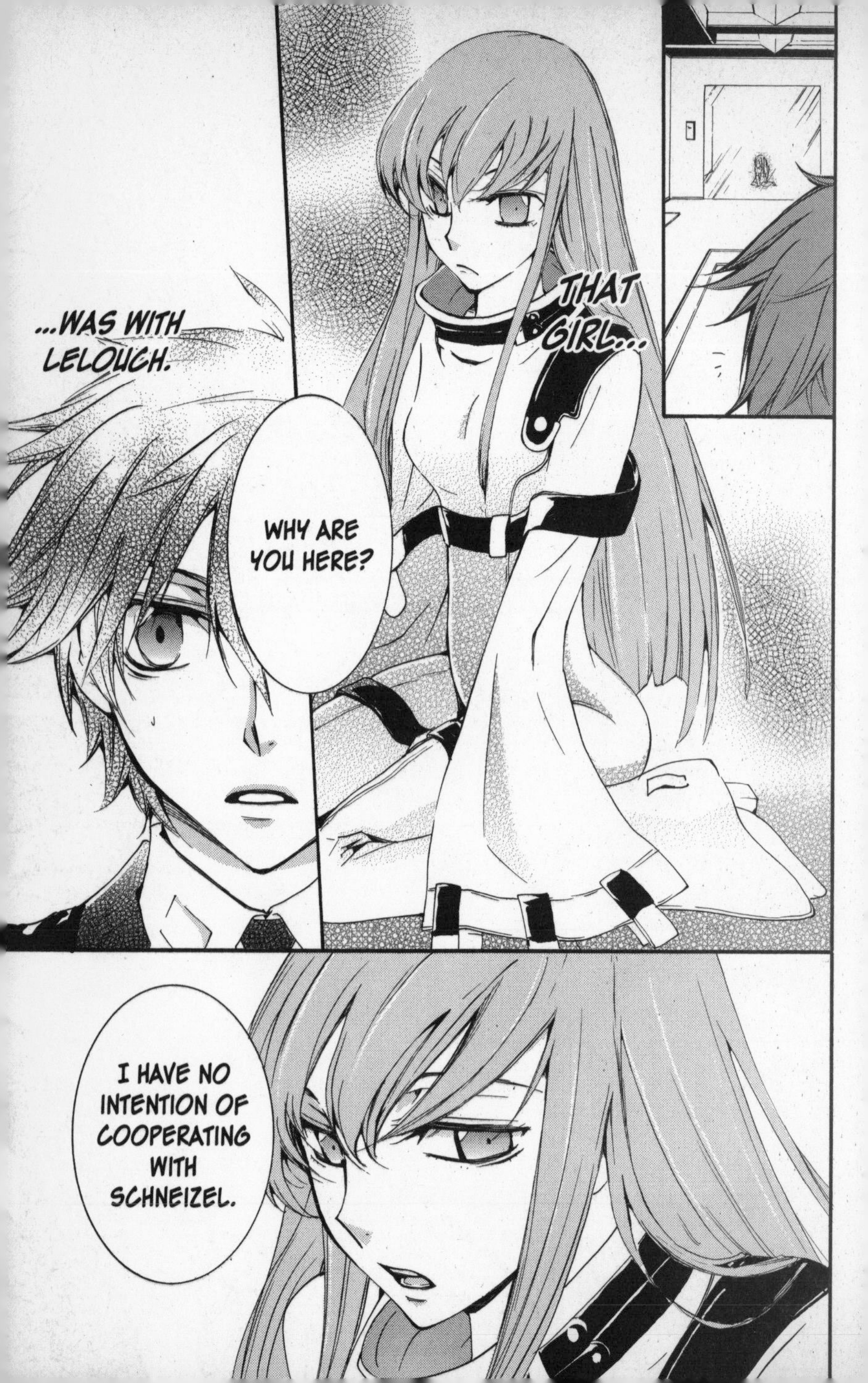
THAT GIRL...
...WAS WITH LELOUCH.
WHY ARE YOU HERE?
I HAVE NO INTENTION OF COOPERATING WITH SCHNEIZEL.

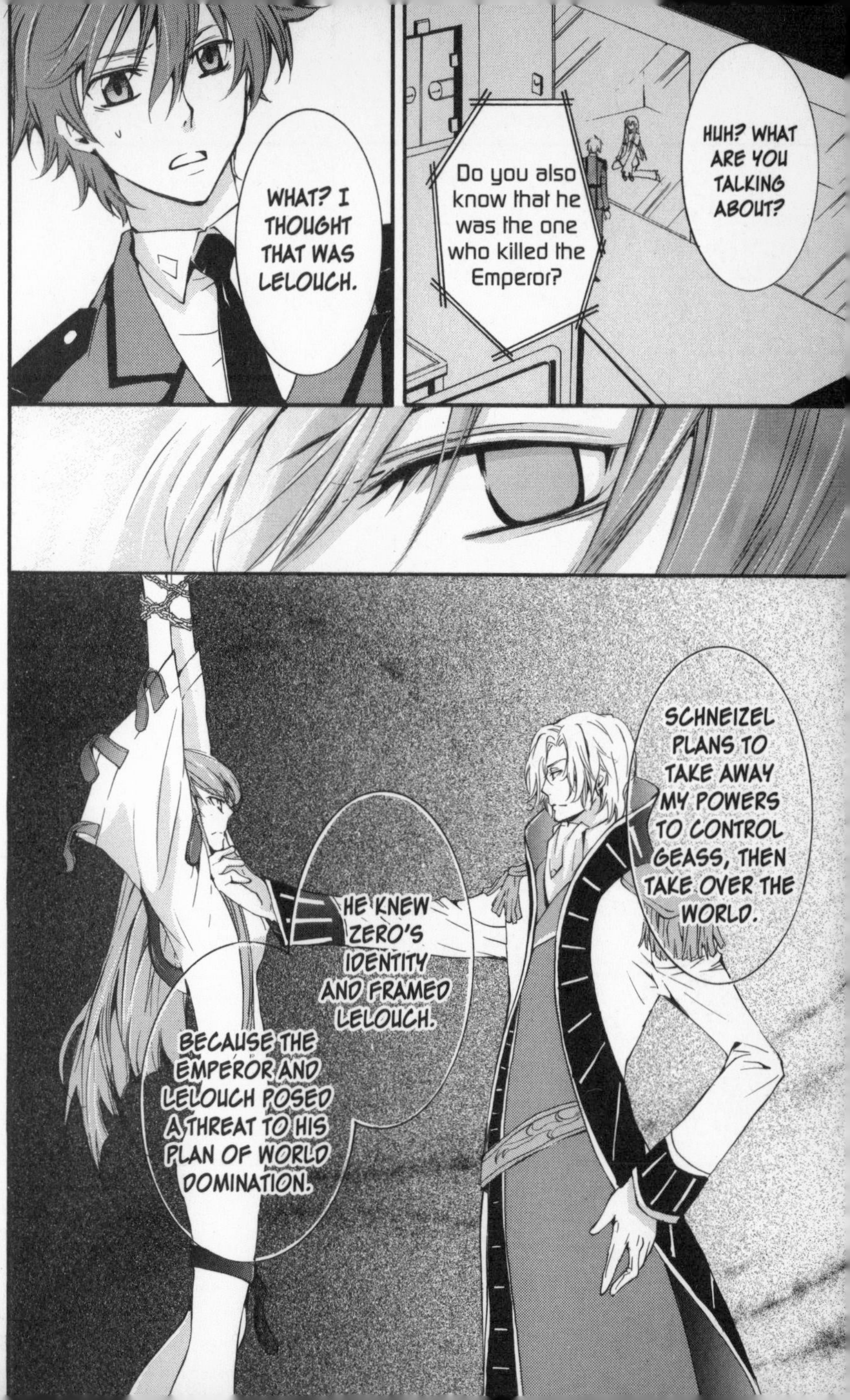
HUH? WHAT ARE YOU TALKING ABOUT?
Do you also know that he was the one who killed the Emperor?
WHAT? I THOUGHT THAT WAS LELOUCH.
SCHNEIZEL PLANS TO TAKE AWAY MY POWERS TO CONTROL GEASS, THEN TAKE OVER THE WORLD.
HE KNEW ZERO'S IDENTITY AND FRAMED LELOUCH.
BECAUSE THE EMPEROR AND LELOUCH POSED A THREAT TO HIS PLAN OF WORLD DOMINATION.

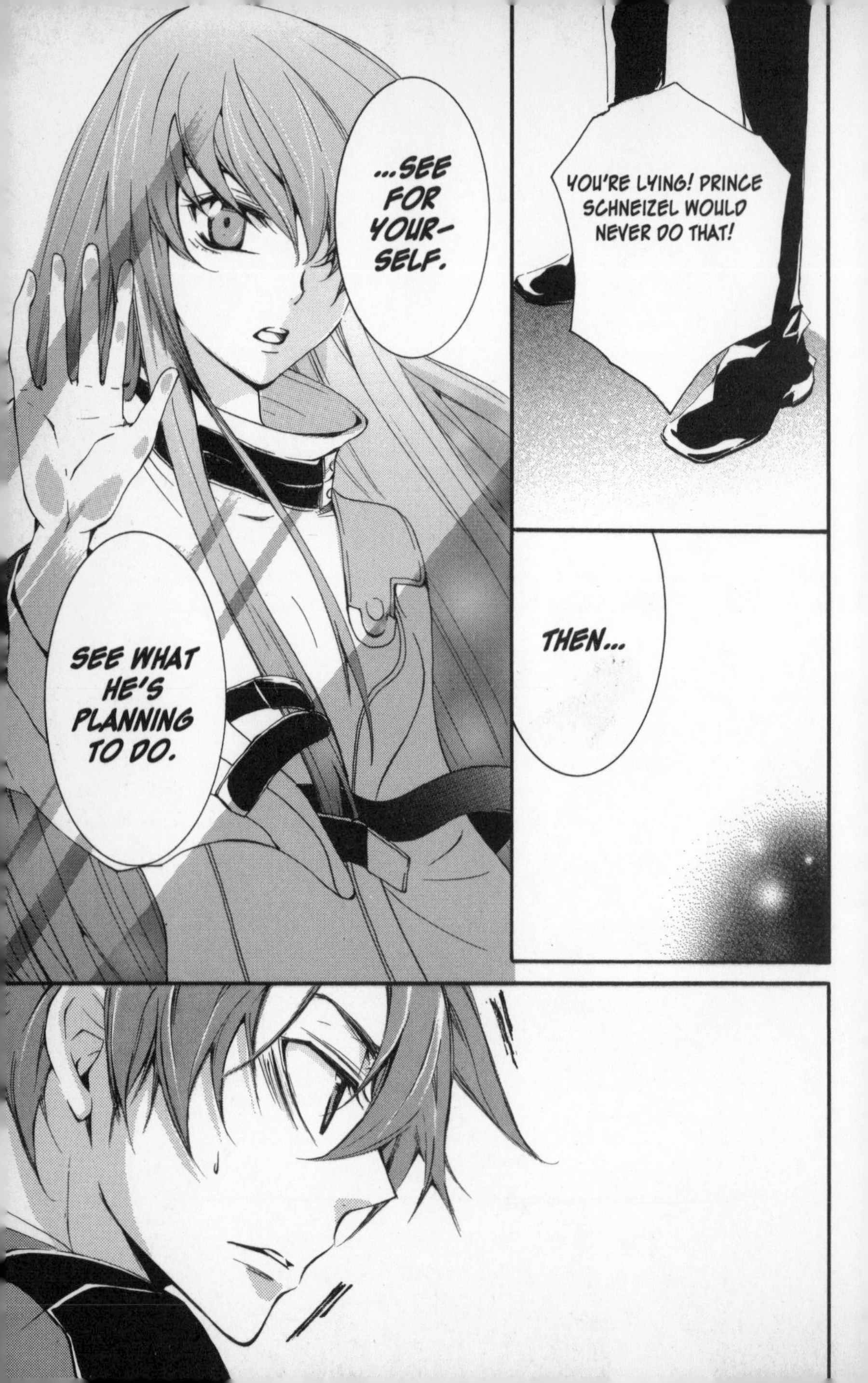
YOU'RE LYING! PRINCE SCHNEIZEL WOULD NEVER DO THAT!
THEN...
...SEE FOR YOUR-SELF.
SEE WHAT HE'S PLANNING TO DO.

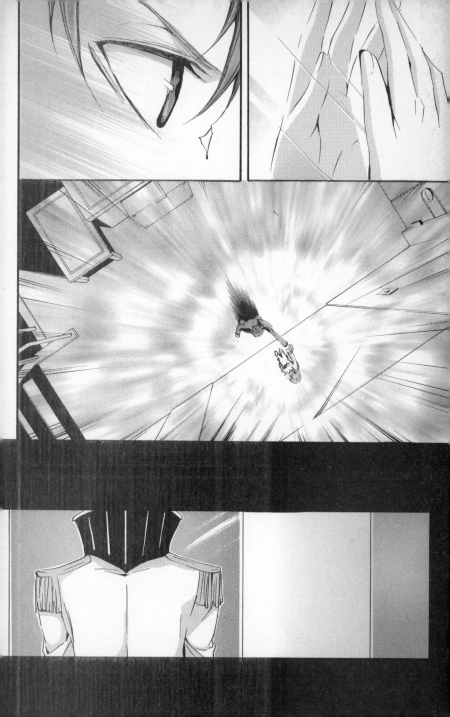

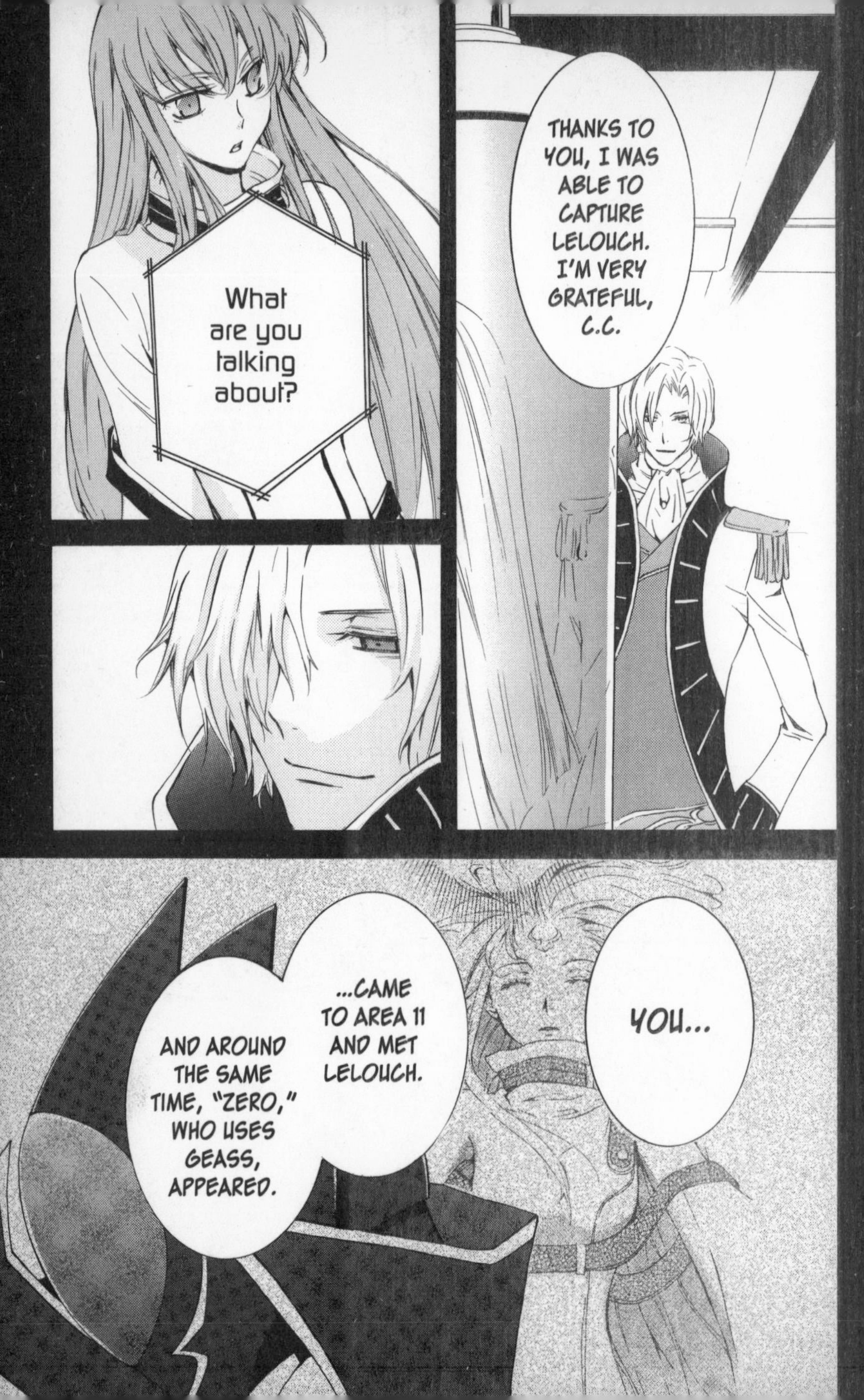
THANKS TO YOU, I WAS ABLE TO CAPTURE LELOUCH. I'M VERY GRATEFUL, C.C.
What are you talking about?
YOU...
...CAME TO AREA 11 AND MET LELOUCH.
AND AROUND THE SAME TIME, "ZERO," WHO USES GEASS, APPEARED.

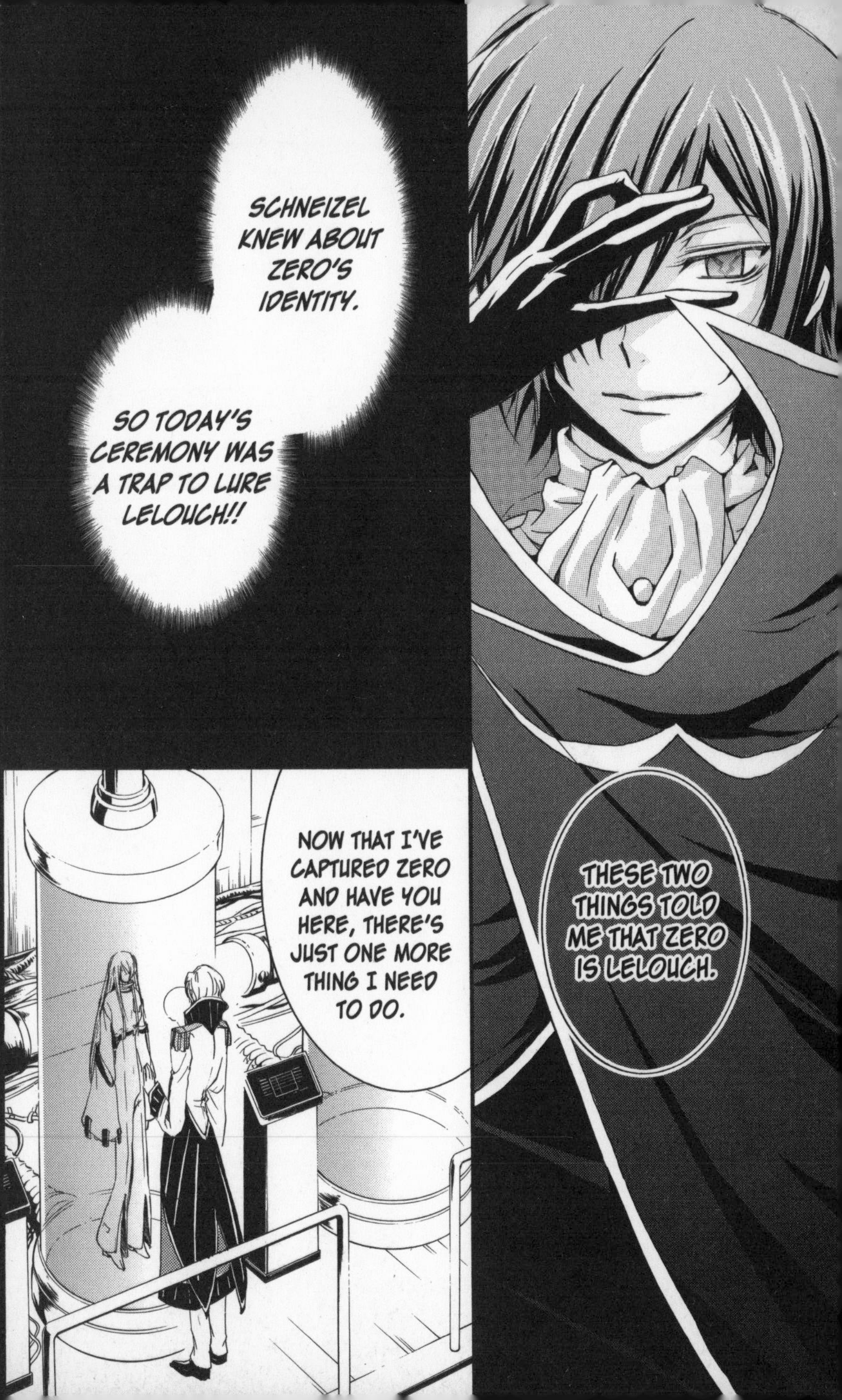
THESE TWO THINGS TOLD ME THAT ZERO IS LELOUCH.
SCHNEIZEL KNEW ABOUT ZERO'S IDENTITY.
SO TODAY'S CEREMONY WAS A TRAP TO LURE LELOUCH!!
NOW THAT I'VE CAPTURED ZERO AND HAVE YOU HERE, THERE'S JUST ONE MORE THING I NEED TO DO.

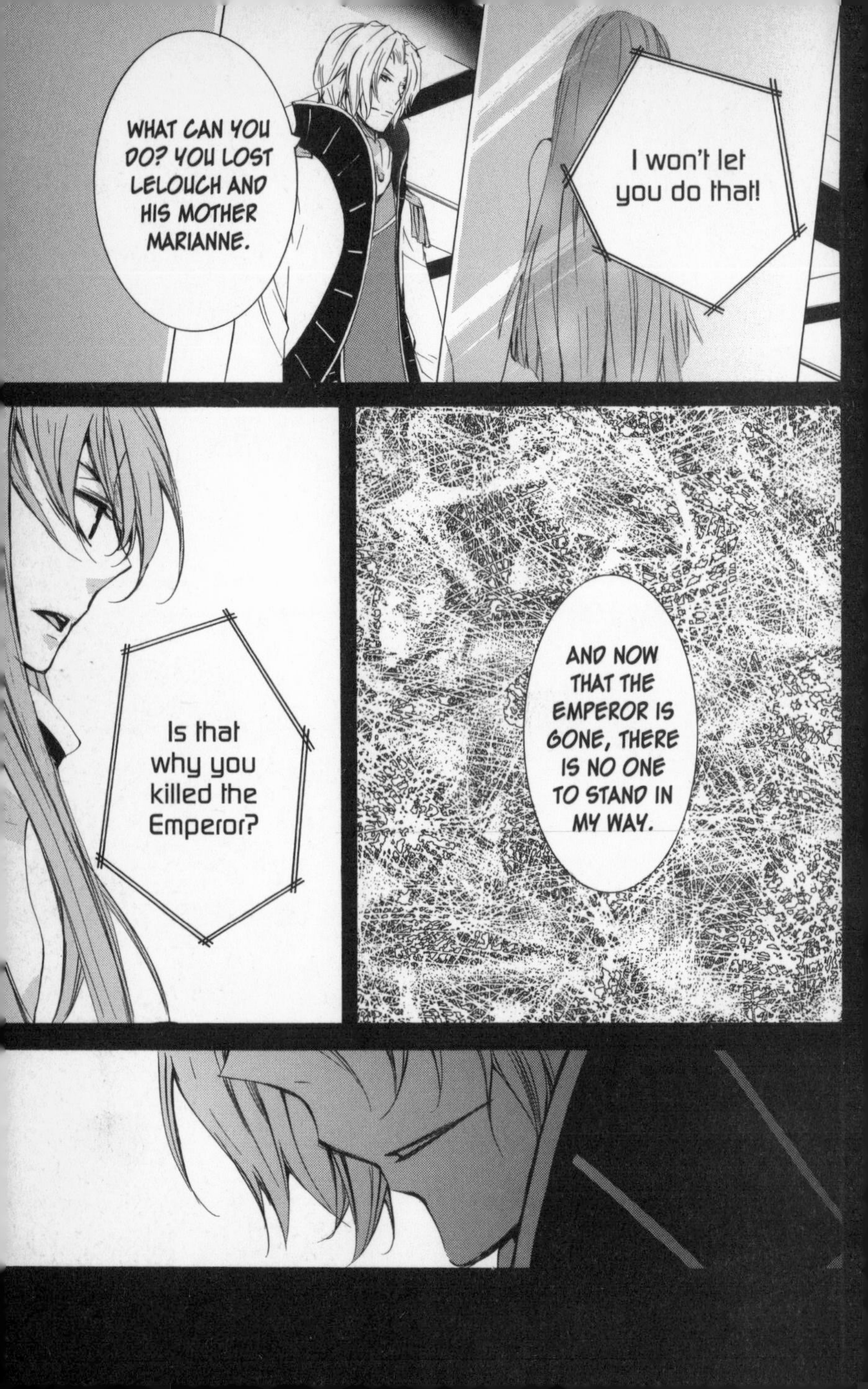

I won't let you do that!
WHAT CAN YOU DO? YOU LOST LELOUCH AND HIS MOTHER MARIANNE.
AND NOW THAT THE EMPEROR IS GONE, THERE IS NO ONE TO STAND IN MY WAY.
Is that why you killed the Emperor?

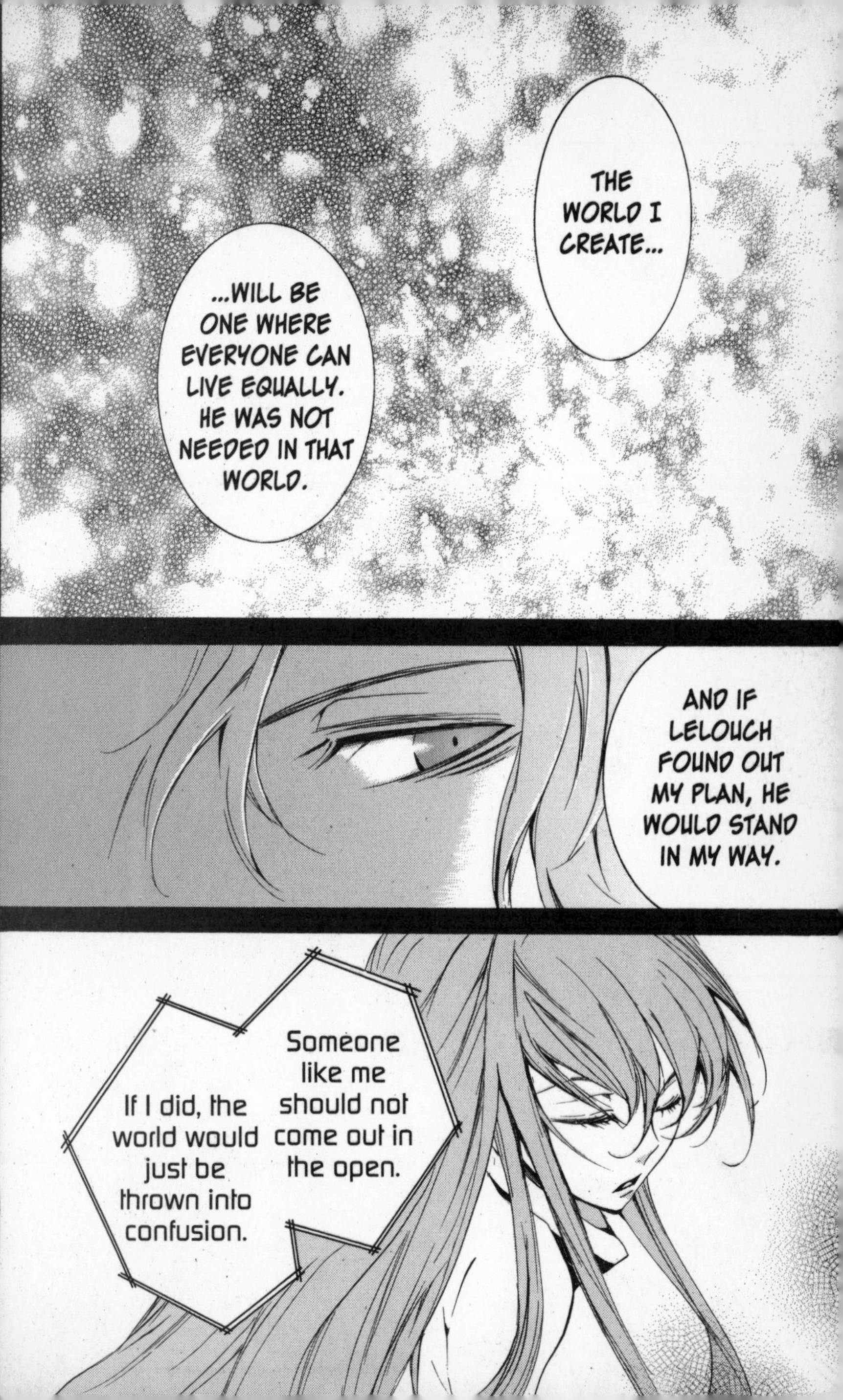
THE WORLD I CREATE...
...WILL BE ONE WHERE EVERYONE CAN LIVE EQUALLY. HE WAS NOT NEEDED IN THAT WORLD.
AND IF LELOUCH FOUND OUT MY PLAN, HE WOULD STAND IN MY WAY.
Someone like me should not come out in the open.
If I did, the world would just be thrown into confusion.

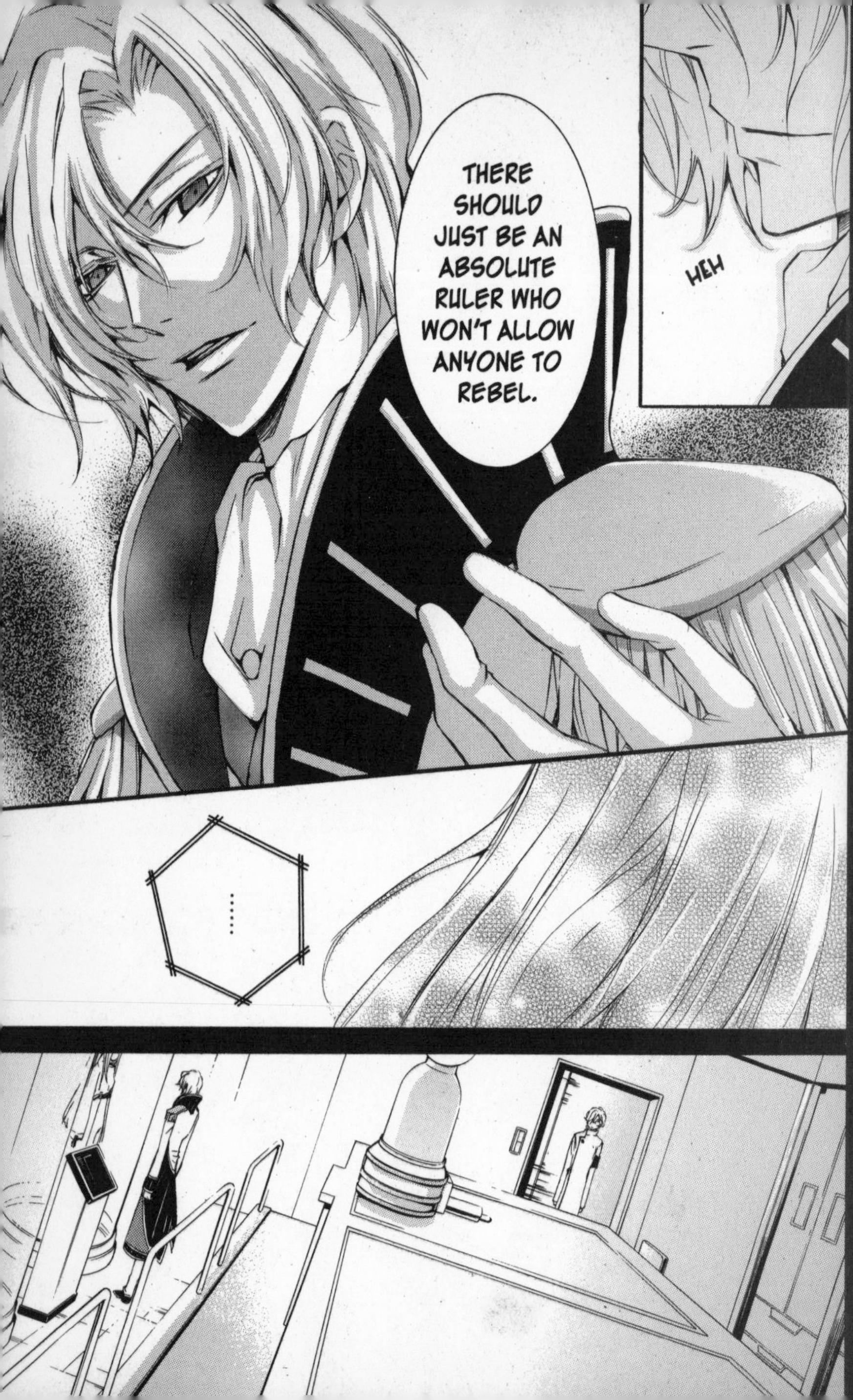
HEH
THERE SHOULD JUST BE AN ABSOLUTE RULER WHO WON'T ALLOW ANYONE TO REBEL.
......

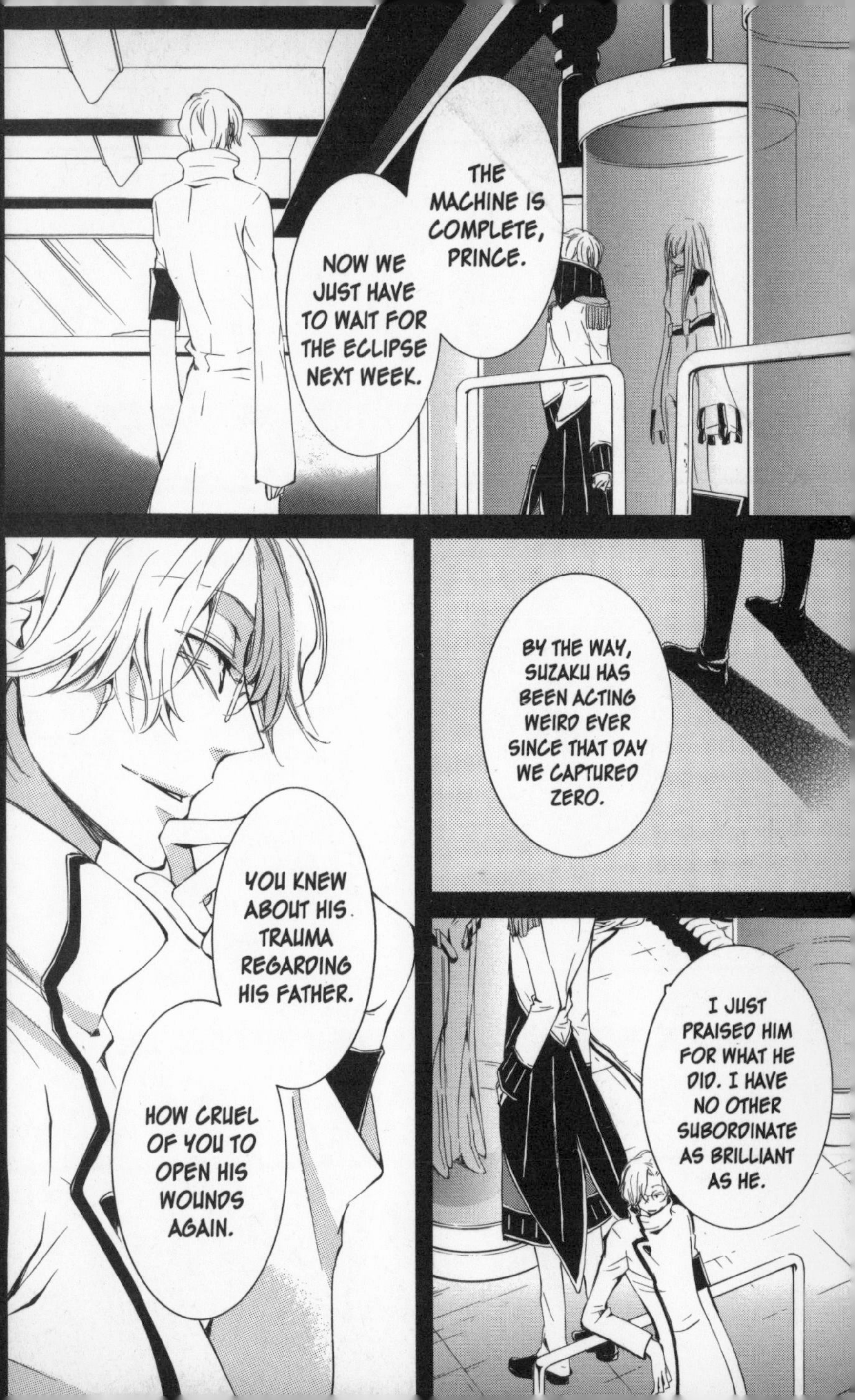
THE MACHINE IS COMPLETE, PRINCE.
NOW WE JUST HAVE TO WAIT FOR THE ECLIPSE NEXT WEEK.
BY THE WAY, SUZAKU HAS BEEN ACTING WEIRD EVER SINCE THAT DAY WE CAPTURED ZERO.
I JUST PRAISED HIM FOR WHAT HE DID. I HAVE NO OTHER SUBORDINATE AS BRILLIANT AS HE.
YOU KNEW ABOUT HIS TRAUMA REGARDING HIS FATHER.
HOW CRUEL OF YOU TO OPEN HIS WOUNDS AGAIN.

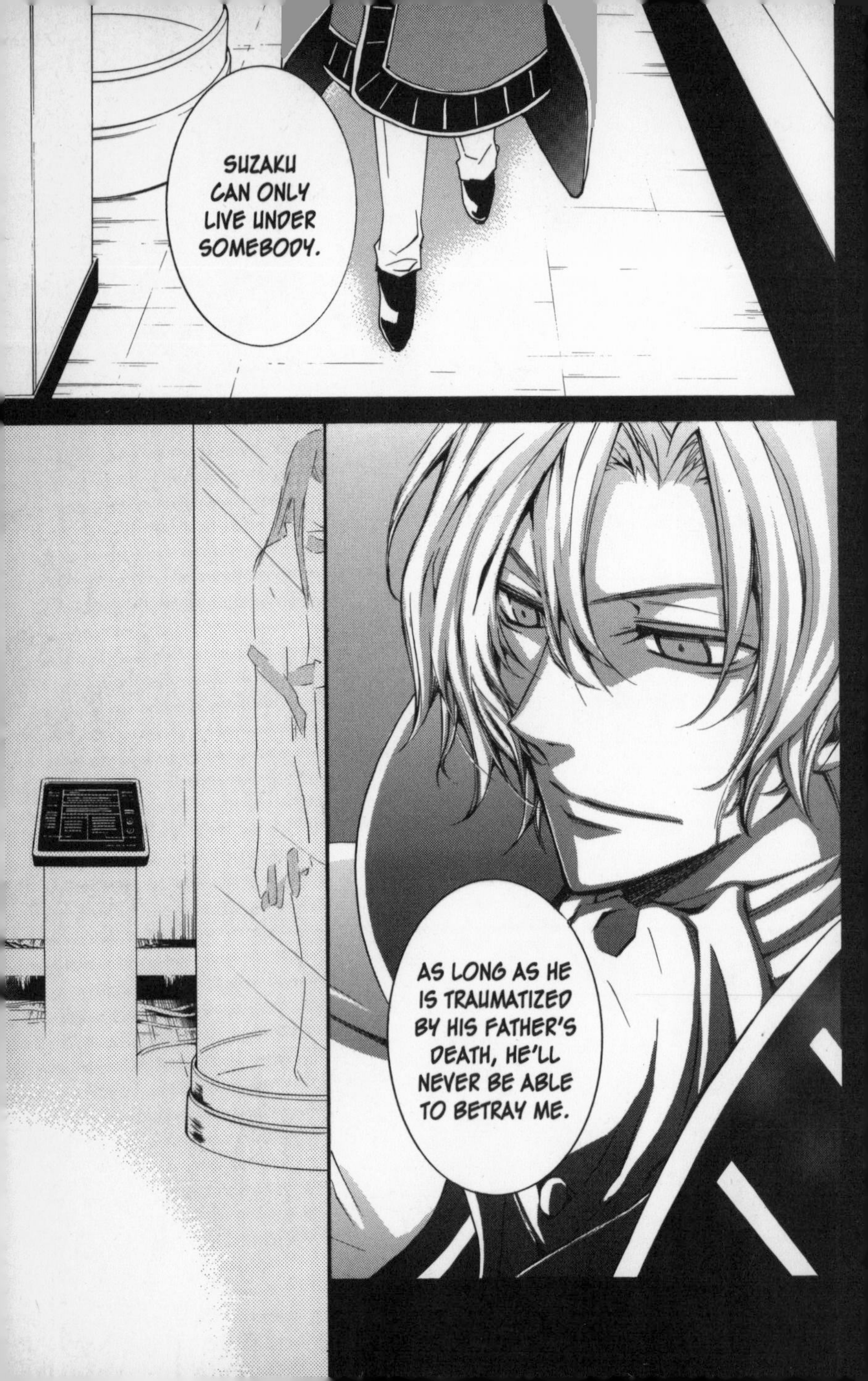
SUZAKU CAN ONLY LIVE UNDER SOMEBODY.
AS LONG AS HE IS TRAUMATIZED BY HIS FATHER'S DEATH, HE'LL NEVER BE ABLE TO BETRAY ME.

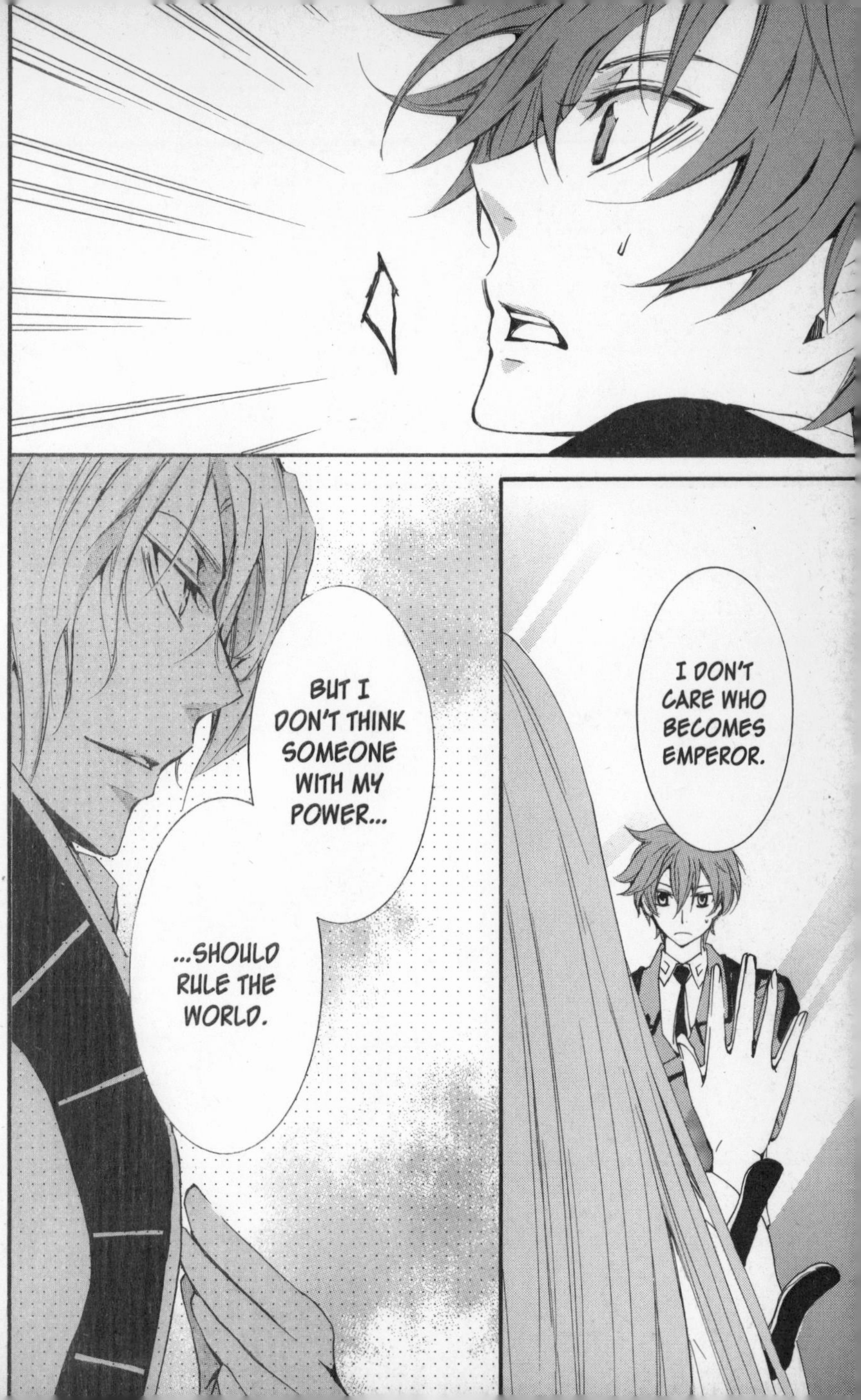
I DON'T CARE WHO BECOMES EMPEROR.
BUT I DON'T THINK SOMEONE WITH MY POWER...
...SHOULD RULE THE WORLD.

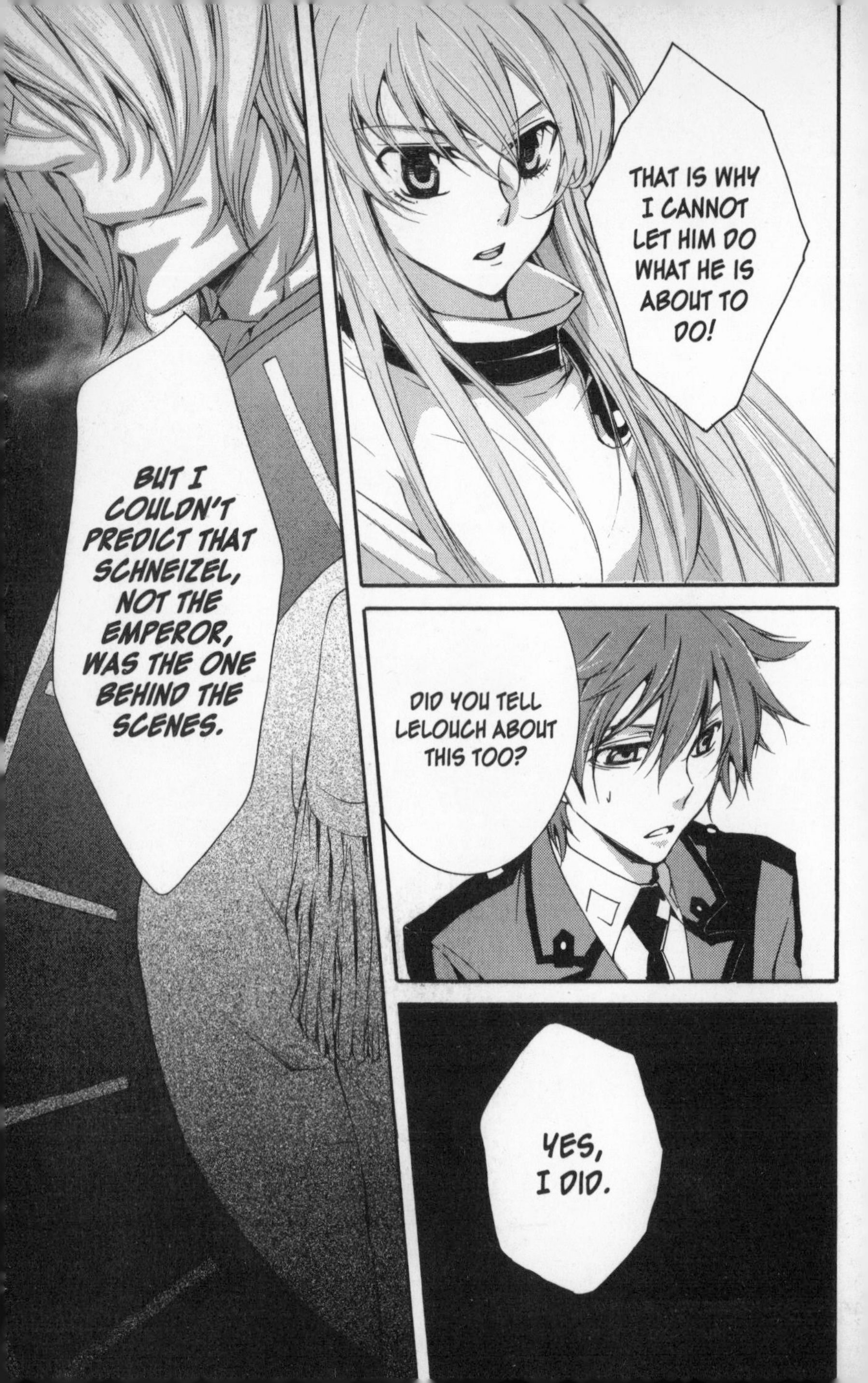
THAT IS WHY I CANNOT LET HIM DO WHAT HE IS ABOUT TO DO!
DID YOU TELL LELOUCH ABOUT THIS TOO?
YES, I DID.
BUT I COULDN'T PREDICT THAT SCHNEIZEL, NOT THE EMPEROR, WAS THE ONE BEHIND THE SCENES.

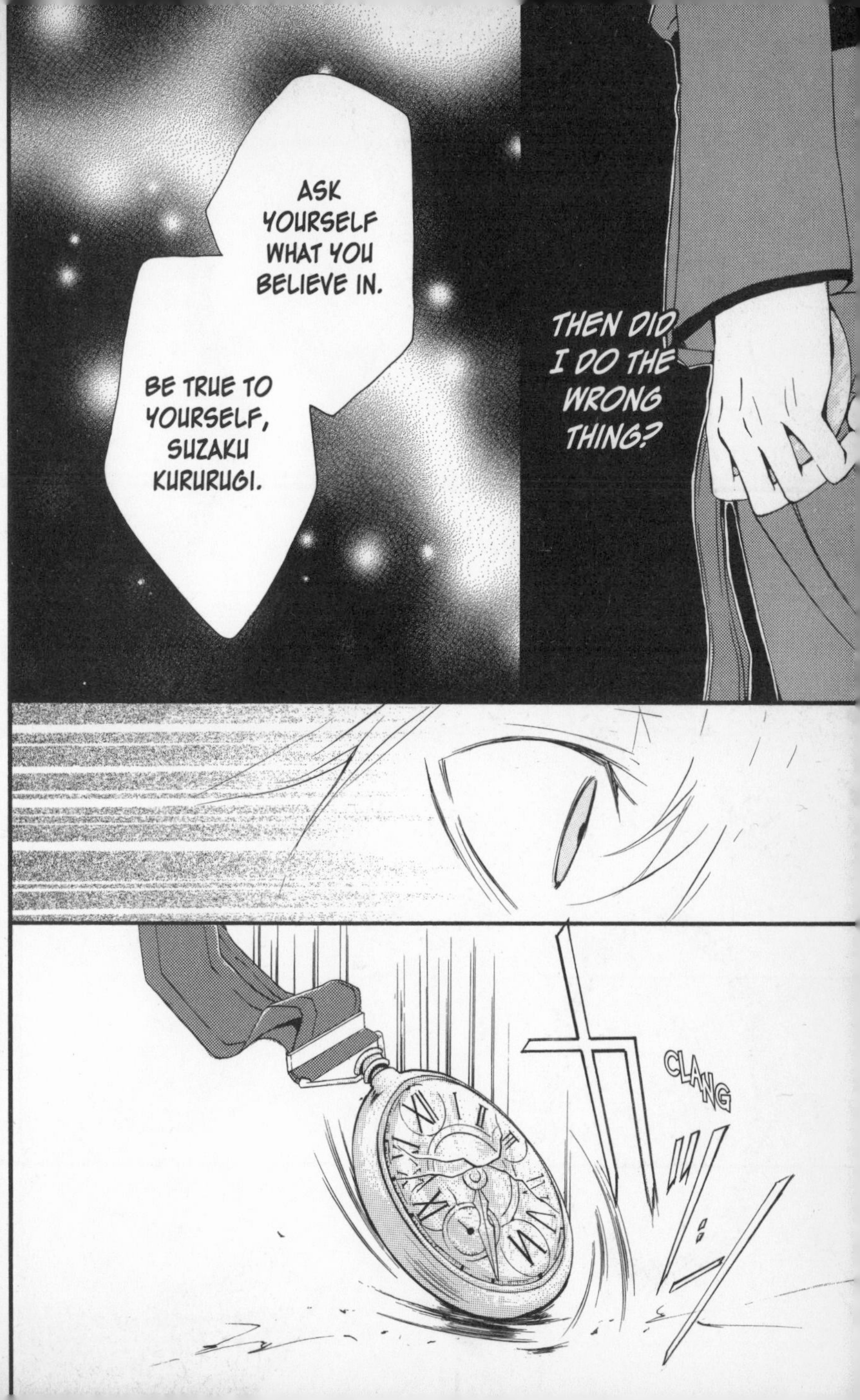
THEN DID I DO THE WRONG THING?
ASK YOURSELF WHAT YOU BELIEVE IN.
BE TRUE TO YOURSELF, SUZAKU KURURUGI.
CLANG

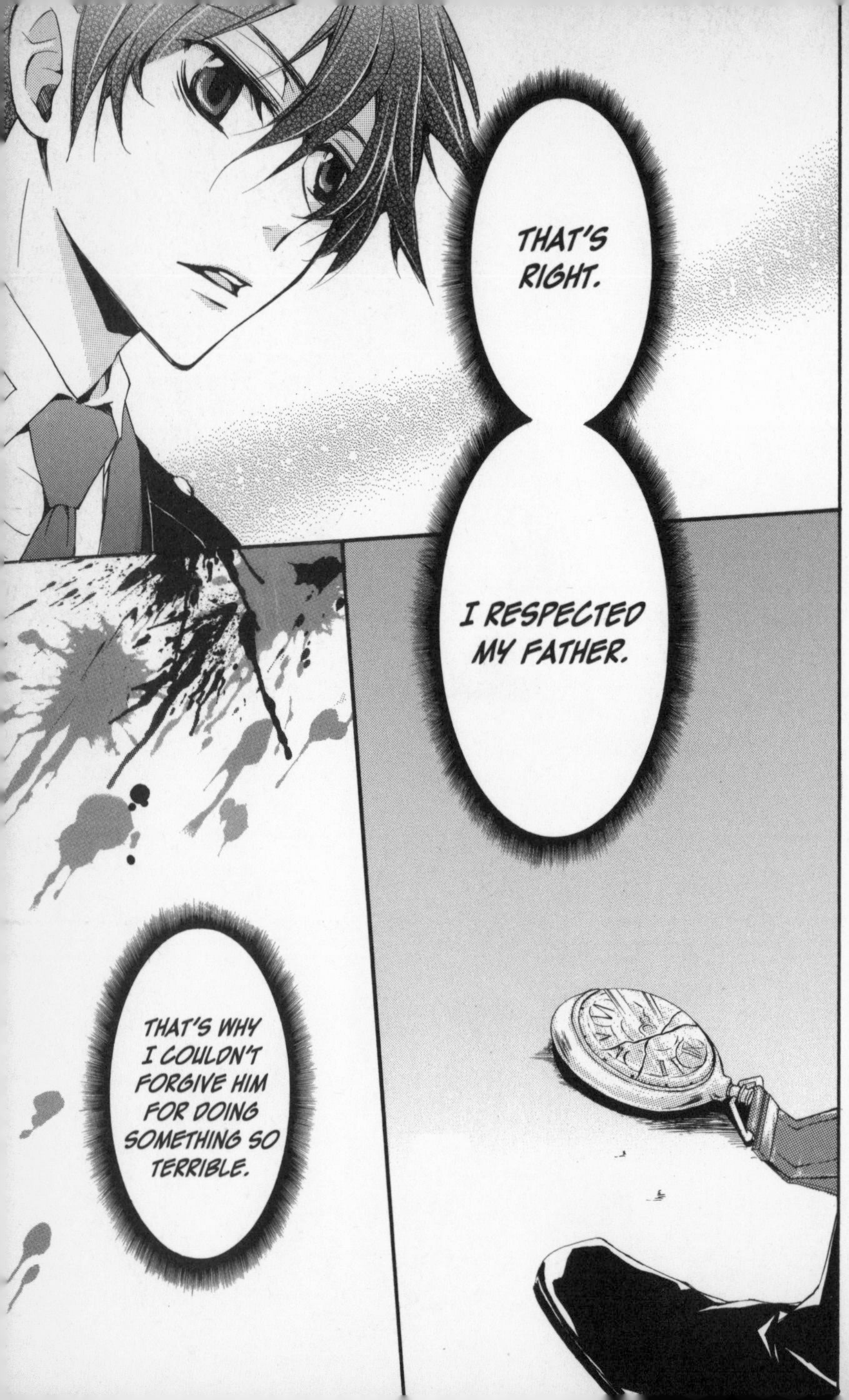
THAT'S RIGHT.
I RESPECTED MY FATHER.
THAT'S WHY I COULDN'T FORGIVE HIM FOR DOING SOMETHING SO TERRIBLE.

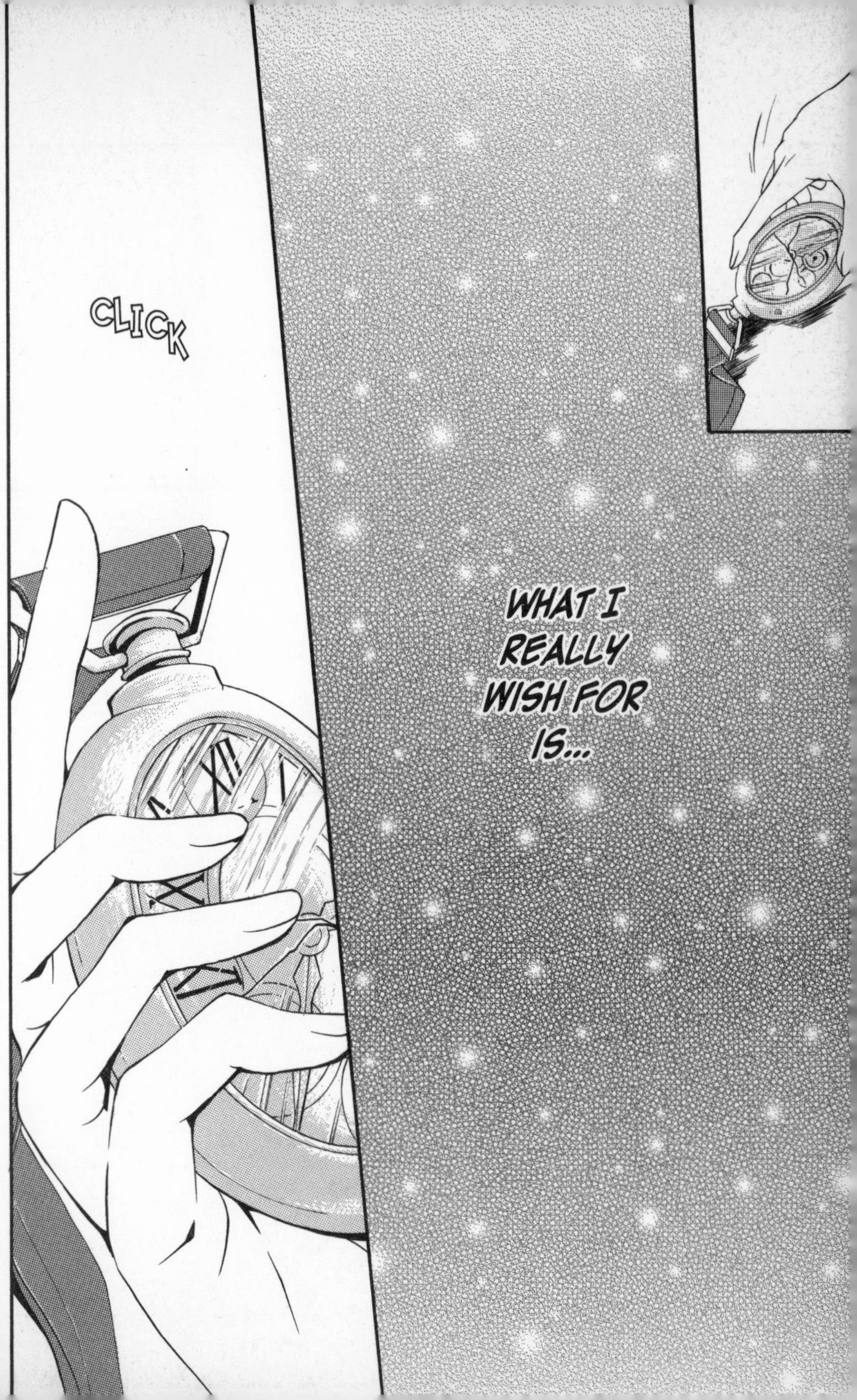
WHAT I REALLY WISH FOR IS...
CLICK

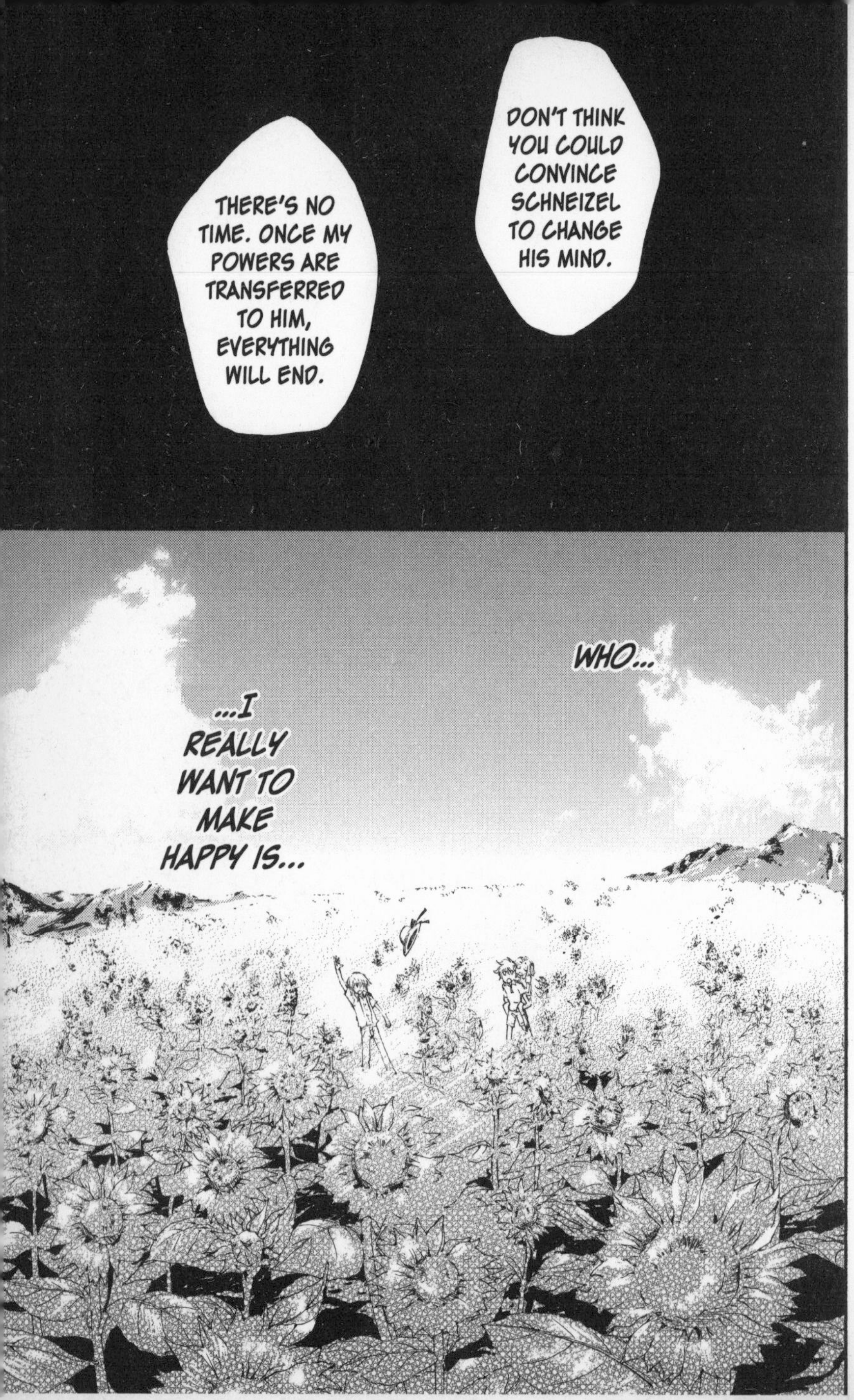
DON'T THINK YOU COULD CONVINCE SCHNEIZEL TO CHANGE HIS MIND.
THERE'S NO TIME. ONCE MY POWERS ARE TRANSFERRED TO HIM, EVERYTHING WILL END.
WHO...
...I REALLY WANT TO MAKE HAPPY IS...

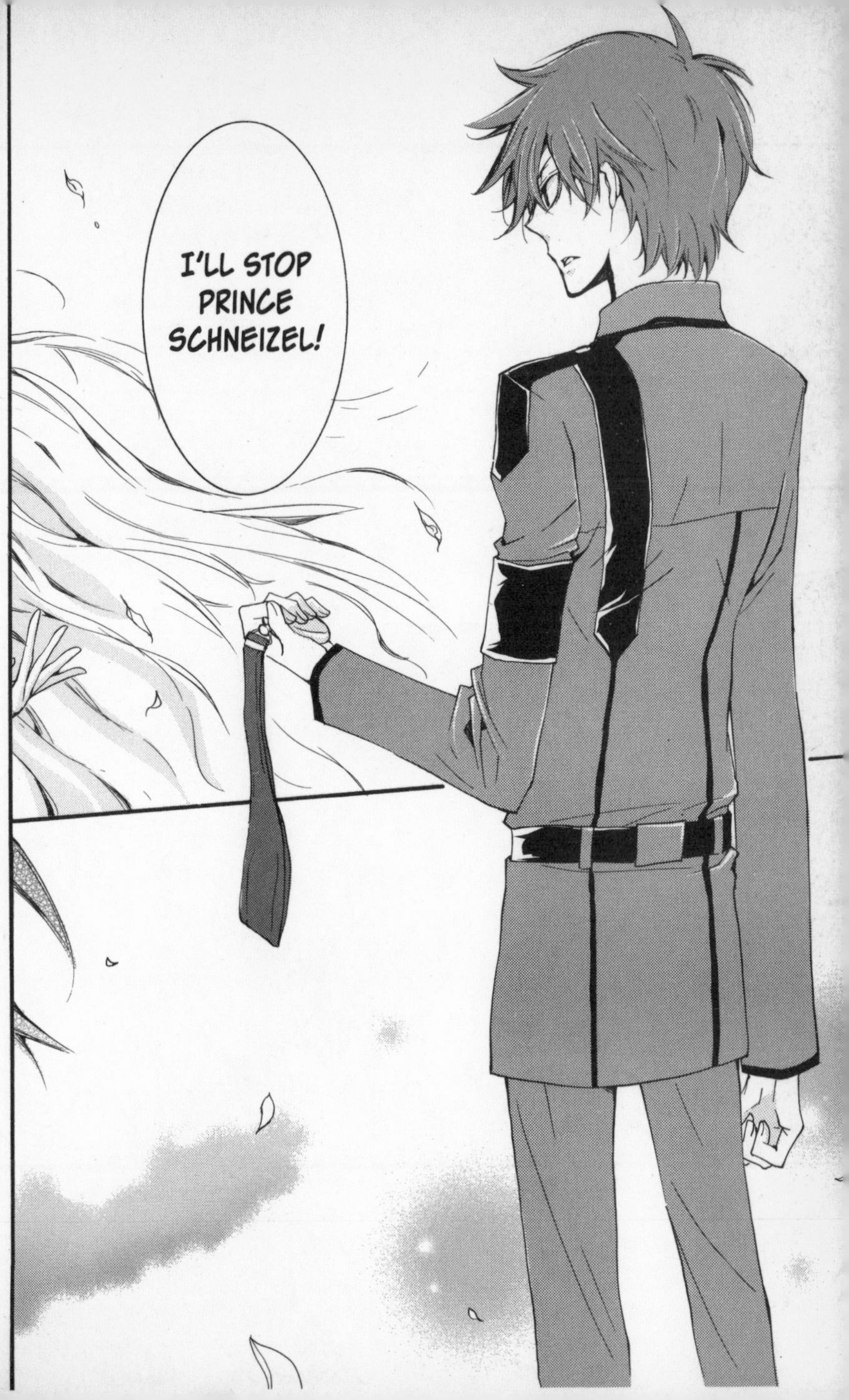
I'LL STOP PRINCE SCHNEIZEL!

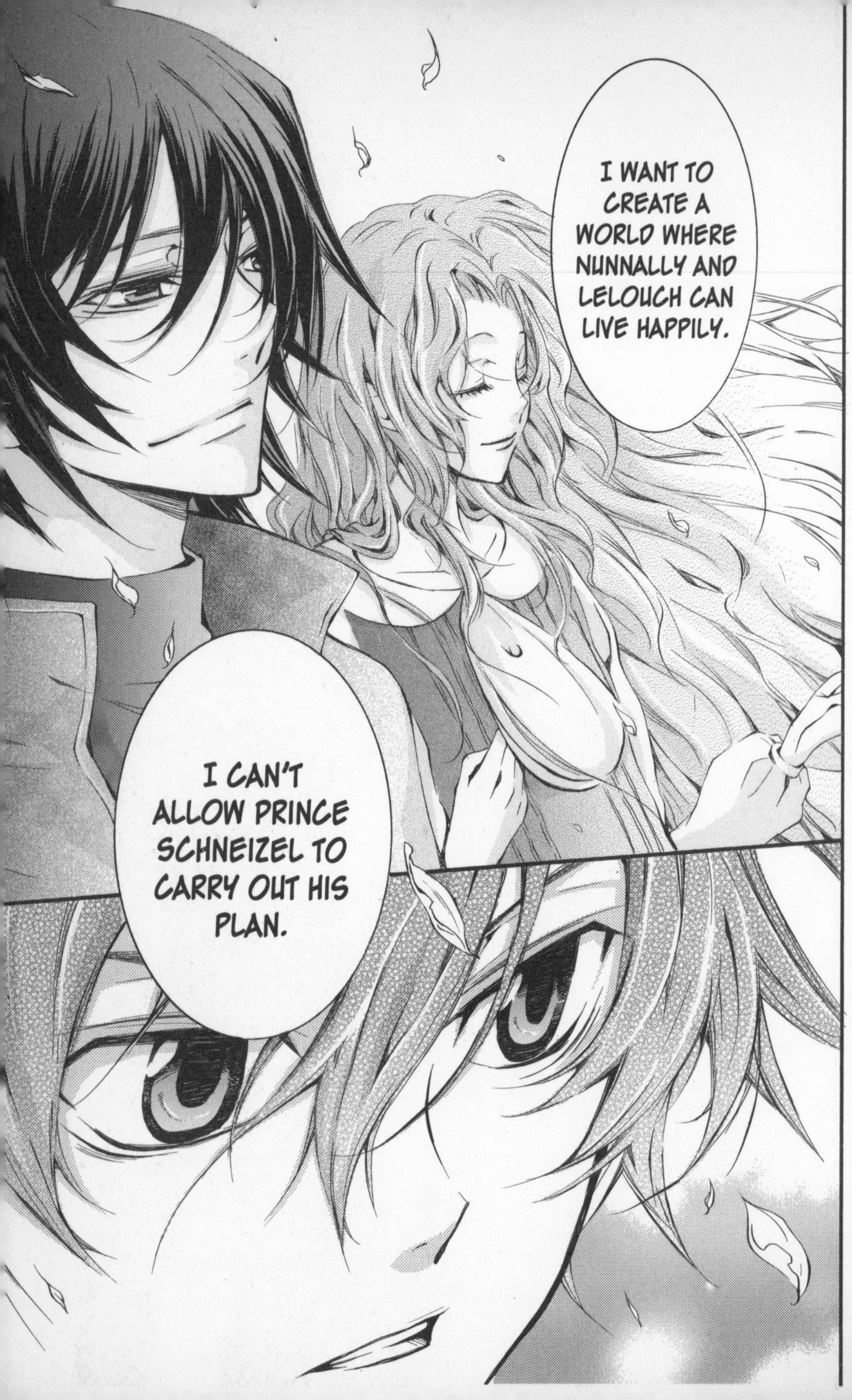
I WANT TO CREATE A WORLD WHERE NUNNALLY AND LELOUCH CAN LIVE HAPPILY.
I CAN'T ALLOW PRINCE SCHNEIZEL TO CARRY OUT HIS PLAN.

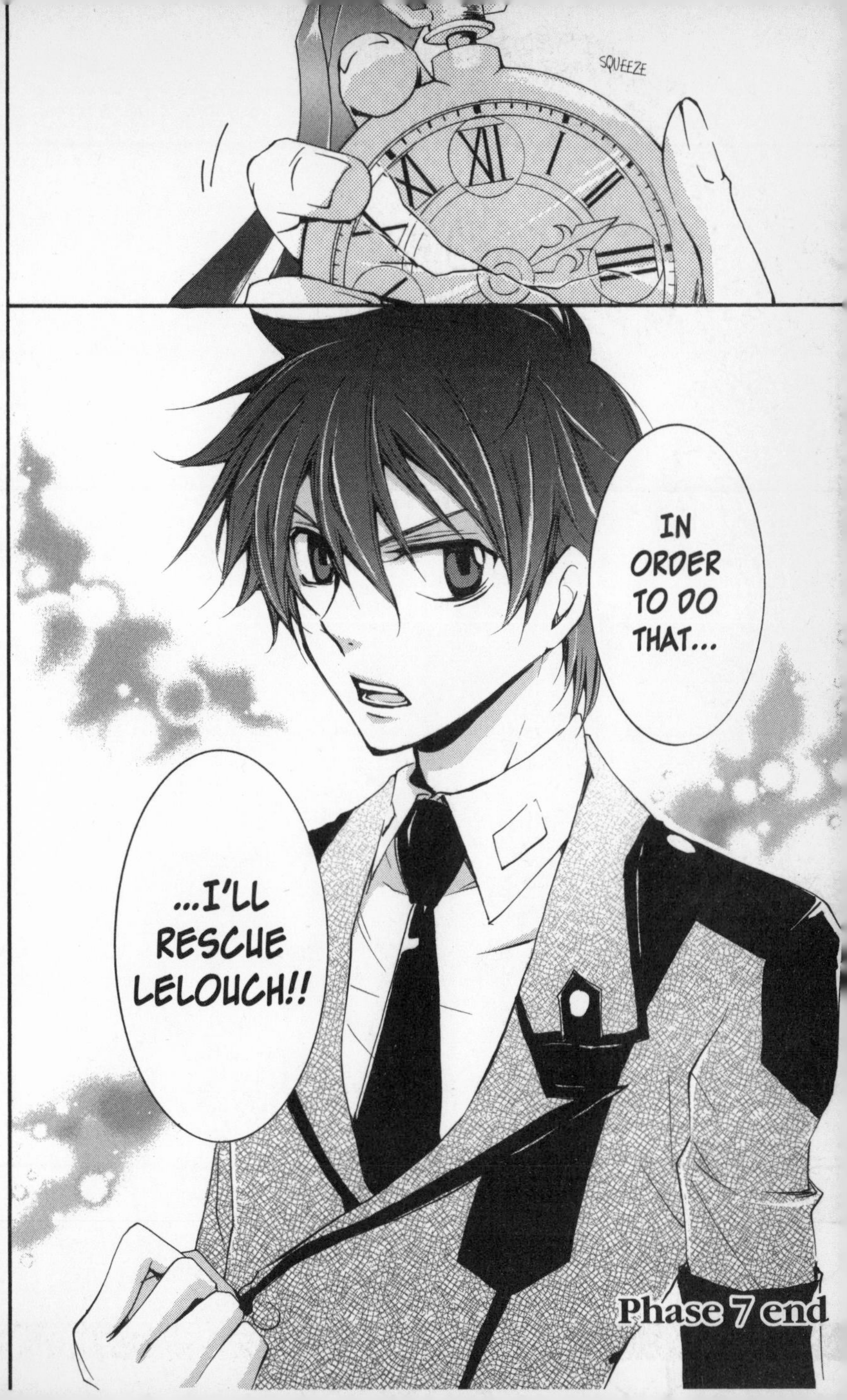
SQUEEZE
IN ORDER TO DO THAT...
...I'LL RESCUE LELOUCH!!
Phase 7 end

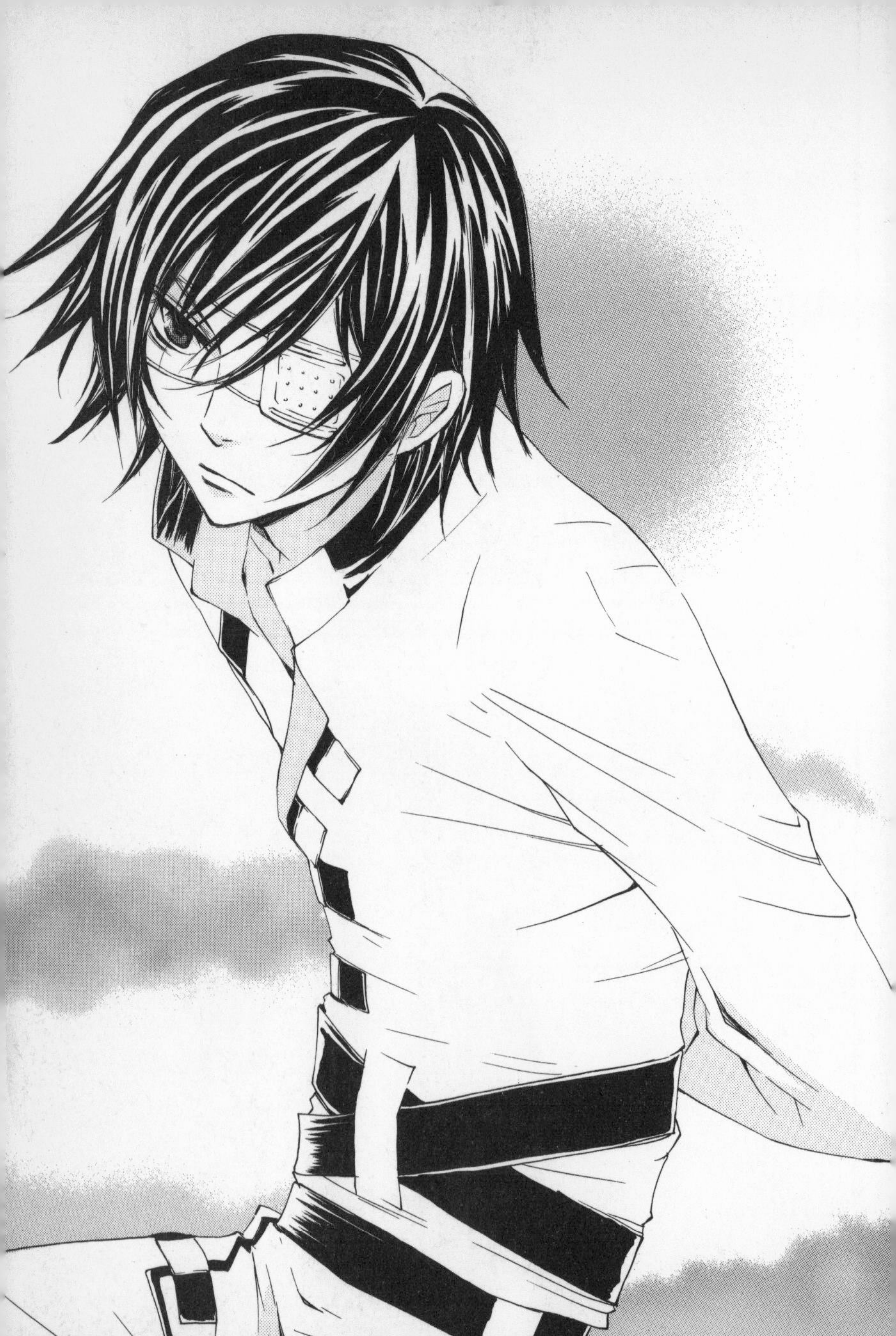

Last Phase

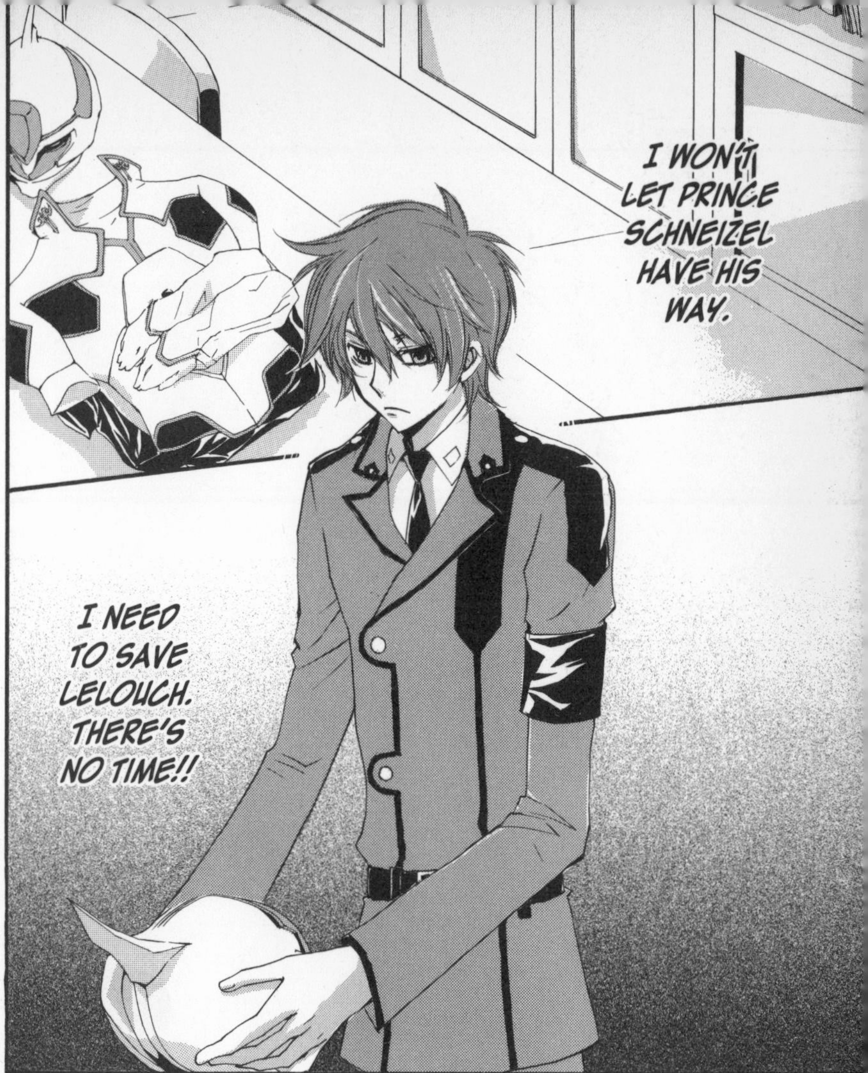
I WON'T LET PRINCE SCHNEIZEL HAVE HIS WAY.
I NEED TO SAVE LELOUCH. THERE'S NO TIME!!

They changed the slot that the anime is airing in and now it's on Sundays at 5 PM, so it's really hard to watch it on TV. I've had to watch it at my friend's house...

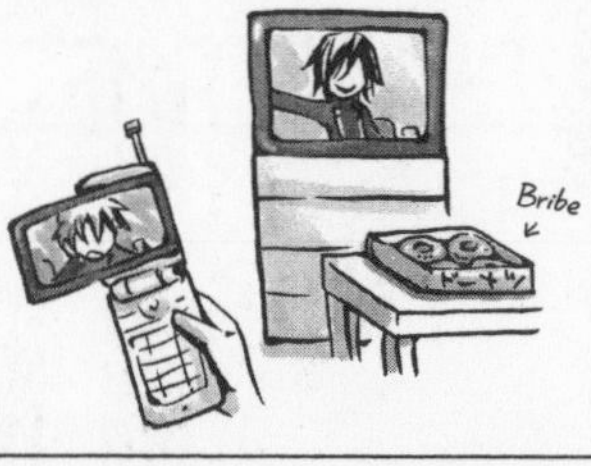
Bribe

...or watch it on my cell phone. I have a hard time catching it. Come to think of it, for the 555 Festival there is no way I can see it live!

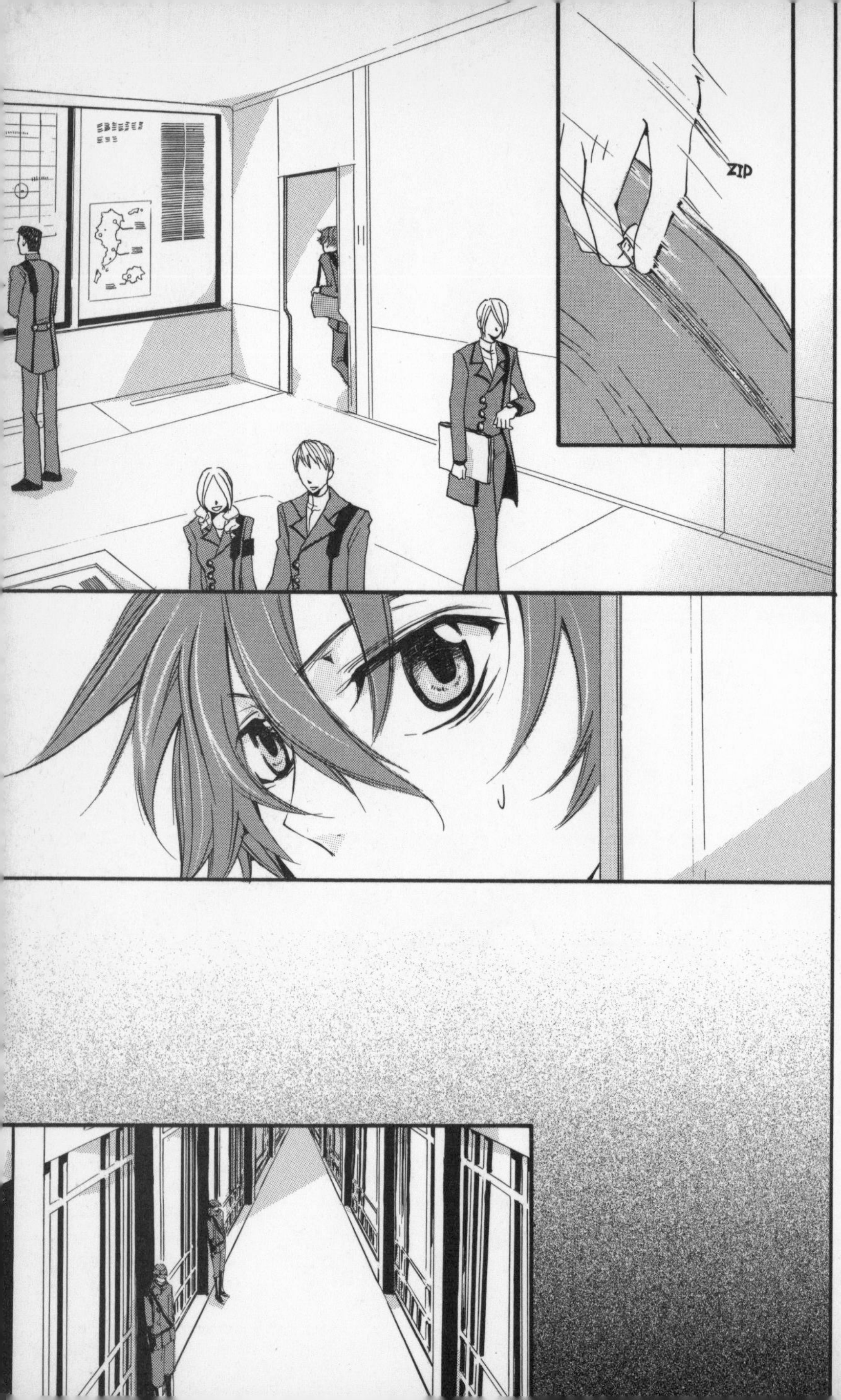
ZIP

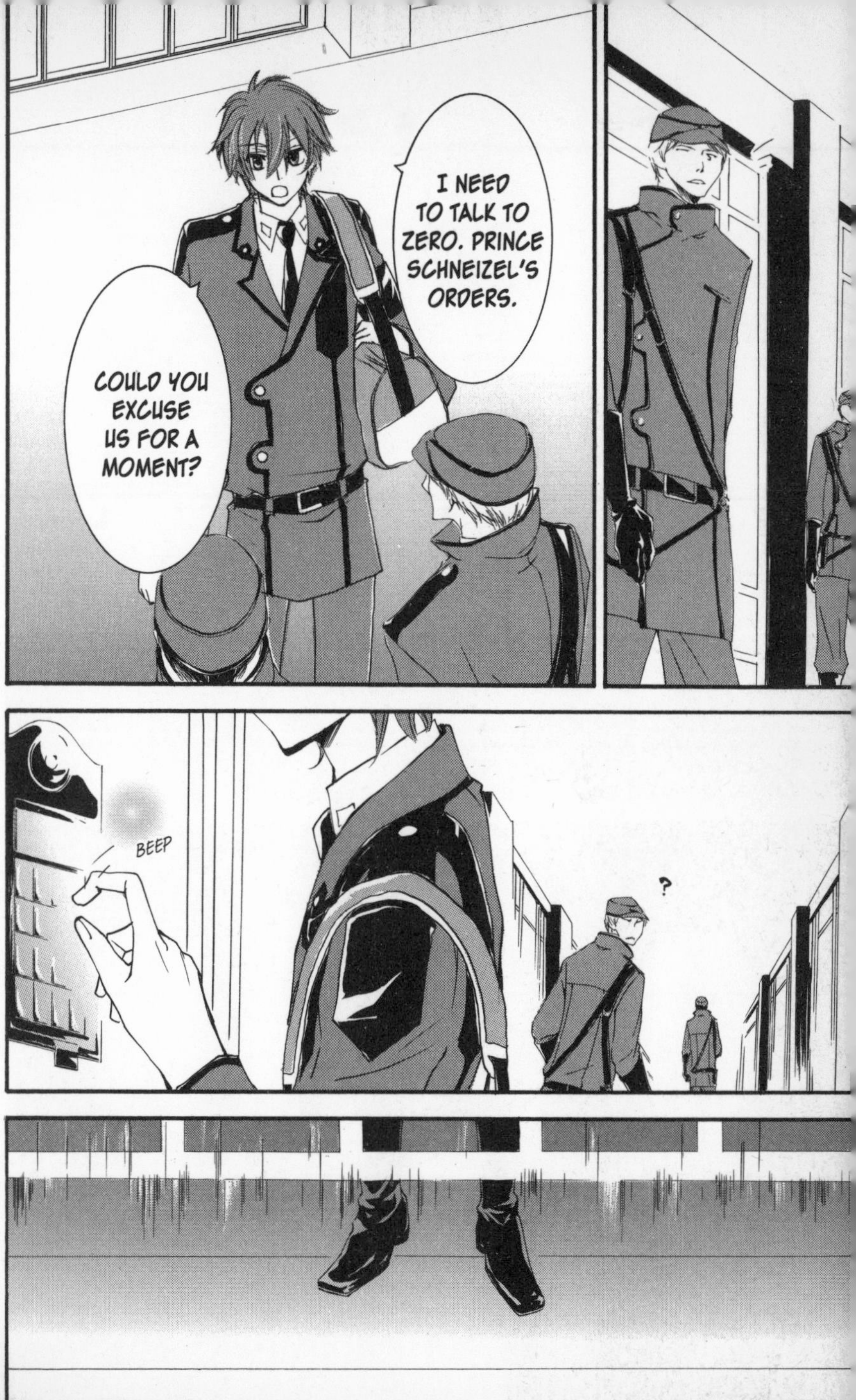
I NEED TO TALK TO ZERO. PRINCE SCHNEIZEL'S ORDERS.
COULD YOU EXCUSE US FOR A MOMENT?
?
BEEP

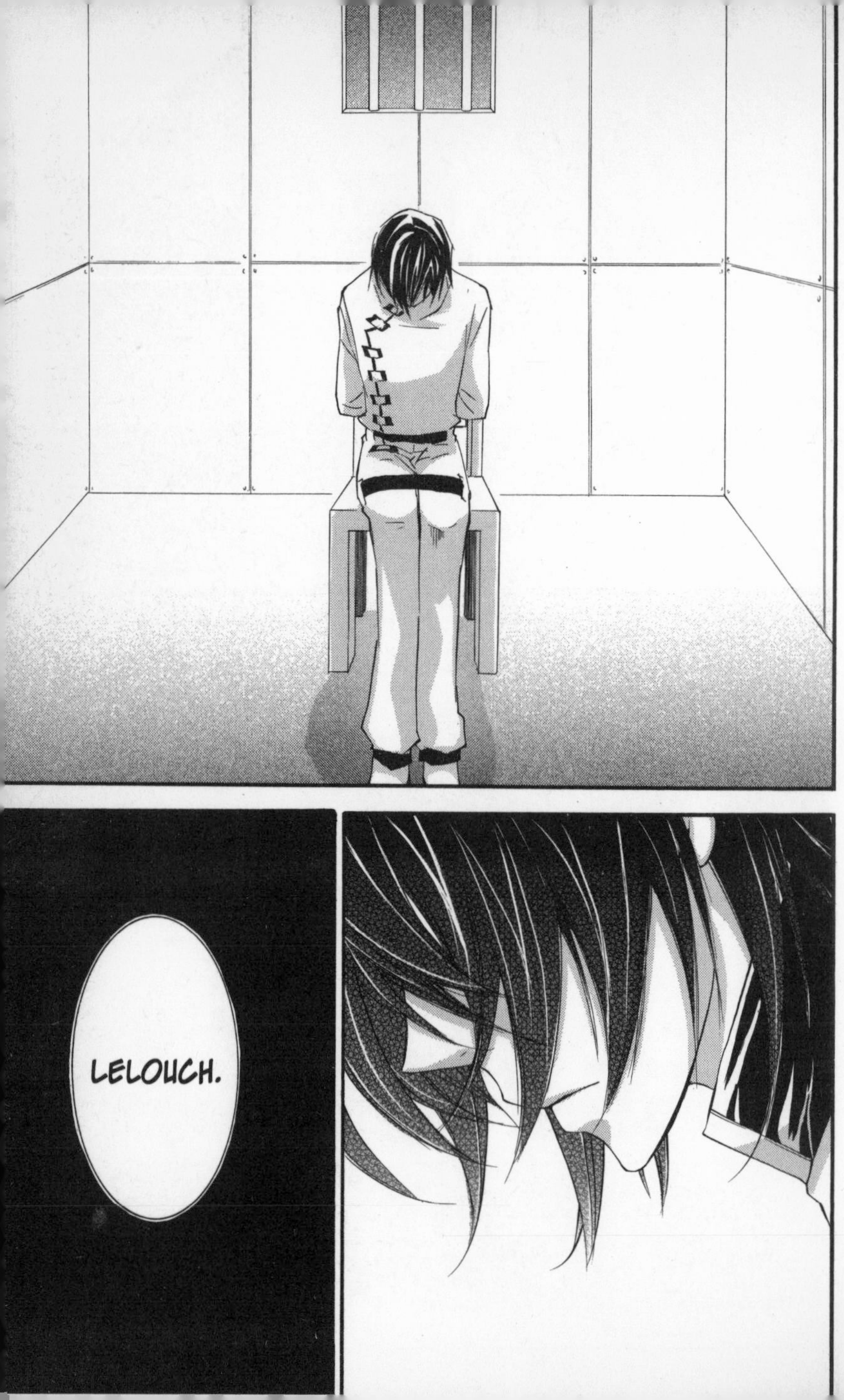
LELOUCH.

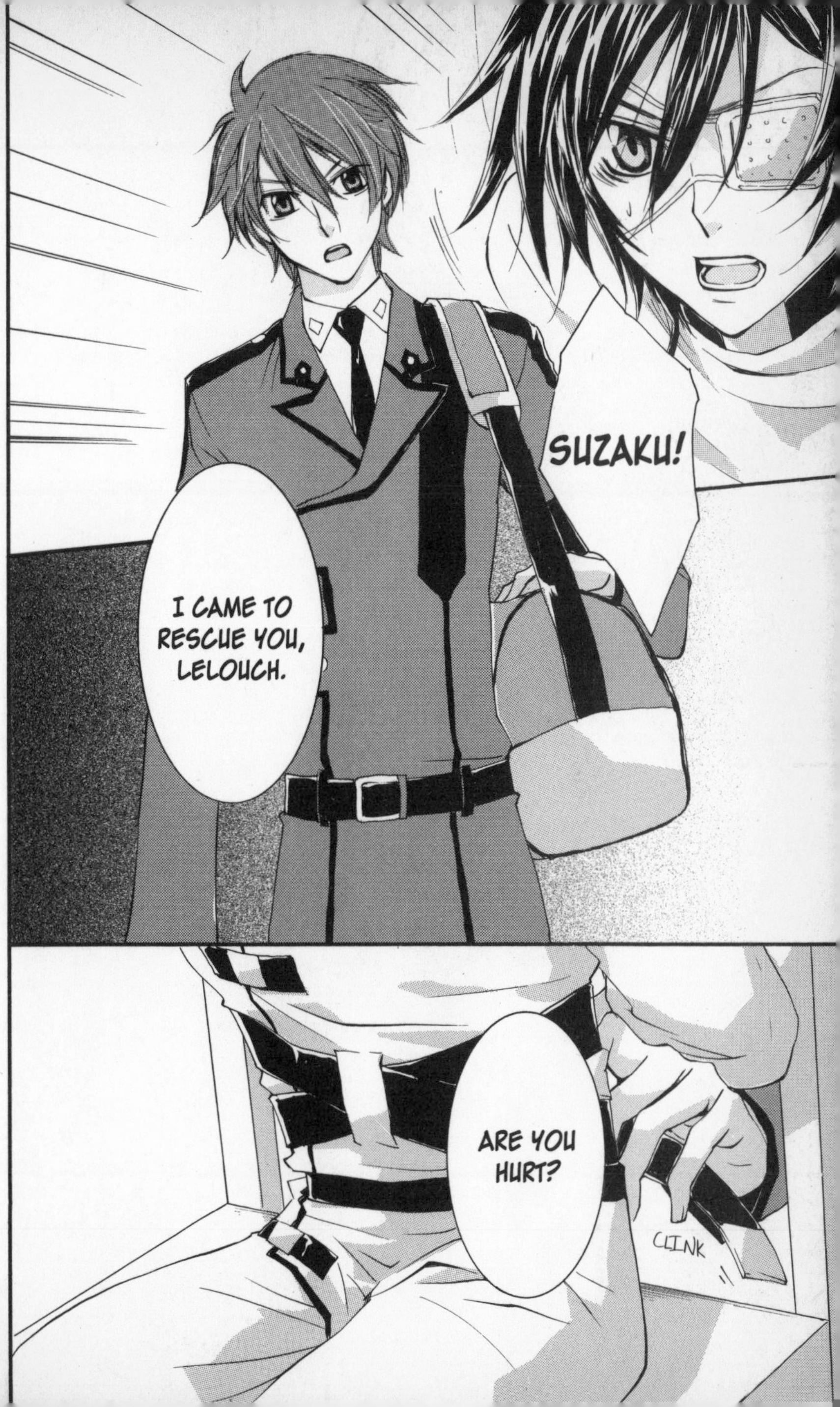
SUZAKU!
I CAME TO RESCUE YOU, LELOUCH.
ARE YOU HURT?
CLINK

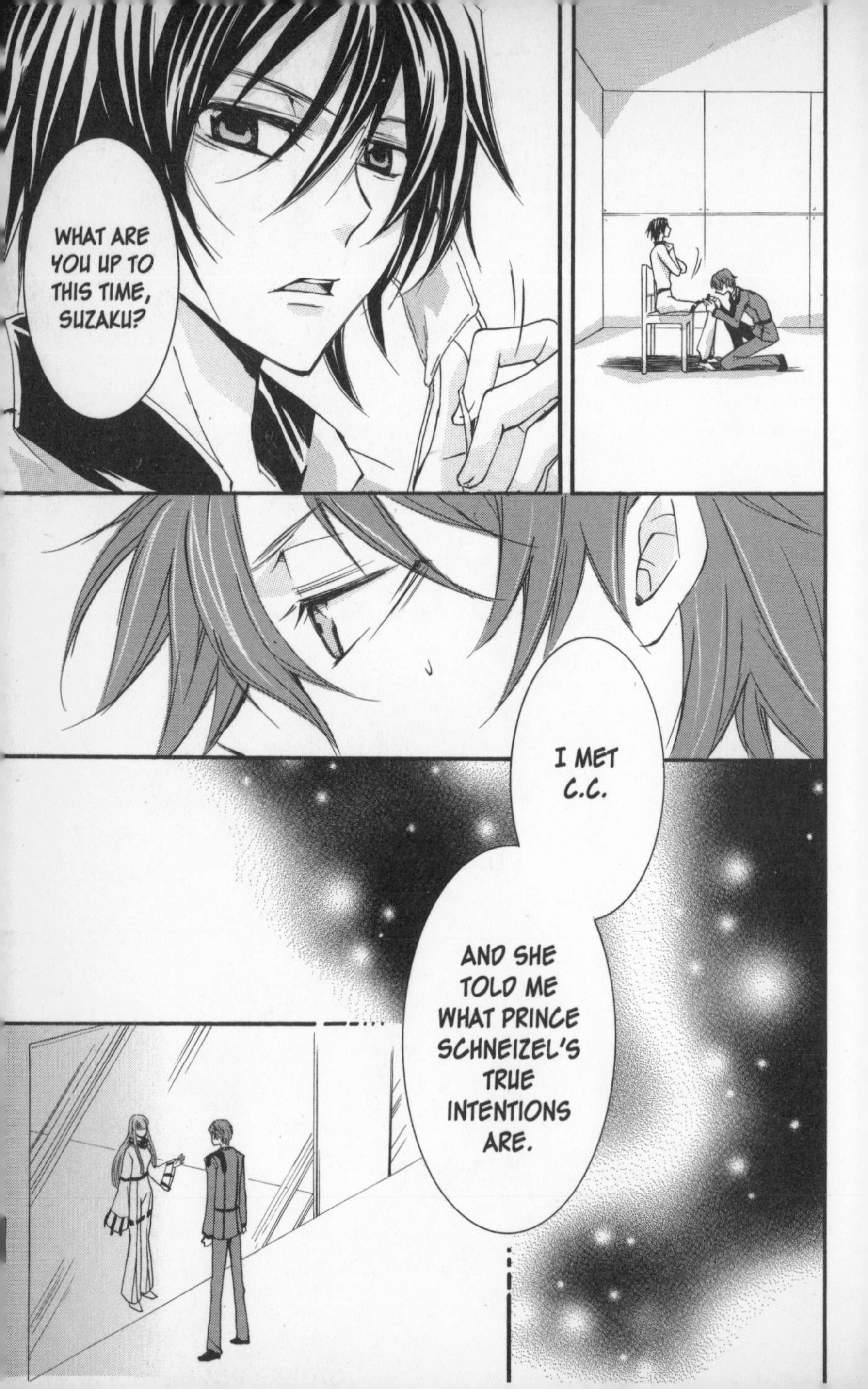
WHAT ARE YOU UP TO THIS TIME, SUZAKU?
I MET C.C.
AND SHE TOLD ME WHAT PRINCE SCHNEIZEL'S TRUE INTENTIONS ARE.

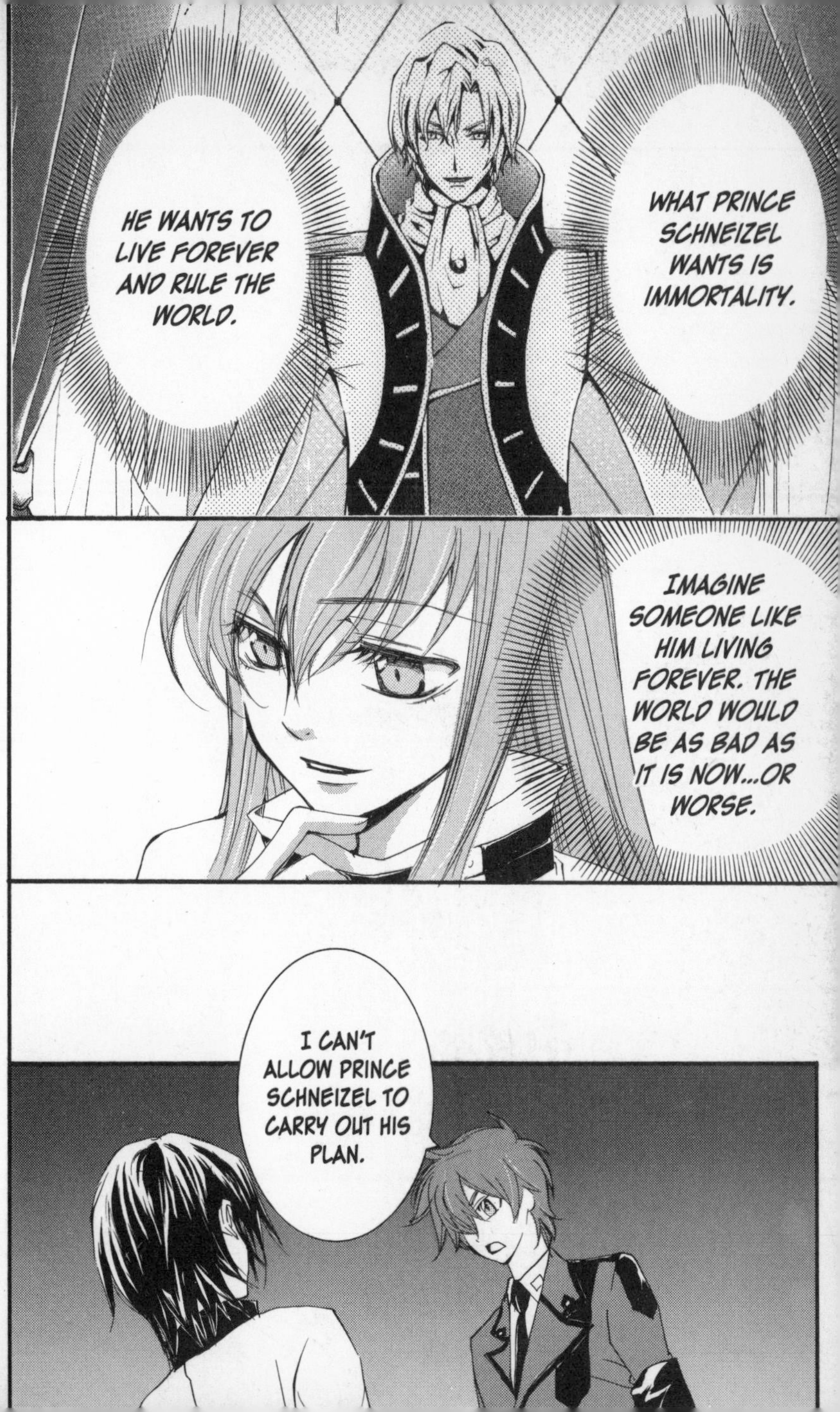
WHAT PRINCE SCHNEIZEL WANTS IS IMMORTALITY.
HE WANTS TO LIVE FOREVER AND RULE THE WORLD.
IMAGINE SOMEONE LIKE HIM LIVING FOREVER. THE WORLD WOULD BE AS BAD AS IT IS NOW...OR WORSE.
I CAN'T ALLOW PRINCE SCHNEIZEL TO CARRY OUT HIS PLAN.

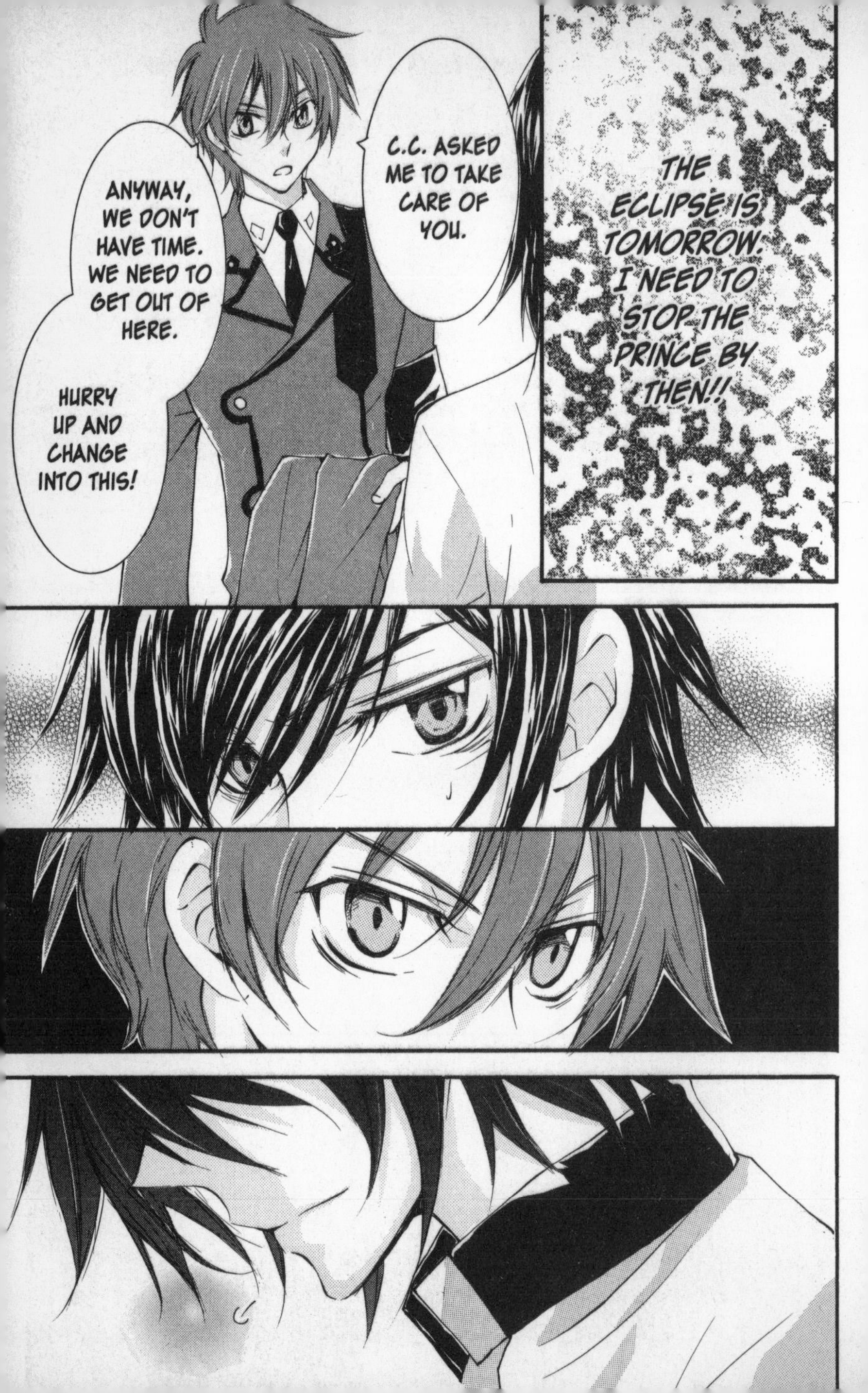
THE ECLIPSE IS TOMORROW. I NEED TO STOP THE PRINCE BY THEN!!
C.C. ASKED ME TO TAKE CARE OF YOU.
ANYWAY, WE DON'T HAVE TIME. WE NEED TO GET OUT OF HERE.
HURRY UP AND CHANGE INTO THIS!

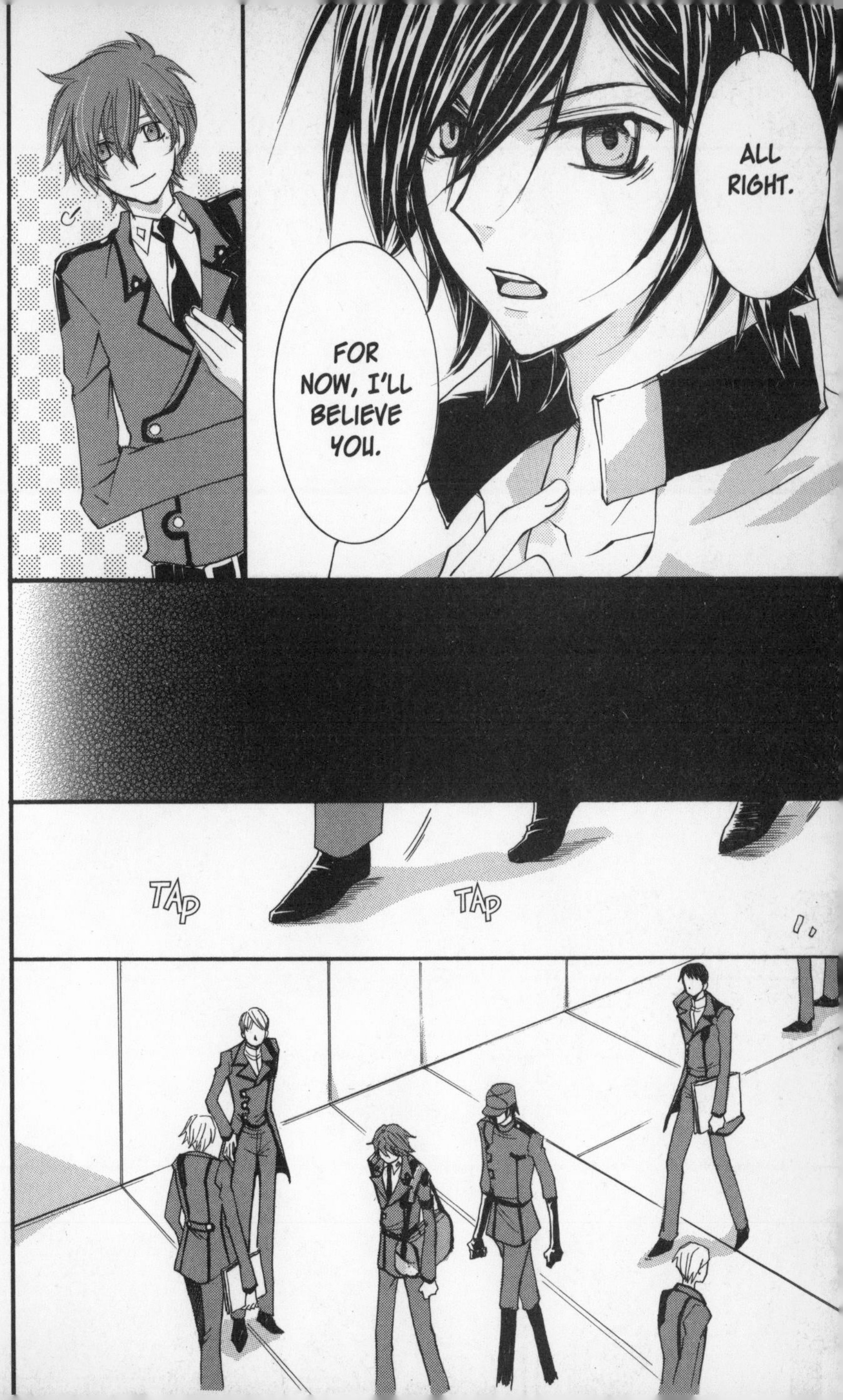
ALL RIGHT.
FOR NOW, I'LL BELIEVE YOU.
TAP
TAP

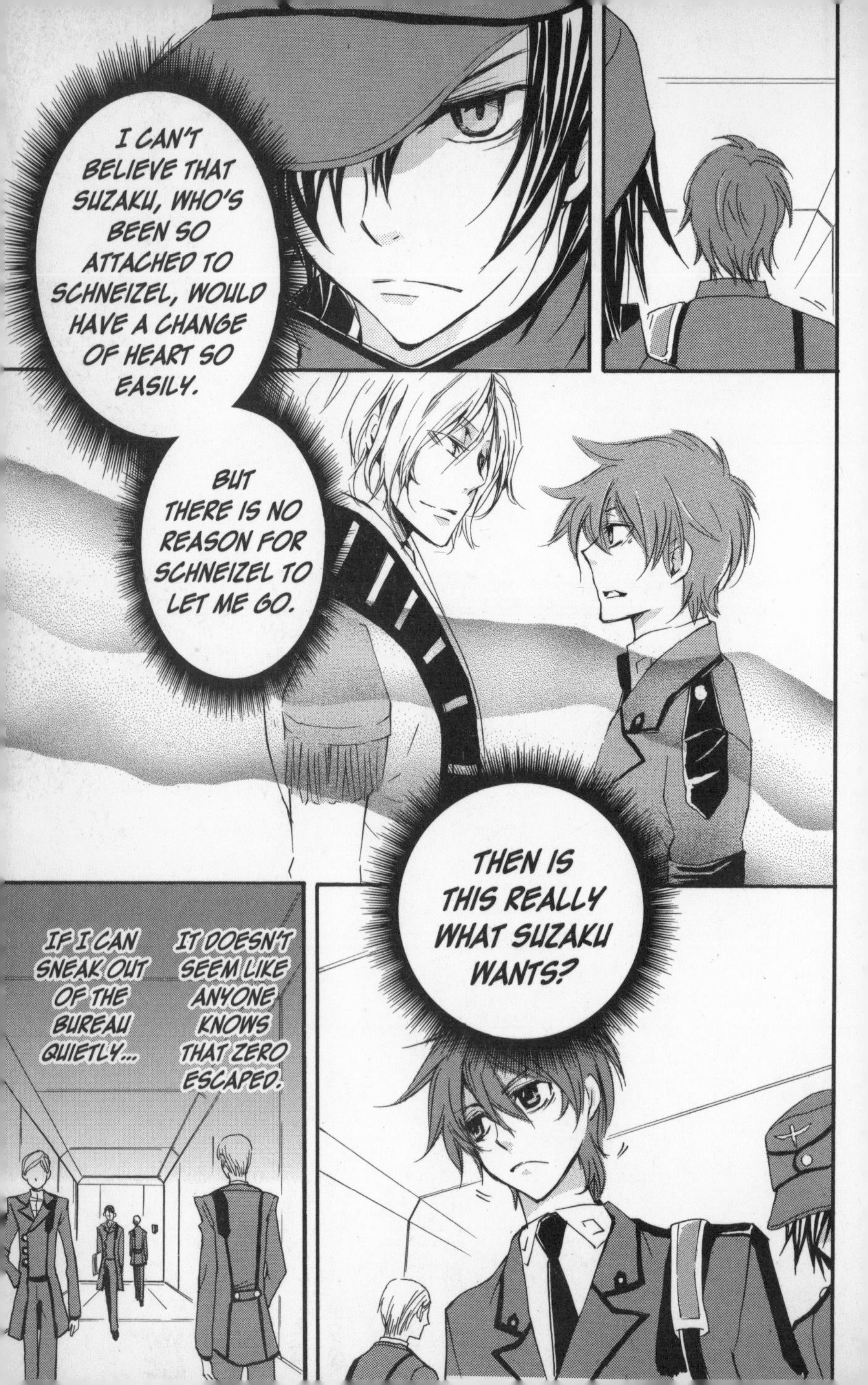
I CAN'T BELIEVE THAT SUZAKU, WHO'S BEEN SO ATTACHED TO SCHNEIZEL, WOULD HAVE A CHANGE OF HEART SO EASILY.
BUT THERE IS NO REASON FOR SCHNEIZEL TO LET ME GO.
THEN IS THIS REALLY WHAT SUZAKU WANTS?
IT DOESN'T SEEM LIKE ANYONE KNOWS THAT ZERO ESCAPED.
IF I CAN SNEAK OUT OF THE BUREAU QUIETLY...

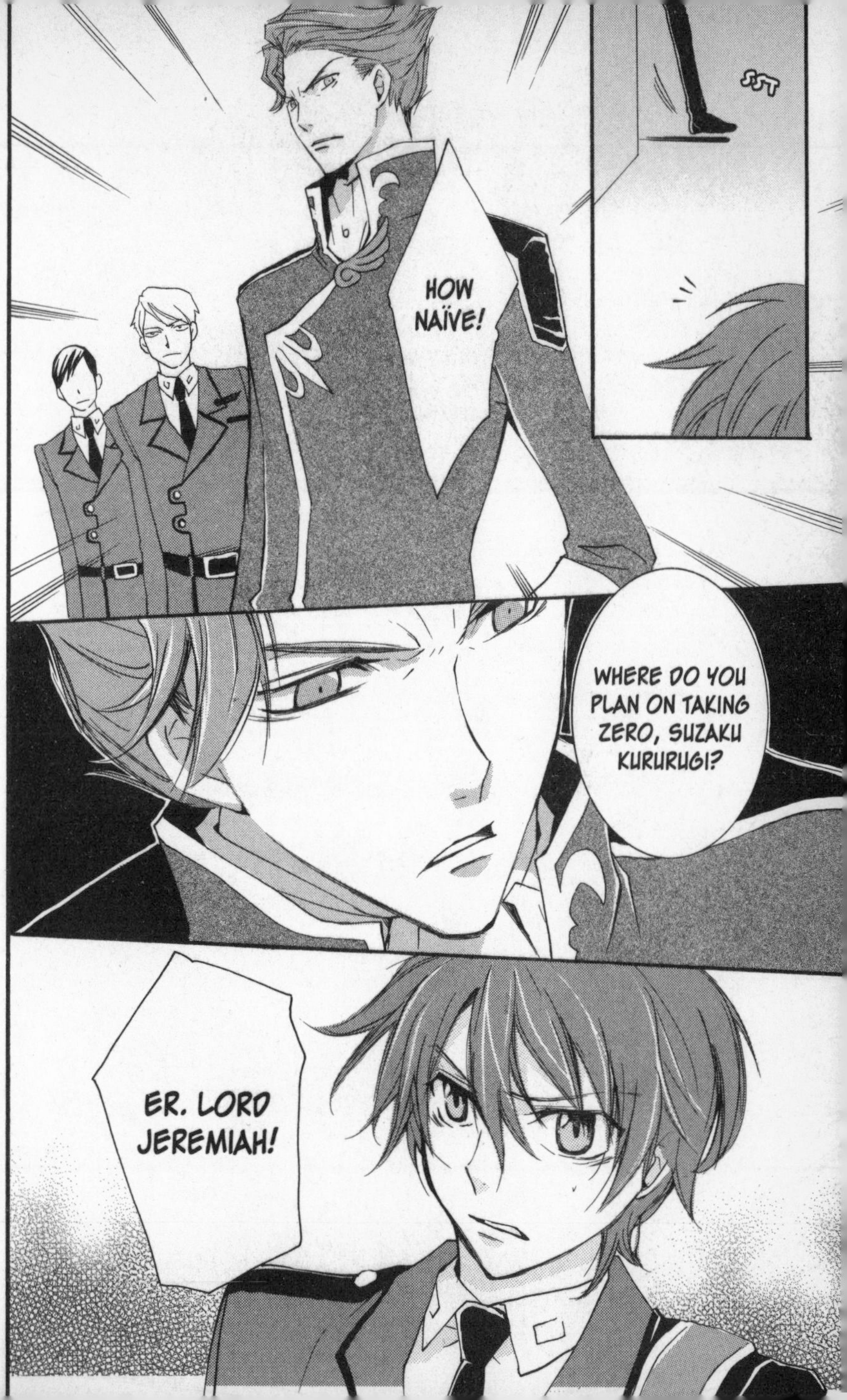
SST
HOW NAÏVE!
WHERE DO YOU PLAN ON TAKING ZERO, SUZAKU KURURUGI?
ER. LORD JEREMIAH!

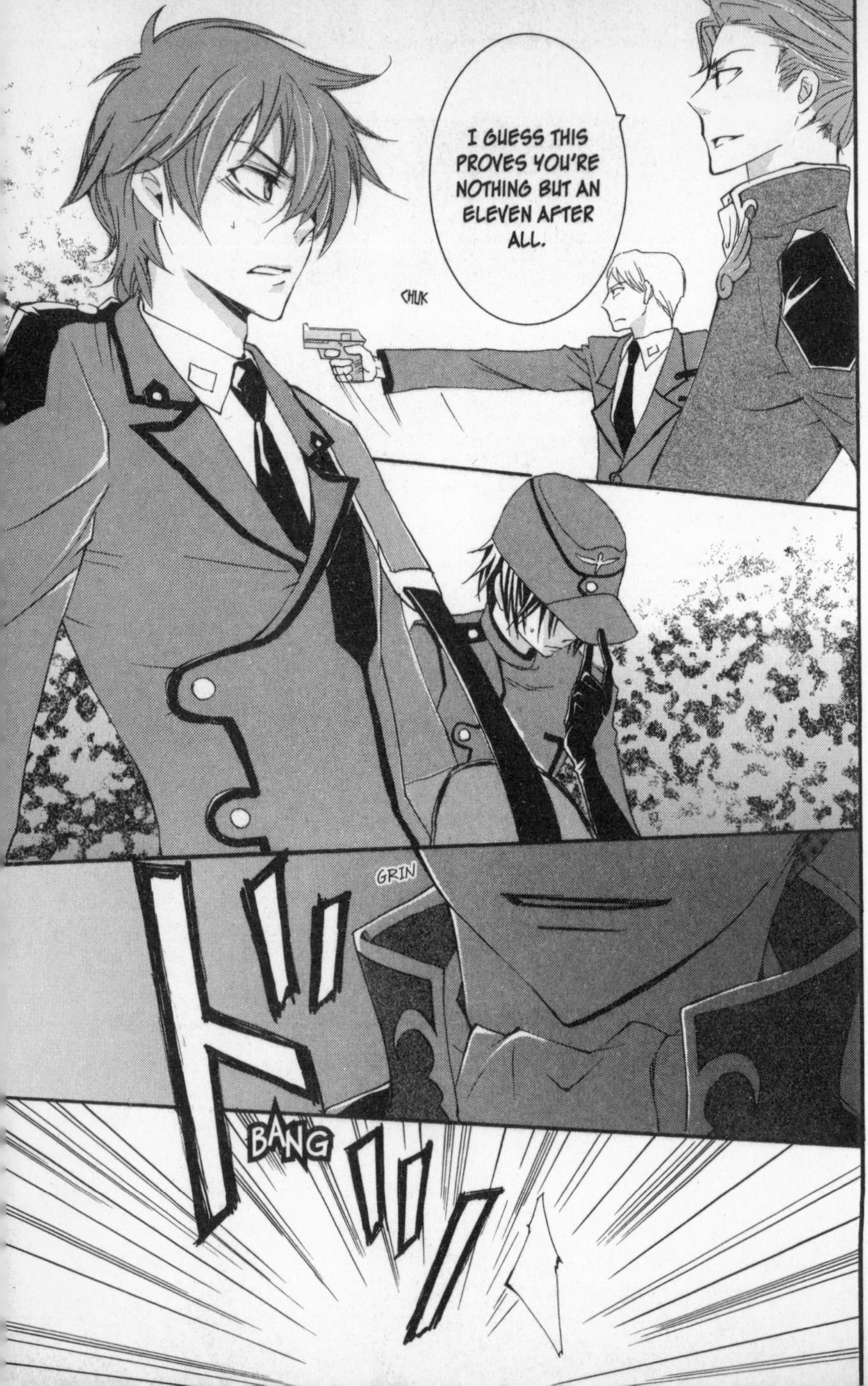
I GUESS THIS PROVES YOU'RE NOTHING BUT AN ELEVEN AFTER ALL.
CHUK
GRIN
BANG

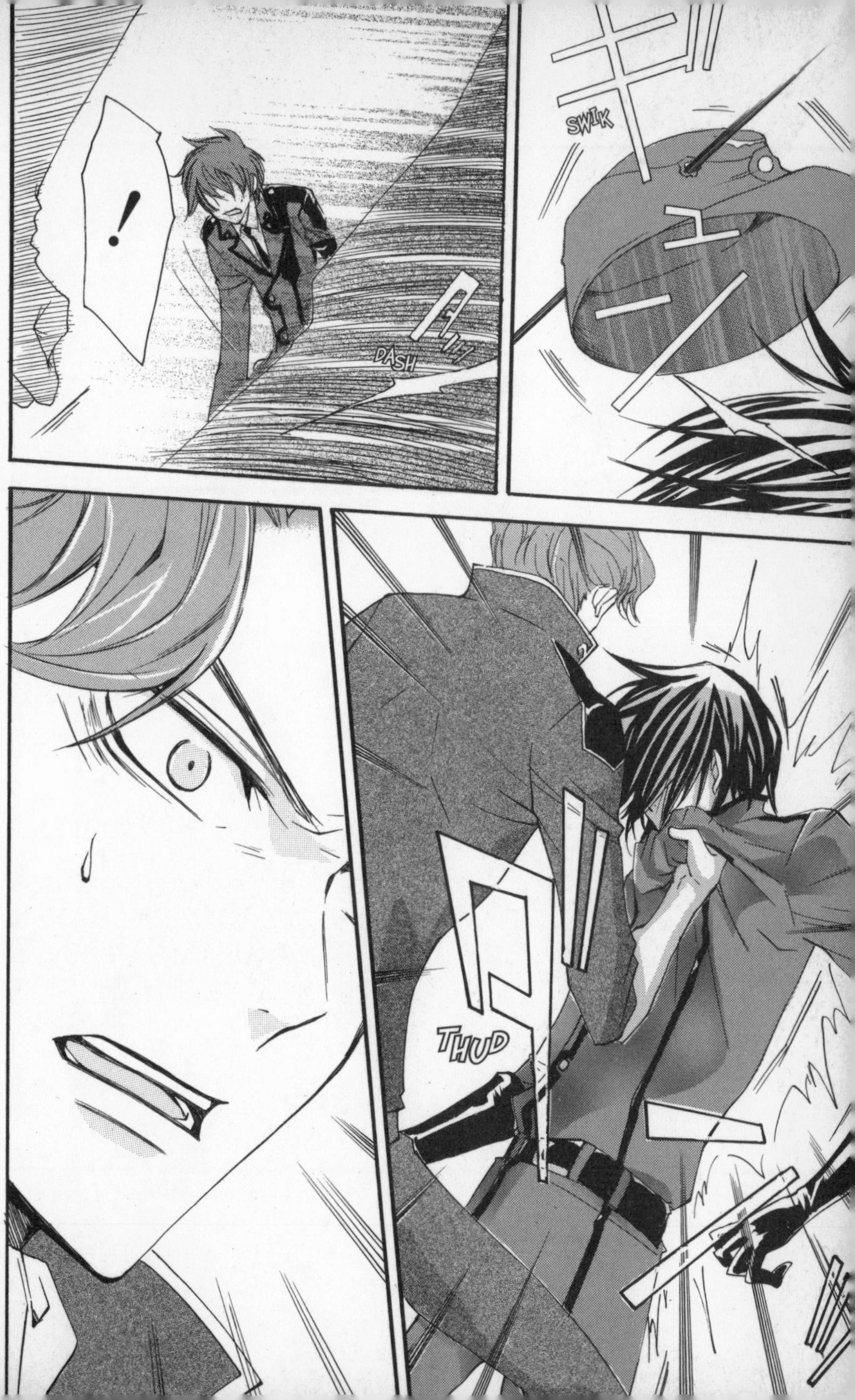
SWIK
!
DASH
THUD

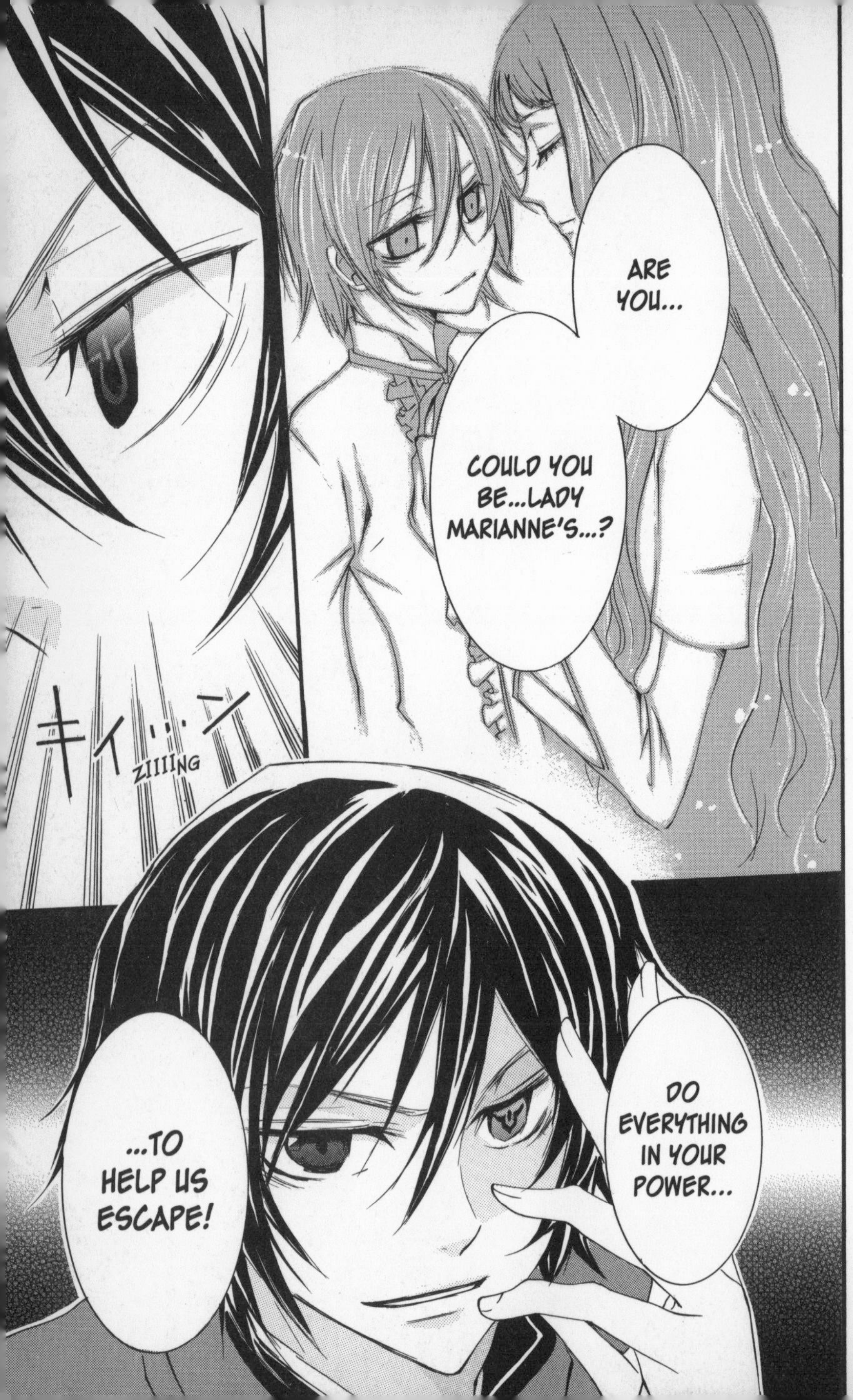
ARE YOU...
COULD YOU BE...LADY MARIANNE'S...?
キィーン
ZIIIING
DO EVERYTHING IN YOUR POWER...
...TO HELP US ESCAPE!

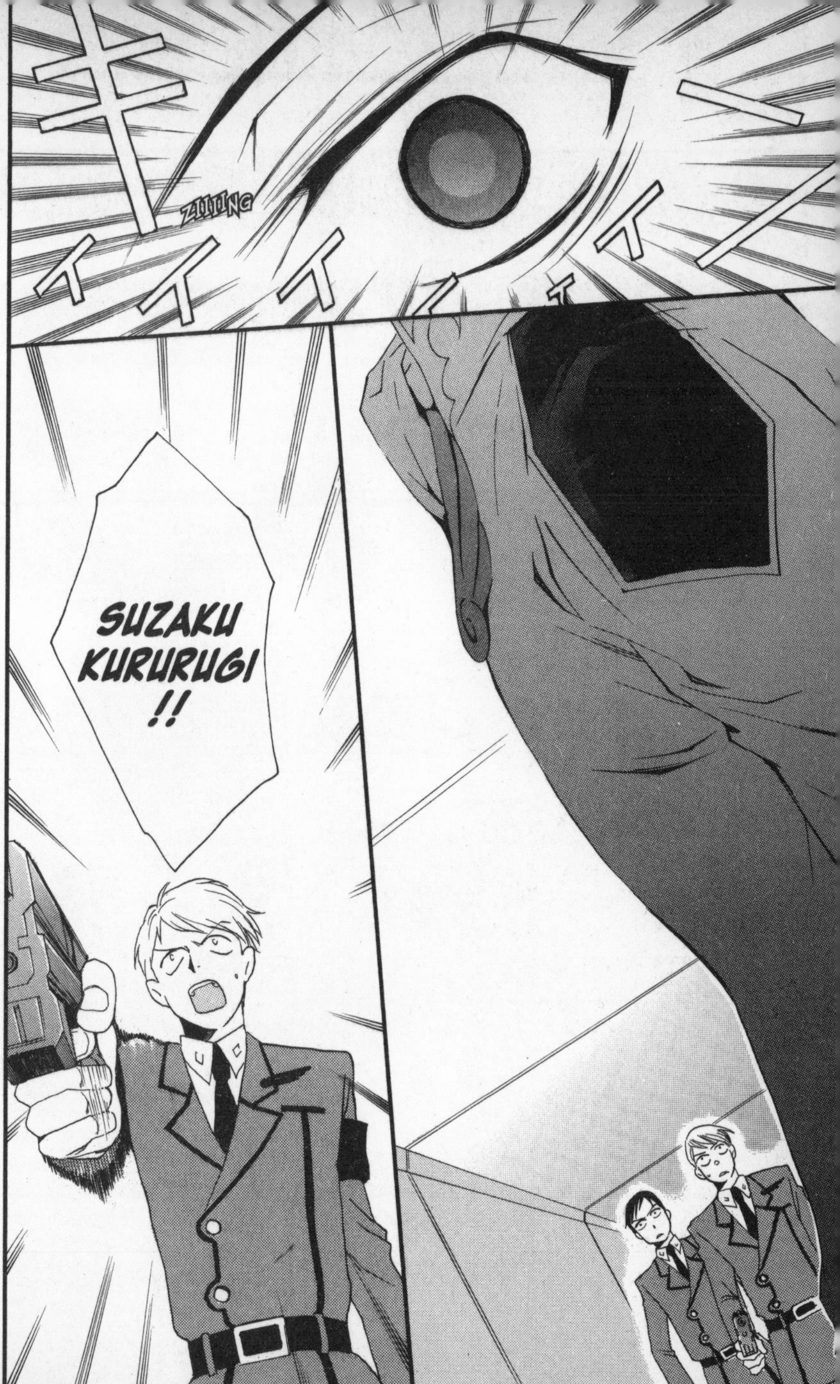
キイイイイイーン
ZIIIING
SUZAKU KURURUGI !!

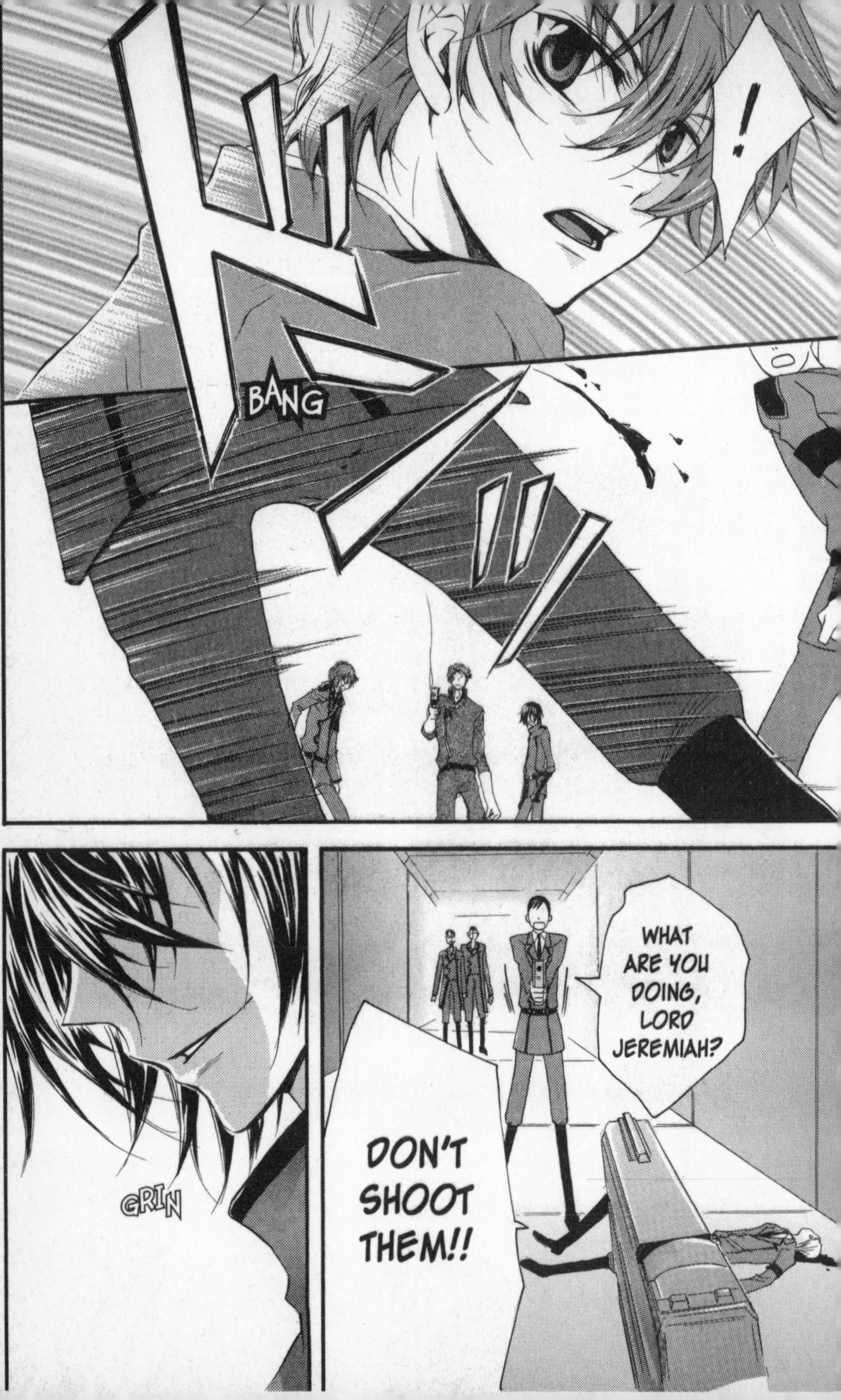
!
BANG
WHAT ARE YOU DOING, LORD JEREMIAH?
DON'T SHOOT THEM!!
GRIN

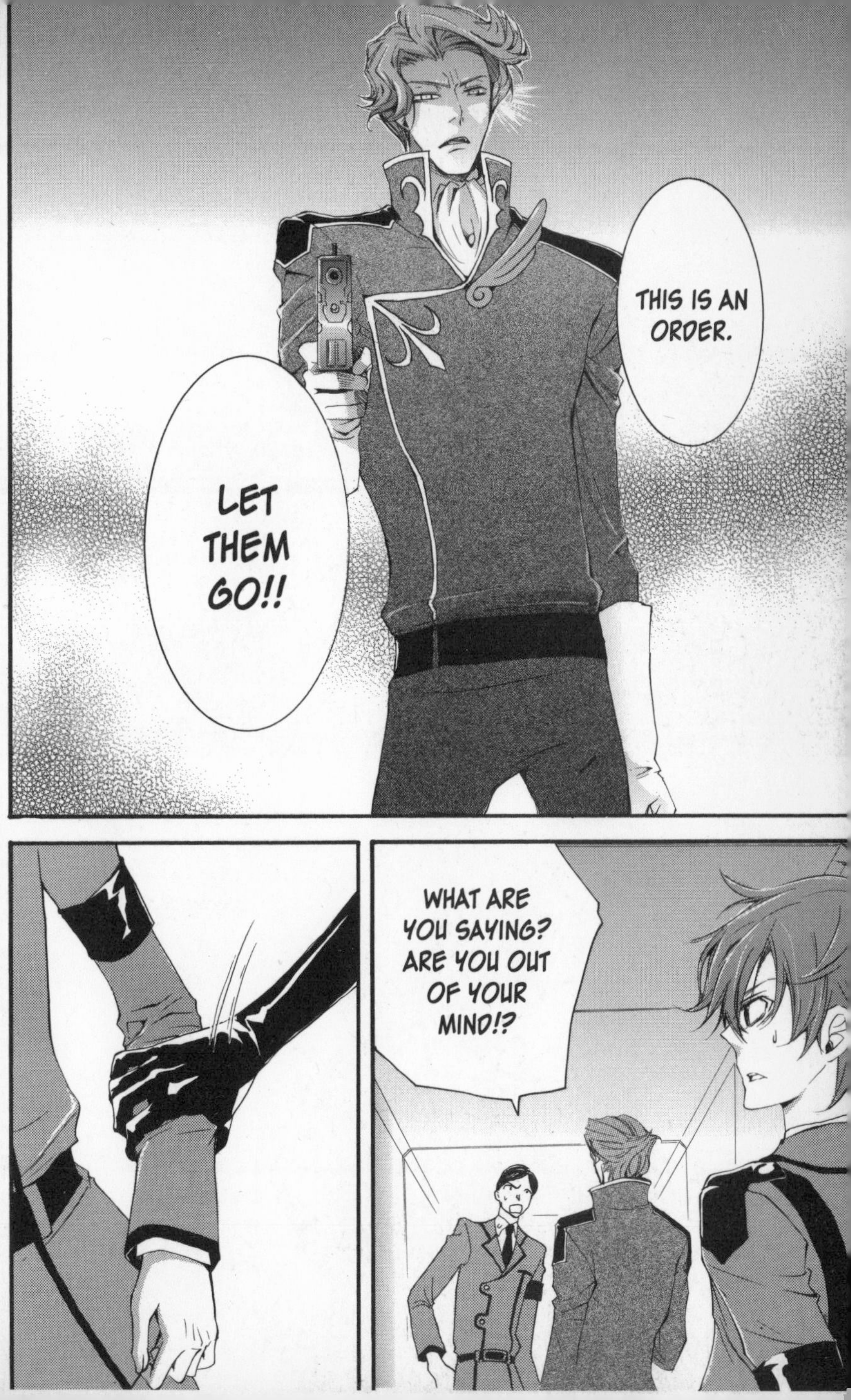
THIS IS AN ORDER.
LET THEM GO!!
WHAT ARE YOU SAYING? ARE YOU OUT OF YOUR MIND!?

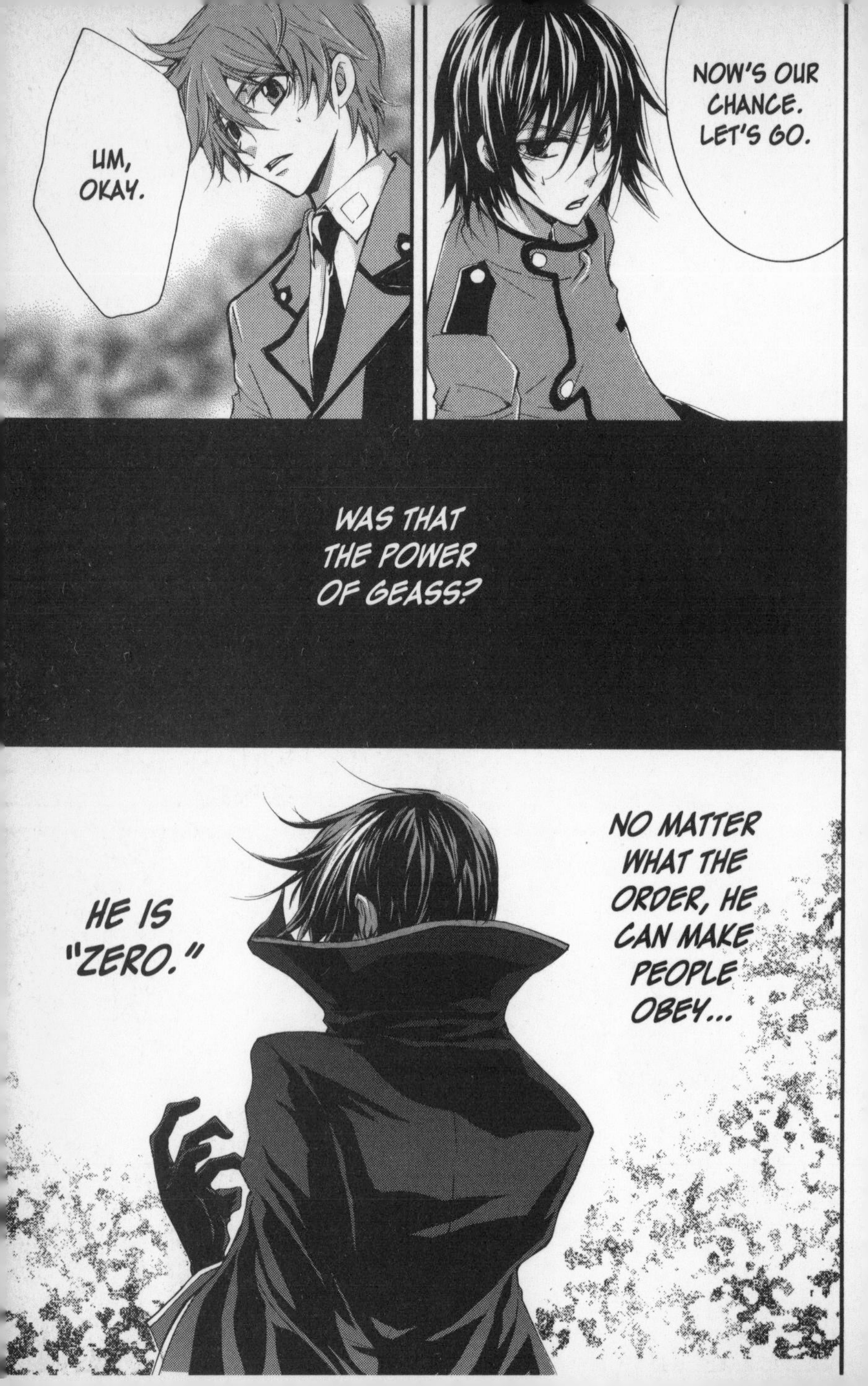
NOW'S OUR CHANCE. LET'S GO.
UM, OKAY.
WAS THAT THE POWER OF GEASS?
NO MATTER WHAT THE ORDER, HE CAN MAKE PEOPLE OBEY...
HE IS "ZERO."

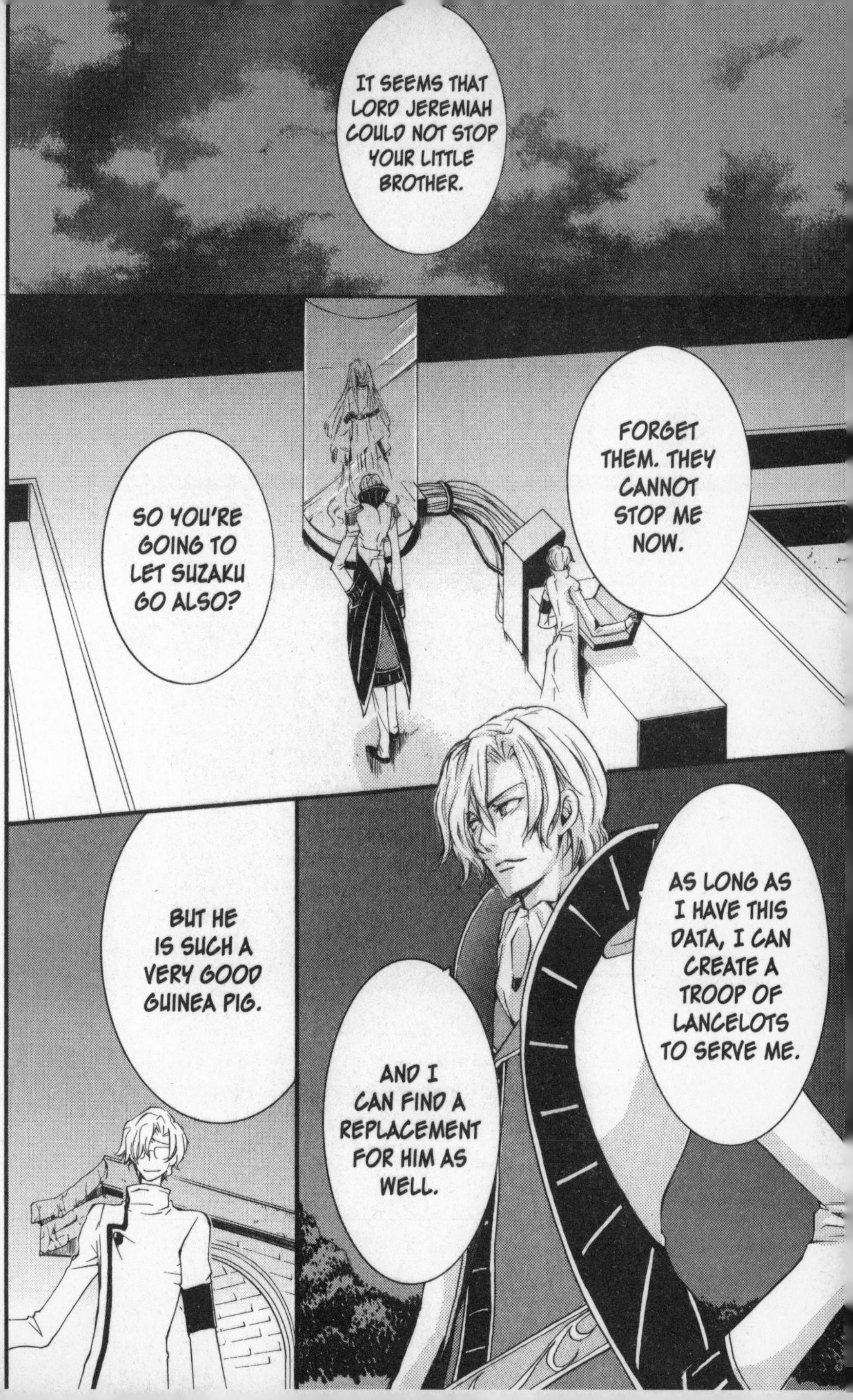
IT SEEMS THAT LORD JEREMIAH COULD NOT STOP YOUR LITTLE BROTHER.
FORGET THEM. THEY CANNOT STOP ME NOW.
SO YOU'RE GOING TO LET SUZAKU GO ALSO?
AS LONG AS I HAVE THIS DATA, I CAN CREATE A TROOP OF LANCELOTS TO SERVE ME.
AND I CAN FIND A REPLACEMENT FOR HIM AS WELL.
BUT HE IS SUCH A VERY GOOD GUINEA PIG.

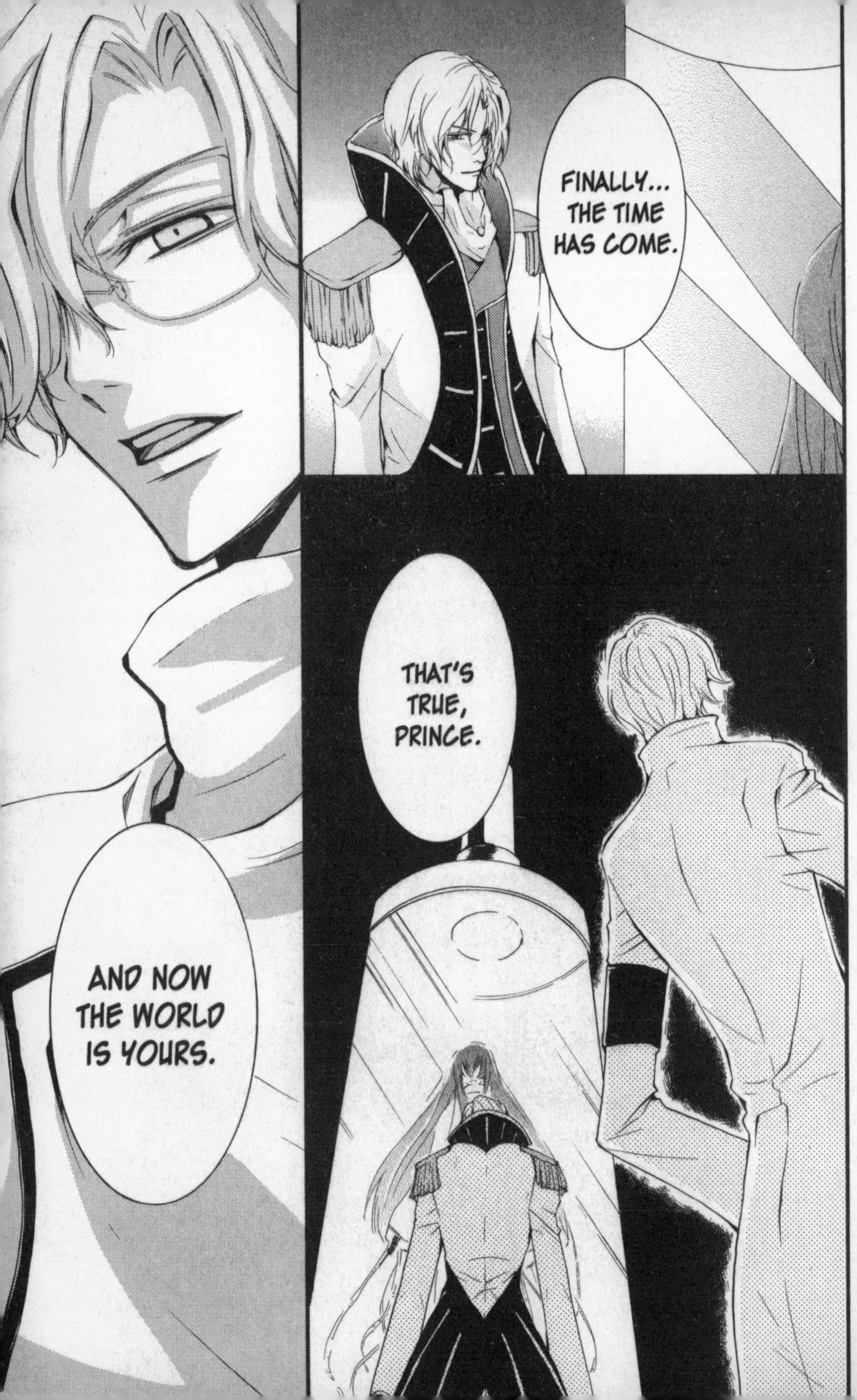
FINALLY... THE TIME HAS COME.
THAT'S TRUE, PRINCE.
AND NOW THE WORLD IS YOURS.

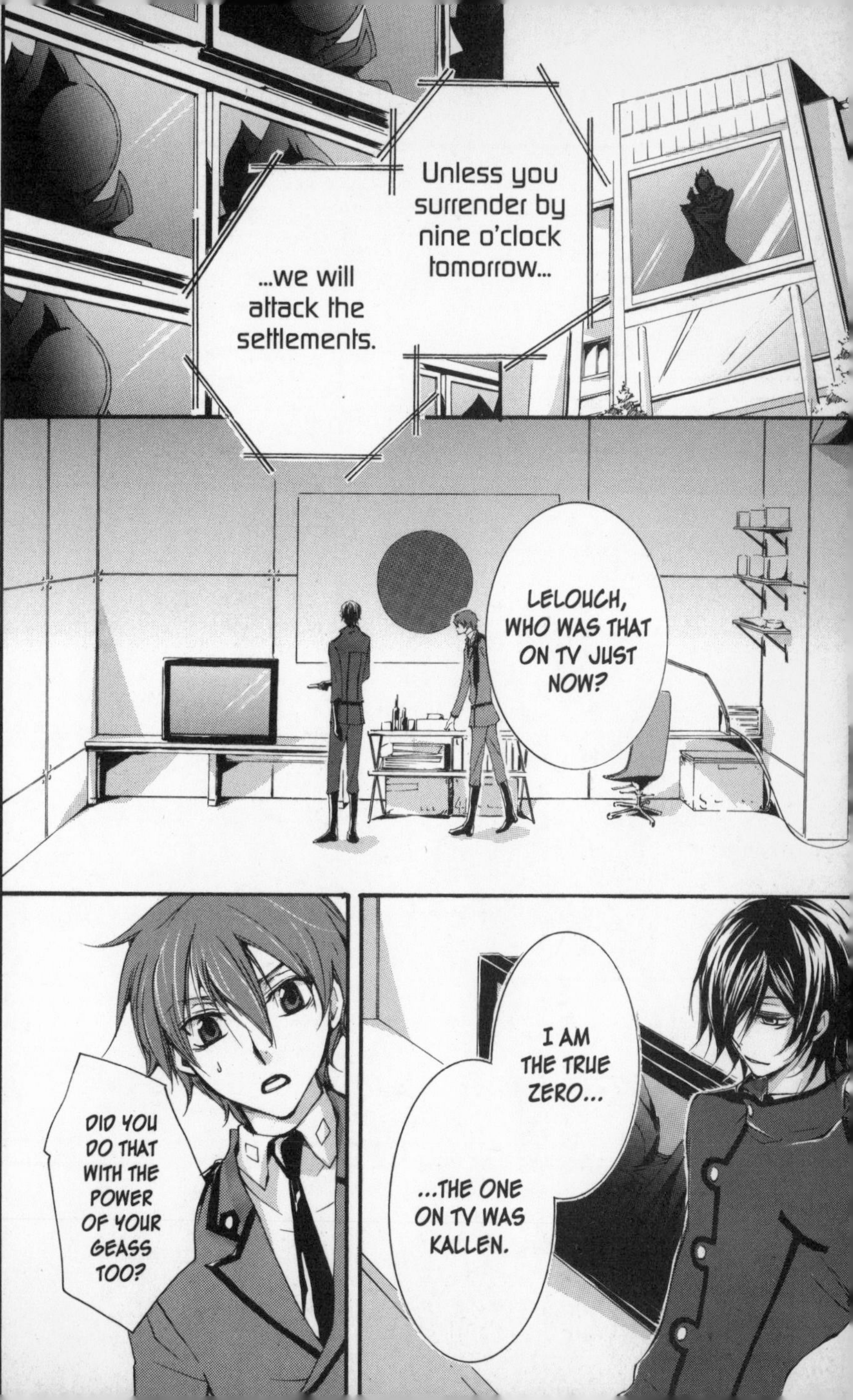
Unless you surrender by nine o'clock tomorrow...
...we will attack the settlements.
LELOUCH, WHO WAS THAT ON TV JUST NOW?
I AM THE TRUE ZERO...
...THE ONE ON TV WAS KALLEN.
DID YOU DO THAT WITH THE POWER OF YOUR GEASS TOO?

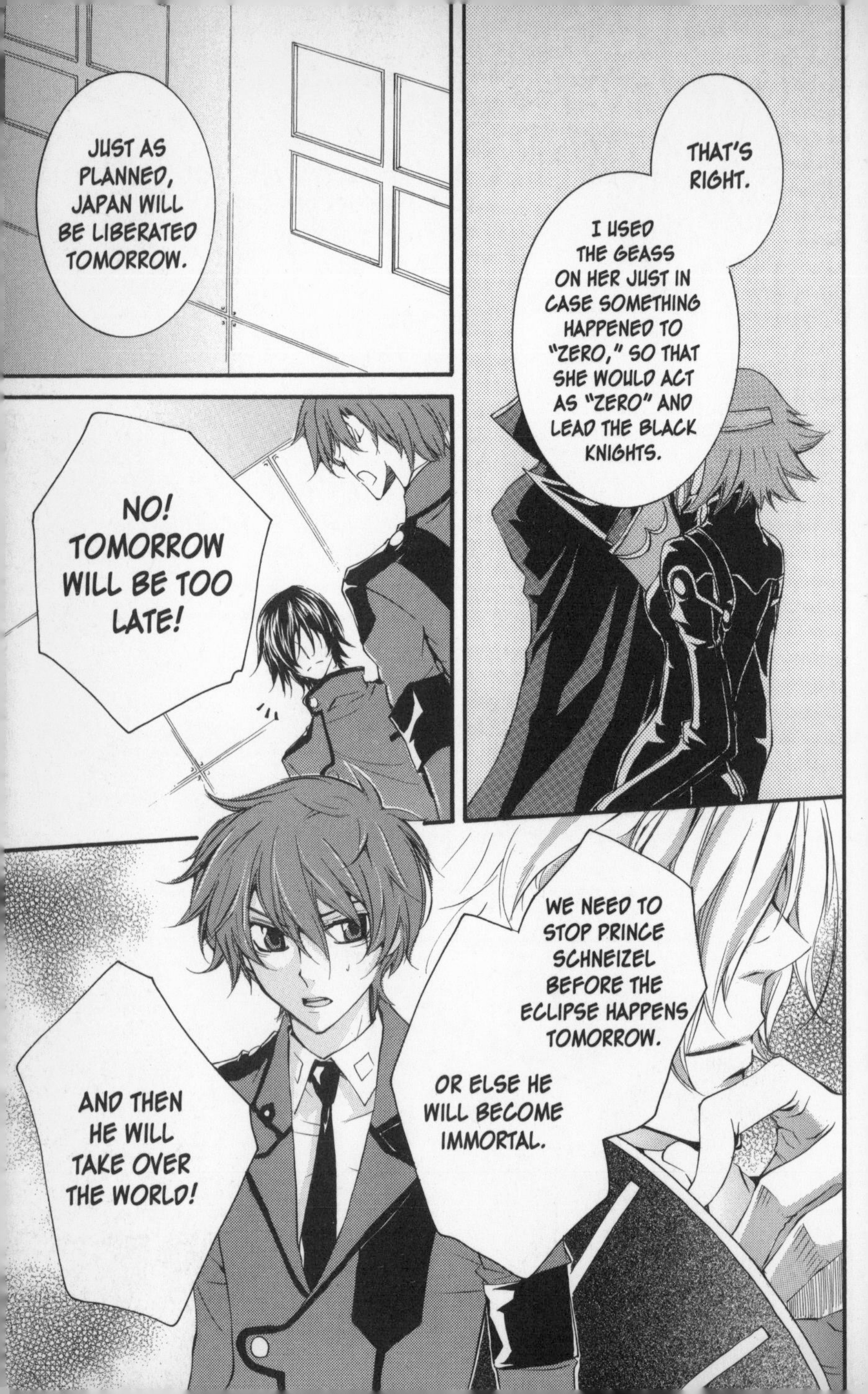
THAT'S RIGHT.
I USED THE GEASS ON HER JUST IN CASE SOMETHING HAPPENED TO "ZERO," SO THAT SHE WOULD ACT AS "ZERO" AND LEAD THE BLACK KNIGHTS.
JUST AS PLANNED, JAPAN WILL BE LIBERATED TOMORROW.
NO! TOMORROW WILL BE TOO LATE!
WE NEED TO STOP PRINCE SCHNEIZEL BEFORE THE ECLIPSE HAPPENS TOMORROW.
OR ELSE HE WILL BECOME IMMORTAL.
AND THEN HE WILL TAKE OVER THE WORLD!

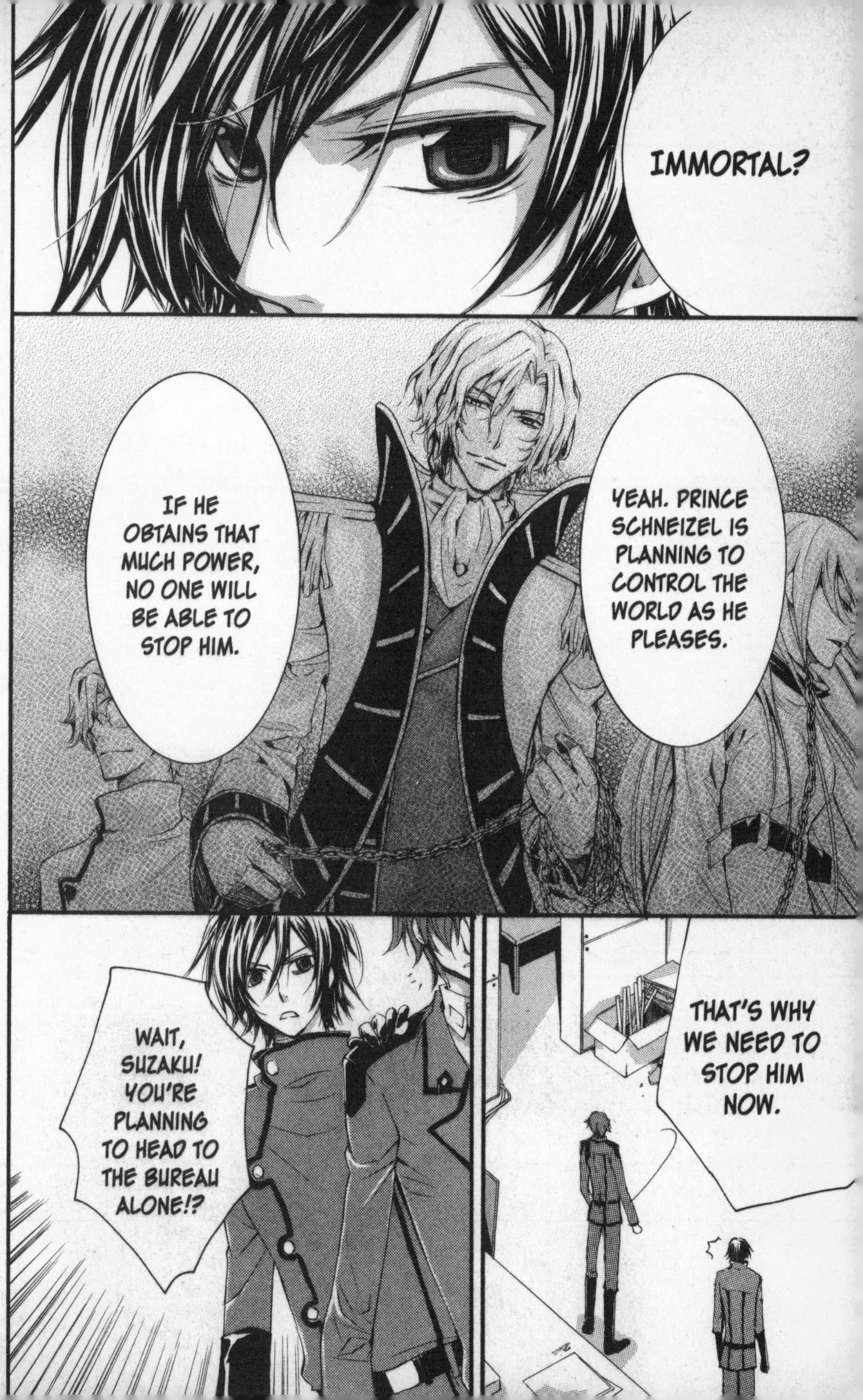
IMMORTAL?
YEAH. PRINCE SCHNEIZEL IS PLANNING TO CONTROL THE WORLD AS HE PLEASES.
IF HE OBTAINS THAT MUCH POWER, NO ONE WILL BE ABLE TO STOP HIM.
THAT'S WHY WE NEED TO STOP HIM NOW.
WAIT, SUZAKU! YOU'RE PLANNING TO HEAD TO THE BUREAU ALONE!?

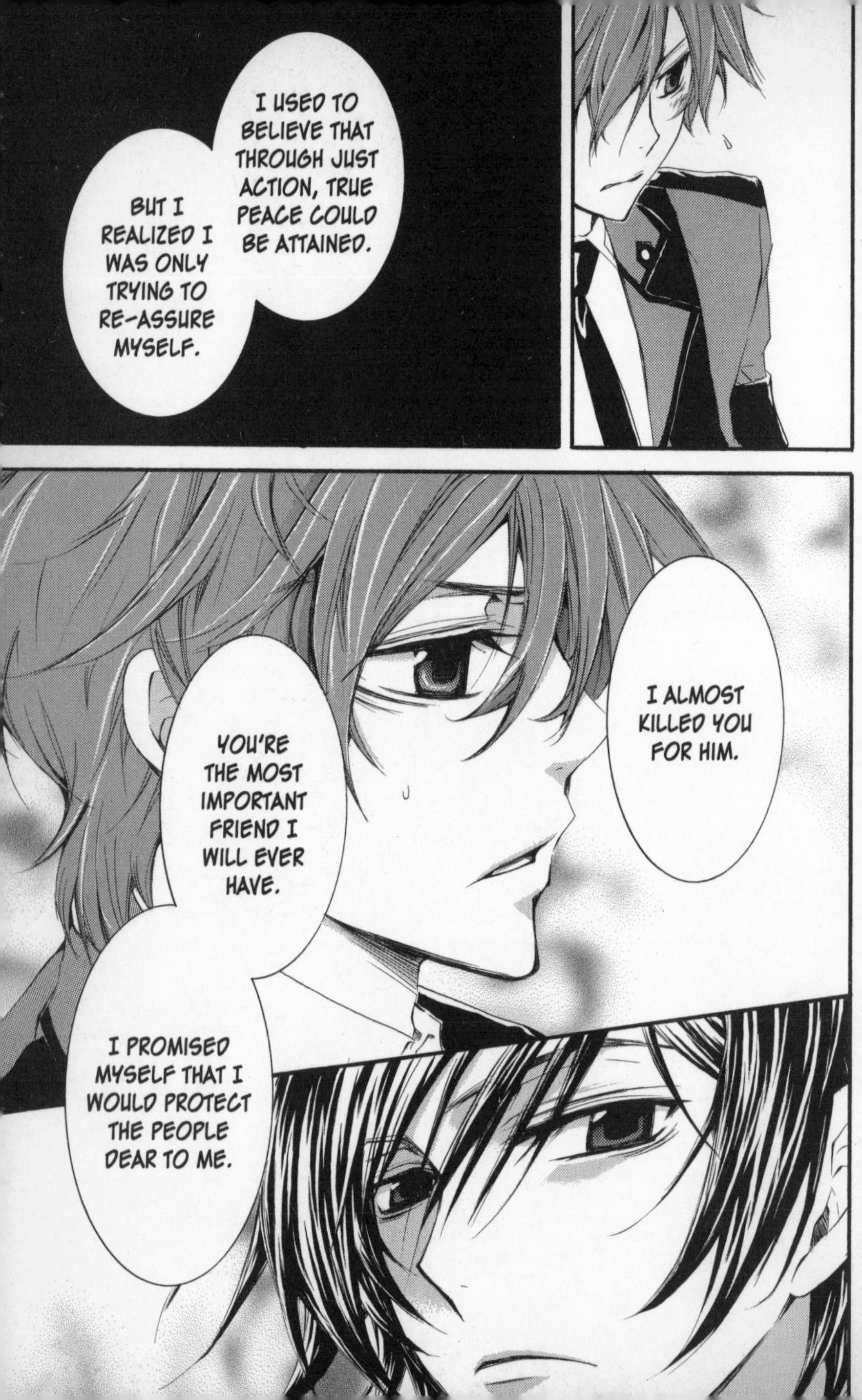
I USED TO BELIEVE THAT THROUGH JUST ACTION, TRUE PEACE COULD BE ATTAINED.
BUT I REALIZED I WAS ONLY TRYING TO RE-ASSURE MYSELF.
I ALMOST KILLED YOU FOR HIM.
YOU'RE THE MOST IMPORTANT FRIEND I WILL EVER HAVE.
I PROMISED MYSELF THAT I WOULD PROTECT THE PEOPLE DEAR TO ME.

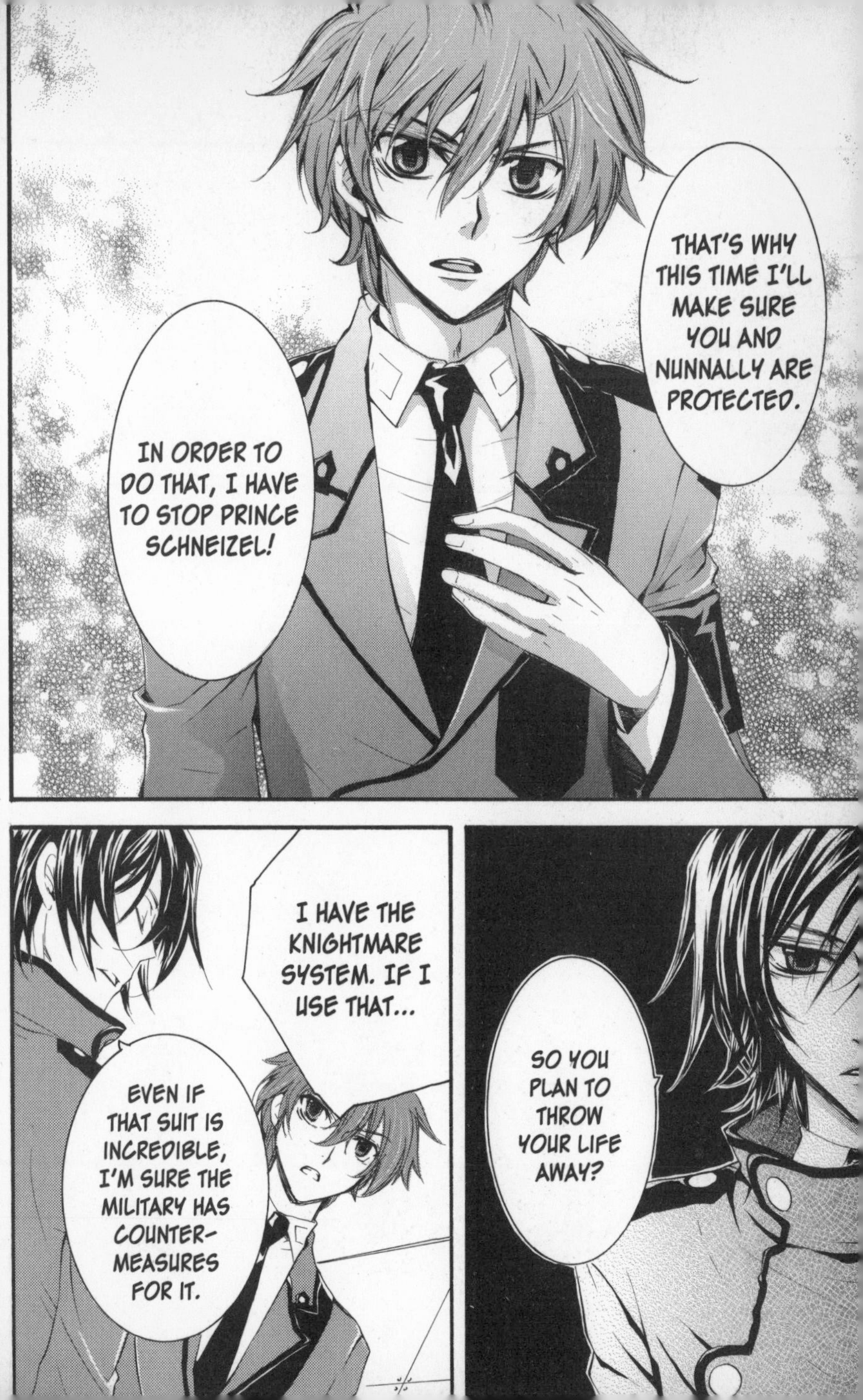
THAT'S WHY THIS TIME I'LL MAKE SURE YOU AND NUNNALLY ARE PROTECTED.
IN ORDER TO DO THAT, I HAVE TO STOP PRINCE SCHNEIZEL!
SO YOU PLAN TO THROW YOUR LIFE AWAY?
I HAVE THE KNIGHTMARE SYSTEM. IF I USE THAT...
EVEN IF THAT SUIT IS INCREDIBLE, I'M SURE THE MILITARY HAS COUNTER-MEASURES FOR IT.

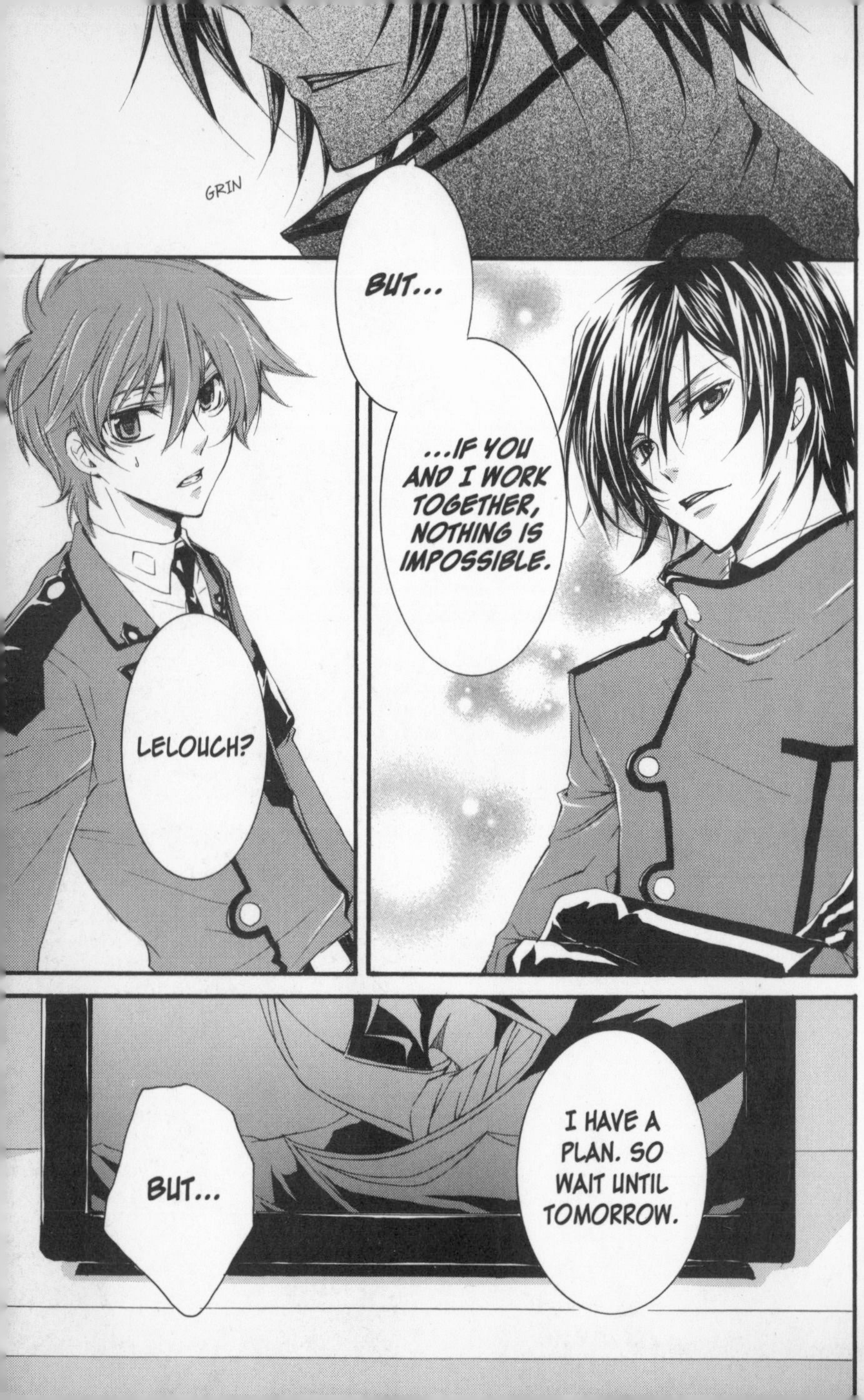
GRIN
BUT...
...IF YOU AND I WORK TOGETHER, NOTHING IS IMPOSSIBLE.
LELOUCH?
I HAVE A PLAN. SO WAIT UNTIL TOMORROW.
BUT...

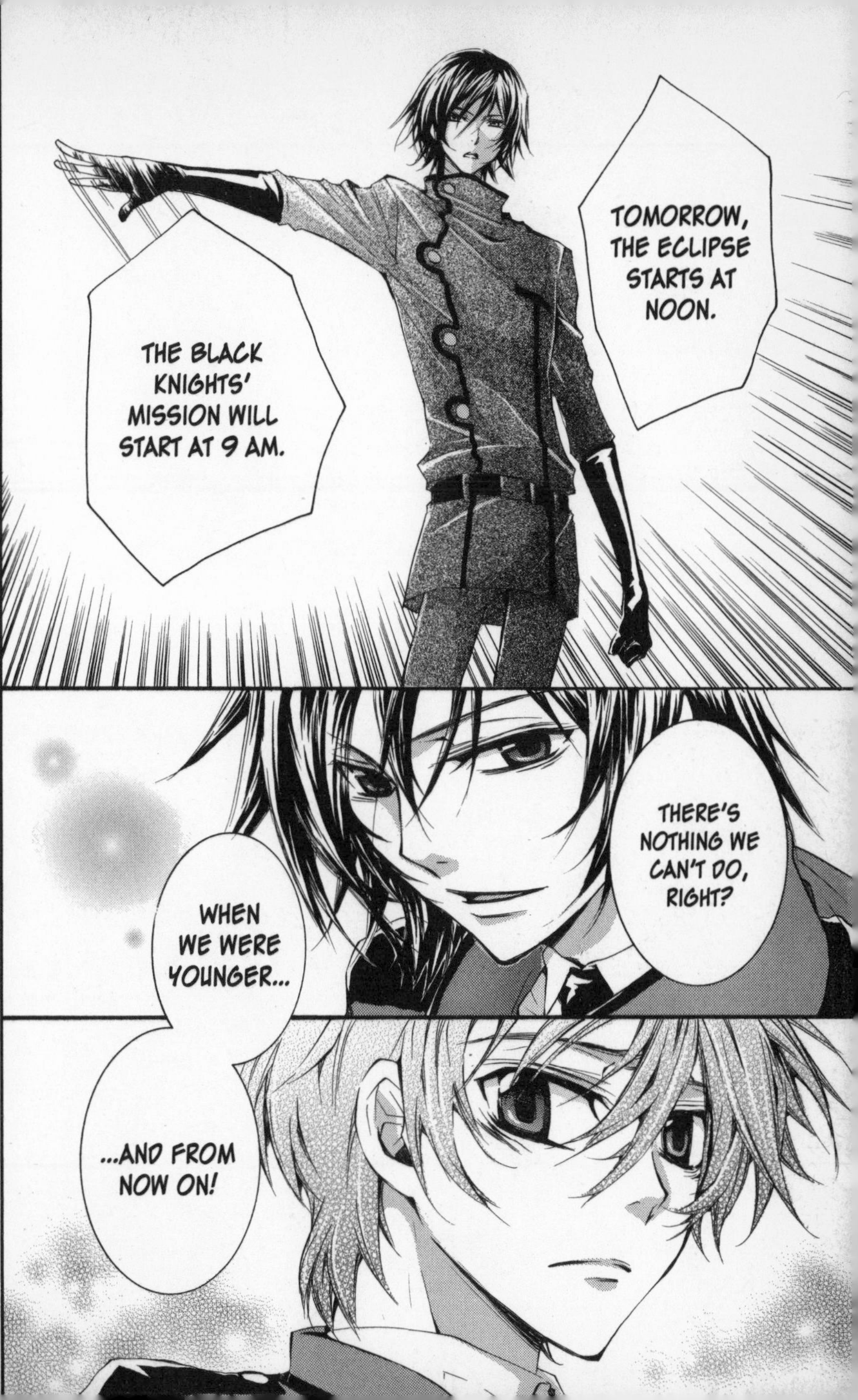
TOMORROW, THE ECLIPSE STARTS AT NOON.
THE BLACK KNIGHTS' MISSION WILL START AT 9 AM.
THERE'S NOTHING WE CAN'T DO, RIGHT?
WHEN WE WERE YOUNGER...
...AND FROM NOW ON!

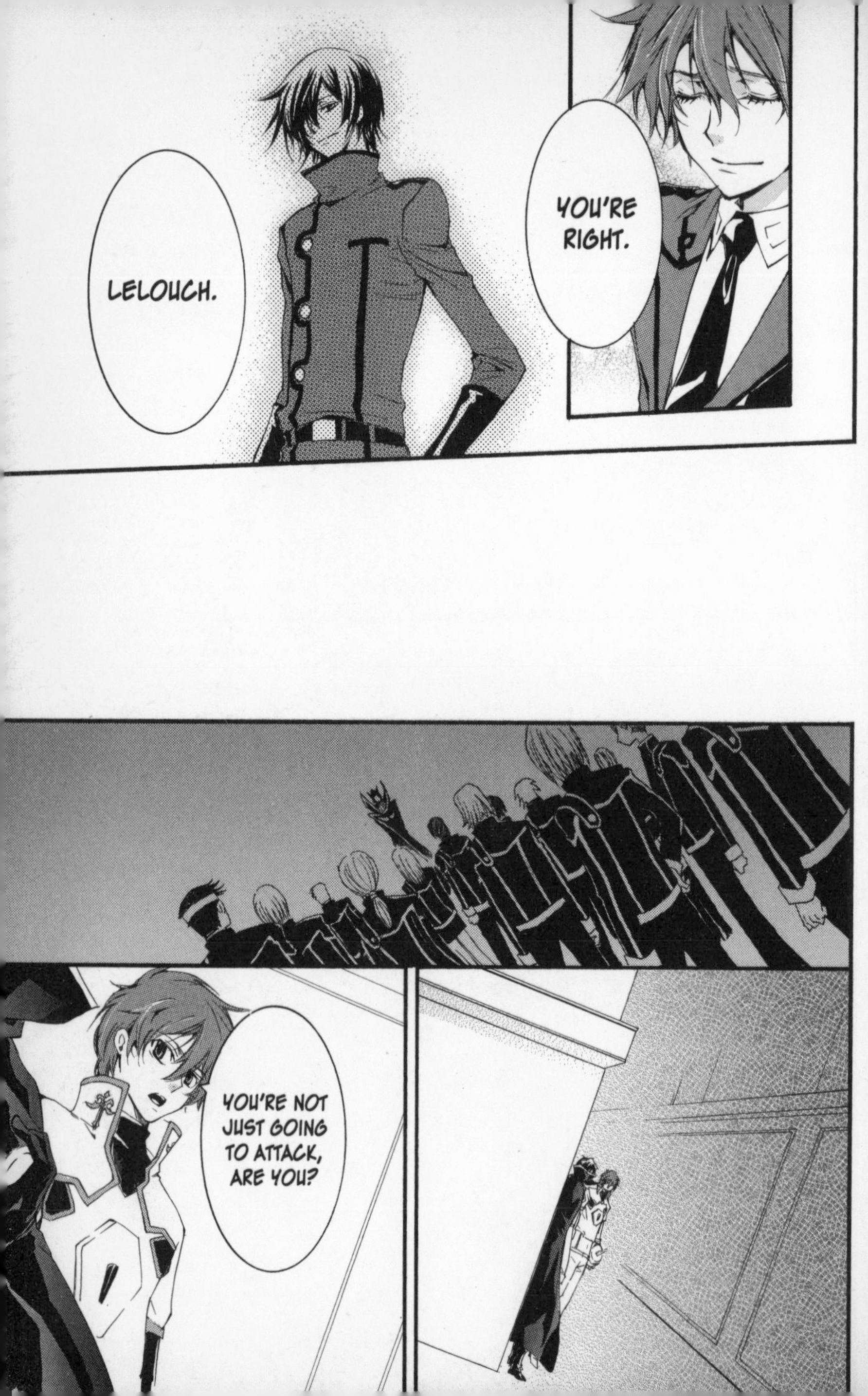
YOU'RE RIGHT.
LELOUCH.
YOU'RE NOT JUST GOING TO ATTACK, ARE YOU?

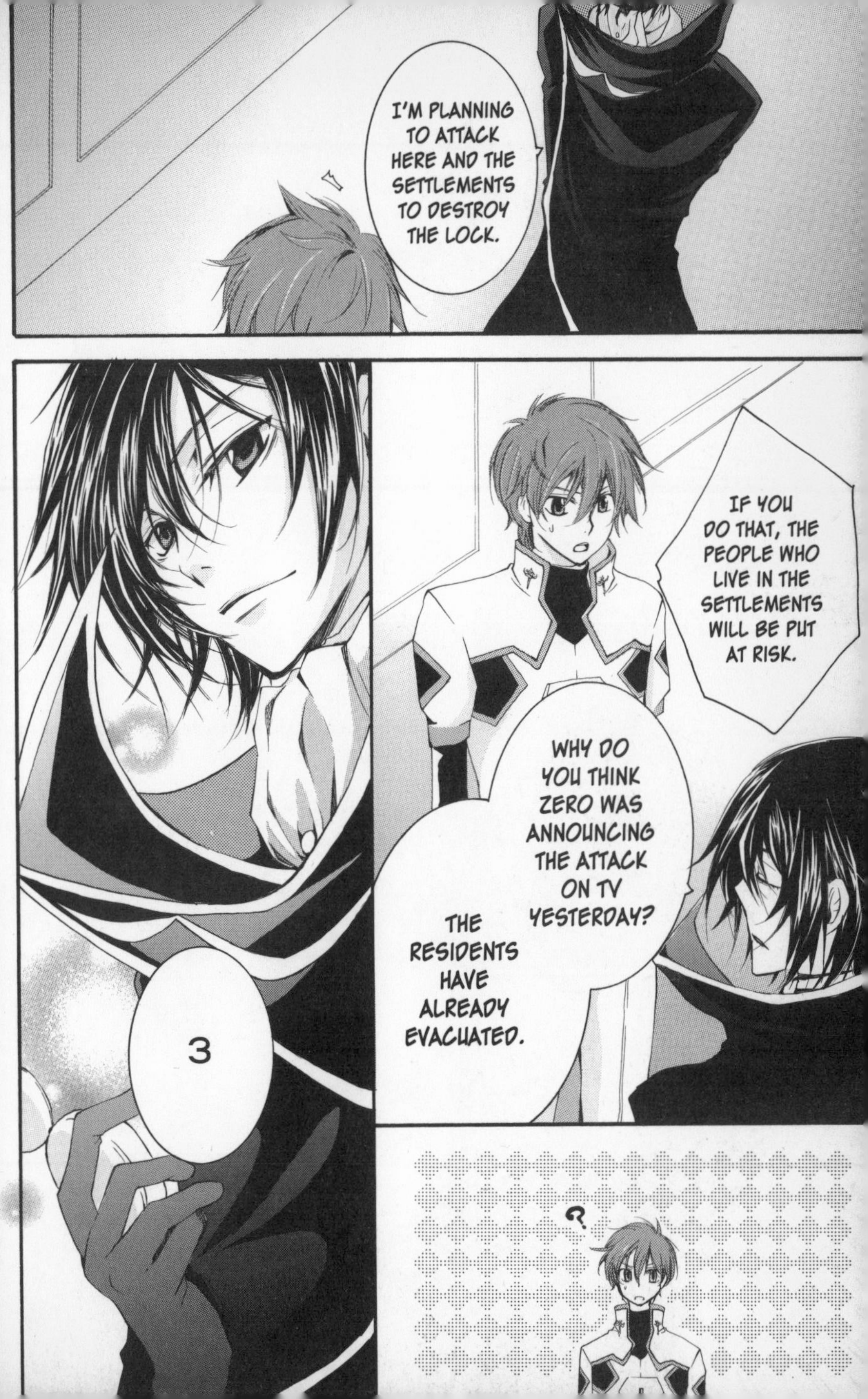
I'M PLANNING TO ATTACK HERE AND THE SETTLEMENTS TO DESTROY THE LOCK.
IF YOU DO THAT, THE PEOPLE WHO LIVE IN THE SETTLEMENTS WILL BE PUT AT RISK.
WHY DO YOU THINK ZERO WAS ANNOUNCING THE ATTACK ON TV YESTERDAY?
THE RESIDENTS HAVE ALREADY EVACUATED.
?
3

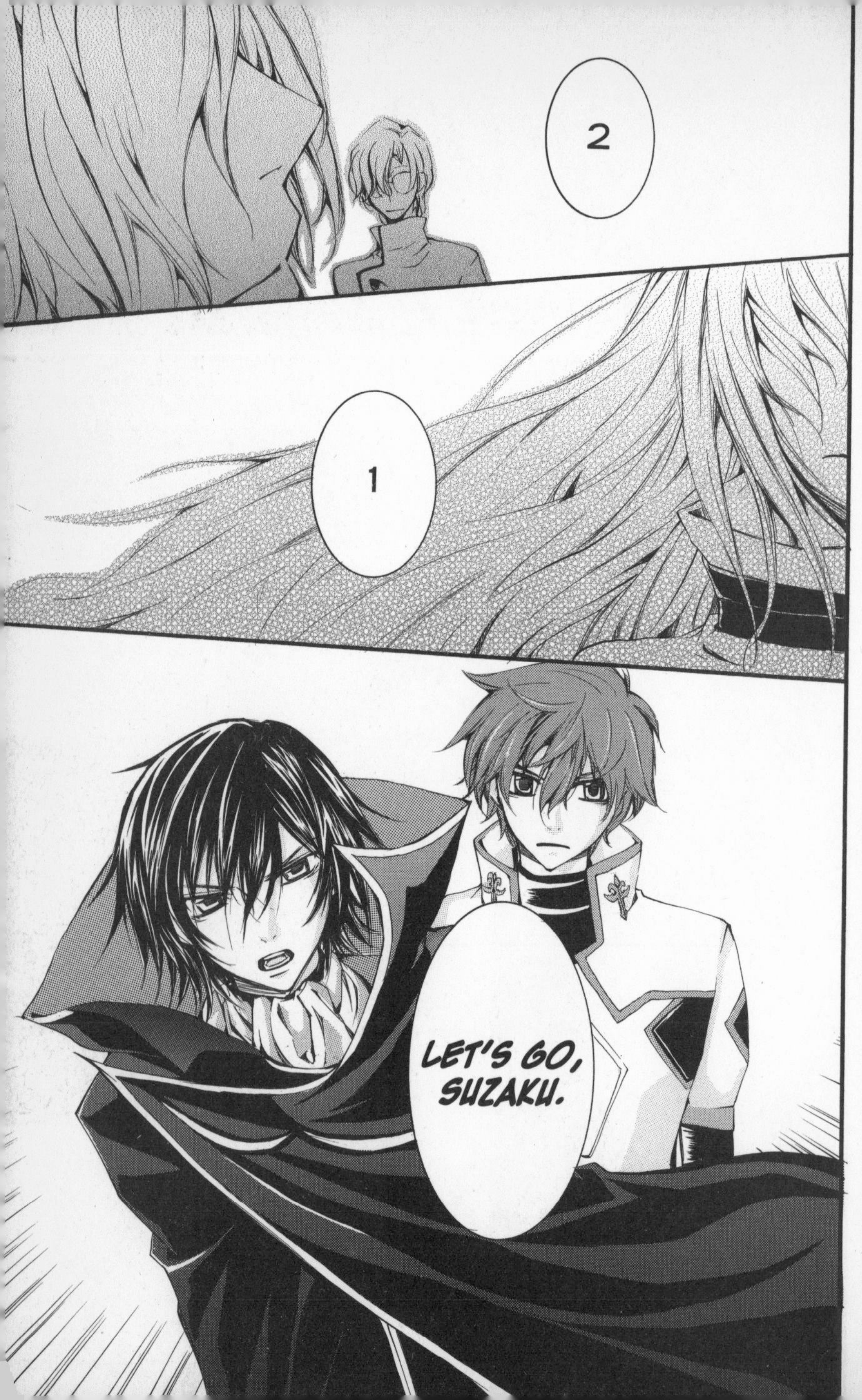
2
1
LET'S GO, SUZAKU.

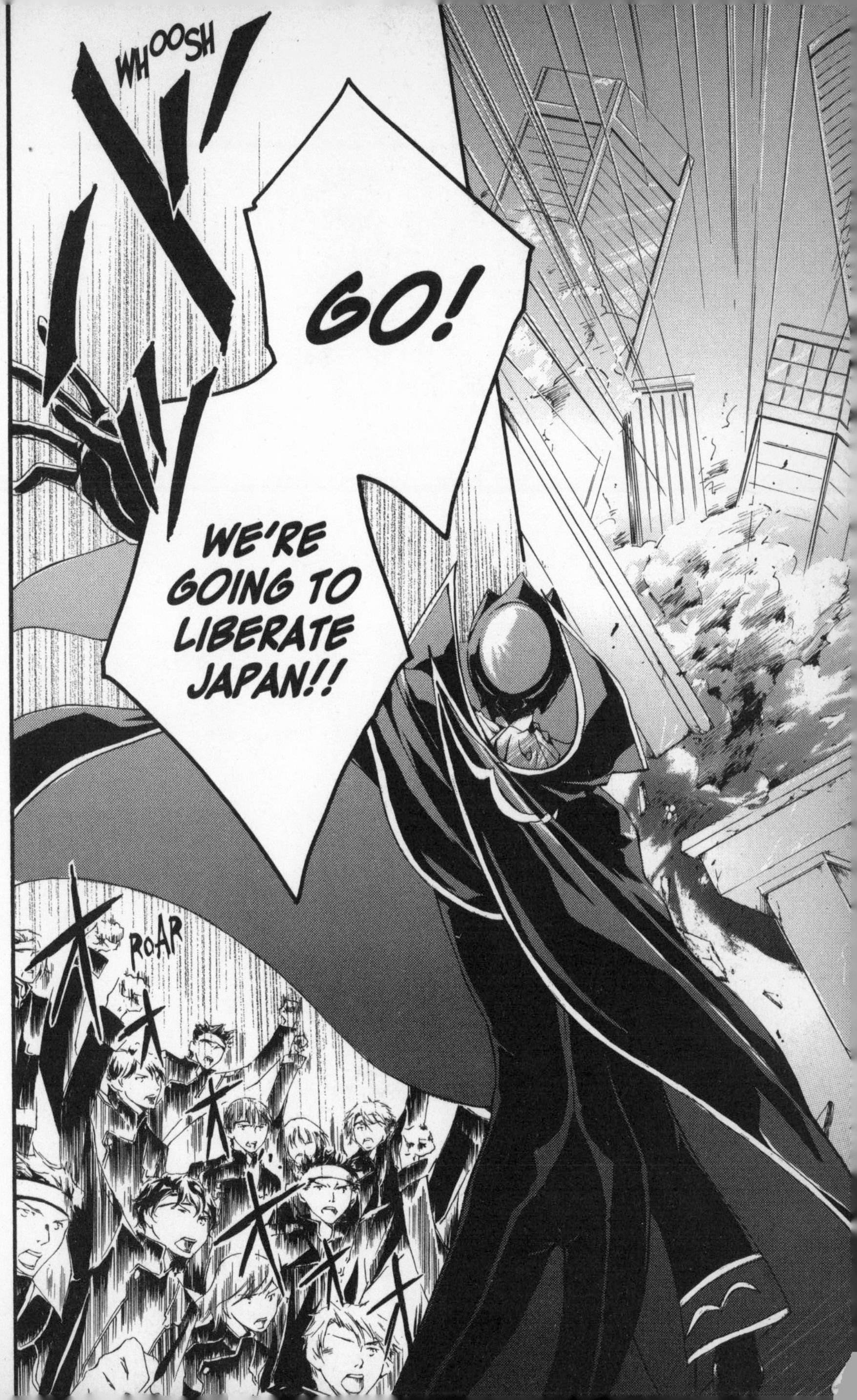
WHOOSH
GO!
WE'RE GOING TO LIBERATE JAPAN!!
ROAR

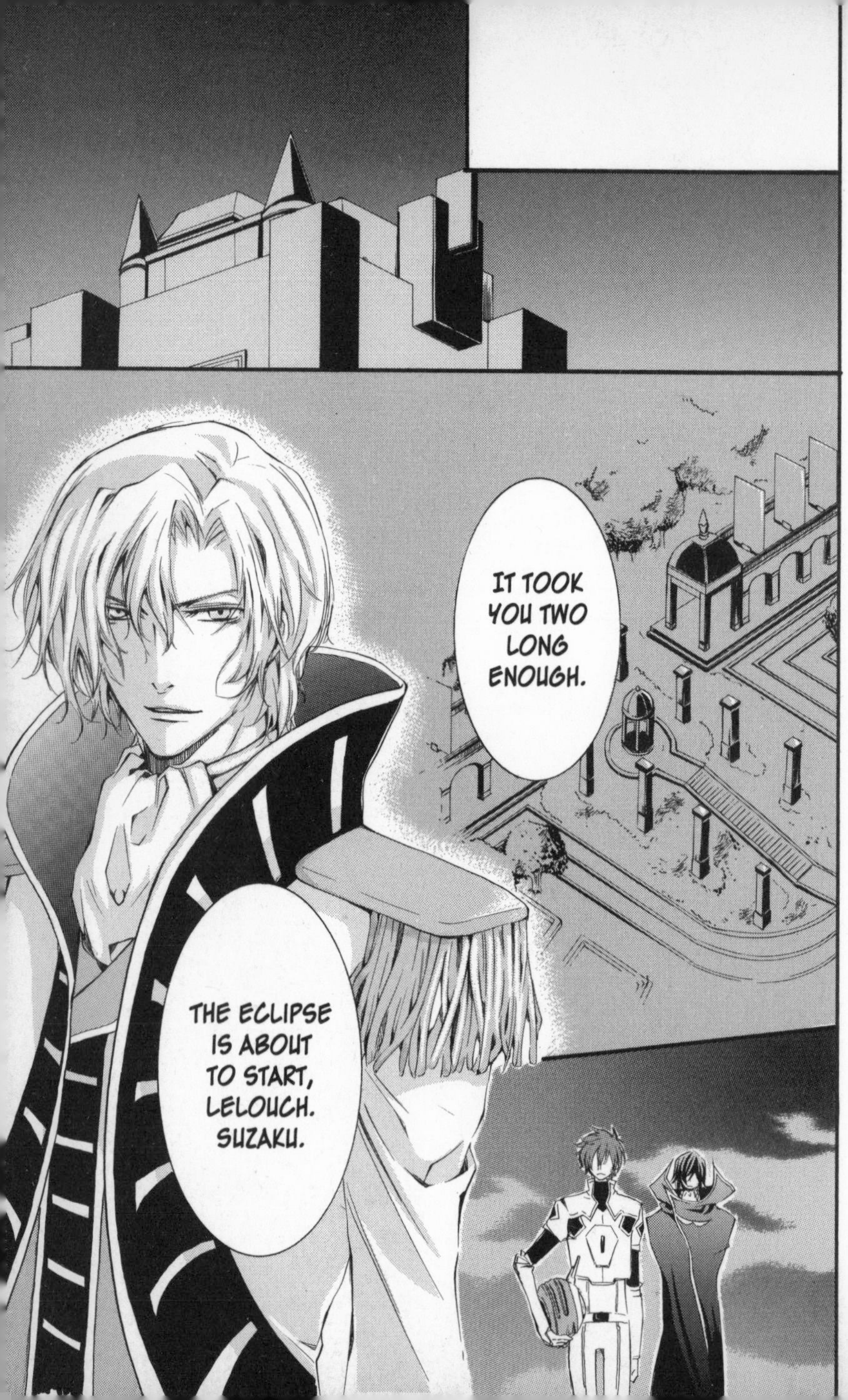
IT TOOK YOU TWO LONG ENOUGH.
THE ECLIPSE IS ABOUT TO START, LELOUCH. SUZAKU.

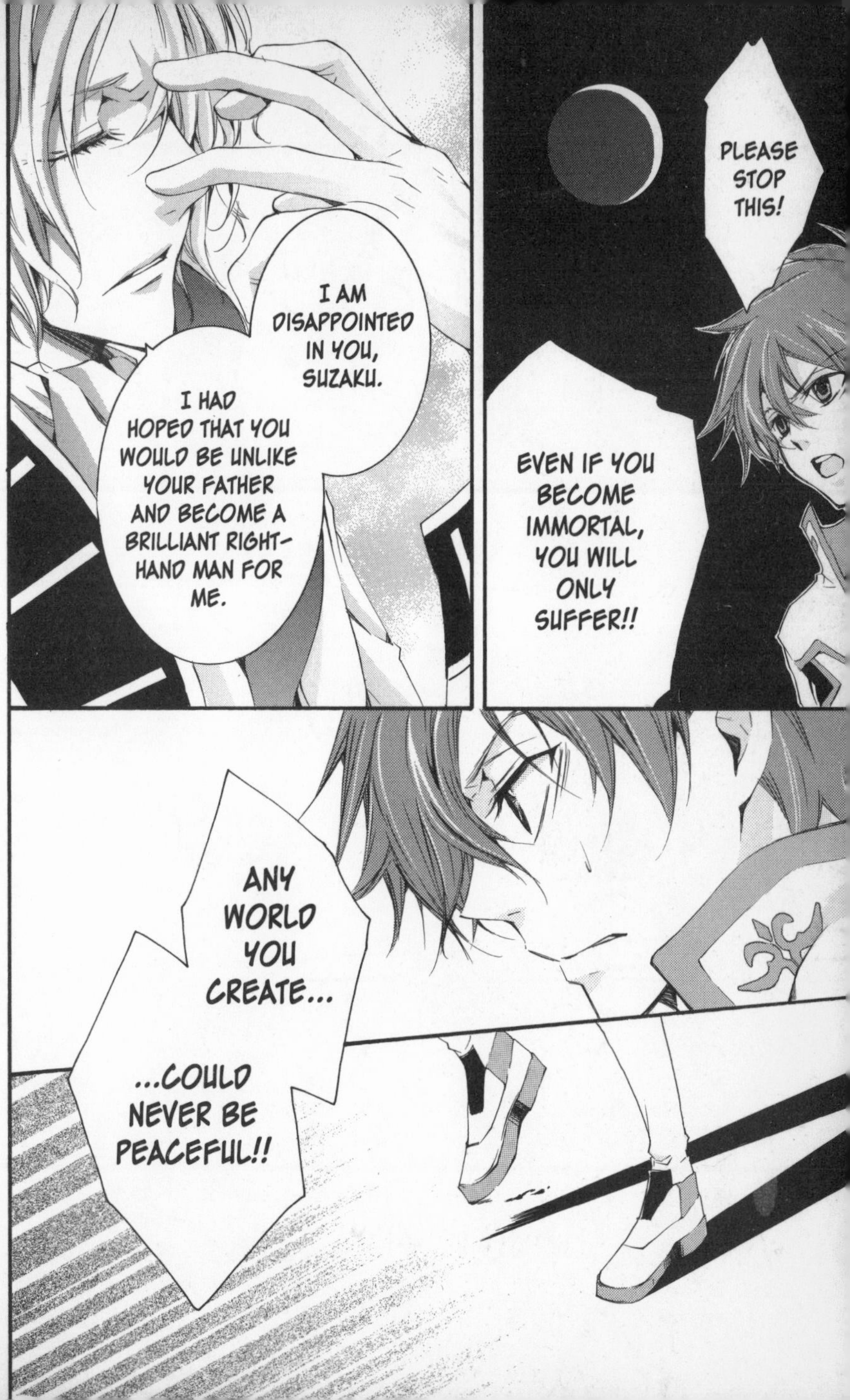
PLEASE STOP THIS!
EVEN IF YOU BECOME IMMORTAL, YOU WILL ONLY SUFFER!!
I AM DISAPPOINTED IN YOU, SUZAKU.
I HAD HOPED THAT YOU WOULD BE UNLIKE YOUR FATHER AND BECOME A BRILLIANT RIGHT-HAND MAN FOR ME.
ANY WORLD YOU CREATE...
...COULD NEVER BE PEACEFUL!!

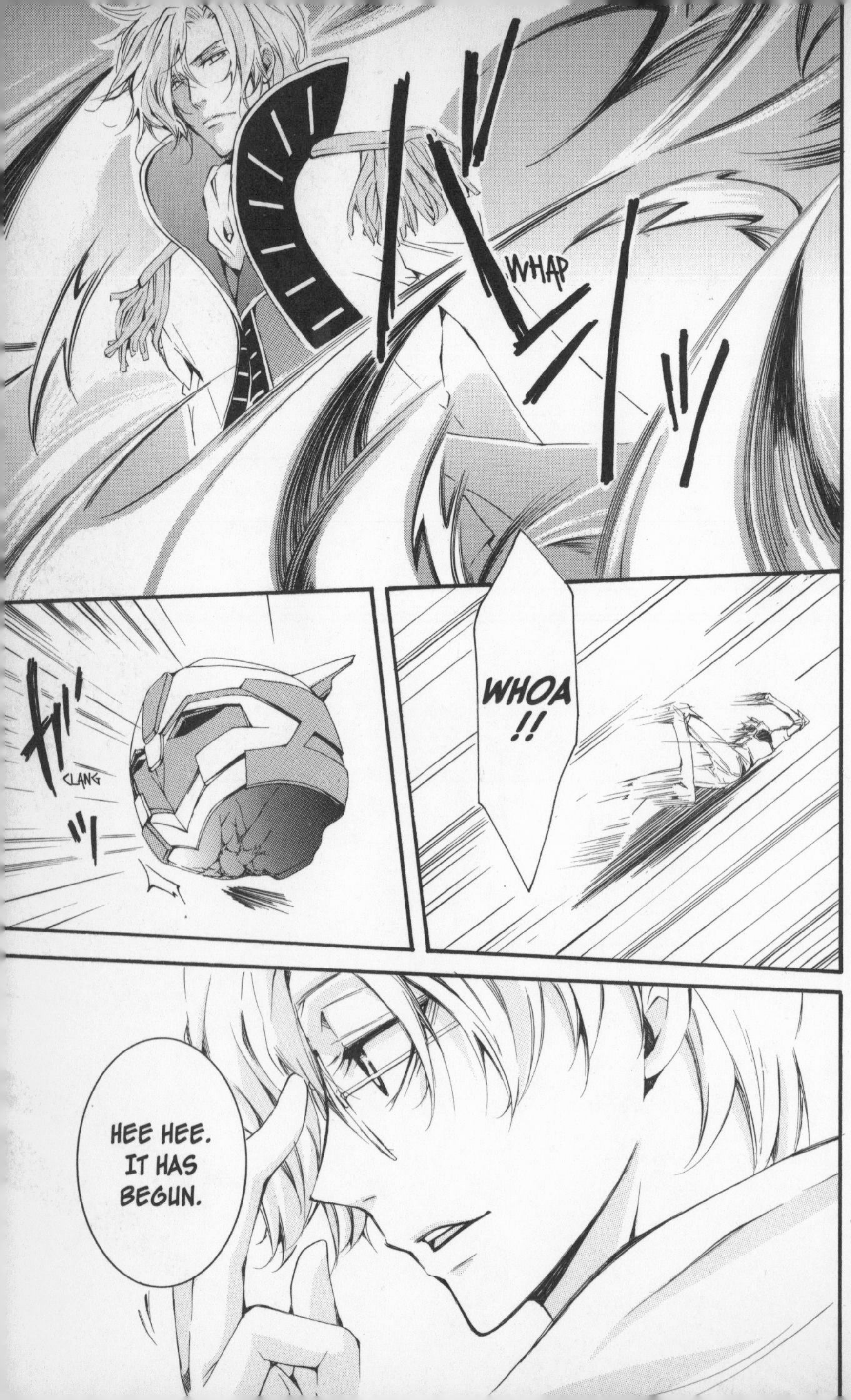
WHAP
WHOA !!
CLANG
HEE HEE. IT HAS BEGUN.

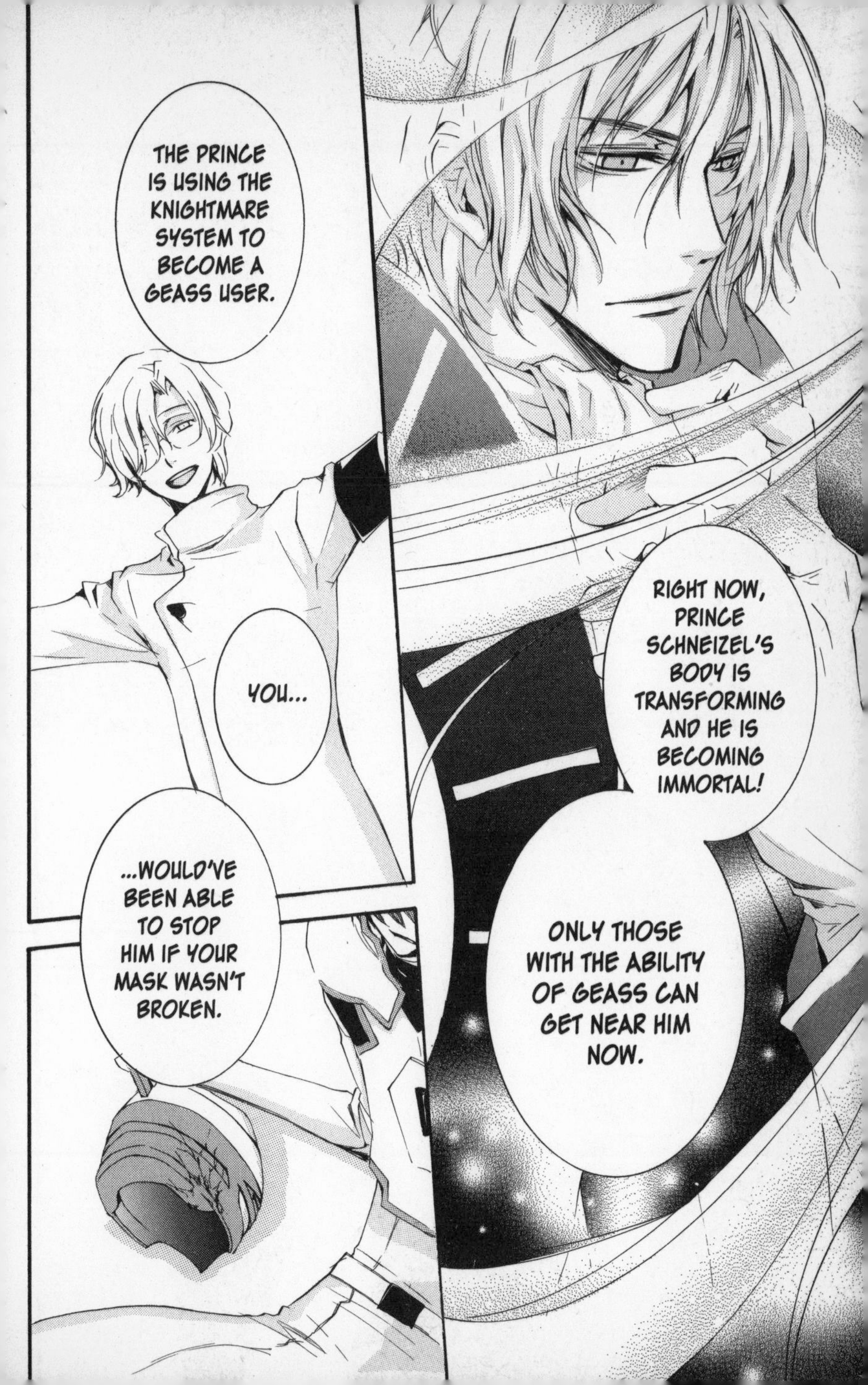
RIGHT NOW, PRINCE SCHNEIZEL'S BODY IS TRANSFORMING AND HE IS BECOMING IMMORTAL!
ONLY THOSE WITH THE ABILITY OF GEASS CAN GET NEAR HIM NOW.
THE PRINCE IS USING THE KNIGHTMARE SYSTEM TO BECOME A GEASS USER.
YOU...
...WOULD'VE BEEN ABLE TO STOP HIM IF YOUR MASK WASN'T BROKEN.

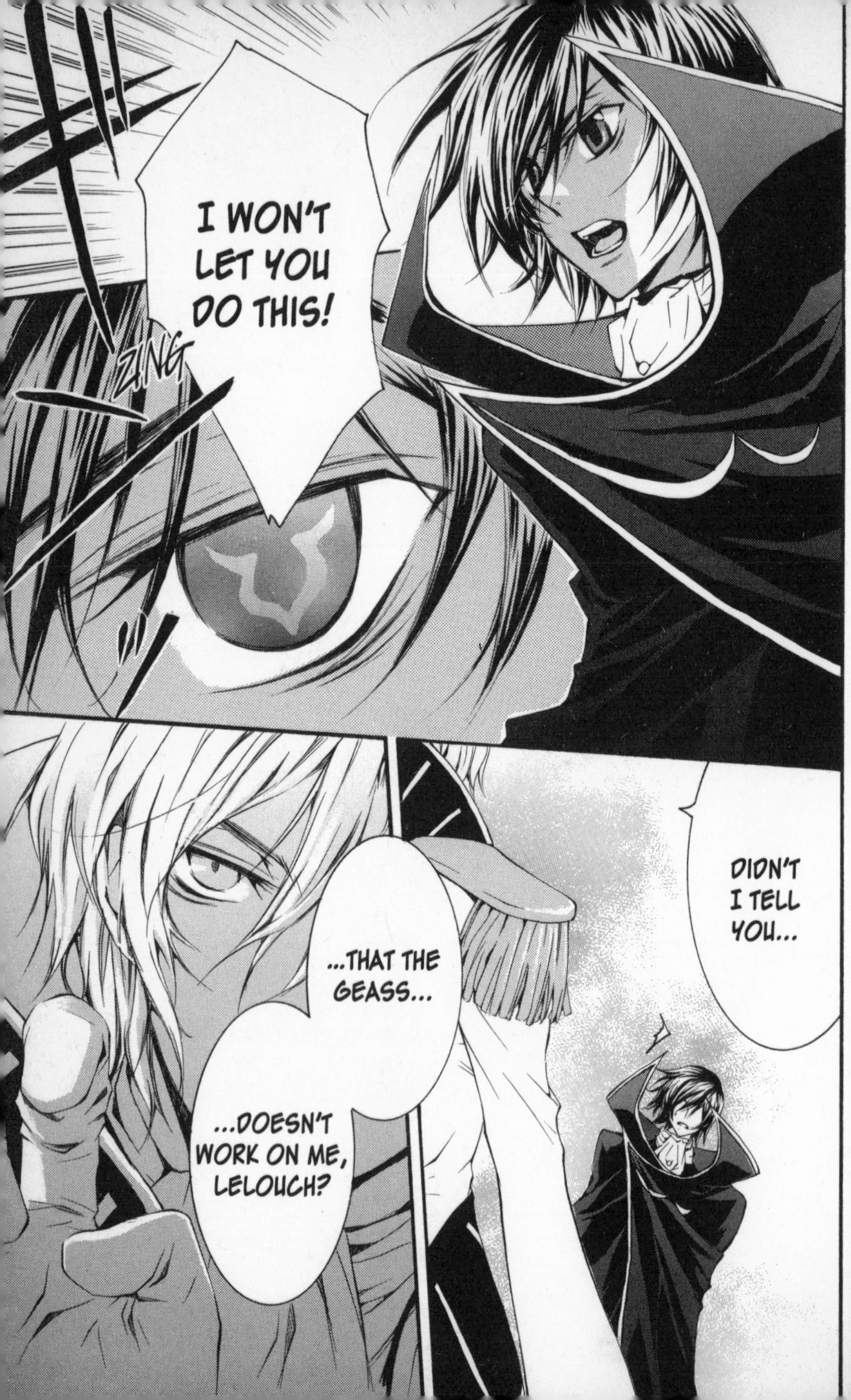
I WON'T LET YOU DO THIS!
ZING
DIDN'T I TELL YOU...
...THAT THE GEASS...
...DOESN'T WORK ON ME, LELOUCH?

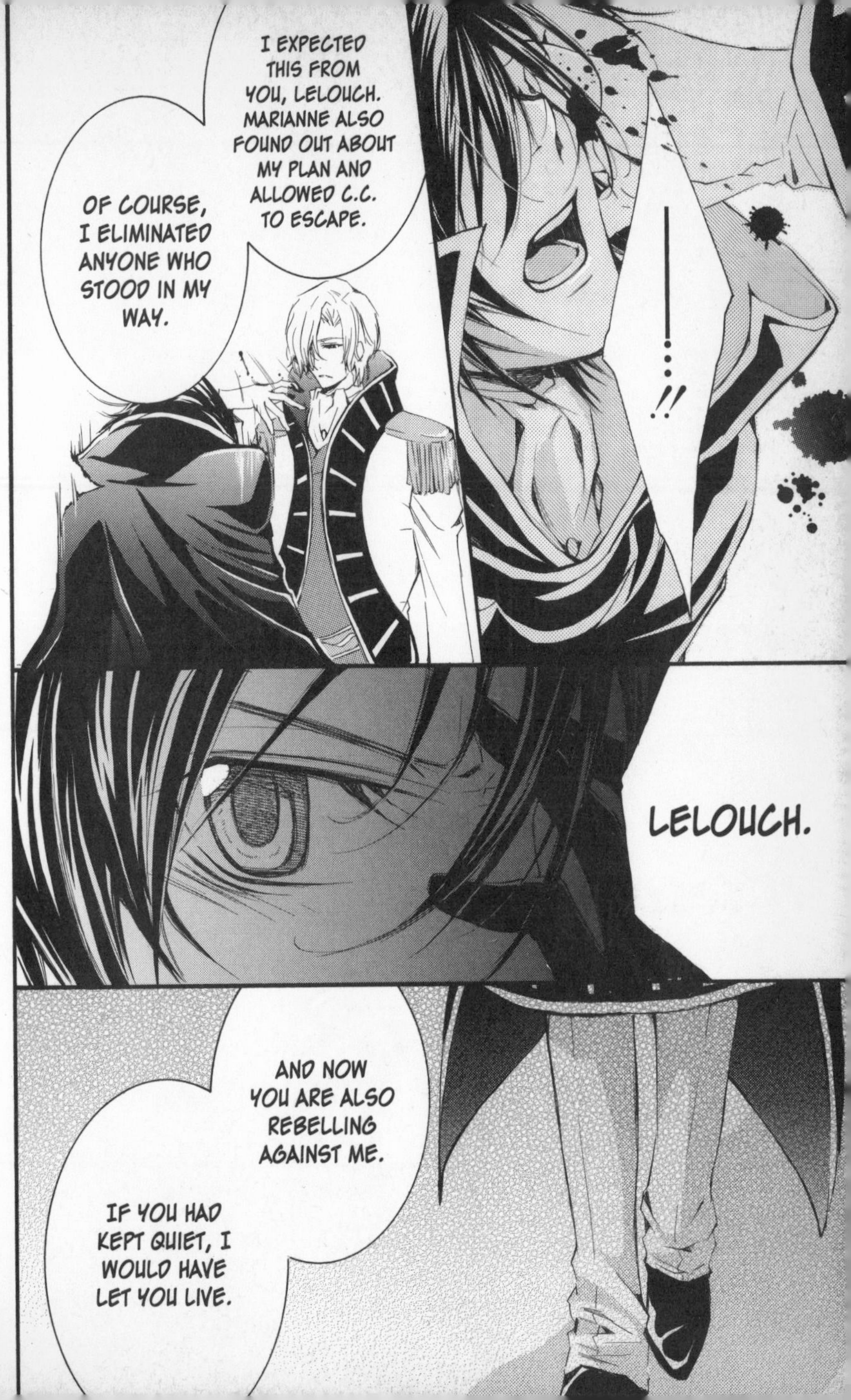
!......!!
I EXPECTED THIS FROM YOU, LELOUCH. MARIANNE ALSO FOUND OUT ABOUT MY PLAN AND ALLOWED C.C. TO ESCAPE.
OF COURSE, I ELIMINATED ANYONE WHO STOOD IN MY WAY.
LELOUCH.
AND NOW YOU ARE ALSO REBELLING AGAINST ME.
IF YOU HAD KEPT QUIET, I WOULD HAVE LET YOU LIVE.

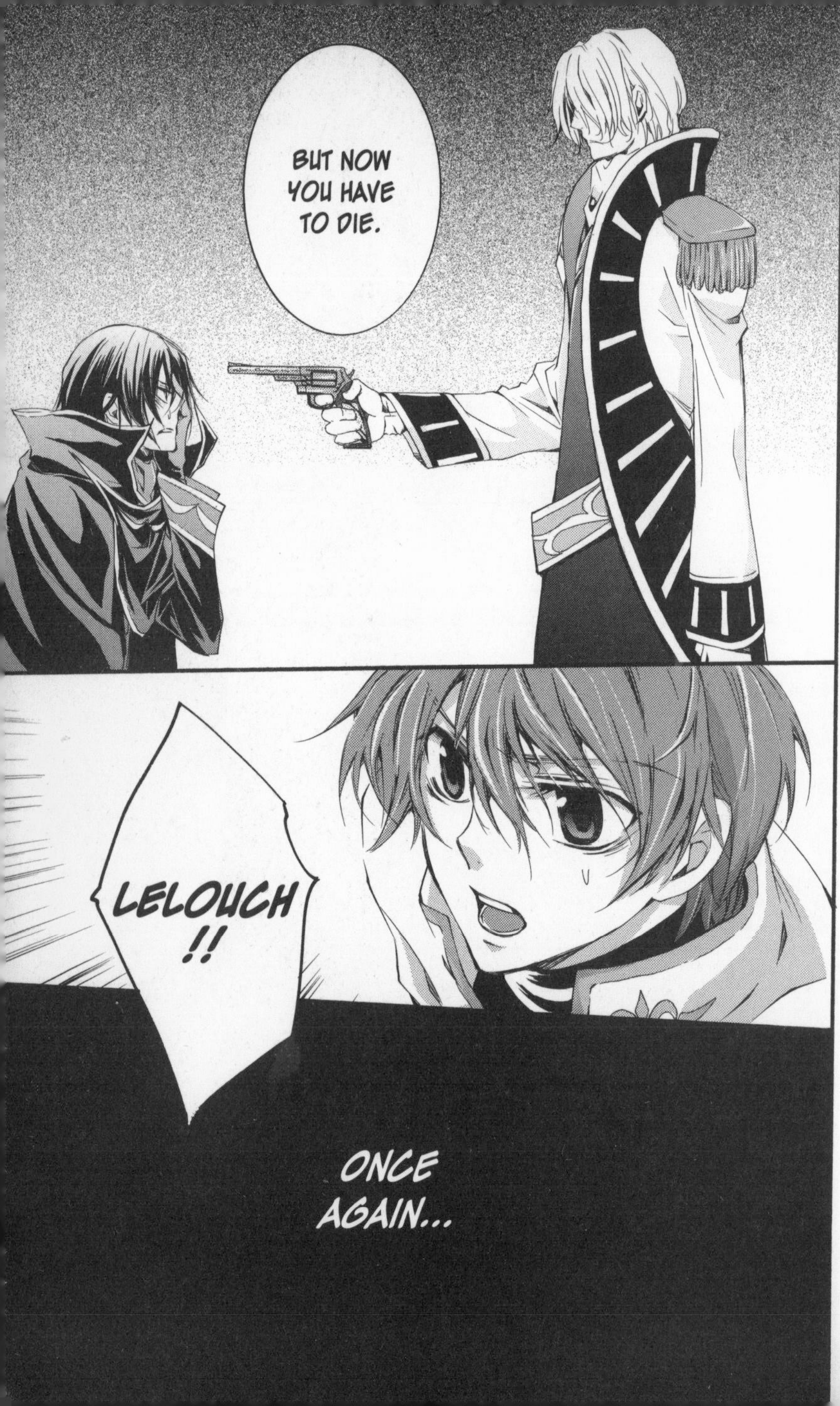
BUT NOW YOU HAVE TO DIE.
LELOUCH !!
ONCE AGAIN...

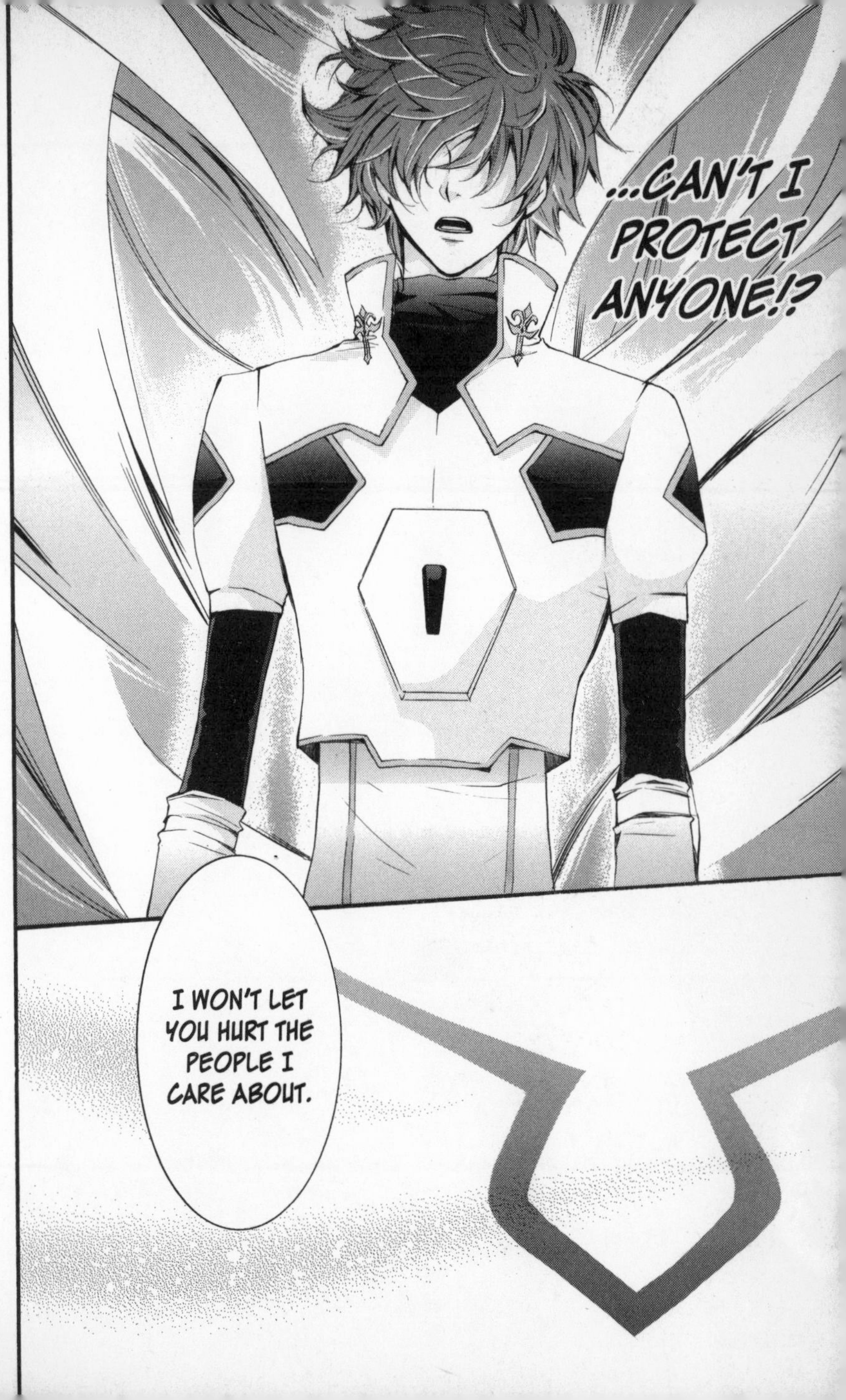
...CAN'T I PROTECT ANYONE!?
I WON'T LET YOU HURT THE PEOPLE I CARE ABOUT.

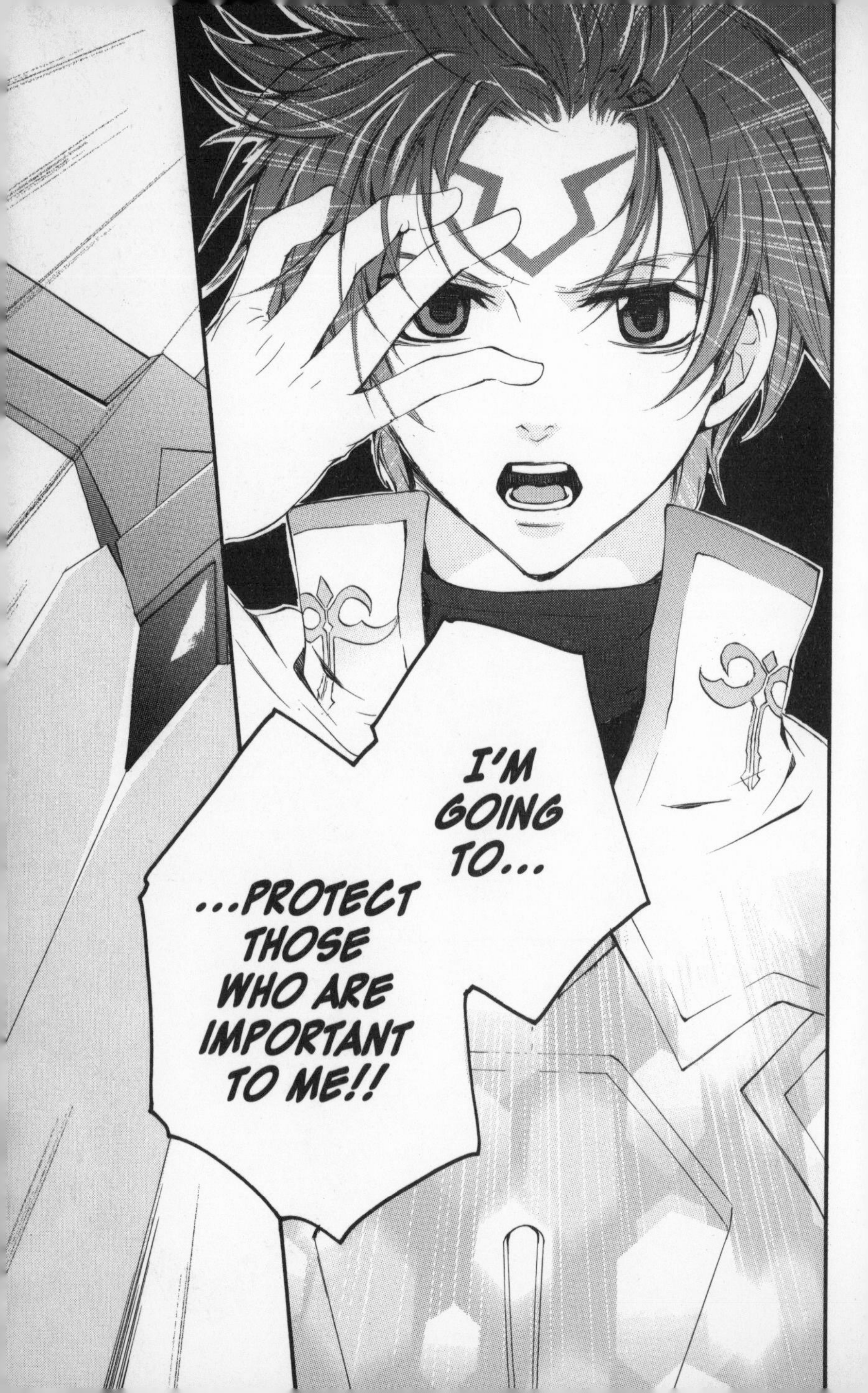
I'M GOING TO...
...PROTECT THOSE WHO ARE IMPORTANT TO ME!!

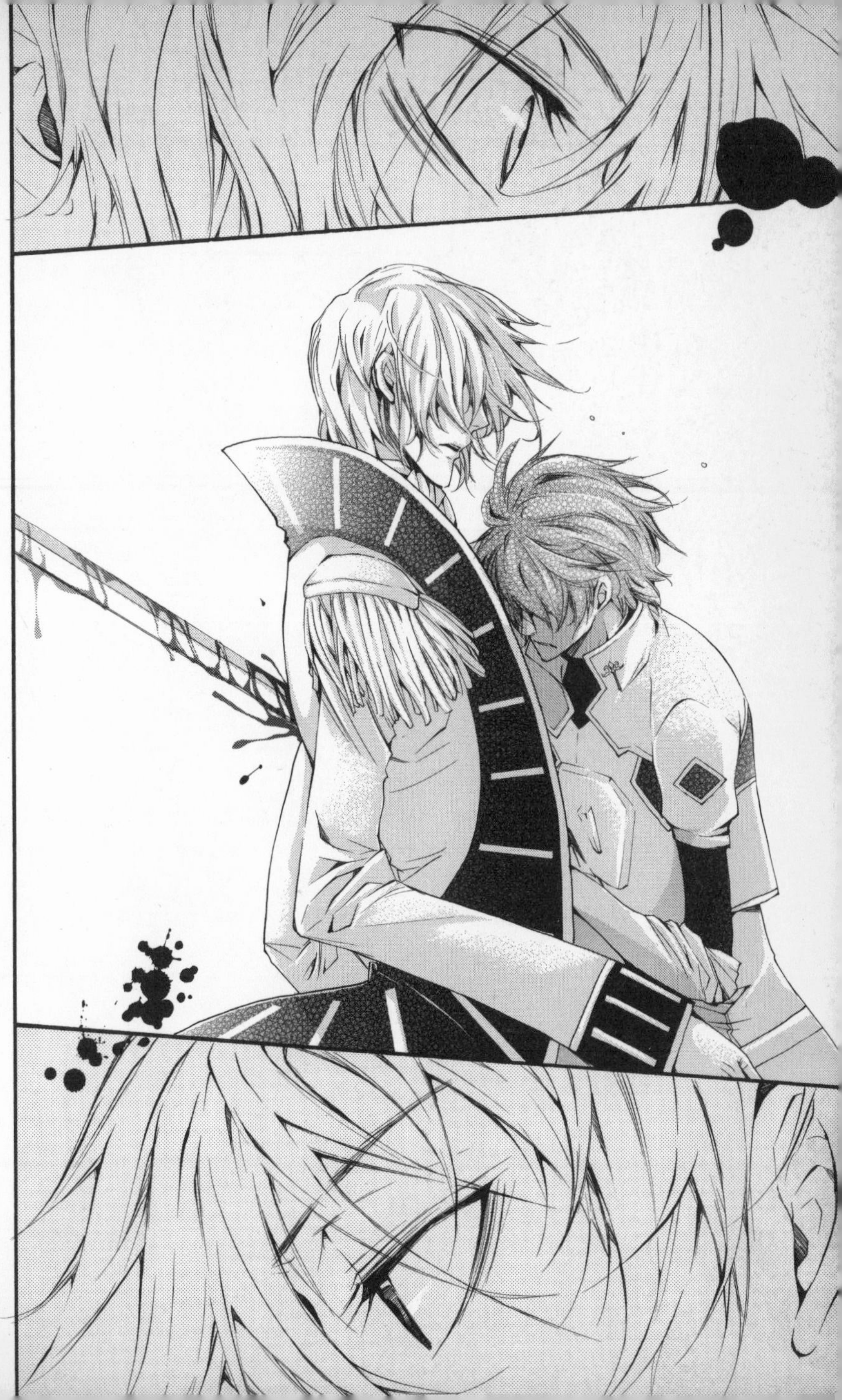

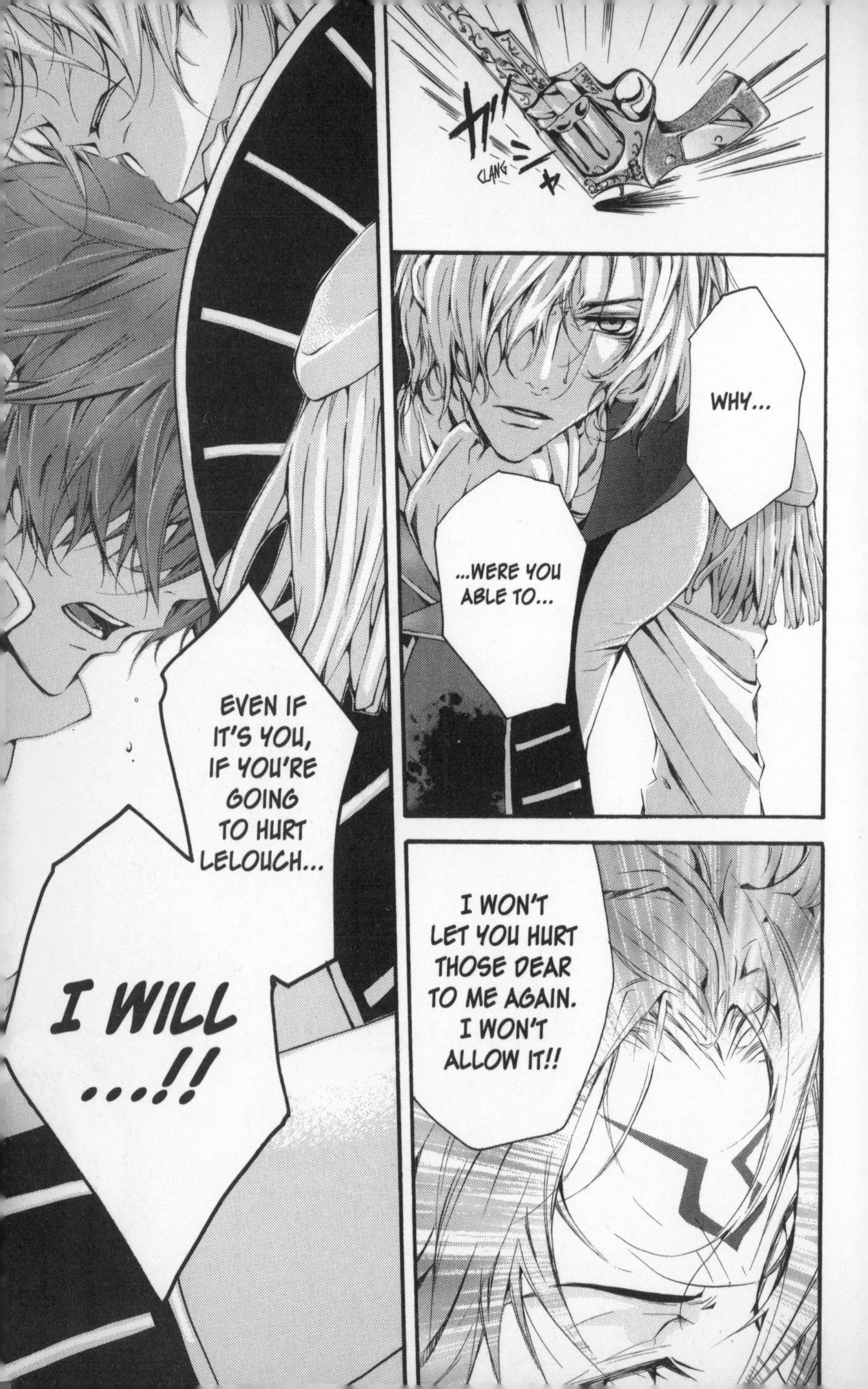
CLANG
WHY...
...WERE YOU ABLE TO...
I WON'T LET YOU HURT THOSE DEAR TO ME AGAIN. I WON'T ALLOW IT!!
EVEN IF IT'S YOU, IF YOU'RE GOING TO HURT LELOUCH...
I WILL ...!!

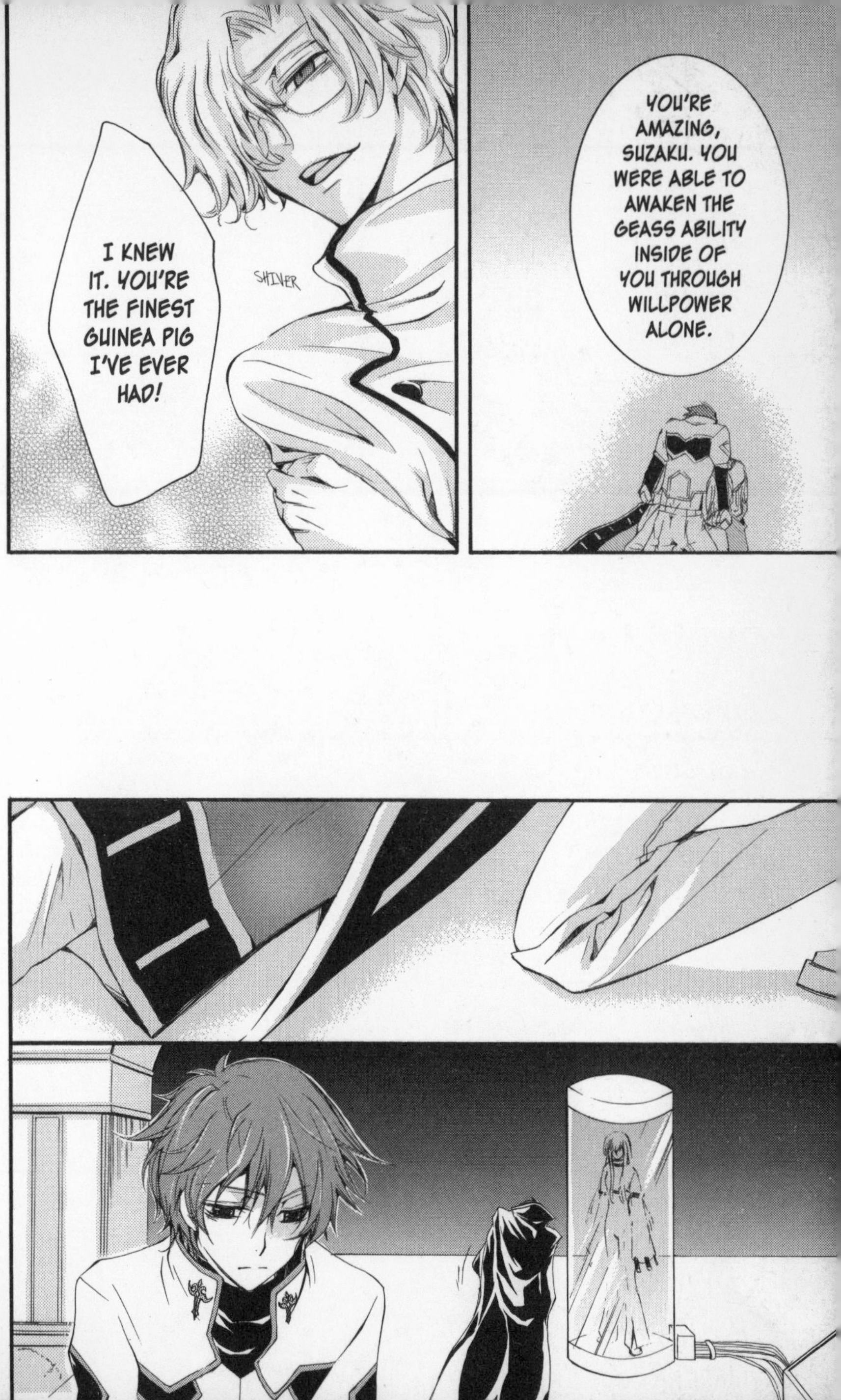
YOU'RE AMAZING, SUZAKU. YOU WERE ABLE TO AWAKEN THE GEASS ABILITY INSIDE OF YOU THROUGH WILLPOWER ALONE.
I KNEW IT. YOU'RE THE FINEST GUINEA PIG I'VE EVER HAD!
SHIVER

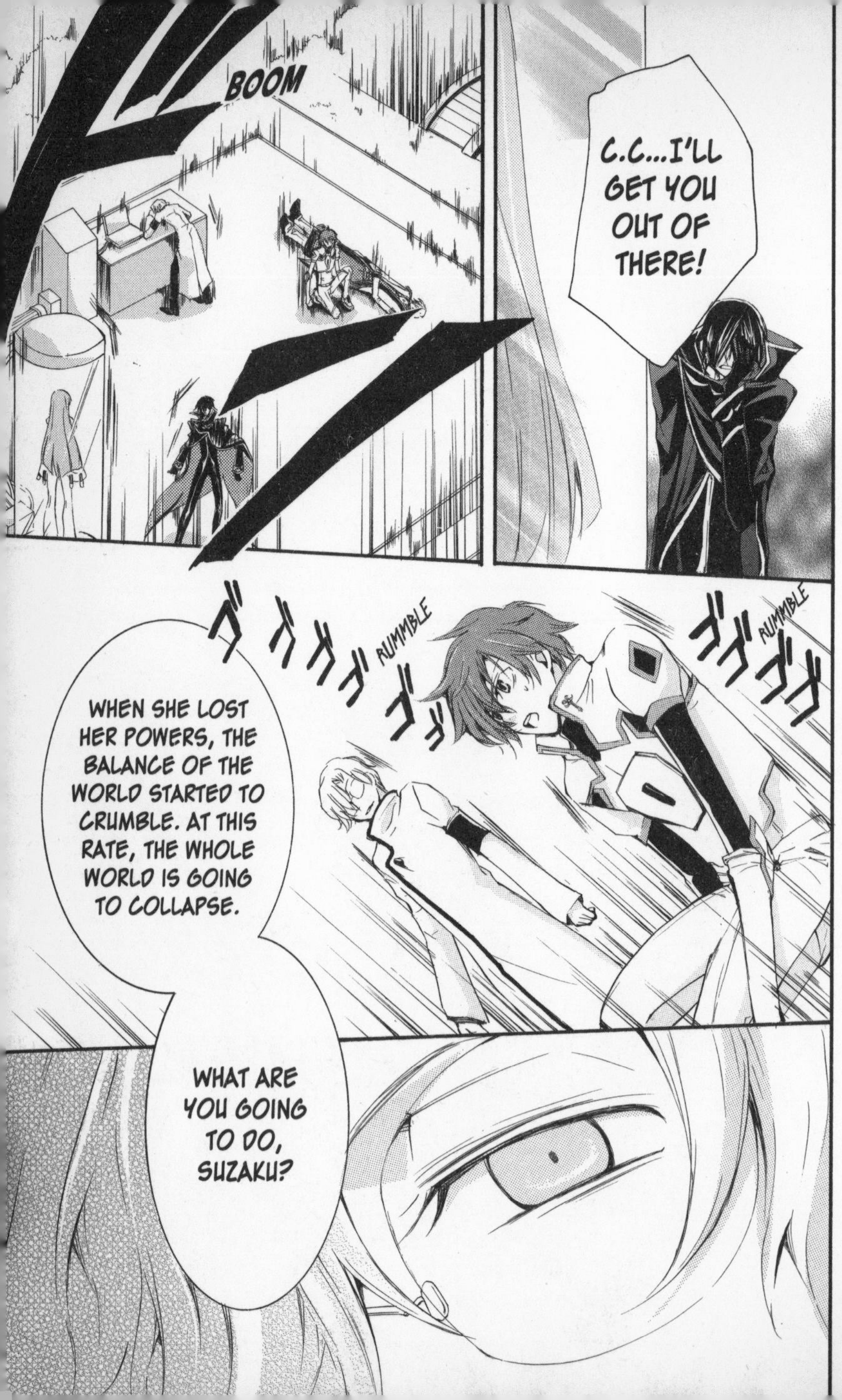
C.C...I'LL GET YOU OUT OF THERE!
BOOM
RUMMBLE
RUMMBLE
WHEN SHE LOST HER POWERS, THE BALANCE OF THE WORLD STARTED TO CRUMBLE. AT THIS RATE, THE WHOLE WORLD IS GOING TO COLLAPSE.
WHAT ARE YOU GOING TO DO, SUZAKU?

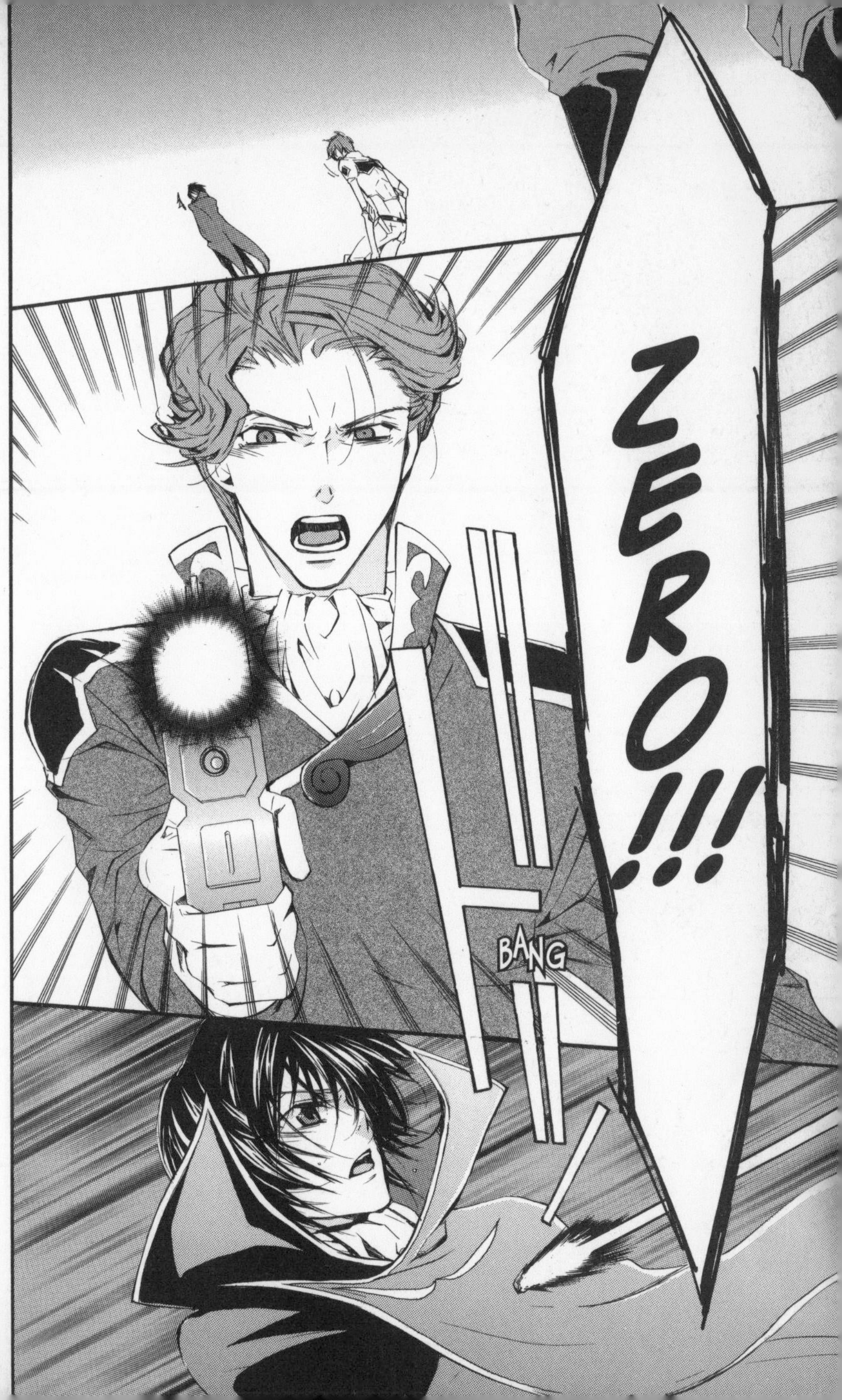
ZERO!!!
BANG

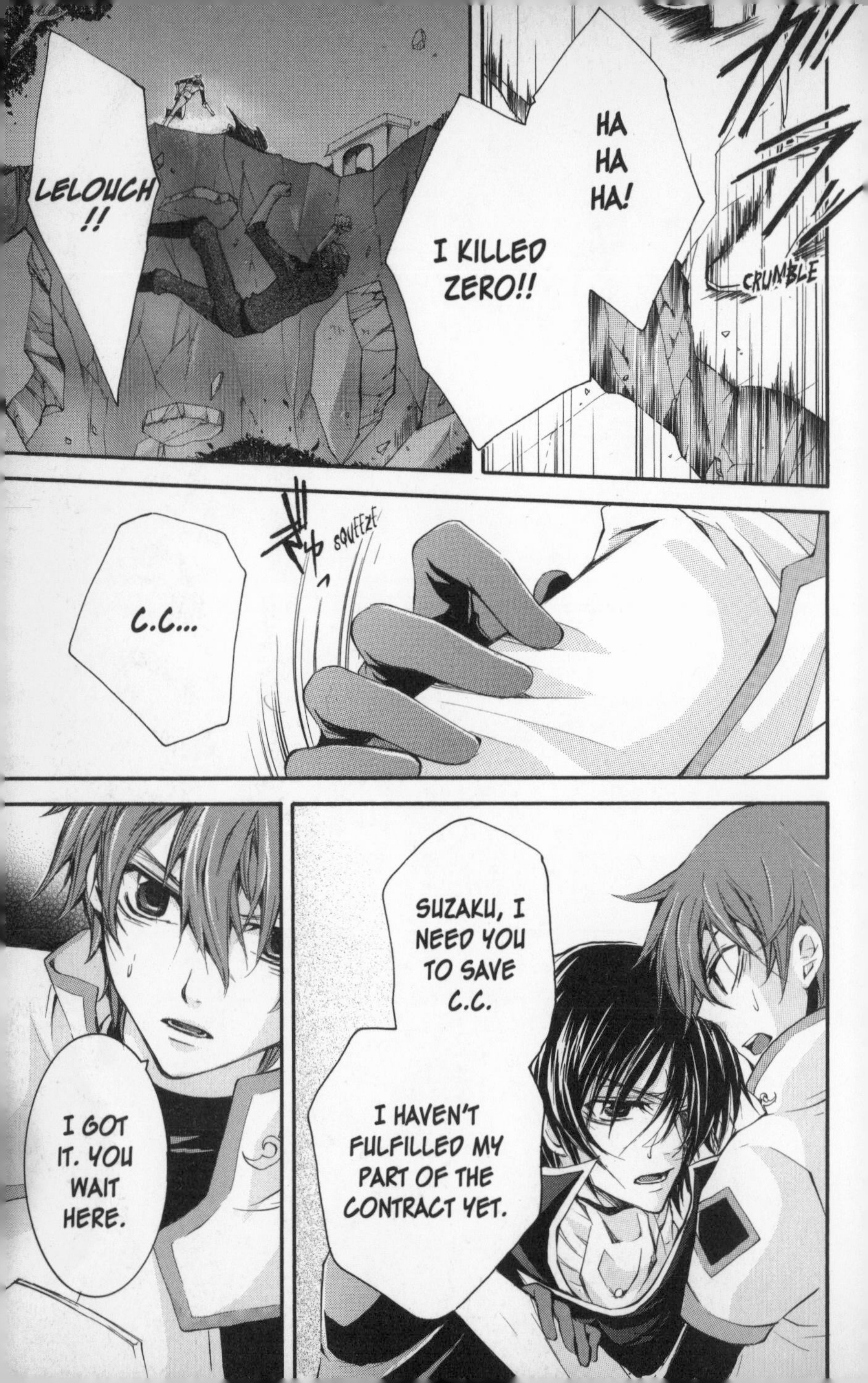
HA HA HA!
I KILLED ZERO!!
CRUMBLE
LELOUCH!!
SQUEEZE
C.C...
SUZAKU, I NEED YOU TO SAVE C.C.
I HAVEN'T FULFILLED MY PART OF THE CONTRACT YET.
I GOT IT. YOU WAIT HERE.

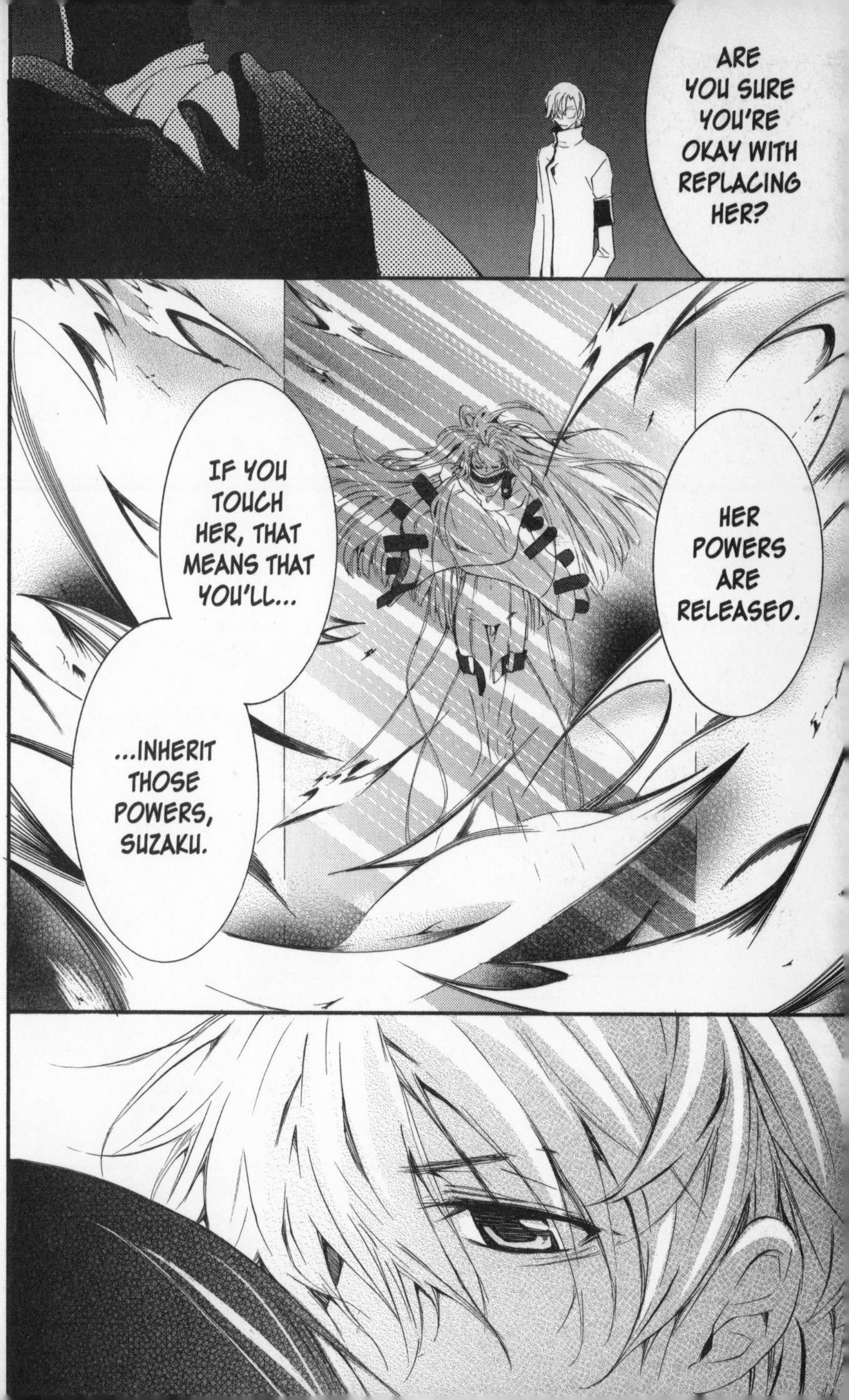
ARE YOU SURE YOU'RE OKAY WITH REPLACING HER?
HER POWERS ARE RELEASED.
IF YOU TOUCH HER, THAT MEANS THAT YOU'LL...
...INHERIT THOSE POWERS, SUZAKU.

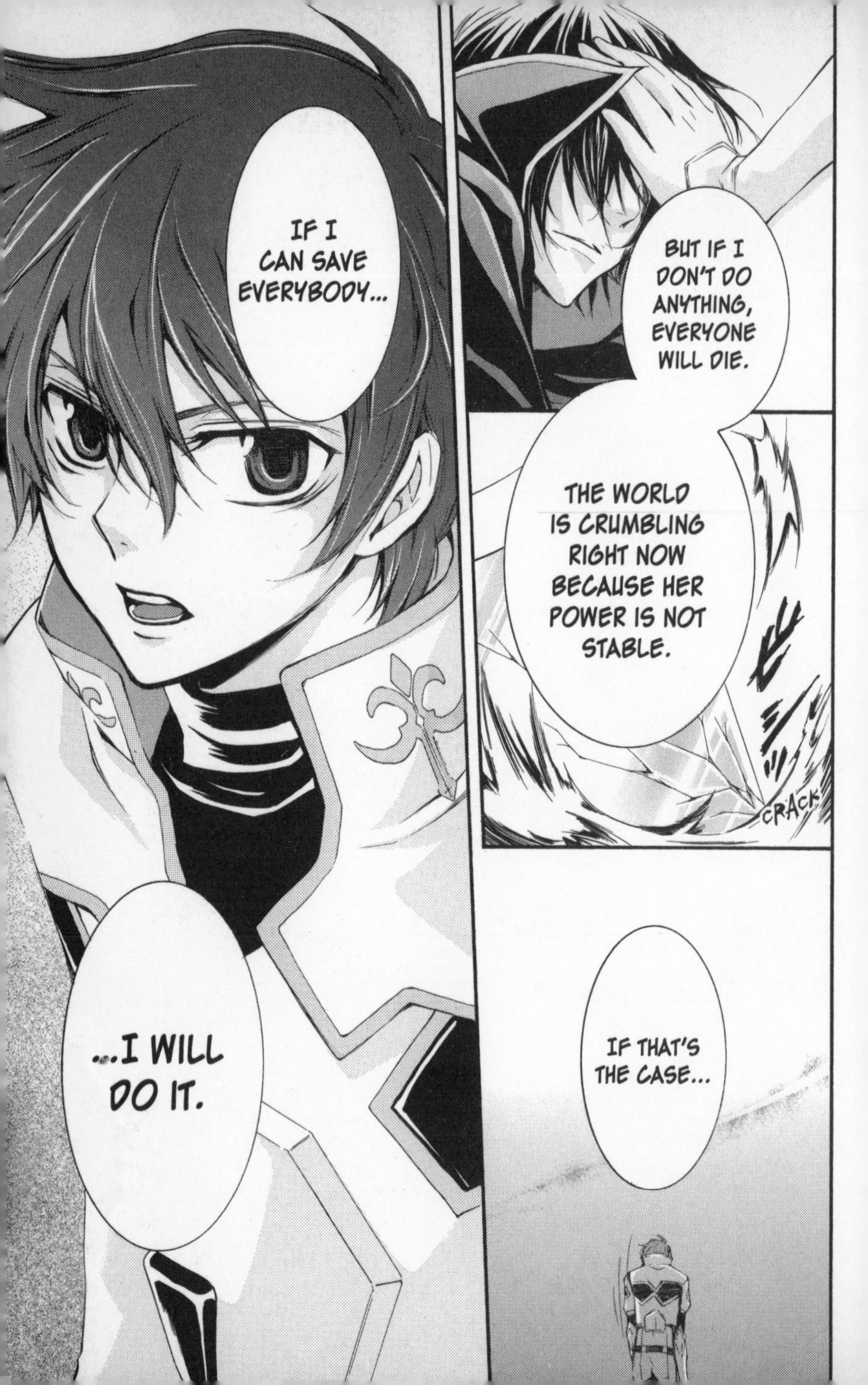
BUT IF I DON'T DO ANYTHING, EVERYONE WILL DIE.
THE WORLD IS CRUMBLING RIGHT NOW BECAUSE HER POWER IS NOT STABLE.
CRACK
IF THAT'S THE CASE...
IF I CAN SAVE EVERYBODY...
...I WILL DO IT.

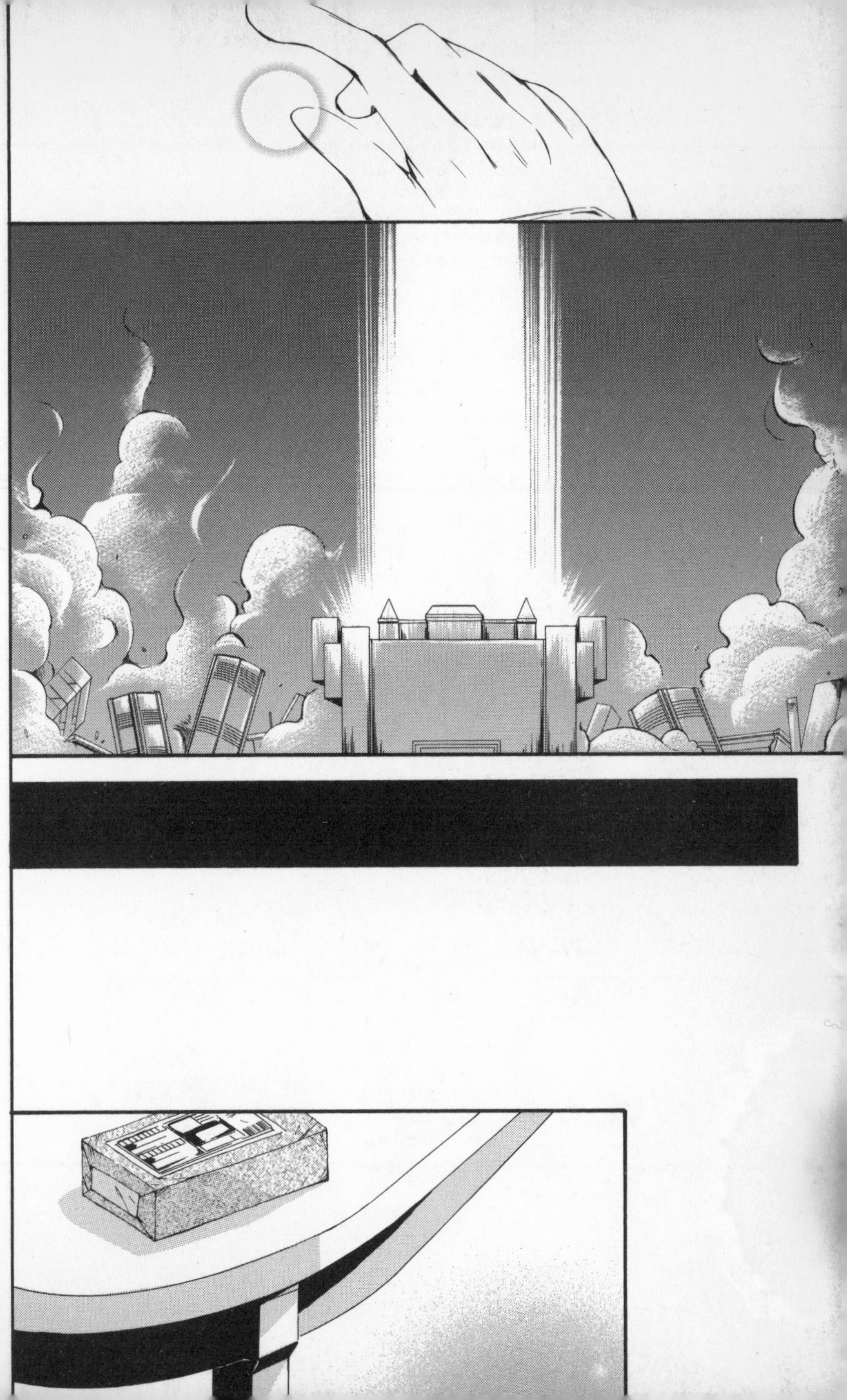

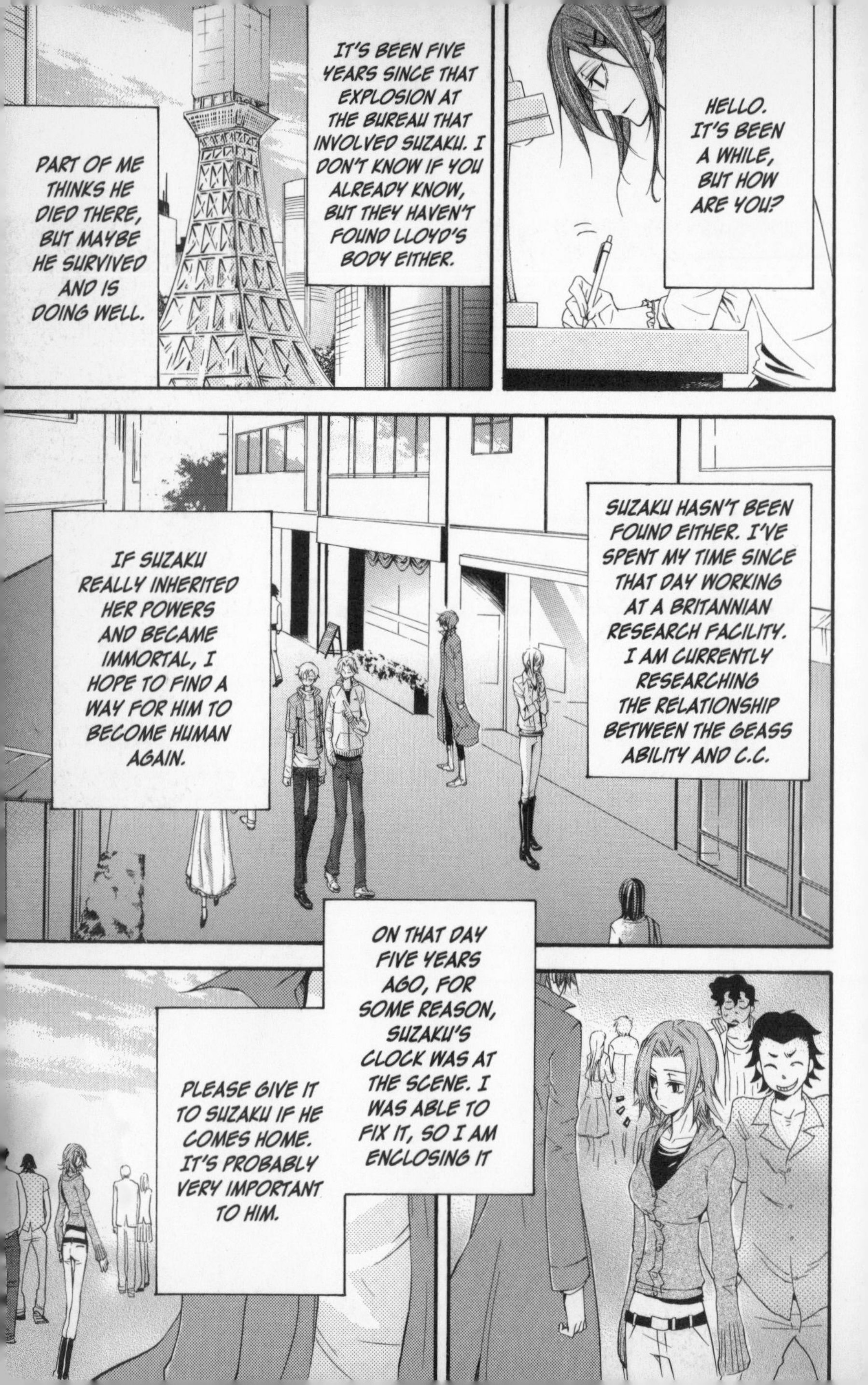
HELLO. IT'S BEEN A WHILE, BUT HOW ARE YOU?
IT'S BEEN FIVE YEARS SINCE THAT EXPLOSION AT THE BUREAU THAT INVOLVED SUZAKU. I DON'T KNOW IF YOU ALREADY KNOW, BUT THEY HAVEN'T FOUND LLOYD'S BODY EITHER.
PART OF ME THINKS HE DIED THERE, BUT MAYBE HE SURVIVED AND IS DOING WELL.
SUZAKU HASN'T BEEN FOUND EITHER. I'VE SPENT MY TIME SINCE THAT DAY WORKING AT A BRITANNIAN RESEARCH FACILITY. I AM CURRENTLY RESEARCHING THE RELATIONSHIP BETWEEN THE GEASS ABILITY AND C.C.
IF SUZAKU REALLY INHERITED HER POWERS AND BECAME IMMORTAL, I HOPE TO FIND A WAY FOR HIM TO BECOME HUMAN AGAIN.
ON THAT DAY FIVE YEARS AGO, FOR SOME REASON, SUZAKU'S CLOCK WAS AT THE SCENE. I WAS ABLE TO FIX IT, SO I AM ENCLOSING IT
PLEASE GIVE IT TO SUZAKU IF HE COMES HOME. IT'S PROBABLY VERY IMPORTANT TO HIM.

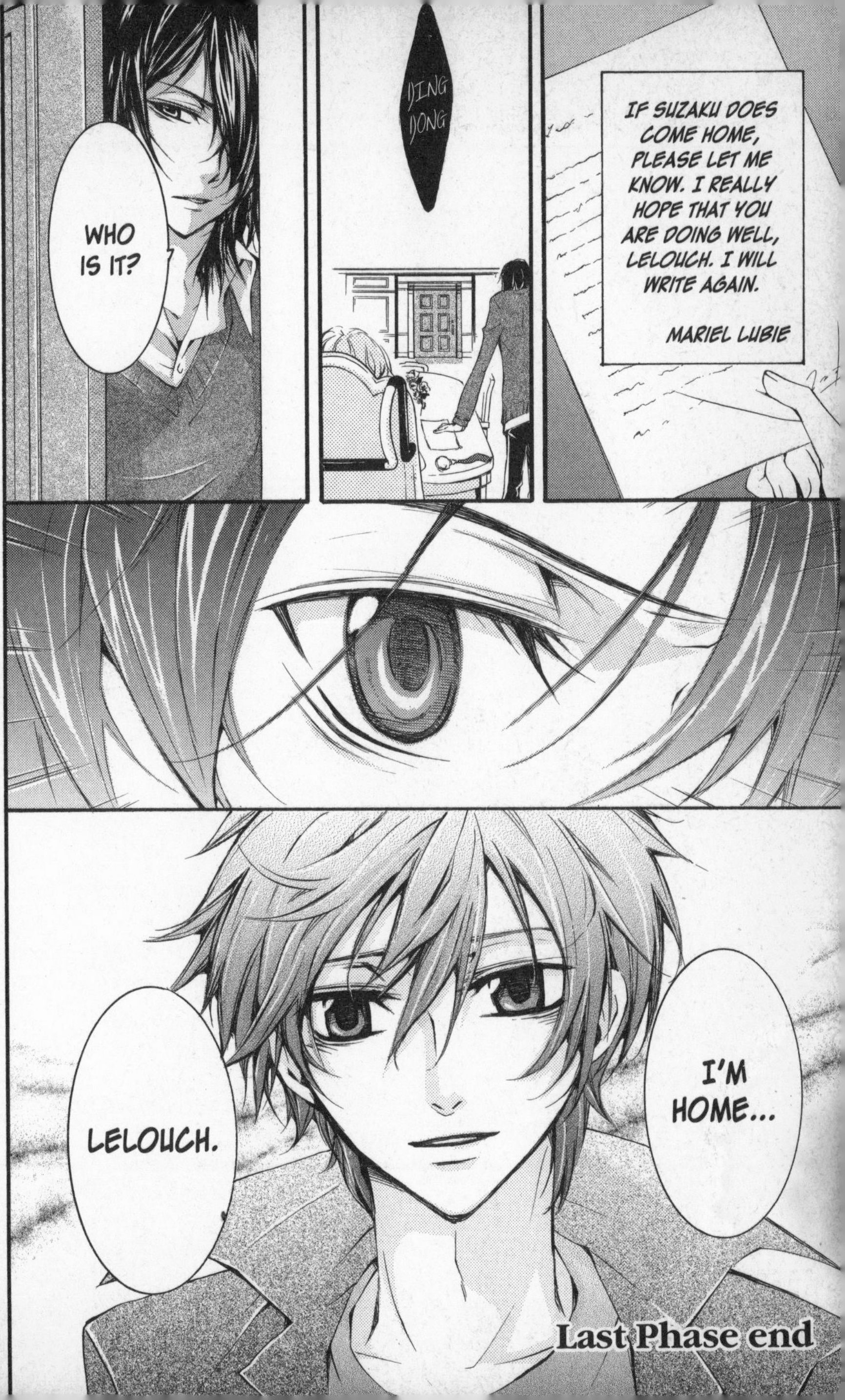
IF SUZAKU DOES COME HOME, PLEASE LET ME KNOW. I REALLY HOPE THAT YOU ARE DOING WELL, LELOUCH. I WILL WRITE AGAIN.
MARIEL LUBIE
DING DONG
WHO IS IT?
I'M HOME...
LELOUCH.
Last Phase end

CODE GEASS
Suzaku of
the Counterattack

AFTERWORD

Suzaku of the Rebellion R2 Part 1

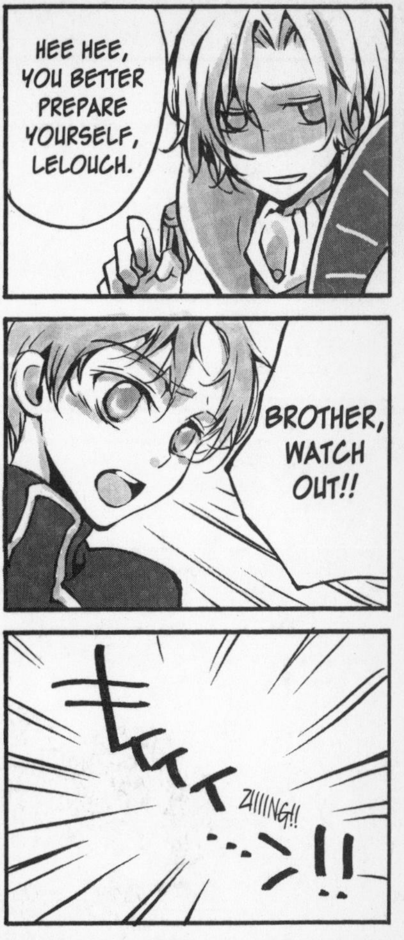
HEE HEE, YOU BETTER PREPARE YOURSELF, LELOUCH.
BROTHER, WATCH OUT!!
ZIIIING!!
I TOLD YOU THAT THE GEASS DOESN'T WORK ON ME.
I'M GOING TO DRAW ON HIM NOW.

Suzaku of the Rebellion R2 Part 2

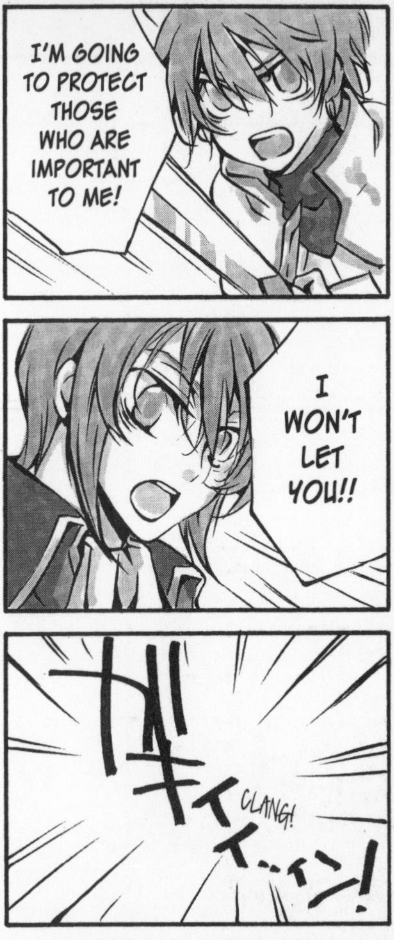
I'M GOING TO PROTECT THOSE WHO ARE IMPORTANT TO ME!
I WON'T LET YOU!!
CLANG!
THANK YOU AS ALWAYS, KANON.
ARE YOU OKAY, PRINCE? I WEAR A STEEL BREASTPLATE FOR TIMES LIKE THESE.
No way!